The Civil War Party System

The Civil War Party System

The Case of Massachusetts, 1848–1876

by Dale Baum

The University of North Carolina Press

Chapel Hill and London

Library of Congress Cataloging in Publication Data

Baum, Dale, 1943–
   The Civil War party system.

   Bibliography: p.
   Includes index.
   1. Political parties—Massachusetts—History—19th
century.   2. Elections—Massachusetts—History—19th
century.   3. Massachusetts—Politics and government—Civil
War, 1861–1865.   I. Title.
JK2295.M42B28   1984   324.2744′009   83-19687
ISBN 0-8078-1588-8

Portions of this work have appeared in somewhat different
form in the *Journal of American History* 64, no. 4 (March
1978) and *Civil War History* 26, no. 2 (June 1980).

To the memory of my grandmother,
Alma Hinrichs Baum, 1887–1978

Contents

Tables

Acknowledgments

It is a pleasure to acknowledge the assistance given to me by many individuals and institutions during the years this book has been in preparation. My greatest debt is to Peyton McCrary, who guided this work through each of its many stages, from the initial formulation of the topic to the final revisions. This book also owes a great deal to Germaine A. Hoston, who helped me draw a circle of definition around my subject; to Maria Turner, whose blue pencil improved nearly every page; and to Lawrence D. Cress, whose perceptive comments came at a crucial time. I am also grateful for the suggestions for improvement made by two anonymous readers for the University of North Carolina Press and by George D. Green and Kinley J. Brauer, who directed the dissertation from which this book was developed. I am, of course, completely responsible for the errors and inadequacies that remain.

Parts of Chapters 2 and 5 originally appeared in different form in the *Journal of American History* and *Civil War History*, and are incorporated here with the editors' permission.

In the course of my research I received prompt and cordial assistance from the library staffs of the American Antiquarian Society, the Bapst Library of Boston College, the Boston Public Library, the Dinand Library of the College of the Holy Cross, the Rutherford B. Hayes Library, the Houghton Library of Harvard University, the Manuscript Division of the Library of Congress, the Massachusetts Historical Society, the Massachusetts State House Library and Archives, and the State Historical Society of Wisconsin.

I wish to thank the scholars who read parts of earlier drafts of the manuscript and helped clarify either ideas or style: Terry H. Anderson, Colleen Cook, Henry C. Dethloff, Paul Goodman, Michael F. Holt, Arnold P. Krammer, Charlene Muehlenhard, and Kevin M. Sweeney. For contributions to the quantitative aspects of the book I owe a special debt of gratitude to Clark L. Miller. In this regard I also wish to thank William H. Flanigan, J. Morgan Kousser, Albert C. E. Parker, W. Phillips Shively, and Nancy H. Zingale. Denise Duncan helped me with the task of coding election returns. The computer centers at the University of Minnesota and Texas A&M University were indispensable in providing programming assistance and computer time. Carole R. Knapp, Mary Watson, Margaret R. Lauer, and Pat Rodrigue skillfully typed various drafts of the manuscript. I wish also to thank Stevie Glass Champion for her meticulous editing.

Finally, I would like to thank my parents, Bobbe and Bill Allen, and my sister and brother, Gail and Jim. Through their love and understanding they have made possible whatever I have been able to accomplish thus far, including this book.

The Civil War Party System

Introduction

It may be argued with great plausibility that the American Civil
War and its aftermath constituted the only genuine revolution
in the history of the country.—*Walter Dean Burnham*, The
American Party Systems: Stages of Political Development

During the late 1840s, a few like-minded Massachusetts men began
meeting on Saturday afternoons to discuss politics. The issue that
invoked the greatest concern was the prospect of an expansion of slavery into the western territories. The group usually gathered together
for dinner at a Boston hotel where their host was Frank Bird, a political ally of Charles Sumner and the antislavery Whigs. By 1850 out-
siders had dubbed this informal group the "Bird Club," and acknowledged its reputation as the most dedicated and resourceful antislavery
faction within the newly formed Free-Soil party. The influence of Bird
and his associates grew extensively during the next turbulent decade
when their party was absorbed by the new Republican party. By 1860
they elected a member of their group, John Andrew, to the governorship of the Bay State. Andrew's inauguration propelled this clique of
former Free-Soilers to dizzying political heights. For the next and crucial decade these men not only dominated the politics of their state, but
also had a significant impact on the Republican party and on national
policy. Representing the Sumner wing of the Massachusetts Republican party, they constituted, in theory and practice, the radical Republican establishment.

The antislavery position of the Bird Club radicals vastly influenced
public opinion and national politics. From the late 1840s Bird and his
colleagues continually denounced southern slaveholders and their
"dough-faced" supporters in the North. Their belief in the irrecon-
cilability of slavery and freedom convinced them of the need to prepare
for battle with the South, so they conspired to harbor fugitive slaves,
presided over abolitionist meetings, and subsidized John Brown's activities in Kansas and his invasion of Virginia. They welcomed the se-

cession crisis, believing that the Union was not worth the sacrifice of antislavery principles.

Events following the outbreak of the Civil War strengthened the Bird Club's position within the Republican party. Stubbornly defending the principle of equal rights under the law irrespective of race, color, or creed, they saw the campaign against the Confederacy as an opportunity to destroy legalized slavery and to remodel southern society according to their own notions of democracy. Convinced that the defeated Confederacy's leaders would never grant justice to their former slaves, the Bird Club radicals supported a Reconstruction policy solidly backed by federal power to secure racial equality and equal rights in the former rebel states—even if that meant stationing troops in the Old South.

By the end of the 1860s the influence of the Bird Club members began to decline. Their views on total equality for the southern blacks aroused less enthusiasm than had their earlier antislavery rhetoric. Northern voters, believing that the issues stemming from the war had been resolved by the passage of the Thirteenth, Fourteenth, and Fifteenth amendments, turned their attention to other issues that did not define party lines but cut across them. Loyalty to the Republicans remained strong, but radicalism as a political ideology failed to unite the party.

Radicalism could no longer be sustained by events in the 1870s as it had been a generation earlier. Thus it seemed natural that in 1872 Bird abandoned the Republican party that he had helped to create. By then Bird and most of his colleagues feared that the Republican party had degenerated into a vehicle for the advancement of ambitious politicians, that the party was no longer the conduit for the promotion of that great and noble idea: the political equality of all men. Power shifted abruptly from the Bird Club to those dedicated to keeping Republicans in office and to preserving the party organization.

Bird and his associates were unique figures in American political history. Their style of politics was unusually doctrinaire, reformist, and emotional in contrast to the normal "give and take" of professionally managed politics. Historically, the major parties have practiced the art of pragmatic, as opposed to ideological politics. They have made nondogmatic and inoffensive appeals for the support of all voters, while skillfully minimizing, by compromise and accommodation, differences in viewpoint. They have promoted few enduring policy commitments of their own, and have demonstrated a remarkable ability to appeal to voters on each new issue. Given this traditional brokerage operation of the major parties, it is easy to overlook a time when ideological politics was important, even taking precedence over pragmatic politics.

Unlike most eras in American history, the Civil War and Reconstruction witnessed Republicans and Democrats offering clear ideological alternatives to the voters. The parties stared at each other over the chasm of a single issue: what was to be the status in the nation of millions of descendants of black Africans? The issue touched the foundation of the Great Republic. Had the founding fathers labored at Philadelphia to establish a government that forever institutionalized the political power of white men? In defense of the status quo the Democrats charged that the radical Republicans were abolitionists who would sink the nation to the infernal depths of a racially amalgamated republic. The radical Republicans answered by claiming that the Declaration of Independence promised the brotherhood of all men in the new nation. They were determined to perfect the Union of their fathers by extending Jefferson's principles of 1776 to include emancipation and civil equality for blacks.

The sweeping views of the Bird Club members transcended the merely "political." Bird and his allies had little interest in minimizing differences of opinion and compromising their principles merely to win votes on election day. They refused to espouse vague platitudes and pieties. Rather, the Bird Club members exposed the slavery issue that divided voters. They were interested in defining and sharpening political differences, and then attracting support for their revolutionary propositions about racial equality, equal rights, and the enforcement of federal law to secure both. For these men, the cause was everything. Principles, rather than politics, absorbed their energy.

The members of the Bird Club were depicted by their enemies as single-minded ideologues, "Jacobins," and "drunken mutineers" who had seized the Massachusetts ship of state. There was a time when historians used these terms of opprobrium to describe the radical Republicans. Sumner, the best known member of the Bird Club, was characterized by generations of writers as a fanatic trying to impose a harsh, vindictive, and hypocritical Reconstruction policy upon the defeated and defenseless South. During the Civil War centennial and civil rights movement of the 1960s, historians again became interested in the radicals, the war, and Reconstruction; but the focus of the newer studies, while taking issue with earlier characterizations of the radicals, remained on national policies and racial problems of the freedmen. This revisionist scholarship did make a contribution by demonstrating that the failure of Reconstruction was linked to the decline of radicalism as a viable political ideology in the North. Since the 1970s, however, historians have begun to reevaluate the politics of the northern states before, during, and after the Civil War.

The following study of the radical Republicans thus ventures into relatively unexplored territory. It analyzes the internal dynamics of Massachusetts politics, which produced the Bird Club and maintained its members in positions of power and influence. In a larger view, the study also assesses the structure of the Republican party in the context of the Civil War party system, including innovations in party strategy, electoral behavior, and voter perceptions of the political system. It investigates the social basis of support for the major parties and traces how that support changed. It describes the tactics the radicals used to stay in power and outlines the factors contributing to the postwar resurgence of the Democrats. By analyzing politics at the grass-roots level, this book asks fundamental questions dealing with the rise of the radical Republicans and their influence on America: what was the role of ideology in forming popular support for the Republican party, and what was to become of an ideologically conceived party when the era of ideological politics had passed?

The Bay State presents an excellent case study of the political activities of the radical Republicans in their own bailiwick. The state's politics presents two facets of a major problem: the dilemmas posed by the unwillingness of the radicals to compromise on issues to win votes, and the limitations of ideological appeals in sustaining voter enthusiasm. Moreover, the state censuses are exceptionally rich in the data needed to examine the social and economic bases of party support. Indeed, few states during this era have ever collected as detailed demographic information as Massachusetts.

This study relies on a variety of quantitative and traditional historical methods. Sophisticated statistical techniques have been used to unravel the inner workings of the two major parties. Interpretations of voting rest on an analysis of election returns using a method historians have rarely adopted until recently: regression estimation of voter transition probabilities in contingency tables. By employing this device, estimates of the percentages of voters moving across party lines have been obtained for every sequential pair of presidential, congressional, and gubernatorial elections in Massachusetts from 1854 to 1876. For all of these elections, these are the first estimates based on this statistical method. Yet quantitative techniques alone cannot explain why men voted as they did or how politicians interpreted the results at the polls. Thus, more traditional evidence, such as pamphlets, newspapers, manuscripts, and other archival material, has been surveyed.

The findings of this study offer a reinterpretation of Massachusetts politics during the Civil War era. The earlier portrait of the political realignment of the 1850s has been distorted: historians have exaggerated the importance of nativism in the forging of Republican majorities. In Massachusetts the Know-Nothing movement, with its dislike of immigrants and Catholics, played a minor role in the shift from Whigs to Republicans. The vote cast during the Civil War years was not a reflection of an earlier period of religious antagonism within a developing industrial, working-class society. Many scholars have argued that differences between Republicans and Democrats in the northern states resulted from a clash of religious values between pietistic and liturgical church denominations. But the partisan cleavage of the Civil War era, at least in Massachusetts, did not follow exclusively the fault lines of cultural conflict. Scholars have also assumed that support for the major parties remained stable throughout the late nineteenth century; but Bay State voters were reshuffled across party lines in the 1870s, more so than in the 1890s, a fact suggesting that the second Grant election resulted in a significant electoral realignment.

This book, then, is a history of the dramatic rise, subsequent domination, and eventual decline of the Massachusetts radical Republicans. On a broader level, it is also a study of voting behavior and the endurance of radical ideology in the politics of one of the most important northern states before, during, and after the Civil War. As such, its findings help to explain the circumstances that enabled this unique episode of ideological politics to occur in American history and help us to comprehend its dynamics and limitations.

Chapter 1
Critical Election Theory and the Realities of Massachusetts Presidential Politics, 1848–1908

The search for a single election in a series is . . . akin to the vain quest for principal causes that has so concerned philosophers of history.—*John L. Shover, "Emergence of a Two-Party System"*

Generations of Americans have transmitted party preferences to their children, but none have done so as successfully as the voters of the Civil War era. When antislavery journalist William S. Robinson, or "Warrington" as he was known to the readers of the Springfield *Republican*, returned home from casting his vote in the 1864 presidential election, he brought back with him extra Republican and Democratic ballots. Summoning his children outside into the garden, "he stuck the McClellan ticket on a hook, and set fire to it, while the children gave three cheers for 'old Abe.'" His behavior was intended to teach his children "their political duty in their youth."[1]

Undoubtedly, such fathers and sons would rely on party loyalty when making future choices at the polls. Observers later in the century commented on this retention of voter allegiance. The "great mass of voters," wrote George S. Merriam, are bound to their party because of "habit, sentiment, and finally of inheritance; so that John Smith is a Republican or a Democrat because his father was one before him; and hardly asks himself seriously why he prefers his party any more than he asks why he prefers Mrs. John Smith to other women, or John Smith, Junior, to other boys."[2]

This deep-seated commitment to parties provides a clue to understanding the Massachusetts electorate and the political history of the state in the second half of the nineteenth century. Voter loyalties were formed during the most disruptive and divisive period of American politics, encompassing the slavery controversies of the 1850s and eventual secession and war. During the Civil War, fundamental disagreements between Republicans and Democrats over the use of federal power to sustain the campaign against the Confederacy polarized the two parties. Radicals within the Republican party and reactionaries within the Democratic party identified two opposite ends of an ideological spectrum. Most Republicans supported the conscription act that mobilized men into the Union army, legal tender acts that created a government-controlled currency, direct taxation to defray the cost of war, and emancipation of the slaves. Most Democrats opposed these measures, believing they were unconstitutional, if not revolutionary, and fearing that they would lead to a dangerous increase in federal power that would alter American society. The real or perceived threat of radical social change was the major issue separating the two parties.[3]

Voters, then, strongly identified themselves with a political organization and this is central to the idea of electoral eras or "party systems." Historians within the past decade have used this concept to study parties, elections, and voters from the genesis of American politics to the present. The party system literature divides the evolution of national politics into stable periods disrupted periodically by brief, yet intense, realigning phases of the electorate, resulting in five distinct party eras. The first or so-called "pre-party" system from 1789 to 1820 prefaced the creation of truly national and competitive partisan organizations, such as the Democratic and Whig parties. These parties flourished during the second period, from 1824 to the massive reshuffling of voters in the 1850s. The third party era was the Civil War party system, which was fully in place by 1860 with the rise to power of the first purely sectional party, the Republicans. During the 1890s, a new electoral era resulted from agrarian discontent in the South and West coupled with urban dissatisfaction with the Democrats in the Northeast. Finally, the New Deal marked the last party system, resulting from the economic depression of the 1930s and persisting until the Great Society of Lyndon Baines Johnson.[4]

Each electoral era consists of a stable period that begins and ends with fluctuation and results in realignment. During stability, individuals continually vote for the same party, and so party loyalty remains constant. Voters seldom cross party lines between elections and the political balance remains unchanged. The placid equilibrium is destroyed by one or a few "critical" or "realigning" elections in which many voters abruptly shift their party allegiance. This change results from many factors, the most important being the emergence of new issues that cut across old party alignments. Individuals are aroused to reassess their political beliefs and party preferences, and new coalitions of voters are formed along with another political balance between the two main parties. Realignment provokes changes in party platforms, policies, and approaches to issues. More important, the public now may form different ideas or perceptions about the nation's political process.[5]

The notion of critical realignments and party systems provides the theoretical basis that underlies the research strategy of this study. A fresh approach is taken, however, in calculating voting returns. The analysis of voter participation and behavior includes those who chose not to vote—defined as nonvoters and abstainers.[6] This additional measurement results in a more accurate assessment of critical realignment. Studies of electoral change that compute party support on the conventional basis of the number of ballots cast have ignored citizens who entered or quit the active or participating electorate, individuals who can be crucial in forming new coalitions or destroying old constituencies.[7] It is possible, for example, for realignments to involve primarily not the conversion of opposition loyalists but the mobilization of previous nonvoters: not one voter has to cross partisan lines to alter an electoral outcome if one party benefits exclusively from a dramatic rise in voter turnout. In incorporating nonvoters into the analysis of election returns, political analysts must not confuse the apolitical citizen with the unfranchised. It is one thing if an individual could not meet the voting qualifications, another if he had the vote but chose not to exercise it.

An understanding of the laws governing elections in nineteenth-century Massachusetts is first necessary in order to characterize nonvoters. The state's original constitution of 1780 gave voting rights to every twenty-one-year-old male resident who received an annual income of three pounds from a freehold or who held any estate worth sixty pounds. In 1821 the property qualification was eliminated and the suffrage was extended to all taxpayers. Residence requirements included one year in the state and six months in the voting area. A poll tax of one or two dollars also was required. The obligation to pay the poll tax—a capitation tax assessed on every twenty-one-year-old male whether a citizen or alien—remained after 1891 when the tax was abolished as a voter registration requirement. Because the costs of collecting the tax were as high as the levy itself, there were few, if any, prosecutions of poll-tax delinquents. In fact, the tax proved even more difficult to collect after it was abolished as a prerequisite for voting because this eliminated the most important incentive to pay it.[8]

On the recommendation of the 1855 anti-immigrant, Know-Nothing legislature, the voters in 1857 adopted a constitutional amendment inaugurating a voter literacy test. The amendment denied future voting rights to anyone unable to read the Constitution and to write his name, but exempted those who already had the suffrage. Another nativist-inspired amendment ratified in 1859 required a foreign-born citizen to meet an additional residence requirement of two years after receiving final naturalization papers, but this amendment was repealed during the Civil War.[9]

Massachusetts never excluded any man from voting on account of color or race. Along with Maine, Vermont, New Hampshire, and Rhode Island, it was one of five New England states where blacks enjoyed equal voting privileges with whites. The same rights were granted to Indians, except those living on communal land and exempt from the poll tax. The state's original inhabitants were not granted citizenship and voting rights until after the Civil War. Citizens born in Asia, many of whom were the servants of the state's wealthy China merchants, also had voting rights. The federal courts in Massachusetts had violated the letter of the law by misinterpreting the "white only" clause and ruling that the Chinese were "white" within the meaning of the naturalization statutes.[10]

Nevertheless, many people did not possess the right to vote. Women could not cast the ballot except in some local school board elections. Aliens, convicts, and those labeled by the courts as "idiots" and "paupers" were excluded. Others who had the suffrage were at times effectively barred from voting. For example, Massachusetts made no provisions for its own soldiers stationed out of state. No absentee ballots were distributed in the field except for presidential electors and congressional candidates, even during the Civil War. An amendment allowing soldiers to vote in state elections while away from home on active duty was not ratified until 1890.[11]

The literacy test did not discourage many uneducated or non-English-speaking citizens from registering and voting. It was common practice for local party workers to examine applicants on the steps of city hall and then vouch for them before the city clerk, who assumed that a respected citizen would not present any applicant who could not pass the examination. City officials did not abuse their power by refusing registration without cause, nor did they turn the test into an inquisition designed to humiliate the citizenry. Thus, they tried to avoid denying applications on the basis of illiteracy.[12] Similarly, the poll tax did not prevent poor men from voting. Before the day of an election, especially a presidential election, city hall vestibules were crowded with citizens lined up to pay their taxes so their names would be on the final "check-lists" used to admit voters to the polls. Both political parties commanded the national machinery needed to raise money to pay the taxes of poorer citizens in order to attract their votes. (Because the poll tax could accumulate for two years, an additional burden fell upon the parties if a voter had failed to pay his tax the previous year.) Just before the poll tax was abolished as a prerequisite for registering and voting, the Democrats were spending approximately $50,000 a year on poll taxes alone throughout the state.[13]

The true impact of the poll tax on voter registration is problematic. The testimony of contemporaries of the period is questionable because it was given during heated partisan debate. Democrats denounced the tax, convinced that they suffered from it more than the Republicans did. In 1869 an inquiry determined that 43 percent of those eligible to vote had been assessed only a two-dollar tax. Using tortured logic, Democratic members of the state legislature interpreted this to mean that more than one-fourth of the potential vote could be mobilized by abolishing the levy. They also believed that newly registered voters would disproportionally support their party.[14]

Equally unreliable testimony on the impact of "poll-tax voters" was offered by reform-minded and educated elites who frequently dominated political commentary through their control of newspapers, trade journals, and learned journals. Their views often reflected the prejudices of property-conscious and conservative citizens who believed that eventually political power would fall into the hands of the poor, landless, untaxed workers who were becoming more visible in the industrial cities and towns. This prospect alarmed the state's articulate aristocrats. To them it meant the destruction of town-meeting democracy run by Protestant yeomanry who could be counted upon to exercise moral restraint and sound judgment. According to one such man, Brooks Adams, a mere poll-tax voter could cast his ballot one year "to swamp his town with debt" and the following year "move away, after he has pocketed his share of the spoil."[15]

A precise piece of evidence at one point in this period, a list of poll-tax voters in every city and town in 1869, is amenable to statistical techniques designed to infer individual behavior from data available only for geographic units (see Table 1.1). A comparison of voting patterns in the 1868 presidential election between poll-tax voters and voters also assessed property taxes reveals that the rate of abstention or nonvoting was higher among those assessed property taxes (see Table 1.1.A). The same phenomenon existed in the 1869 gubernatorial election (see Table 1.1.B). The estimates also indicate that the partisan preferences of poll-tax voters in 1868 were about equally divided between Republicans and Democrats; in the 1869 election, they were evenly split between the Democrats and their Republican and Labor Reform opponents. The poll-tax voters, however, were not as important in the Republican coalitions as they were in the Democratic. About one-third of the 1868 Republican presidential vote was composed of poll-tax voters, whereas slightly over two-thirds of the ballots cast for Democrats came from those who paid only the required poll tax. In brief, the results suggest that poorer poll-tax voters were split between the parties and wealthier, propertied voters expressed a decidedly pro-Republican preference. More importantly, poorer men exercised their right of suffrage with more frequency than did citizens with a property stake in their communities.

Indifference to voting was particularly prevalent among Boston's richer classes. Reputable Bostonians, who surfaced periodically to protest the unfairness of taxes levied on their "over-burdened" real estate or to support candidates for local political office, were often embarrassed by newspaper stories pointing out their failure to register and vote in Boston. Many of them left Boston in the spring to establish temporary residences in the country before the first day of May. In this way they avoided paying assessments on their personal property in Boston and were taxed in some small town where, through fraudulent arrangements with local assessors, they paid less taxes. Hiding wealth through perjury and deception lowered the state's total valuation and caused taxes to soar higher in every city and town, except in those that benefited from systematic tax chiseling. Such ploys left the men who engaged in them off the tax and voting lists in Boston and other cities where assessors had reputations for being honest and incorruptible.[16]

Nevertheless, richer citizens were not disfranchised by dodging taxes because traveling to their temporary residences in early November to vote presented no insurmountable barrier. For example, the seaside community of Nahant, dubbed "the tax-payers' paradise" by Boston's assessors, flourished as a tax haven for the Hub's wealthy citizens. The town had steadily enticed potential tax dodgers by promising lower assessments. By the 1870s it had become a fashionable "permanent resident" summer resort for those anxious to evade their fair share of taxes in Boston where they lived most of the year. Turnout rates for presidential elections from 1860 to 1900 were higher in that small town than statewide averages, with the exception of 1872 and 1876.[17]

Boston Brahmins might have avoided being on the city's tax and therefore voting list, but the city's poor, especially the immigrants, did

TABLE 1.1
A Comparison of the Voting Behavior of "Poll-Tax Voters"
and Voters Assessed Both Property and Poll Taxes
(by percent of 1869 electorate)

A. Estimated Relationships Between Taxpayer Category and
Voting in the 1868 Presidential Election

	Taxpayer Category in 1869		
Party in 1868 Presidential Election	Assessed Poll Taxes Only	Assessed Both Property and Poll Taxes	Percent of 1869 Electorate
Democratic	15	7	22
Republican	17	35	52
Abstained	8	15	23
Not Eligible in 1868	3	0	2
Percent of 1869 Electorate	43	57	100

B. Estimated Relationships Between Taxpayer Category and
Voting in the 1869 Gubernatorial Election

	Taxpayer Category in 1869		
Party in 1869 Gubernatorial Election	Assessed Poll Taxes Only	Assessed Both Property and Poll Taxes	Percent of 1869 Electorate
Democratic	12	7	19
Republican	9	19	28
Labor Reform	3	2	5
Abstained	20	28	48
Percent of 1869 Electorate	43	57	100

Sources: Voting returns for the 1868 presidential and 1869
gubernatorial elections are the official totals. The source for
the number of "legal" voters paying only a poll tax in 1869 is
Massachusetts, General Court, Journal of the House of
Representatives, H.Doc. 82 (February 1870), pp. 1-11.

Note: Actual N = 335. To adjust for the varying populations of
cities and towns, variables used in the analysis are "weighted"
by the number of "legal" voters. For a discussion of the
regression technique used to generate the cell entries in the
above contingency tables, see Langbein and Lichtman, Ecological
Inference, pp. 53-55. Rounding procedures occasionally produce
totals greater or less than 100 percent.

not. Aliens were quickly converted into voters, regardless of party allegiance. If Republicans and Democrats competed to naturalize aliens, there should have been a strong association between party competition and the degree to which the foreign-born population had taken out naturalization papers and become American citizens. But that was not the case. Nor did the ratio of foreign-born voters to the entire foreign-born population in cities in 1875 deviate substantially from the statewide average of 16 percent.[18] The rate at which aliens obtained citizenship, then, appears to have been a function of the enforcement of the naturalization laws.

Laws for naturalization and subsequent voting were straightforward and uncomplicated. An alien who sought citizenship had to be over the age of eighteen and to have lived three years in the United States. He then could file his declaration to be a citizen and two years later receive his second or final papers. An honorably discharged soldier who had not voted prior to his enlistment was not automatically a citizen upon his release; but he easily became naturalized by producing his discharge papers along with the statements of two citizens who had known him for one year. The total amount of time normally required to become a citizen, however, was five years.[19]

During the antiimmigrant, Know-Nothing period of the mid-1850s, debates over the naturalization laws occurred frequently. After the demise of Know-Nothings, neither the operation nor the substance of the laws was a partisan issue. Party chieftains considered it dangerous to tamper with the naturalization laws. One Worcester County Republican, for example, admitted that minor violations sometimes occurred and that Irish-Americans voted against his party. Still, he reminded his colleagues that many other nationalities who supported the Republicans would be offended by changes designed to make the laws more stringent.[20]

The mechanics of voting often disfranchised citizens as effectively as any law directly relating to suffrage qualifications. Before the adoption of the state ballot in 1889, local party committees bore the responsibility of printing and distributing ballots. Improper ballots or an insufficient supply of one party's ticket could hinder voter choice. In theory, a voter could prepare his own ballot and vote for candidates of different parties, thus splitting his ticket. But, in practice, this usually was not done because it was inconvenient, and the voter would be easily spotted as a "bolter," one not voting the party ticket. "Scratching," erasing, or altering names on the partisan ballots were noticed by party activists who diligently peddled their ballots in an excited atmosphere in front of the polls. One observer in Cambridge witnessed a "man's coat torn off his back, crowds pushing voters away and ballots taken out of men's hands and others substituted."[21]

There was no secrecy in casting the party ballot. A voter gave his name to election officials in the presence of party poll watchers; he was admitted unless successfully challenged, and then required to hold his ballot, open and unfolded, above the box to avoid double voting. Newspaper reporters were able to count the vote as the distinctively marked or cut party ballots were deposited in the boxes. During close elections party workers often applauded or hissed depending on the ballot cast. The balloting process enormously strengthened the institution of the political party, for a candidate had no hope of victory without local supporters outside the polls.[22]

The Australian ballot, adopted in 1888, significantly altered the voting process in Massachusetts. The state took over the function of printing and supplying ballots, preventing the political parties from distributing their ballots at the polls. Critics of party-distributed ballots alleged that there was often a prearranged agreement: voters cast ballots to repay political favors owed to local party leaders. Supposedly, the new ballot would encourage greater voter independence at the polls. Also, the new state ballot would effectively disfranchise voters who could not read, although election officials were required to aid illiterates who had been qualified before passage of the 1857 "reading and writing" amendment. Zealous party workers armed with sample ballots had to coach all other unlettered voters before they stepped into the privacy of the voting booths.[23]

The Australian ballot affected voting in two important ways: split-ticket voting increased as did the tendency of voters to mark their ballot for prestigious offices, such as president and governor, but not for lower offices, such as county commissioners of insolvency. The latter phenomenon, called "roll-off," resulted from using the office bloc, rather than the party column, format of the ballot. There is little indication that the secret ballot was responsible for a decline in voter participation. In 1892, the first presidential election in which the Australian ballot was used, turnout was higher than in any presidential election since 1868.[24]

During the second half of the nineteenth century, who, then, accurately could be called a nonvoter or abstainer? Many who met the suffrage requirements were effectively disfranchised by illiteracy, nonpayment of the poll tax while it remained a prerequisite for registering, absence from the state, failure to meet the local residence requirement, and sickness. Consequently, the percentage prevented from voting at any time probably constituted, according to contemporaries of the period, anywhere from 10 to 15 percent of the legally eligible voters. The number of "legal" Massachusetts voters, therefore, represented the ultimate possible voting strength of the state.[25] For the purpose of determining voter turnout or nonvoting and party support, all election statistics (both here and elsewhere unless specified) have been calculated on the basis of the number of legal or potentially eligible voters. The contours of the presidential vote in the Bay State from 1848 to 1908 are shown in Table 1.2.

TABLE 1.2
Turnout and Proportion of "Legal" Voters Casting Ballots for Each Party in the Massachusetts Presidential Elections, 1848-1908

Presidential Election Year	Turnout	Whig/Fillmore-American/Constitutional Union	Free-Soil/Republican	Democratic	Others	Abstained
1848	79.4%	36.1%	22.5%	20.9%	.0%	20.6%
1852	67.9	28.1	15.0	23.8	1.0[d]	32.1
1856	81.4	9.5	52.4	19.0	.4	18.6
1860	75.9	10.0	47.7	15.4	2.9[b]	24.1
1864	72.6	--	52.4	20.2	.0	27.4
1868	75.7	--	52.8	22.9	.0	24.3
1872	63.5	--	44.0	19.5	--	36.5
1876	72.2	--	41.8	30.3	.2	27.8
1880	71.6	--	41.9	28.4	1.3[c]	28.4
1884	70.1	--	33.9	28.3	7.9[c]	29.9
1888	72.4	--	38.7	31.9	1.8[d]	27.6
1892	74.8	--	38.8	33.8	2.2[e]	25.2
1896	70.2	--	48.8	15.8	5.6[f]	29.8
1900	67.5	--	38.8	25.5	3.1[g]	32.5
1904	67.2	--	38.9	25.0	3.3[h]	32.8
1908	64.8	--	37.7	22.1	4.9[i]	35.2

Sources: All calculations are my own, based on interpolations from lists of "legal" voters and the official manuscript returns for presidential electors on file in the Archives Division of the Commonwealth of Massachusetts, State House, Boston. A growth rate formula that assumed a curvilinear pattern of both increase and decline in population was used to estimate the number of potentially eligible voters in the years for which registration data were not readily available. For the actual formulas used, see Dollar and Jensen, Historian's Guide to Statistics, pp. 130-32.

[a]Constitutional Union ticket pledged to Daniel Webster and scattered returns.

[b]Breckinridge Democrats and scattered returns.

[c]Greenback, Prohibition, and scattered returns.

[d]Prohibition and scattered returns.

[e]Prohibition, Populist, Socialist Labor, and scattered returns.

[f]People's, National (Gold) Democratic, Prohibition, Socialist Labor, and scattered returns.

[g]Democratic Social, Socialist Labor, Prohibition, and scattered returns.

[h]Socialist, Prohibition, Socialist Labor, People's, and scattered returns.

[i]Independent League, Socialist, Prohibition, Socialist Labor, and scattered returns.

The idea of a Civil War party system has become the central organizing motif for studying American electoral history from 1856 to 1896. Within this period historians have further divided the system into subperiods: a realigning or unstable phase from 1856 to 1874 and a stable or normal sequence from 1874 to 1892. A massive national realignment occurred during the 1850s when the Whigs vanished and new political factions in the North and border states replaced them as the opponents of the Democrats. In the South the Whig demise resulted in increased Democratic party dominance. Most authorities agree that this realignment was completed in the northern states by 1860, and that the final collapse of traditional party loyalties in the South occurred in the winter of 1860–61 during the balloting for delegates to state secession conventions.[26]

The economic depression of 1873 marked the beginning of the end of the first phase of the Civil War party system. In the great upset of 1874, Republican hegemony was shattered by Democratic congressional victories. Nevertheless, the Democrats were not able to establish dominance, and this led to intense competition with Republicans throughout the late 1870s and 1880s. This electoral rivalry characterized the second phase of the Civil War party system. Minor political parties, such as the Greenbackers and Prohibitionists, arose along with factions such as the Mugwumps. Contemporaries perceived these groups as important because they might be able to tip the balance of power in closely contested elections.[27]

Political analysts regard the 1890s as another great period of national realignment, which is also important to this study of an earlier period. Standard accounts of this turbulent decade blame the panic of 1893 for the erosion of Democratic support in congressional elections the following year. This disaffection crystallized in 1896 when the Democrats selected an agrarian populist from Nebraska, William Jennings Bryan, as their presidential nominee. While the differences in the campaign appeared to be geographic and economic, involving a deflationary gold policy favored in the Northeast versus one of inflationist silver popular in the West and South, there also were social and religious issues. Recent studies demonstrate that Bryan's fundamentalist Protestant zeal alienated many members of liturgical churches who traditionally supported the Democrats. Naturally, historians differ over the importance of sectional, economic, or ethnocultural issues in Bryan's defeat, but most agree that the realignment of the 1890s transformed the anatomy and public image of the Democratic and Republican parties, and finally destroyed the Civil War party system.[28]

Massachusetts provides an excellent test of electoral changes during the nineteenth century. By analyzing the presidential vote from 1848 to 1908 one can support or reject the conventional periodizations of critical election theory. Unfortunately, the existing studies of the state's politics are not helpful, for most are biographical, tracing the movements and machinations of prominent politicians or articulate elites. None systematically analyzes voting patterns for the entire second half of the nineteenth century.[29]

In any two successive elections one can divide all legal voters into five categories: those who voted in both elections for the same party; those who voted in both elections but switched parties or crossed party lines; those who cast ballots in the first election but not in the second; those who did not vote in the first election but did in the second; and those who abstained from voting in both elections. By examining the size of these groups in pairs of elections, one can explain changes in voter alignments between elections. In addition, it is possible to uncover the critical elections in which many abruptly shifted parties, and to discover the occurrence of subtle changes in voter preferences that slowly developed over many elections.

This information can be computed by using regression estimation of cell entries in contingency tables. Scholars struggling with the task of inferring individual behavior from voting returns available only for geographical areas have recently experimented with this technique and have begun to employ it creatively in the analysis of past politics. In the variation used here, partisans and abstainers are treated as subgroups of the state's legal voters, and regressions on these subgroups produce estimates of individual behavior such as the movement between parties between elections.[30]

When using ecological regressions to analyze the Massachusetts presidential vote, one must maintain a constant voting population. Ideally, the analyst uses data on the number of previous nonvoters who attained eligibility at the time of the second election, as well as data on the number of men who belonged to the electorate at the time of the first election, but who, because of death, migration, or some other reason, were no longer part of the voting population at the time of the second election. In this manner more accurate estimates can be computed for the number of voters belonging to the categories of those voting in the first election but not in the second, and those voting in the second but not in the first. Unfortunately, most of this information does not exist for this period. Still, the analysis is strengthened by using the increase in the voting population between elections as a measure of previously ineligible or "new voters." This creates an additional subgroup, which, when used in regression equations, produces more accurate estimates of voting between pairs of elections.[31]

Naturally, any analysis contains some problems. In this study, city and town boundary changes over the years complicated the gathering of voting returns. Consequently, when boundary changes in any city or town made comparison between one election and the next impossible, the city or town was simply dropped from the analysis of the pair of elections involved.[32]

In the analysis of Massachusetts presidential elections, all sequential elections, both successive and alternate, are compared from 1848 to 1908 (see Table 1.3). The goal is to derive estimates of the five subgroups of the total electorate in each pair of elections. Each row in the following table presents estimates of the size of electoral categories.

Individuals who either voted in one election only or who switched parties (total instability) and those who voted for the same party or who did not vote in both elections (total stability) are marked by parentheses.[33]

The table demonstrates that voter turnout fluctuated, and that in the late nineteenth century turnout was as important in shaping the outcome of presidential elections as voters switching parties. In every set of comparisons, individuals who crossed party lines comprised less than 10 percent of the electorate after 1864 in any successive or alternate pair of elections. Voters leaving or entering the active electorate between 1856 and 1896 always outnumbered those who switched parties. Consequently, those who "came into" or "dropped out of" the active electorate affected presidential outcomes as much as those who crossed party lines. Even a one-way defection of Democrats into Republican ranks could have been countered by former Republican voters who abstained or by the influx of new voters such as immigrants who voted disproportionally for the Democrats.

The Bay State electorate was extremely volatile before but not after the Civil War. An unusually large segment of voters switched parties between the 1848 and 1860 elections. For the purpose of analysis, the Republican party is treated as the Free-Soil party under another name. However, the votes cast for John C. Breckinridge on the "splitter" Democratic ticket in 1860 were not combined with those cast for Stephen A. Douglas, the candidate for the "regular" Democrats. The Know-Nothing party is not treated as a continuation of the Whig party, and in the 1860 election the Constitutional Union party also is considered separately (and not as the Know-Nothing party under another name). The percentage of the electorate switching parties between 1852 and 1856 was unusually high, 34 percent. But this is not true if both 1848 and 1852 Whigs and Free-Soilers voting for John C. Frémont are regarded as repeating their anti-Democratic party preferences. Then, the percentage switching parties declines to 12 percent and the percentage switching between 1848 and 1856 drops to 21 percent, making the 1852–56 period equivalent to the degree of electoral volatility that both preceded it in 1848–52 and followed it in 1856–60 (see Table 2.9). When viewed from this vantage point, the period of the Know-Nothing imbroglio had no disproportionate impact upon the regrouping of voters that occurred between 1848 and 1860.

In contrast to the electoral instability of the late antebellum period, the most durable voter coalitions demonstrated in Table 1.3 were forged in the wartime presidential election of 1864. Between that year and 1868 an insignificant number of voters crossed party lines. About 86 percent of the Massachusetts electorate repeated their exact behav-

TABLE 1.3
Transition Probabilities of Voting Behavior in Sequential Presidential Elections in Massachusetts, 1848-1908
(by percent of electorate)

Election Pair	Actual Number of Cases	Switching Parties	Voting in First Election Only	Voting in Second Election Only	(Total Instability)	Repeating a Party Vote	Not Voting in Both Elections	(Total Stability)
Sequential Successive Presidential Elections, 1848-1908								
1848-1852	301	14	7	5	(26)	51	24	(75)
1852-1856	321	34	0	16	(50)	30	19	(49)
1856-1860	325	15	9	10	(34)	51	15	(66)
1860-1864	332	10	9	11	(30)	52	18	(70)
1864-1868	332	0	3	11	(14)	65	21	(86)
1868-1872	334	6	9	8	(23)	50	27	(77)
1872-1876	338	2	3	21	(26)	48	25	(73)
1876-1880	341	2	4	10	(16)	60	24	(84)
1880-1884	344	6	7	12	(25)	52	23	(75)
1884-1888	346	8	2	11	(21)	54	25	(79)
1888-1892	350	2	6	13	(21)	59	20	(79)
1892-1896	351	7	8	10	(25)	54	22	(76)
1896-1900	352	3	8	10	(21)	54	25	(79)
1900-1904	353	1	3	7	(11)	59	30	(89)
1904-1908	353	5	5	7	(17)	53	30	(83)
Sequential Alternate Presidential Elections, 1848-1908								
1848-1856	301	37	1	17	(55)	27	18	(45)
1852-1860	322	32	4	21	(57)	23	20	(43)
1856-1864	324	7	11	14	(32)	51	16	(67)
1860-1868	332	11	4	15	(30)	50	20	(70)
1864-1872	331	1	13	18	(32)	44	24	(68)
1868-1876	331	6	1	19	(26)	47	26	(73)
1872-1880	337	1	7	29	(37)	41	21	(62)
1876-1884	342	5	5	16	(26)	50	23	(73)
1880-1888	343	3	6	19	(28)	51	21	(72)
1884-1892	346	9	2	19	(30)	47	23	(70)
1888-1896	350	7	7	16	(30)	46	24	(70)
1892-1900	350	2	3	6	(11)	59	30	(89)
1896-1904	352	4	7	13	(24)	49	26	(75)
1900-1908	353	3	7	12	(22)	49	28	(77)

Sources: The 1852 and 1860 official returns were supplemented by unofficial tallies in instances where the votes from certain towns were excluded because of a mere technicality, such as the failure of the report of votes to arrive in Boston before a certain deadline. Otherwise, all returns are the official totals.

Note: Logically but not statistically impossible estimates falling slightly outside of the 0 to 100 percent range were arbitrarily set at their respective minimum or maximum limits, and the values of the remaining estimates were then adjusted according to the restraints of the marginal values of the contingency tables. This procedure eliminated negative estimates from a few of the tables. In following this procedure, however, no modifications were made in the logical estimates of voters repeating a vote for the same party in both elections. Estimates of the percentage of abstainers in the first election who subsequently did not vote in the second election were also unaffected by this procedure provided the original estimates fell similarly within the 0 to 100 percent range. For the reasons to have more confidence in these estimates than in others, see Shively, "'Ecological'Inference," p. 1191. For the purposes of this analysis, the Republican party was treated as a continuation of the Free-Soil party, while the Whig, Fillmore-American, Constitutional Union, and Breckinridge constituencies were regarded as separate and distinct parties. The Democratic vote in 1896 included only those voting for William Jennings Bryan on the "regular" Democratic ticket.

ior in both elections; that is, they either supported the same party twice or they did not vote in both elections. This indicates a remarkable degree of stability; however, it did not endure. The 1872 and 1876 elections again were marked by instability.

Another observation derived from the table contradicts the notion that the 1896 election was a critical election. In Massachusetts there was more permanent reshuffling of voters in either the 1870s or 1880s than in the 1890s. A comparison of one election with those eight years before or after allows us to distinguish permanent and temporary changes. Using this approach, the 1890s emerge as a stable era in the state's electoral politics. The temporary disruption in 1896 does not significantly affect this pattern. If the period between 1892 and 1896 witnessed a fundamental realignment, the election of William McKinley should mark the beginning of a series of elections that are unrelated to the previous election in 1896. This is not the case. Voters did not alter their allegiances between 1892 and 1900, exactly the opposite of what would be predicted by advocating the critical election hypothesis. Only about 2 percent switched parties between 1892 and 1900, while approximately 89 percent either voted for the same party twice or sat out both elections. In other words, the 1900 election reestablished the earlier coalitions of 1892, rather than continuing the reorientation of preferences initiated during the 1896 contest.

This is not to say, however, that the Democratic and Republican parties were not affected by the first Bryan-McKinley contest. On the contrary, differential rates of turnout shaped the 1896 outcome and, as a consequence, the election realigned the Democratic party. In 1888 and 1892 the Democrats attracted about 32 percent and 34 percent, respectively, of the potential vote, figures that fell to 16 percent after the Bryan debacle (see Table 1.2). By 1900 and 1904 the party's fortunes improved, but it still could not attract a full one-third of the electorate. Thus, in 1896 the Democratic party suffered a disastrous decline in support that it was not able to regain. For the Republicans, the election proved to be a deviating one, since McKinley could not maintain the additional support he received under the stimulus of Bryan's first campaign. The enhanced Republican majorities of 1900 and 1904 were due primarily to the persistence with which many Democrats stayed away from the polls after 1892, rather than to the conversion of former Democrats to Republicans.[34]

Massachusetts voting trends throughout the second half of the nineteenth century reject the conventional description of national and northern state voting patterns. The state's voting behavior in presidential elections from 1848 to 1908 does not conform to critical election theory because its presidential politics do not support the idea of a Civil War party system at the national level. The behavior of the electorate does not exhibit an unstable phase lasting from 1856 to 1874 and a stable phase from 1874 to 1892, a pattern which voters permanently shattered in 1896. Nor does a single election or a "critical" period hold the key to understanding the complexities of electoral change processes that occurred in the 1850s and 1890s. These negative findings, however, are not cause for discouragement. The major issue, after all, is to describe as accurately as possible how all potential voters responded to parties and candidates and how their behavior changed from one election to the next. Only then can the relationship between voter realignments and other aspects of the political system be explored. It is time to confront that task by analyzing Massachusetts politics during the turbulent decade of the 1850s.

Chapter 2
The Political Realignment
of the 1850s: Know-Nothingism
and the Emergence of a
Republican Majority

The political history of Massachusetts from 1846 to 1865 is, in
general, the history of the share of the Commonwealth in the
great National contest with Slavery; the beginning and growth
of the Free Soil or Republican Party and the putting down of
the Rebellion. The rise and dominion for three years, and final
overthrow of the Know-Nothing Party . . . is an episode which
might be omitted without injury to the sense.—*George Frisbie
Hoar*, Autobiography of Seventy Years

From 1848 to 1856 political developments in Massachusetts were
chaotic. Determined to make expansion of slavery an issue after
the Mexican War, dissidents in the Whig and Democratic parties along
with former Liberty party men organized the Free-Soil party. An anti-
Whig alliance of Free-Soilers and Democrats controlled the state government from 1850 to 1852. Although the Whigs made a successful
comeback in 1853, they soon found their party in shambles during the
Know-Nothing embranglement. In the mid-1850s, the Commonwealth
fell under the temporary sway of the antiimmigrant and anti-Catholic
Know-Nothing or American party. The heir to the Free-Soil party, a
new antislavery Republican party, emerged during the years of Know-
Nothing dominance and successfully competed with former Whigs and
die-hard Know-Nothings for the mantle of the anti-Democratic movement. When the Republicans finally captured the governorship in 1857,
a measure of predictability was restored to Massachusetts electoral
politics. By 1860, political hegemony passed to the radical faction of the
Republicans who dominated state politics throughout the next decade.
   Massachusetts thus experienced a major political realignment in the

late antebellum period. This involved a drastic reorganization of mass voting behavior that resulted in a dramatic shift in the focus of political power. The old Whig leadership was replaced with original Free-Soil party men, such as Charles Sumner, John Andrew, and Frank Bird, who prior to 1860 were not accustomed to being on the winning side on election day. The problem in analyzing the realignment of the 1850s, however, lies not with describing the nature of the change in political leadership so much as with accurately describing the behavior of the voters at the grass-roots level who brought it about.[1]

In 1852 the Free-Soilers grappled with the argument put forward by their political opponents that the Compromise of 1850 represented a final settlement to sectional differences. Both the Whig and Democratic parties adopted resolutions endorsing the Compromise and the Fugitive Slave Law, and declared their intention to resist all further efforts to renew debate on the slavery issue. Furthermore, both major parties made efforts to lure the 1848 Free-Soilers back to their previous party loyalties. As the 1852 election approached, some Free-Soil politicians favored a union with the Democrats on a slate of presidential electors, but the Bay State Free-Soil party stoically resolved to take an independent stand knowing that it would be unlikely to duplicate its strong, second-place finish of 1848 in the presidential balloting. On the other hand, many Free-Soilers looked happily upon the thinning of their ranks, especially if the result would lead to an increased emphasis on antislavery extensionism rather than on petty political intrigues at home. Because of the tendency of many Free-Soilers to place the antislavery cause above the very survival of their own party organization, Democratic and Whig party chieftains dubbed the Free-Soilers "the most unreasonable faction" in state politics. "They deal with morals as with mathematics," complained Senator Daniel Webster, "and they think what is right may be distinguished from what is wrong, with the precision of an algebraic equation."[2]

Although nationally the Democratic party regained its majority position with the election of Franklin Pierce in 1852, in Massachusetts it managed to outpoll the Free-Soil party and finish second in the balloting. Historians have assumed that, on the national level, the increase in the Democratic popular vote by some 380,000 over 1848 was largely attributable to Martin Van Buren or "Barnburner" Democrats returning to the party.[3] In Massachusetts—where about one-third of the 1848 Free-Soil vote was composed of former Democrats—there is insufficient quantitative evidence to support the notion that Democratic party leader Marcus Morton led the return of "a large group of Massachusetts Free Soilers to the Democratic party in 1852."[4] An insignificant number of 1848 Free-Soilers voted for Pierce in 1852 (see Table 2.1). Thus, in Massachusetts Democratic gains at the polls in 1852 did not represent "Van Burenites" returning to their antecedent loyalties, the party of Andrew Jackson. Whereas about 70 percent of the 1848 Free-Soilers repeated a Free-Soil vote in 1852, about one-fourth of them voted for Whig candidate Winfield Scott. Presumably, many Free-Soilers perceived Scott as a more realistic antislavery candidate than their own candidate, John P. Hale, and in 1852 temporarily jumped to the Whigs.

The fact that the Whigs carried Massachusetts for Scott in 1852 has obscured the amount of disaffection in the party's rank and file in that election (see Table 2.1). Whig conversions to the Democrats are usually assumed to have occurred mainly in the southern states rather than in New England, but in 1852 there were sizable Whig defections to the Democrats in Massachusetts. Apparently, many Bay State Whigs deferred to Webster who, brokenhearted after his failure to receive his party's nomination for president, made known his wish that his supporters vote for Pierce. There was a tendency for 1848 Whigs to sit out the 1852 election or, perhaps, to "scratch" Scott from their ballots. If Webster had lived, according to his political enemies, his persistent friends would have easily given him as many as 10,000 votes. As it turned out, an electoral ticket pledged to the deceased Webster polled 1,670 votes and about 11,200 1848 Whigs voted for Pierce. The result was that the Whigs were able to marshal the support of only about 64 percent of their 1848 constituency for Scott.[5]

By claiming that the Know-Nothing movement had immense significance for the emergence of the Bay State Republican party, historians have placed the coalition of voters brought together under the American party banner in a pivotal position in the story of the realignment of parties in the 1850s.[6] Although Republicans were often angered by Irish Catholic opposition to the antislavery crusade, the connection between Massachusetts Republicans and nativism was complex. In 1854 there was no consensus among Free-Soil politicians over the significance of nativism as a force in state politics. Henry Wilson genuinely hoped to make the plebeian and populistic Know-Nothing movement a vehicle for a strong antislavery program, but Charles Francis Adams and many other Free-Soilers were disgusted by such an endeavor, considering it yet another instance of sacrificing antislavery principles for political expediency. Sumner even feared that nativism might divert the attention of voters from slavery and unite the North and South on the basis of hatred of foreigners and Catholics.[7]

The ambivalent attitudes of antislavery politicians toward the

TABLE 2.1
Crossover Voting Between the 1848 and 1852 Presidential Elections
(by percent of 1852 electorate)

Candidate in 1852	Candidate in 1848			Not Voting for President 1848	Not Eligible 1848	Percent of 1852 Electorate
	Taylor	Cass	Van Buren			
Scott	21	2	5	0	0	28
Pierce	6	16	0	1	2	25
Hale	0	0	14	2	0	15
Webster[a]	1	0	0	0	0	1
Not Voting for President 1852	5	1	1	16	8	31
Percent of 1852 Electorate	33	19	20	19	10	100

Note: Actual N = 301. To adjust for the varying populations of cities and towns, variables used in regression equations are "weighted" by the potential voting population. The figures above represent the percentage of eligible voters, not the conventional percentage of ballots cast. The marginals are the actual figures, not estimates; thus the sum of the percentages of eligibles voting for Scott (28%), Pierce (25%), Hale (15%), and Webster (1%) equals the turnout for the 1852 election (69%). Both here and elsewhere in the tables, rounding procedures occasionally produce totals greater or less than 100 percent. To avoid giving the impression that the estimates are actual numbers that can be measured with precision, all figures in the tables have been rounded to the nearest whole percentage.

[a]Constitutional Union ticket pledged to Daniel Webster.

Know-Nothings were understandable, for unlike the narrow, anti-foreign focus of Know-Nothingism in many other states, the Massachusetts American party was composed of a diverse collection of voters. For awhile it seemed that the confusion in party positions on the slavery issue following the passage of the Kansas-Nebraska Act was the catalyst bringing together the motley assortment of nativist political groups in the state in 1854. Politically adventurous and conservative Whigs flocked to the American party banner, seeking an alternative to unacceptable antislavery principles and hoping to forge a new, truly national party on the foundations of anti-Catholic and antiforeign sentiment. Equally opportunistic, reform-minded Democrats, along with many Free-Soilers, moved into the new American party with hopes of taking it over and converting it to their own purposes. In almost every case where a former Whig, Democratic or Free-Soil politician entered a "black lantern" lodge of the secret order in search of votes, political advantages outweighed religious bigotry and ethnic intolerance. Even the Know-Nothing mayor of Boston, J. V. C. Smith, while in office in 1854 continued his close business relationships with his Irish Catholic friends.[8]

The Know-Nothing party drew its strongest support from rapidly growing areas of the state most affected by industrialism, urbanization, and immigration. The drab new factory towns around Boston, like Watertown and Somerville, were caught up in the Know-Nothing craze; towns off the beaten track in the Berkshire Mountains in the western part of the state, like New Ashford, were virtually untouched. Know-Nothings ran best where, not surprisingly, their followers were organized in nativist secret societies. Native-born Protestant workers filled the membership lists of these lodges. Yet the impulse toward reform was always important to the success of the party. Even in towns where native-born workers rushed to join the nativist party for fear of job competition from poverty-stricken Irish immigrants willing to work for less pay, the new party was often promoted as a labor reform movement with goals wider than just placing legal restrictions on immigrants. For example, the Know-Nothing legislators restricted child labor, enacted a mechanics lien law, and showed interest in, yet failed to pass, a law to limit the workday to ten hours.[9]

There is a sense in which the Know-Nothing party can be considered a successor to the anti-Whig Coalition of Free-Soilers and Democrats that swept the state elections in 1850. The program of the Coalition had been inspired by a reformist impulse similar to the one contributing to the success of the Know-Nothings. Both the Coalition and the Know-Nothing party, moreover, brought into public office many men of relatively humble backgrounds. These men were ridiculed for their lack of social polish and education by wealthy Beacon Hill and Back Bay Bostonians who exercised a dominant influence in the Whig party. Wilson, the architect of the Coalition, had once been a cobbler in Natick; the leading Democrat fusionist, Nathaniel P. Banks, had once been a bobbin boy in a Waltham factory. Both men played important roles in the Know-Nothing party.[10]

The glue that held the Coalition together proved as weak as that later uniting the disparate groups that flocked to the Know-Nothing party. Serious conflicts arose among Free-Soil leaders regarding the basic purpose of the anti-Whig alliance. In Wilson's words, the Coalition was formed in 1850 to give Massachusetts both "a state government not under control of powerful corporations, and a senator who would wake up the echoes of freedom in the Capitol of the nation." The Coalition's most consequential accomplishment was giving Webster's old seat in the United States Senate to Sumner. But many upper-class Free-Soilers, such as Charles F. Adams and John G. Palfrey, had little enthusiasm for Coalition-inspired economic reforms. They especially protested when the Coalition began mobilizing the people of the Massachusetts countryside against Whiggish Boston. The city contained the business leaders, the wealth, and the institutions, such as Harvard College, that gave the old-fashioned, conservative, compromise Union Whigs their power in state politics.[11]

Some profusionist Free-Soilers were wary of the reform measures sponsored by the Coalition, fearing the reformist response to the evil of slavery in the South would become sidetracked in its zeal to correct abuses at the local and state levels. Bird, the leader of the Sumner faction of the state's political antislavery forces, hoped that the Coalition would indoctrinate the Democratic party with antislavery ideology and that, when the alliance ended, the departing Free-Soilers would take a large portion of the Democratic party with them. According to Bird, only "the humbug" of state reform kept up the pretext of the Coalition's existence after the election of Pierce to the presidency. When the new administration in Washington insisted that Massachusetts Democrats avoid all alliances that might offend the South, the Coalition, in Bird's opinion, could never be brought back to life.[12]

The desire for reform produced a new state constitution, which, if it had been approved by the voters, would have institutionalized most of the previous assaults made by the Coalition upon everything it believed contributed to the power and influence of the wealthy, conservative Boston Whigs. The proposed constitution aimed at giving greater representation in the legislature to rural areas. There, Whig strength was weakest, whereas the opposite was true in Boston, long considered the bastion of Websterism. But in 1853 voters rejected the constitution by a narrow margin in a statewide referendum (see Table 2.2). Many Coalitionists blamed the constitution's defeat on the opposition of Irish voters. The Irish had objected to the increased political representation given to rural districts at the expense of the cities, and especially to a suggested amendment barring the use of state funds for religious schools. The opposition of the "Cotton" Whigs was taken for granted, but the "treason" of the Irish Democrats was unforgivable. It was commonly believed that a "Cotton and Catholic Coalition" forged by Whig purchases of Irish votes in and around Boston had defeated the new constitution. When the nativist, Know-Nothing movement emerged the following year, many considered it to be controlled by old Coalitionists seeking political revenge for the Irish who voted en bloc against the constitution.[13]

The defeat of the constitution by slightly over 5,000 votes was the result of many factors. Analysis of voting patterns in the 1852 presidential election and in the 1853 constitutional initiative suggests that defections from the ranks of those who voted for Pierce, whether Irish or others, equaled about 2 percent of the electorate in 1853 or about 3,840 voters (see Table 2.2). The Irish, therefore, were not totally responsible for the defeat of the constitution. When the Democratic defectors are, in turn, combined with the number of 1852 Free-Soilers who decided to vote against the proposed constitution, the defeat could

TABLE 2.2
The Defeat of the Coalition-Inspired Constitution: Estimated Relationships Between Voting
Patterns in the 1852 Presidential Election and the 1853 Constitutional Referendum
(by percent of 1853 electorate)

1853 Referendum	Candidate in 1852				Not Voting for President 1852	Not Eligible 1852	Percent of 1853 Electorate
	Scott	Pierce	Hale	Webster[a]			
For	0	18	14	0	1	0	33
Against	27	2	2	1	3	1	36
Abstained	1	5	0	0	24	1	31
Percent of 1853 Electorate	28	25	15	1	28	2	100

Note: Actual N = 312.

[a]Constitutional Union ticket pledged to Daniel Webster.

easily be credited to "independent" Free-Soilers and Democrats. At least one newspaper account reached this conclusion. The rate of abstention of 1852 Democrats also played a crucial role in shaping the outcome. This suggests that the Pierce administration's warning against further Democratic collaboration with Massachusetts Free-Soilers— especially Attorney General Caleb Cushing's famous "ukase" threatening the loss of all national patronage—kept many Democrats from participating in the referendum. On the other hand, the united stand of the Whigs in opposing the new constitution was no less important in determining the result: a remarkably high 97 percent of those who voted in 1852 for either Winfield Scott or Daniel Webster also cast ballots against the Coalitionist-inspired constitution. This perhaps, in the final analysis, ensured its defeat.[14]

The Whig resurgence in 1853 was short-lived for in the fall of 1854 the American party swept into power. In its first statewide appearance the new nativist party polled an unprecedented majority of the popular vote, electing its entire state ticket, all of the state's members of Congress, the entire state senate, and almost all of the lower house. In spite of the antiparty spirit of Know-Nothingism and the large number of young political amateurs who were elected to the state legislature under its banner, the Massachusetts organization at the top was dominated by three experienced politicians: the incoming governor, Henry J. Gardner, had been an active Whig; Banks had been a longtime Democrat; and Wilson had been a prominent Free-Soil party leader. The former Coalitionists Banks and Wilson worked together effectively, but neither could work with their new governor. Gardner, a former Boston dry-goods merchant, sincerely hoped that nativism could divert attention from slavery in the South and reform at home, and that it would become the basis for a new, enduring national political party.

Know-Nothing
reforms

Soon after the opening of the 1855 legislative session, a leading Know-Nothing newspaper complained that the conduct of governmental affairs was not being directed by those dedicated to the true principles of the American party.[15]

The reform-minded Know-Nothing legislature passed measures recognizing the property rights of married women, requiring compulsory vaccination and attendance for public school children, and abolishing imprisonment for debt. But the more conservative Governor Gardner vetoed many of its other constructive accomplishments. Although the Know-Nothing party's antiimmigrant achievements—such as the abolishment of all foreign-born military companies and the deportation of a number of aliens—were largely inconsequential, the unsavory, if not farcical, investigation of the state's nunneries by nativist members of the legislature served to discredit the new party in the eyes of many Bay State voters. Those who had the true principles of the American party at heart wanted to ban all foreign-born citizens from holding office, deprive aliens of the vote, and delay naturalization of immigrants for at least twenty-one years after their arrival in the country. But these proposals failed to distract attention from more dangerous sectional animosities. When the Know-Nothing legislature passed a school integration law, tried to impeach a slave-returning judge, and enacted a personal liberty law making the Fugitive Slave Law practically impossible to enforce in Massachusetts, an irrevocable breach opened between Gardner and the antislavery elements in his own party.[16]

Some historians have assumed that the same impulse toward reform that ushered in Know-Nothingism produced the Massachusetts Republican party, and that this reformist urge was basically an outgrowth of the values and beliefs of native-born Protestant voters.[17] During the nineteenth century the notion was widespread that progress in movements for the promotion of temperance, moral reform, antislavery, public education, and scientific knowledge depended on the absence of ritual, dogma, and superstition in religion. Many Protestants believed that Christianity was capable of stimulating the greatest possible mental and moral development only in direct proportion to its elimination of atavistic Roman Catholic doctrines and practices. But the presumption that anti-Catholicism and antislavery moved in tandem demands refinement.

Historians must differentiate carefully between nativism as an intolerant attitude toward Irish Catholicism—which undoubtedly many abolitionists, Free-Soilers, and Republicans shared—and nativism as a vote-getting force in politics.[18] Abolitionists and antislavery zealots were seldom found among the nativists, even though many of them probably shared to some degree the conviction that enlightened and progressive thought could flourish only in the absence of the pernicious influence of the Catholic church. Abolitionists, especially the Garrisonians, were usually found among those who bitterly denounced the nativists and Know-Nothings. The historical record is replete with examples of such denunciations by individual abolitionists and antislavery politicians. Speaking in Fall River at the height of the Know-Nothing craze that swept over the city, Senator Sumner pleaded with his listeners as the "descendants of the Pilgrims of another generation," not to turn their backs now on the "Pilgrims of the present."[19]

Conversely, Sumner's antislavery speeches often failed to generate any interest among Know-Nothings. The Bay State American party won support from many who were either indifferent or antagonistic to antislavery. Many Know-Nothings, moreover, were also hostile to the antiliquor crusade. Antislavery and prohibition issues cut across the lines of nativism and frequently exposed the inner tensions within the Know-Nothing coalition. The Know-Nothing mayor of Worcester in 1854 characterized the men who elected him as "tired of talk about rum and talk about niggers."[20] Virulent nativism proved attractive to many hard-drinking, lower-class workingmen who despised Irish immigrants, but it did not serve as a channel from one political party to another.

Although a few prominent antislavery men became Know-Nothings, their behavior was an unreliable guide to the behavior of otherwise anonymous voters who did not always take their cues from elites. Wilson, the former Free-Soil fusionist in Coalition politics, believed that the new American party was a step toward building a genuinely antislavery party. As the 1854 gubernatorial candidate of the debilitated Free-Soil or "Republican" party, he had entered into a liaison with Gardner and the Know-Nothings before the election. After receiving the amazing news of the Know-Nothing sweep at the polls, Whig Senator Edward Everett recorded in his diary that the entire Bay State Free-Soil organization merged itself in the new American party. One historian has estimated that 78 percent of the Massachusetts Free-Soilers voted the Know-Nothing ticket, an estimate that agrees with the conclusions of election "postmortems" by contemporaries.[21]

Even though most former Free-Soilers and Democrats voted for Gardner in 1854, there is no support for the commonly accepted notion that Free-Soil party men, to a greater extent than Whigs or Democrats, rushed into the ranks of the new American party (see Table 2.3). About 60 percent of the 1852 Free-Soilers actually had voted for Gardner and the Know-Nothings, but former Democrats, at least those who voted for Pierce in 1852, voted the Know-Nothing ticket at a slightly greater rate. Only about 41 percent of the 1852 Whigs, including those who threw away their votes for Webster, voted for Gardner. Significantly, many Free-Soilers, who undoubtedly felt "sold out" by Wilson's political opportunism, stayed away from the polls in 1854. The highest rate of voter abstention in the gubernatorial election was among 1852 Free-Soilers. In net results, Free-Soilers composed slightly over one-fifth of the Know-Nothing vote, whereas former Democrats and Whigs made up the bulk of Gardner's total. In other words, the vast majority of Massachusetts Know-Nothings were not former Free-Soilers.[22]

The analysis of voting returns substantiates the suspicions of contemporaries of the period that the American party attracted thousands of previous nonvoters into its rank and file. It has been claimed by one authority that the success of the Know-Nothing party in Massachusetts "rested upon thousands of new men drawn into politics by nativism."[23] Although the American party's margin of victory had not depended on the new voters who were drawn to the polls by religious bigotry or by other concerns for the first time in 1854, still it appears that about 12 percent of those who cast ballots for Gardner and the Know-Nothings either had not voted in the previous presidential election or were not eligible to vote in 1852 (see Table 2.3). This would constitute an even more remarkable finding had not the 1852 presidential contest witnessed a relatively low turnout primarily due to Whig disaffection with Scott. But, on the other hand, 1854 was also a relatively low turnout election, a "fact" often obscured by Know-Nothing capture of the large share (nearly 63 percent) of the actual number of ballots cast.[24]

Was the group of voters brought together under the Know-Nothing banner in 1854 a recrudescence of the coalition of voters who had tried unsuccessfully to ratify the proposed new constitution in 1853? Apparently not. The appeal of the new nativist party easily sliced through the political divisions of the previous years that were formed by the debates over the constitution (see Table 2.4). As many 1854 Know-Nothings had opposed the constitution as had favored it and almost one out of every ten Know-Nothings had sat out the balloting on the referendum. Otherwise, the past behavior of 1854 Whigs, Democrats, and "Republicans" was consistent with the basically party-line vote cast in the 1853 referendum: virtually all of what remained of the Whig constituency in 1854 had rallied to defeat the constitution, whereas almost none of the 1854 Democrats and "Republicans" had cast ballots against the measure.

TABLE 2.3
Estimated Relationships Between the 1852 Presidential Election and Subsequent Voting
in the 1854 Gubernatorial Election
(by percent of 1854 electorate)

Party in 1854	Party in 1852 Whig	"Webster" Whigs	Democratic	Free-Soil	Not Voting for President 1852	Not Eligible 1852	Percent of 1854 Electorate
Whig	13	1	0	0	0	0	14
Democratic	0	0	6	1	0	0	7
Free-Soil	0	0	0	2	1	0	3
American	12	0	15	9	4	1	41
Not Voting for Governor 1854	3	0	3	3	25	1	34
Percent of 1854 Electorate	28	1	24	15	30	2	100

Note: Actual <u>N</u> = 312.

Although the anti-Whig Coalition, at least at the grass-roots level, was hardly a progenitor of the Know-Nothing party, in historical accounts the suspicion remains that it prefaced in one way or another the rise of the Republican party.[25] Massachusetts antislavery politicians who refused to join the Know-Nothings in 1854 led the movement, the following year, to rebuild a new Republican party uncontaminated by nativism. After the national Know-Nothing organization split over the status of slavery in the territories, many of the antislavery men who had cooperated with the Know-Nothings in 1854 switched in 1855 to the new revitalized and ideologically uncompromising Republican party. Whereas the Whig and Know-Nothing state party platforms went no further than to demand the restoration of the Missouri Compromise line, the Republicans declared against the admission of any more slave states to the Union. Wilson, now in the United States Senate, and seven out of eleven of the state's congressmen demonstrated that they put antislavery above the principles of the nativist party by supporting the Republican gubernatorial candidate, Julius Rockwell, against the incumbent Gardner. Many antislavery men felt that the confusion in state politics would come to an end with the successful inauguration of the Republican movement because subsequently there would be a true division of voters into parties based on their standing on the slavery issue. Despite many predictions of a Republican victory in the election of 1855, Rockwell failed to carry the state against Gardner and the Know-Nothings.[26]

The estimated relationships between voting patterns in the 1855 gubernatorial contest and those in the 1852 presidential election are

TABLE 2.4
Estimated Relationships Between the 1854 Gubernatorial Election and Prior Voting
in the 1853 Constitutional Referendum
(by percent of 1854 electorate)

Party in 1854	1853 Referendum			Not Eligible 1853	Percent of 1854 Electorate
	Against	For	Abstained		
Whig	15	0	0	0	14
Democratic	0	6	1	0	7
Free-Soil	0	3	0	0	3
American	18	18	4	1	41
Not Voting for Governor 1854	2	4	27	1	34
Percent of 1854 Electorate	35	32	31	2	100

Note: Actual N = 314.

consistent with the commonly-held notion that Republican voting strength geographically had come from the old Free-Soil areas in Franklin and Worcester counties and from the old Whig areas in western Massachusetts (see Table 2.5.A). As expected, former Free-Soilers flocked to the Republican party at a higher rate than did former Whigs. But Rockwell won virtually no support from 1852 Democrats, even though former Governor George S. Boutwell, one of the state's prominent Democratic leaders, had declared his adherence to the Republicans. Nor did Rockwell's candidacy attract any significant number of previously apolitical citizens who in 1854 were pulled into, or perhaps back into, the political arena by the nativist appeal. Of all the candidates in the governor's race, Rockwell fared the best among voters who in 1853 had rallied in a losing cause to adopt the Coalition-inspired constitution (see Table 2.5.B). However, about 28 percent of his total vote consisted of those who had voted against the document, many of them presumably former Whigs.[27]

If the 1855 Republican vote was not reassemblage of the old Free-Soil/Democratic coalition, neither was it a mere subgroup of 1854 Know-Nothings (see Table 2.6). Although Rockwell did manage to attract the support of about one-fifth of those who had voted for Gardner and the Know-Nothings in the previous gubernatorial election, 1854 Know-Nothings did not comprise the bulk of Republican voters in 1855. On the contrary, in its first credible debut the Republican party was composed of as many men who had voted against, as had voted for, Gardner and the American party in 1854.

The changed profile of support for Gardner in 1855 is also revealing, for it foreshadowed the unraveling of the American coalition. In 1855

TABLE 2.5
The Antecedents of Republican Party Support in 1855
(by percent of 1855 electorate)

A. The 1852 Presidential Election and the 1855 Gubernatorial Contest
(Actual $\underline{N}$ = 312)

Party in 1855	Party in 1852					
	Whig[a]	Democratic	Free-Soil	Not Voting for President 1852	Not Eligible 1852	Percent of 1855 Electorate
Whig	4	0	0	2	1	7
Democratic	1	13	2	0	1	17
Republican	10	0	9	0	0	18
American	7	9	3	4	2	26
Not Voting for Governor 1855	6	2	0	21	3	32
Percent of 1855 Electorate	28	24	15	27	7	100

B. The 1853 Referendum and the 1855 Gubernatorial Contest
(Actual $\underline{N}$ = 314)

Party in 1855	1853 Referendum				
	Against	For	Abstained	Not Eligible 1853	Percent of 1855 Electorate
Whig	7	0	0	0	7
Democratic	5	9	2	1	17
American	14	5	4	2	26
Republican	5	14	0	0	18
Not Voting for Governor 1855	3	3	24	2	32
Percent of 1855 Electorate	34	31	30	5	100

[a]Ballots cast for Daniel Webster have been added to the totals received by Winfield Scott to equal the Whig presidential vote in 1852.

Gardner's vote fell off sharply among all 1852 partisans (see Tables 2.3 and 2.5.A). Democratic disaffection with the Know-Nothings was particularly heavy: whereas over 60 percent of the 1852 Democrats had defected in 1854 to the Americans, only about 38 percent of them persisted in voting in 1855 for Gardner and the Know-Nothings. An even more dramatic decline in Gardner's support occurred among 1854 Know-Nothings who in 1853 had voted for the constitution (see Tables 2.4 and 2.5.B). Whereas about 56 percent of those voting "yea" in the 1853 referendum favored Gardner in 1854, only approximately 16 percent of them voted for him in 1855. Thus, by 1855 the Know-Nothing party was largely deserted by its old reformist elements: only about one-fifth of Gardner's supporters had voted for the constitution. In running for a second term, Gardner attracted only about 56 percent of those who initially had supported him, and, except for small numbers

TABLE 2.6
As Many 1855 Republicans Opposed as Favored the Know-Nothings in 1854:
The 1854 and 1855 Governor's Races
(by percent of 1855 electorate)

Party in 1855	Party in 1854				Not Voting for Governor 1854	Not Eligible 1854	Percent of 1855 Electorate
	Democratic	Whig	American	Free-Soil			
Democratic	7	2	6	1	1	0	17
Whig	0	4	0	0	2	1	7
American	0	2	23	0	1	0	26
Republican	1	4	8	3	2	0	18
Not Voting for Governor 1855	0	2	3	0	27	1	32
Percent of 1855 Electorate	7	14	41	3	33	2	100

Note: Actual N = 320.

of Whigs and those who did not vote in 1854, he picked up no new support (see Table 2.6). In net results, almost 90 percent of the vote Gardner received in 1855 was cast by those who had voted for him in 1854.

The guerrilla warfare in Kansas, Preston Brooks's assault upon Sumner, and the first national campaign of the Republicans added considerable drama to the 1856 presidential race. The new northern antislavery party possessed such vitality in Massachusetts that many suspected it not only would sweep the state but also might elect John C. Frémont to the presidency. "Bleeding Kansas" and "Bleeding Sumner" provided Massachusetts Republicanism with emotional issues that the party could convert into votes in the November election. Still, party leaders were uncertain of their actual strength. Rather than risk alienating Know-Nothing votes from Frémont and their candidates for Congress, the Republicans refrained from making any nominations for state offices, thus ensuring Gardner's election as governor for a third term. In return Gardner promised to support Frémont rather than Millard Fillmore, the American or Know-Nothing candidate for the presidency. Gardner's failure to win a place on the national American party ticket had estranged both him and his loyal followers from Fillmore, setting the stage for this Republican "deal" with the Gardnerites in 1856. The "straight" Americans, composed mostly of Boston Whigs, ran George W. Gordon against Gardner for the governorship on a Fillmore-American ticket.[28]

Dissident antislavery radicals under the leadership of Frank Bird fielded their own "Honest Man's" ticket on election day to protest the Frémont-American ballot. Bird's colleague, William S. Robinson or

"Warrington," wrote in disgust that the Republican deal with the American party chieftains was made "by men who threw away the election of 1856 by dabbling in the dirty pool of Know-Nothingism." He was referring to Banks and Wilson who, more than any other Frémont supporters, had caused the Republican "capitulation" to the Know-Nothing Gardnerites. Bird and his circle of friends were convinced that nonextension of slavery in the territories, not nativism, was the most salient issue in the minds of the voters.[29]

The results of the November election suggest that the Republicans lacked a moral strength in their basic antislavery appeal commensurate with their voting strength at the polls. In 1856, just over half (approximately 56 percent) of the 1855 Republicans cast ballots for Gardner; the rest either voted for Bird's protest candidate, wrote in the name of their own choice for governor, or did not vote for governor (see Table 2.7). Gardner ran 15,705 votes behind Frémont, suggesting that the 1855 Republicans who abstained in the 1856 governor's race "scratched" Gardner's name from Frémont-American ballots (see Table 2.8). When this Republican disaffection with Gardner is taken together with the popular swing to Frémont's candidacy, it can easily be argued that the Republicans committed a major tactical blunder by not fielding a slate of candidates for state offices in the 1856 general election.

In winning Massachusetts's electoral votes in 1856, Frémont managed to attract virtually all surviving voters who had cast a ballot for Van Buren in 1848, plus slightly over half of the 1848 Whigs and almost half of the 1848 Democrats (see Table 2.9.A). In net results, former Van Buren men constituted about 35 percent of Frémont's total, whereas 1848 Democrats and 1848 Whigs equaled about 46 percent of the Frémont-American vote. The remainder of Frémont's coalition consisted of new voters who either had been ineligible to vote in 1848 or who had not yet become part of the "potential" electorate as measured by the number of legal voters.

The shredding of the old Whig voter coalition is dramatically revealed by looking backward from the 1856 election. The 1848 Whigs who did not vote for Frémont were roughly divided between the Democratic and Fillmore-American columns, although a small proportion sat out the balloting altogether (see Table 2.9.A). Remarkably, one-fifth of the voters who backed Zachary Taylor in 1848 supported James Buchanan and the Democrats eight years later. In terms of voter alignments in the 1852 election, Frémont captured well over 80 percent of the 1852 Whigs (see Table 2.9.B). By comparison, in the Know-Nothing sweep of 1854 slightly over 40 percent of the 1852

TABLE 2.7
Many 1855 Republicans Did Not Vote for Gardner in 1856: The 1855 and 1856 Governor's Races
(by percent of 1856 electorate)

Party in 1856	Party in 1855				Not Voting for Governor 1855	Not Eligible 1855	Percent of 1856 Electorate
	Democratic	Whig	Republican	American			
Democratic	14	0	0	3	2	0	19
Whig	0	1	0	2	0	0	3
Fillmore-American	0	1	0	3	1	0	5
Fremont-American	4	5	10	18	7	1	45
"Honest Man's"	0	0	4	0	0	0	3
All Others	0	0	1	0	0	0	1
Not Voting for Governor 1856	0	0	2	0	21	2	24
Percent of 1856 Electorate	17	6	18	25	31	2	100

Note: Actual N = 320.

TABLE 2.8
Split-Ticket Voting in the 1856 General Election: The Presidential and Gubernatorial Races
(by percent of 1856 electorate)

Presidential Candidate in 1856	Party in 1856 Gubernatorial Election						Not Voting for Governor 1856	Percent of 1856 Electorate
	Democratic	Whig	Fremont-American	Fillmore-American	"Honest Man's"	All Others		
Buchanan	18	0	0	0	0	0	0	19
Fillmore	0	3	0	5	0	0	1	10
Fremont	1	0	45	0	3	1	4	53
All Others	0	0	0	0	0	0	1	0
Not Voting for President 1856	0	0	0	0	0	0	18	18
Percent of 1856 Electorate	19	3	45	5	3	1	24	100

Note: Actual N = 320.

Whigs voted for Gardner (see Table 2.3). Thus, at least half of the 1852 Whigs on their way into Republican ranks had avoided any connection with the Know-Nothings.

During 1848–56 support for the Democratic party was in considerable turmoil. This was not a period of deviating change, as old combinations of voters never again reassembled. A large percentage of those who voted Democratic in 1856 had not done so in 1848 and many who had voted Democratic in 1848 were not in the Democratic column in 1856 (see Table 2.9.A). The majority of 1852 Democrats had been pulled into the American party during Know-Nothing excitement in 1854, but most of them returned to the party fold by 1856 (see Tables

TABLE 2.9
Voter Realignment in Presidential Politics Between 1848 and 1856
(by percent of 1856 electorate)

A. Crossover Voting Between the 1848 and 1856 Presidential Elections
(Actual N = 301)

Candidate in 1856	Candidate in 1848					
	Taylor	Cass	Van Buren	Not Voting for President 1848	Not Eligible 1848	Percent of 1856 Electorate
Buchanan	6	9	0	1	3	19
Fremont	16	8	18	5	5	52
Fillmore	7	0	0	1	2	10
Not Voting for President 1856	1	0	0	10	8	19
Percent of 1856 Electorate	30	17	18	17	18	100

B. Crossover Voting Between the 1852 and 1856 Presidential Elections
(Actual N = 321)

Candidate in 1856	Candidate in 1852						
	Scott	Pierce	Hale	Webster	Not Voting for President 1852	Not Eligible 1852	Percent of 1856 Electorate
Buchanan	1	16	0	0	1	1	19
Fremont	22	6	14	0	6	4	52
Fillmore	3	1	0	1	2	2	10
Not Voting for President 1856	0	0	0	0	17	2	19
Percent of 1856 Electorate	26	23	14	1	26	9	100

2.3 and 2.9.B). Yet over one-fourth of the 1852 Democrats defected permanently into the ranks of the new Republican party (see Tables 2.9.B and 2.15.A), the American party undoubtedly serving as a halfway station for some.

In 1857 the Republicans finally captured the governor's chair, despite a bitter factional split in their party. The Republican platform had taken a firm and unequivocal antislavery stand, but Banks, the party's gubernatorial nominee, symbolized to the Sumner wing of the Massachusetts Republicans the conservative, "time serving" nativist element in their party. Consequently, a few "pure" antislavery Republicans withheld their support. Unable to forget Banks's role in the Republican capitulation to the Gardnerites in the previous year, Bird once again bolted the party and ran a token rival candidate for governor who received an inconsequential 213 votes. But Wilson, whose soul Wendell Phillips once remarked could be "made out of the sweepings of a caucus room," believed Banks's moderate antislavery position, former Know-Nothing affiliation, and support for an aggressive American foreign policy, were distinct advantages that promised to win support for the Republican ticket from the broadest possible array of voters. A professional politician himself, Banks skillfully combined his own personal popularity, his identification with the "Young America" movement, and a firm commitment to antislavery expansion to easily win a plurality of the vote in the three-way contest for the governorship.[30]

In running against Banks for a fourth term on the American party ticket, Gardner was forced to offer the voters a lackluster program of nativism, retrenchment, and Unionism tailored to attract any nativist, conservative, or "doughface" whether American, Whig, or Democrat. Thus, the metamorphosis of the American party from a working-class, populist movement with genuine grass-roots appeal to a conservative party dominated by Gardner and other former Whigs was completed by 1857. In defeat Gardner managed to mobilize the support of approximately half of those who had voted for him in 1855 (see Table 2.10.A). The day of the Know-Nothing party was evidently over in Massachusetts. As for Gardner, the pro-Republican press hoped that the Know-Nothings, like the Mongolians, would bury their chief "with his horse, weapons, vestments, and soldiers." When Banks ran for reelection the following year he won by a clear majority over the Democrats and what was left of the American party, now without Gardner as its gubernatorial nominee (see Table 2.10.B).[31]

By 1858, the original 1854 coalition of Know-Nothings was in complete disarray. A large share of the 1854 Know-Nothings sat out the 1858 gubernatorial election (see Table 2.11). Previous historians have fostered misconceptions about the subsequent behavior of the original Know-Nothings by considering only the percentage of them who participated in later elections. For example, of the 1854 Know-Nothings who voted in 1858, about two-thirds cast Republican ballots. Because only slightly over half of them turned out for this election, they played a much smaller role in the Republican coalition than if all of them had taken part. The voters who originally had been drawn into the American party in 1854, including some Free-Soilers temporarily misled by Wilson's political maneuverings, made up less than half of the total Republican vote for governor in 1858, just as had been the case in 1855 (see Tables 2.6 and 2.11).

It will be recalled that, although Gardner and the Know-Nothings had carried the state against a revitalized Republican party in 1855, the American party vote in that election was not inflated by genuine antislavery votes as it had been in 1854. Therefore, one would expect the 1855 Know-Nothings to be less important to Republicans in later elections than the 1854 Know-Nothings. Indeed, this was precisely the

TABLE 2.10
The Effect of Banks's Candidacy in Attracting Former Know-Nothings
(by percent of 1857, 1858, and 1859 electorates)

A. Crossover Voting Between the 1855 and 1857 Gubernatorial Elections

Party in 1857	Party in 1855				Not Voting for Governor 1855	Not Eligible 1855	Percent of 1857 Electorate
	Democratic	Whig	Republican	American			
Democratic	11	0	0	3	1	0	15
Republican	5	2	16	4	1	1	29
American	1	3	0	12	1	1	18
Not Voting for Governor 1857	0	1	1	5	28	3	38
Percent of 1857 Electorate	16	6	17	24	31	5	100

B. Crossover Voting Between the 1855 and 1858 Gubernatorial Elections

Party in 1858	Party in 1855				Not Voting for Governor 1855	Not Eligible 1855	Percent of 1858 Electorate
	Democratic	Whig	Republican	American			
Democratic	11	0	0	3	3	1	18
Republican	6	2	13	7	3	1	32
American	0	1	0	4	1	1	6
Not Voting for Governor 1858	0	3	5	10	23	4	45
Percent of 1858 Electorate	16	6	17	24	30	7	100

C. Crossover Voting Between the 1855 and 1859 Gubernatorial Elections

Party in 1859	Party in 1855				Not Voting for Governor 1855	Not Eligible 1855	Percent of 1859 Electorate
	Democratic	Whig	Republican	American			
Democratic	10	0	0	3	2	1	16
Republican	5	1	11	7	2	1	27
American	0	2	0	4	0	1	7
Not Voting for Governor 1859	1	3	6	9	25	5	50
Percent of 1859 Electorate	16	6	17	23	30	8	100

Note: Actual N = 320.

case: Banks never captured more than one-third of the 1855 Know-Nothing vote in any year he ran for governor (see Table 2.10). These findings do not support the widely accepted notion that after 1856 the Massachusetts Know-Nothings "were absorbed in the tremendous growth of the new [Republican] party, and Banks led the remnants to the Republicans in 1857–58 on his election to the governorship."[32] Nevertheless, the belief that northern Know-Nothings, especially in New

TABLE 2.11
Many Original Know-Nothings Abstained from Voting After 1856: The 1854 and 1858 Governor's Races
(by percent of 1858 electorate)

Party in 1858	Party in 1854				Not Voting for Governor 1854	Not Eligible 1854	Percent of 1858 Electorate
	Democratic	Whig	American	Free-Soil			
Democratic	5	4	4	0	3	2	18
Republican	2	8	14	2	3	2	32
American	0	1	3	0	1	1	6
Not Voting for Governor 1858	0	0	16	1	24	4	45
Percent of 1858 Electorate	6	13	38	3	31	9	100

Note: Actual N = 320.

England, moved en bloc into the new Republican party remains deeply ingrained in historical interpretations of partisan realignment during the late antebellum period.[33] Massachusetts voting patterns, however, indicate otherwise. After 1854 the nativist forces did not move over to join the Bay State Republican party in strength during the waning of the American party in the late 1850s.

According to the private correspondence of American party leaders, there was considerable antipathy toward Republicans at the top as well as at the bottom of the American party pyramid. Among the many Know-Nothings who lost confidence in Gardner in 1856 was Jonathan Pierce, a Boston manufacturer and one of the original architects of the Bay State American party. In 1857 Pierce favored Banks for the governorship but could not bring himself to be associated with the purely "geographical" or sectionalized party supporting Banks. Consequently, Pierce decided to remain entirely aloof from politics during the fall campaign. After the election of Banks, most Know-Nothing party leaders believed that nothing could be accomplished unless they united with the Democrats. Gardner worked unsuccessfully behind the scenes to find someone whom both Americans and Democrats could endorse for governor. At the American state convention speeches were made openly avowing that a coalition with the Democrats was desirable to prevent Wilson's reelection to the Senate. At the close of the 1850s the only two daily newspapers still supporting the American party divided, one going to the Democracy and the other supporting Banks. Gardner was ready to vote with the Democrats if forced to decide between them and the Republicans.[34]

In the spring of 1859, what remained of the nativist voting bloc in Massachusetts politics found a rallying point. The occasion was the submission to the voters of a proposed state constitutional amendment designed to counteract immigrant naturalization achieved through false oaths on the eve of elections, in particular, and to check any "ill-considered" voting by ethnic allegiance, in general. The gist of the amendment was that a foreign-born male, even after he had been granted final citizenship papers, should have no right to vote or hold office in Massachusetts before the expiration of an additional two years' residence in the state. This "two-year" amendment had its origins in the Know-Nothing legislature of 1855 in which extreme nativists had wanted to exclude foreign-born citizens from voting or holding office forever. Governor Gardner proposed an amendment requiring a twenty-one-year waiting period after naturalization before adopted citizens could vote. The antislavery Know-Nothings unsuccessfully opposed the measure, but two successive passages by the legislature were required for constitutional amendments. The 1856 legislature cut the proscriptive twenty-one-year waiting period to fourteen and then in 1857 the Republican radicals defeated the fourteen-year proposal and prevented passage of substitute amendments with slightly lesser terms of probation. In 1858, a two-year amendment passed and was resubmitted in 1859 and passed, thus setting the stage for a popular referendum.[35]

A one-year waiting period would have had the appearance of being consistent with the state law requiring a native-born citizen from another state to be a resident of Massachusetts for one year before he could vote. A Republican state legislator explained rather apologetically why the two-year stipulation passed: "The pressure of know-nothingism and a foolish disposition to conciliate persuaded us to say *two* years." With a presidential year approaching, the amendment soon returned to plague many who had supported it. "The very men in [Massachusetts] who forced the amendment upon us," Bird wrote to Sumner, "are insanely anxious to defeat it." The references to Wilson and Banks were clear. Banks, who had called upon the legislature to pass the amendment, began to suspect that its adoption would injure his chances of receiving the Republican presidential nomination in 1860. Republican leaders in the western states feared that, if their counterparts in Massachusetts allowed the two-year amendment to become law, in the coming presidential election the Democrats would capture the votes of many German, Scottish, and Scandinavian immigrants who normally voted Republican. Already handicapped by his Know-Nothing antecedents, Banks would risk diminishing his influence as a national party spokesman were he to preside over the reinvigoration of nativism in his own state. The Sumner faction of the Massachusetts Republicans, although strongly opposing the two-year amendment, predicted publicly and gloated privately that its adoption politically would destroy the conservative Banks wing of their party.[36]

Estimates of the relationship between voting patterns in the referendum and those in the 1857 and 1859 gubernatorial contests should disprove any notion that Republican voters were responsible for the adoption of the two-year amendment (see Table 2.12). Most Republicans who cast ballots for Banks in either 1857 or 1859 and who voted in the referendum were against ratification. Democrats were similarly split against the amendment. The support for ratification came overwhelmingly from the die-hard Know-Nothings who had voted for Gardner in 1857 in a losing cause against Banks and the Republicans, or from what remained in 1859 of the American party constituency. This small, yet intransigent, nativist voting bloc took part in the referendum to a far greater extent than did either Republicans or Democrats and, as a consequence, was able to secure the amendment's passage.

Only approximately 16 percent of the potential voters participated in the 1859 referendum. At first glance, this is surprising in light of the Massachusetts voters' relatively high interest in the 1851, 1852, and 1853 constitutional referenda in which turnout rates ranged between 67 and 69 percent. Some obvious factors contributed to the extraordinarily low turnout in 1859. Because balloting on the two-year amendment was held in May, it was effectively insulated from the attention it might otherwise have received if it had been scheduled simultaneously with the state's general elections in November. In addition, there is little evidence to suggest that local American, Republican, and Democratic party organizations took responsibility for printing and distributing ballots, although in Boston a few prominent local politicans, apparently acting independently, were observed occasionally as vote distributors outside polling places. Given these circumstances, the conclusion of the Springfield *Republican* that only Know-Nothings or those who really desired to have the proposed amendment adopted were motivated to turn out for the referendum seems to have been basically correct.[37]

Passage of the two-year amendment was similar to the circumstances under which Bay State voters in the spring of 1857 had approved the adoption of another nativist-inspired proposal, the so-called "reading and writing" amendment to the state constitution. Although the establishment of a literacy test for voting affected all new registrants, whether foreign- or native-born, the proposal was based on the unstated assumption of its nativist supporters that many Irish-born citizens could not read or write. Approximately 18 percent of those eligible to vote participated in the 1857 referendum election in which the

TABLE 2.12
Party and Restriction on Immigrant Voting: The 1857 and 1859 Gubernatorial Races
and the 1859 Constitutional Referendum
(by percent of 1859 electorate)

A. The 1857 Governor's Race and the 1859 Constitutional Referendum
(Actual N = 325)

	Party in 1857			Not Voting for Governor 1857	Not Eligible 1857	Percent of 1859 Electorate
1859 Referendum	Democratic	Republican	American			
For	1	1	6	0	1	9
Against	4	3	0	0	1	7
Abstained	9	24	11	37	2	84
Percent of 1859 Electorate	14	28	17	37	4	100

B. The 1859 Governor's Race and the 1859 Constitutional Referendum
(Actual N = 326)

	Party in 1859			Not Voting for Governor 1859	Percent of 1859 Electorate
1859 Referendum	Democratic	Republican	American		
For	3	1	4	2	9
Against	4	2	0	1	7
Abstained	9	24	3	47	84
Percent of 1859 Electorate	16	27	7	50	100

reading and writing amendment easily passed with 63 percent of the ballots cast. An analysis of incomplete returns reported in the newspapers shows that Know-Nothings turned out in the referendum to a greater extent than did Republicans and Democrats and, as expected, voted emphatically in favor of adoption (see Table 2.13). Democratic voters comprised the overwhelming majority of those who voted against the amendment, whereas over 80 percent of the Republicans did not bother to vote in the referendum.[38]

Predictably, the bulk of those who voted for the two-year amendment came from the ranks of those who had cast ballots in favor of the reading and writing amendment (see Table 2.14). Virtually no voter who had opposed the inauguration of a literacy test subsequently voted for the two-year amendment. But conversely, a small percentage of those who voted for the reading and writing amendment later switched to vote against the two-year amendment, which was, at least in theory, a more obviously discriminatory restriction on foreign-born citizens than was a legally impartial literacy test. The discriminatory nature of the two-year amendment influenced the votes of Republicans who participated in the referenda elections. Of the 1857 Republicans

Banks veto
blacks in
state militia

TABLE 2.13
Party and Imposition of a Voter Literacy Test: The 1857 Governor's Race
and the 1857 Constitutional Referendum
(by percent of 1857 electorate)

1857 Referendum	Party in 1857			Not Voting for Governor 1857	Percent of 1857 Electorate
	Democratic	Republican	American		
For	2	4	5	0	11
Against	5	1	1	0	7
Abstained	8	24	12	38	82
Percent of 1857 Electorate	15	29	18	38	100

Note: Actual N = 187. The marginals of the table equal the actual statewide
returns and not the values of the summations of the incomplete city and town
returns used to generate the transition probabilities of voting behavior.

who voted on the reading and writing amendment, the overwhelming
majority of them voted for its adoption, but the 1857 Republicans who
subsequently cast ballots in the 1859 referendum voted 3 to 1 against
ratification of the two-year amendment. Similarly, 1859 Republicans
who voted on the two-year amendment's passage were split 2 to 1
against adoption (see Tables 2.12 and 2.13). These findings call into serious question the argument that passage of the two-year amendment
in Massachusetts was "a climactic example of the association of nativist
sentiment with the Republican party."[39] During the 1860 presidential
campaign, the pro-Democratic press repeatedly made similar changes
to the effect that the Republicans were responsible for the antiimmigrant, two-year amendment. But the voting patterns clearly reveal
that the amendment passed only because the majority of what was left
of the Know-Nothing constituency voted for it.

The notion that in 1859 nativists were influential in the Massachusetts Republican party is compatible with neither the behavior of rank-
and-file Republicans nor the behavior of the party's leadership. Senators Sumner and Wilson and the entire radical antislavery wing of the
party had pleaded with the voters to defeat the antiimmigrant measure. In an attack against Governor Banks's veto of a law authorizing
blacks to enlist in the state militia, Bird summed up the case of the
radicals against the proposed amendment: "I see constant illustrations
of the melancholy fact that when 'one has learned to discriminate between a native and a foreigner, it becomes easy to discriminate between a white man and a [N]egro.'"[40]

The Bird Club radicals rolled out their heaviest artillery against the
nativist spirit of proscription masquerading as patriotism. On their invitation, Carl Schurz, the eloquent mouthpiece of Missouri Teutonic

TABLE 2.14
Imposition of a Voter Literacy Test and Restriction on Immigrant Voting:
The 1857 and 1859 Referenda
(by percent of 1859 electorate)

1859 Referendum	1857 Referendum			Not Eligible 1857	Percent of 1859 Electorate
	For	Against	Abstained		
For	6	0	2	1	9
Against	1	2	3	1	7
Abstained	4	4	74	2	84
Percent of 1859 Electorate	11	6	79	4	100

Note: Actual N = 187. The marginals of the table equal the actual statewide returns and not the values of the summations of the incomplete city and town returns used to generate the transition probabilities of voting behavior.

Republicanism, delivered a speech entitled "True Americanism" in Boston's historic Faneuil Hall a few weeks before the referendum election. The Sumner radicals hoped that speeches by Schurz, Gustave Koerner, and others would have a profound impact upon Massachusetts Republicans. "Carl Schurz *did us good!*" exclaimed a correspondent of Bird. "I would to God every reeking KN hole in the State were stumped until the cursed heresy were rooted out."[41]

But the two-year amendment—"the anti-American, undemocratic, odious, Know-Nothing amendment," as Bird called it—became attached to the Massachusetts Constitution; foreign-born voters did not regain the civil rights they had lost in 1859 until the radical Republicans managed to obtain its repeal during the Civil War years. The act of repeal was passed by successive legislatures of 1862 and 1863 and was sustained by a small majority of the voters in a statewide referendum held in the spring of 1863. Turnout equaled an abysmally low 7 percent. According to the Springfield *Republican*, "few took trouble to vote on a dead and buried issue."[42]

In 1860 the operative center of the uncompromising political antislavery movement in Massachusetts still remained the group of men around Sumner's friend and confidant, Frank Bird, the initiator of both the "Honest Man's" ticket in 1856 and the symbolic bolt against Banks's nomination for governor in 1857. Throughout the 1850s Bird and his followers had despised the Know-Nothings and they had been politely disliked in return. Bird never forgot nor completely forgave the antislavery politicians, such as Wilson and Banks, who entered the clandestine lodges of the Know-Nothings. When John Andrew received the Republican nomination for governor in 1860, "Warrington," the only newspaper writer Bird invited regularly to dine with him, wrote ecstatically that Andrew's nomination represented "a complete and

E le chn ?
J A
in fluence ?
Bird Club

glorious victory over Banks, and the Know-Nothings, old Boston conservatism, and everything bad." Although Sumner and Wilson supported Andrew, he owed his nomination more to Bird than to any other individual. Andrew's subsequent election marked the beginning of an eleven-year period in which the Bird Club, through its control of the Republican state committee and the most important state offices, was virtually able to dictate the strategy of the Massachusetts Republican party.[43]

Although in 1860 Massachusetts abolitionists had little, if any, faith in Abraham Lincoln, they had only complimentary words for Andrew. Antislavery crusader Samuel May, Jr., feared that Lincoln, like Banks, might perform in office "some disgracefully servile and pro-slavery acts," but he described Andrew as "a gentleman who for a long term of years has been an outspoken abolitionist." Moderate Republicans, however, worried that Andrew's radicalism would dampen enthusiasm for the national Republican ticket. Samuel Bowles, for one, editorialized in his Springfield *Republican* that the Republican opposition in the state would use Andrew's abolitionist affiliations and pro-John Brown statements to injure Andrew and hurt Lincoln's chances elsewhere. One month after the Harper's Ferry raid Andrew, at an antislavery meeting in Boston, declared that he did not know whether Brown's attempt to foment a slave insurrection in Virginia was wise or foolish, but he had added: "I only know that . . . John Brown himself is right." His last five words soon provided the litmus paper test for Massachusetts radicalism. To the Boston *Pilot*, the influential Irish immigrant newspaper, Andrew was the candidate of the fanatical "John Brown clique of Republicans" who would "liberate the slaves by fire and sword."[44]

Unlike in New York, Rhode Island, and New Jersey, no fusion ticket was entered against the Republicans in Massachusetts. There was simply no agreement on statewide candidates or on what faction would have dominated any anti-Republican coalition. The prosouthern John C. Breckinridge wing of the Democratic party was comprised primarily of federal officeholders dependent on President Buchanan's administration. Their importance in the state was exaggerated by their control of such newspapers as the Boston *Post*, the New Bedford *Times*, the Salem *Advocate*, and the Lowell *Advertiser*. The Boston *Pilot* supported Stephen A. Douglas and characterized the party-splitting Breckinridge ticket as the work of "traitors," although it gave a nod of approval to the Constitutional Unionists. The Boston *Courier*, the chief organ of the Constitutional Union party, repeatedly told the disunited Democrats that fusion could be accomplished best by voting

for the John Bell-Edward Everett ticket. In the Boston-area congressional districts (Third, Fourth, and Fifth), the Republican opposition united on three Constitutional Unionists: Leverett Saltonstall,
Erastus B. Bigelow, and William Appleton. Its strategy helped the
Fifth District's wealthy Whig industrialist Appleton defeat by a narrow margin the incumbent Republican Anson Burlingame. This was
the only consolation for the anti-Republicans, however, for the Republicans swept to victory elsewhere across the state.[45]

In 1860 Andrew and Lincoln polled over 60 percent of the Massachusetts popular vote for governor and president, respectively. In Lincoln's column was the bulk of Frémont supporters, plus one out of
every seven who had voted in 1856 against the "Pathfinder" (see Table
2.15). Almost all the votes received by Douglas came from those who
had voted for Buchanan. About a tenth of the Buchanan vote was si-
phoned off by the John C. Breckinridge-Joseph Lane ticket. John Bell
corralled over three-fourths of the 1856 Fillmore-Americans. Lincoln
fared poorly among former Fillmore voters. Indeed, it would have
been incongruous if Lincoln's candidacy had attracted a large portion
of those who, in the prior presidential contest, had upheld the individual who succeeded in making his name odious in Massachusetts by
signing the Fugitive Slave Bill.

Because of its close association with many prominent, old-line Boston
Whigs, avoidance of the slavery issue, lackluster candidates, and connection with Boston's Episcopalian establishment, the Bell-Everett
campaign was regarded before the election as, at best, somewhat of an
oddity. According to Wilson, the Constitutional Union party comprised
a "class of simple people who believe that the sun rises in Chelsea,
comes up over State Street, hovers above the State House, and sinks
in the waters of the Back Bay." The Springfield *Republican* characterized the Bell-Everett ticket as "worthy to be printed on gilt-edged
satin paper, laid away in a box of musk, and kept there. . . . It is the
party of no idea and no purpose." Ridicule of the Constitutional Union
party cut deep. "In this quarter, one gets nothing but slurs," complained Robert C. Winthrop, Boston Brahmin and former Massachusetts Whig party leader, adding that the *Courier* was the only Boston
paper that had given Bell and Everett "fair play."[46]

The sources of support for the Constitutional Union party are worth
examining for what they reveal about the final "easing out" of political
nativism from Massachusetts politics on the eve of the Civil War. On
the national level the motive for organizing the Constitutional Union
party was "to furnish a basis on which the patriotic and national and
union loving men of all parties could unite." Realistically, it was hoped

TABLE 2.15
Crossover Voting Between Presidential Elections from 1852 to 1860
(by percent of 1860 electorate)

A. The 1852 and 1860 Presidential Elections
(Actual $\underline{N}$ = 332)

Candidate in 1860	Candidate in 1852				Not Voting for President 1852	Not Eligible 1852	Percent of 1860 Electorate
	Scott	Pierce	Hale	Webster			
Douglas	0	11	1	0	0	3	15
Lincoln	17	7	12	0	6	6	48
Bell	3	1	0	1	2	3	10
Breckinridge	0	2	0	0	1	0	3
Not Voting for President 1860	4	0	0	0	16	4	24
Percent of 1860 Electorate	24	21	13	1	24	16	100

B. The 1856 and 1860 Presidential Elections
(Actual $\underline{N}$ = 325)

Candidate in 1860	Candidate in 1856			Not Voting for President 1856	Not Eligible 1856	Percent of 1860 Electorate
	Buchanan	Fremont	Fillmore			
Douglas	13	1	0	0	2	15
Lincoln	2	38	2	2	3	48
Bell	1	0	7	0	2	10
Breckinridge	2	0	0	1	0	3
Not Voting for President 1860	0	9	0	14	1	24
Percent of 1860 Electorate	18	48	9	17	8	100

that the Bell-Everett ticket would attract enough votes to devolve the national election on the House of Representatives. In Massachusetts the party hoped to divide and drain the Republicans of their radicalism, while at the same time defeating the Democrats if possible. The state party was organized primarily by old "Cotton" Whigs and Know-Nothings late in 1859, shortly after the hanging of John Brown. From the start it suffered from its connections with the discredited American party. In Essex County, for example, only Know-Nothings originally were consulted in the spadework of building the new party, and progress was slow. By the spring of 1860 attempts were made to disassociate the Constitutional Union party from its sub rosa connections with the Americans and to appeal openly to all voters opposed to the Republicans.[47]

Amos A. Lawrence, a former Whig and the sacrificial Know-Nothing gubernatorial candidate in 1858, was a leading organizer of both the

Massachusetts and national Constitutional Union party. Because he believed that the 1856 Frémont vote had been inflated by the votes of Fillmore-Americans and former Whigs, he was certain that a "great reserve vote" in 1860 would rally to a reliable conservative third party if it were truly national in scope. In many respects Lawrence was correct in his assessment that after 1856 many old-line Whigs had become politically apathetic. A vote for the Democrats meant endorsing the policies of the Buchanan administration, whereas a Republican vote was equivalent to supporting a party that tended toward disunion. While many former Whigs found refuge in the American party, probably more resolved their dilemma by not voting. Former Senator Edward Everett, the savvy old Bay State Whig politician and Bell's reluctant running mate in 1860, had abstained from voting in 1857, apparently for the first time in his life. Nor did Everett bother to vote in the 1858 and 1859 elections.[48]

In Massachusetts the Constitutional Union party was more than merely the "last remnant of the old Whig party," as William C. Endicott characterized it.[49] Geographically, support for the Constitutional Unionists came from isolated pockets of conservatism and nativism in the eastern part of the state, especially in the vicinity of Boston. Although Bell received barely 13 percent of the Massachusetts popular vote for president, roughly 40 percent of his support came from those who had voted for adoption of the two-year amendment in the previous year (see Table 2.16.A). Significantly, the majority of those who favored placing restrictions on immigrant voting in 1859 were not found in Lincoln's column, but voted against Lincoln and his party in 1860. Only Bell, among all presidential candidates, received virtually no support from those who had opposed passage of the two-year amendment.

Voting patterns in the 1860 presidential and 1855 gubernatorial elections reveal that Lincoln's vote was not based on a reassemblage of the nativist coalition of voters who had reelected Gardner to the governorship in 1855 over genuine Republican opposition (see Table 2.17.A). Those who voted the Know-Nothing ticket in 1855 comprised about 27 percent of Lincoln's total vote and, as a consequence, the Republican victory in 1860 did not depend on successful capture of the 1855 Know-Nothings. Even the absorption of 1854 Know-Nothings, whose ranks included many men who put antislavery ahead of nativism, was not a prerequisite for the Republican victory (see Table 2.17.B). In other words, if either all the 1854 or all the 1855 Know-Nothings had sat out the 1860 election, Lincoln still would have won, albeit with only a plurality of the vote if every 1854 Know-Nothing had abstained in 1860.

The estimates of voting further reveal that former dedicated nativists in the late 1850s constituted a much larger portion of Bell's small

TABLE 2.16
The Antecedents of Constitutional Union Support in 1860
(by percent of 1860 electorate)

A. The 1860 Presidential Election and the 1859 Constitutional Referendum
(Actual $\underline{N}$ = 326)

Candidate in 1860	1859 Referendum			Not Eligible 1859	Percent of 1860 Electorate
	For	Against	Abstained		
Douglas	2	4	9	1	15
Lincoln	4	2	42	0	48
Bell	4	0	5	1	10
Breckinridge	0	1	2	0	3
Not Voting for President 1860	0	0	24	0	24
Percent of 1860 Electorate	9	7	82	2	100

B. The 1860 Presidential Election and the 1857 Governor's Race
(Actual $\underline{N}$ = 331)

Candidate in 1860	Party in 1857			Not Voting for Governor 1857	Not Eligible 1857	Percent of 1860 Electorate
	Democratic	Republican	American			
Douglas	10	0	0	2	3	15
Lincoln	2	27	9	7	3	48
Bell	0	0	8	2	0	10
Breckinridge	2	0	0	1	0	3
Not Voting for President 1860	0	0	0	24	0	24
Percent of 1860 Electorate	14	27	17	36	6	100

coalition than they did of Lincoln's large coalition (see Table 2.16). Republican dependence on die-hard American party voters unquestionably was slight. However, when 1857 Gardnerites and those favoring restrictions on immigrant voting in 1859 went to the polls in 1860, they were just as likely to vote for Lincoln as for anybody else. Similarly, over 70 percent of the voters in Lincoln's column had not been 1855 Know-Nothings; nevertheless, most 1855 Know-Nothings (about 57 percent) voted for Lincoln (see Table 2.17.A). The splitting of the former Know-Nothings in 1860 caused by the refuge of many nativists in the Constitutional Union party indicates how deeply nationalistic and ethnocentristic biases were held among a small proportion of the electorate. Hostility to Irish Catholic immigrants was so strong among some voters that it made them resistant to the passions that the slavery issue obviously evoked in much larger segments of the population of Massachusetts.

The findings presented here do not support the conclusion that the

TABLE 2.17
Lincoln's Victory in 1860 Did Not Depend on Capturing Former Know-Nothings
(by percent of 1860 electorate)

A. The 1860 Presidential Election Versus the 1855 Governor's Race

Candidate in 1860	Party in 1855				Not Voting for Governor 1855	Not Eligible 1855	Percent of 1860 Electorate
	Democratic	Whig	Republican	American			
Douglas	9	0	0	3	1	2	15
Lincoln	5	3	16	13	7	4	48
Bell	0	1	0	6	1	2	10
Breckinridge	1	0	0	1	1	0	3
Not Voting for President 1860	0	2	0	0	19	2	24
Percent of 1860 Electorate	16	6	16	23	29	10	100

B. The 1860 Presidential Election Versus the 1854 Governor's Race

Candidate in 1860	Party in 1854				Not Voting for Governor 1854	Not Eligible 1854	Percent of 1860 Electorate
	Democratic	Whig	Free-Soil	American			
Douglas	4	1	0	5	1	4	15
Lincoln	2	7	3	24	6	6	48
Bell	0	4	0	2	3	1	10
Breckinridge	1	0	0	0	2	0	3
Not Voting for President 1860	0	0	0	5	18	1	24
Percent of 1860 Electorate	6	12	3	36	30	12	100

Note: Actual N = 320.

Massachusetts Know-Nothings were completely absorbed into the Republican party after their national organization dissolved over the slavery issue in 1856. Nor does the analysis of voting returns demonstrate the existence of a symbiotic relationship between the Know-Nothing decline and the Republican rise in late antebellum Bay State politics. In some northern states the Republican party may have engaged in cunning political standoffs with nativists, knowing that when the nativist appeal had run its course, they, the Republicans, would be winners on election day.[50] But such was not the case in Massachusetts, where the years from 1855 to 1860 witnessed the resolution of the battle between the Bird Club radicals and Know-Nothingism—both inside and outside the Republican party—for control of the anti-Democratic movement. For Bird and his associates, the formation in 1860 of a Republican party disencumbered by nativism was the culmination of years of political labor.

Chapter 3
The Civil War Years:
Ideological Conflict and
Political Polarization

Let the lines be drawn distinctly;—&, with freedom & right on
one side, & slavery & wrong on the other, he is an infidel & an
Atheist who can doubt the final result.—*Samuel Gridley Howe
to Charles Sumner, 20 December 1860*

The control of the government of Massachusetts by the radical Republicans beginning with John Andrew's election to the governorship in 1860, along with the electoral changes that favored the Republican party, was effective in realigning state politics. The transition from
Whig to Republican rule was nowhere more apparent than in this dramatic change in political leadership. The Boston-centered entrepreneurial and cultural elites who had controlled the old Whig party were
now displaced by resourceful and dedicated antislavery men, once outside both social respectability and the law itself in the antebellum
period.[1]

Andrew had been a Liberty party man and Free-Soiler in the 1840s
and early 1850s when to be either was to relinquish hope of achieving
professional success as a lawyer in Boston; for, then, abolitionism was
as abhorred by the city's business and banking circles as it was by the
crowds of "broad-cloth" ruffians in the streets. A contemporary of Andrew, Thomas Wentworth Higginson, described the effect of forging
"attitudes of revolution" in the minds of antislavery men who fought
the recurrent efforts to enforce the Fugitive Slave Law in Massachusetts. He wrote that it was strange to find himself "outside of established institutions; to be obliged to lower one's voice and conceal one's
purposes; to see law and order, police and military, on the wrong side,
and find good citizenship a sin and bad citizenship a duty." When Andrew offered his legal services to Higginson and five others who were

implicated by a United States Senate investigation in John Brown's attempt to foment slave rebellion in Virginia, conservative Bay Staters considered Andrew himself no less a provoker of violence and revolution than were the members of the so-called "Secret Six" he was willing to defend in court.[2]

Ideologically, Andrew and his colleagues in the Bird Club shared considerable common ground with the Garrisonian abolitionists who believed that the Union was a vile compact made to preserve slavery. Even Frank Bird had flirted with symbolic treason by presiding over a disunionist convention in 1857. Neither Bird nor most other members of the Bird Club were abolitionists in the strict meaning of the word because they refused to eschew political action. Yet the club, if not a formal abolitionist organization, was "the next thing to it."[3]

The regular guests at Bird's Saturday afternoon dinner table included Franklin B. Sanborn, subsequently secretary of the Board of State Charities; George L. Stearns, later an assistant adjutant-general responsible for recruiting black regiments from all over the country during the latter half of the war; Samuel Gridley Howe, a philanthropist, abolitionist, and, like Stearns and Sanborn, a member of the Secret Six; Elizur Wright, a founder of the Liberty party; James M. Stone, a former Free-Soil ward boss in Boston and labor reformer; Charles W. Slack, editor of the Boston *Commonwealth*, which served as the club's mouthpiece; William S. Robinson, or "Warrington," of the Springfield *Republican*; and Senators Henry Wilson and Charles Sumner. These men emerged as an unofficial cabinet during Andrew's administration. Bird was known to be Andrew's man in the state legislature, where it was common knowledge that he consulted with Andrew, Wilson, and Sumner before taking a position.[4]

Sumner's biographer claims that members of the Bird Club were "apolitical politicians," citing Andrew's remark that Bird himself could not be "coaxed, bought, told nor bullied." Yet a close colleague of Bird described him as "one of the shrewdest politicians in a party which is not famous for shrewd politicians." The key to understanding this seeming paradox is to acknowledge that Sumner was the dominant influence on Bird's political career. Because he wanted Sumner, as a statesman, free to embody uncompromising moral principles in the nation's capital, Bird felt it necessary for others to protect Sumner's political interests at home. Therefore, Bird's role was necessarily both that of a dedicated ideologue and practical politician. His success was contingent upon the strong grass-roots support that Sumner commanded. "Of course," wrote Warrington, "the great secret after all is the fact that [Sumner] is right, and is with the people in the front rank of the procession; no straggler, and never footsore."[5]

Andrew
prepara-
for war ca/h/
John Murray
Forbes

In the wake of their 1860 victory the Massachusetts radicals crushed efforts within the Republican party to provide concessions to the southern slave states threatening to secede from the Union. Sumner and his allies in the Bird Club fought the attempts of conservative Republicans to placate alienated slaveholders by modifying the state's personal liberty laws. The radicals opposed the adoption of the "Crittenden Compromise" calling for extension of the old 36°30′ line to California. They obstructed the work of the Washington Peace Convention when its deliberations constituted the only remaining hope of averting conflict between North and South. Perhaps some Massachusetts radicals might have allowed the slave states to secede if they had followed legal procedures. But few Bird Club members were disturbed by the prospect of a full-scale civil war, for it promised to resolve finally the problem of slavery. With the question of war or peace unresolved, Governor Andrew prepared for armed conflict with the South by mobilizing the state militia so it could move to defend the nation's capital if called upon by the president. In an emotional address to the state's lawmakers, Andrew, once a pacifist, dramatically kissed the barrel of a musket that had fired one of the first shots at the British at Concord Bridge in 1775, symbolizing the resolve of Bay Staters to fight again, if necessary, for a noble cause.[6]

The radicals proved extremely adept at consolidating their power. Andrew quickly made his administration acceptable to those who initially were uneasy about his antislavery radicalism. He won support in Boston commercial circles by choosing John Murray Forbes, a prominent businessman, as presidential elector-at-large. In a bid for bipartisan support, Andrew appointed leading Democrats to military commands, including Benjamin F. Butler who had run against him for the governorship as a "Breckinridge Democrat." Labor reformers were gratified when Warrington was made clerk of the House of Representatives and elected secretary of the Republican State Committee. Only the Know-Nothing element—both within and outside of the Republican party—received no quarter from the radicals. Andrew demanded that the legislature charter the College of the Holy Cross and then, to the despair of the state's nativists, he attended commencement exercises at the Catholic school just as he did those at Harvard. Moreover, the radicals were willing to use their political influence directly against the conservative nativists in their own party. At one point, Andrew wrote a letter to President-elect Abraham Lincoln advising him that former Republican Governor Nathaniel P. Banks was not worthy of any position in the federal government.[7]

While actively soliciting the support of moderates and conservatives for his administration, Andrew continued to assert forcefully the demands of the antislavery cause. When armed conflict with the South erupted, he refused to let the Lincoln administration view the Civil War as anything short of a revolutionary crusade to destroy slavery and restructure southern society. Andrew was not a man who would be pulled along in the wake of events, or who would, in Warrington's words, "float like a dead fish down the current." Rather, he actively strove to create events and mold public opinion that would eventually "drag Lincoln up to his duty." If the Massachusetts radicals were stuck with Lincoln, whom many of them regarded as a well-intentioned, second-rate politician, then, in Andrew's words, it was imperative that "the men of motive and ideas must get into the lead, *must elect him*, get hold of the machine and 'run it' themselves."[8]

Radical strategy left no room for nonpartisan politics. Attempts of conservative Republicans and some Democrats to suspend partisan debate for the duration of the war were thwarted at the outset by growing Republican radicalism and reactionary Democratic politicians. Richard Henry Dana, Jr., a conservative Republican, argued that separate political organizations were "no longer necessary or desirable, or defensible," and Samuel Bowles similarly urged in the columns of his influential Springfield *Republican* that party lines be ignored because the only issues were successful prosecution of the war and maintenance of the Union. A few prominent Democrats, such as Benjamin F. Hallett and Caleb Cushing, also favored suspending party action until after the war and absented themselves in 1861 from the Democratic state convention. The Democratic party rejected a motion to make no nominations and selected a full ticket to run against Andrew and the Republicans. In an abortive attempt to recognize the sentiment toward a nonpartisan union of all voters in favor of Lincoln, the Republicans at their convention nominated Edward Dickinson, a Bell-Everett man, for lieutenant governor, and Josiah G. Abbott, a prominent Democrat, for attorney general. Both declined spots on the Republican ticket.[9]

The suggestion that there was no difference between Democrats and Republicans, that "at bottom . . . they differed only upon incidentals,"[10] overlooks how the Civil War experience polarized the two parties. Democrats, conservatives, and proslavery sympathizers became increasingly defined by their belief that the aim of the war should be to reestablish the integrity of the Constitution. Yet the Constitution recognized the right to hold property in slaves, a proposition to which the radical Republicans were unalterably opposed. "The false and fatal element of American politics," according to Bird, was the notion in anti-Republican ranks that "the Constitution is the paramount law, and

[that] when it requires us to do certain things contrary to the law of God or the law of our own conscience, we must obey it."[11]

In 1861 the Republicans did not officially take a stand for emancipation even as a military measure, although Sumner had raised the question at the state convention. At the beginning of the war the Lincoln administration carefully announced that the right of slavery was still recognized and even that fugitive slaves would be returned to loyal citizens. Nevertheless, the Massachusetts radicals were not afraid to discuss publicly the question of emancipation. If the South was fighting for the right to hold human beings in perpetual bondage and extend the system of slavery whenever and wherever it wanted, what principle, they asked, was the North fighting for? The South had started a war to sustain slavery outside the Union, and, ironically, the North was apparently doing the same thing within the Union. The radicals claimed the logic of the situation would eventually compel the North to fight for freedom. When that day came, they predicted, it would mean nothing less than "a revolution in the social condition of the slave states!"[12]

How the influence of the Bird Club members grew as the war wore on is legendary.[13] When the most radical policy—which during a revolutionary period is often the most viable and practical policy—was discussed in detail in Washington, the Massachusetts radical Republican establishment had "already robbed it of its terror by making it familiar." When news of the attack on Fort Sumter reached him, Sumner hurried to the White House to advise Lincoln that under the wartime emergency power the president had the authority to free slaves. When Congress voted unanimously that emancipation was not a purpose of the war, Sumner proclaimed that "slavery was perpetual war and that emancipation only was peace." When General Butler allowed the governor of Maryland to deploy Massachusetts troops to suppress possible slave insurrection, Andrew sharply rebuked Butler, informing him that "the matter of servile insurrection among the community in arms against the Federal Union . . . is to be contemplated as one of the inherent weaknesses of the enemy." (Butler promptly labeled the fugitive slaves who came into his lines "contraband of war" and refused to return them to their masters.) In 1862 Andrew penned his memorable letter to Secretary of War Edwin M. Stanton in which he said that Massachusetts men were hesitant to enlist because black men had not been called on to fight. When Andrew finally received authorization in early 1863 to recruit a black regiment, he demanded that a few lieutenancies with opportunity for promotion be reserved for blacks and that the black soldiers receive equal pay.[14]

The radicals soon became exasperated with Lincoln's slowness to implement their proposals. "We are not living in the same *century* now in which Pierce and Buchanan reigned," complained Andrew to Sumner, "and yet, how much Lincoln and all the rest seem to be troubled by some difficulties, which would have been difficulties ten or even two years ago, but which are not now." On the other side, the conservatives, fearing the influence of the radicals on Lincoln, clung to their belief that the only goal of the war was to preserve the Union. Edward Hamilton, a state Democratic party chieftain, was among those, in his words, "who do not believe in the policy of the government in the conduct of the War, [but] who would lay down their lives to save the Union and our institutions." He had only contempt for "the ultra radicals who growl and grumble that the government does not go further in their direction." For the radicals, however, it was not enough to be for the Union and against the Confederacy. An additional issue was moving politics from beneath. As Sumner repeatedly asked his audiences in the 1864 campaign: "Are you for Freedom, or are you for Slavery?" How a man responded to this question, the radicals believed, determined how he would cast his ballot.[15]

The increasing importance of the slavery issue sharpened the separation between the Republicans and their opponents until the older partisan divisions disappeared. Party lines solidified. The percentages of the electorate switching parties between consecutive pairs of "off-year" gubernatorial elections from 1855 to 1865 gradually declined until virtually no one crossed party lines (see Table 3.1). By 1863 the new realignment was firmly in place. The election of that year was not a "critical" election, since it did not register any definite break with traditional sources of party support; it simply completed the reshuffling of voters that had begun in the late 1840s and had continued throughout the 1850s. When Massachusetts voters cast their ballots after 1863, they repeated familiar partisan habits. Consequently, electoral behavior remained extremely rigid, prefacing a continuance of Republican hegemony.

While some Massachusetts Democrats in 1863 remained in their party because of habit, it is questionable whether they still held to their old Jacksonian belief in the preservation of individual liberties and laissez-faire economics. Andrew speculated that the chief motivation to vote Democratic was the belief that the manpower and resources of the North were being sacrificed "simply for the deliverance of black men, whom they do not much like and for whom they would willingly make no sacrifices." Caleb Cushing's dire prediction that white government in the United States would be doomed under the

TABLE 3.1
Party Lines Tighten: Voting Stability in "Off-Year"
Gubernatorial Elections, 1855-1865
(by percent of electorate)

Election Pair	Actual Number of Cases	Percent Switching Parties	Percent Behaving Stably[a]	Gross Change in Turnout[b]
1855-1857	320	18%	70%	12%
1857-1859	331	8	75	17
1859-1861	331	8	72	19
1861-1863	330	4	77	19
1863-1865	330	0	81	20

Note: To adjust for the varying populations of cities and towns, variables used in regression equations are "weighted" by the potential voting population. The figures above are estimates of the behavior of all eligible voters in the second election in each pair of elections. Both here and elsewhere in the tables, rounding procedures occasionally produce totals greater or less than 100 percent.

[a]Those voting for the same party twice or not voting in both elections.

[b]Previous voters who dropped out of the active electorate in the second election plus previous nonvoters and new voters who cast ballots in the second election.

Lincoln administration "to the infernal depths of a black, red or yellow consolidated Republic" seemed to many Democrats a likely reality as the war dragged on. In the first two years of the war, the Republican party had accumulated an antislavery record that revolutionized race relations. Conservative Democrats, who claimed that Lincoln and his party had already gone too far in exercising federal powers, dreaded Republican postwar policies directed at the South.[16]

For radical Republicans, Colonel Robert G. Shaw's ride through the streets of Boston at the head of the all-black 54th Massachusetts regiment was, indeed, a portent of things to come. The newly formed regiment, armed with Enfield rifles, marched to the State House where it was met by Governor Andrew and his staff. "An imposing sight," wrote onlooker Henry Wadsworth Longfellow, "with something wild and strange about it, like a dream." Nine years before, *The Liberator* reminded its readers, the entire military force of Boston had to be used to escort just one runaway slave named Anthony Burns through the city streets to a ship that took him back to the South; now a thousand black troops marched through the same streets on their way to defeat the same slaveholders to whom Burns had been ignominiously returned. Frederick Douglass, along with many members of Boston's small, but influential, black community, mingled and talked with the troops at the pier before their ship steamed out of the harbor. Black and white abolitionists would later try to express their feelings triggered by the sight of the armed black soldiers, but most would remember best the words uttered by Governor Andrew at the formal presentation of regimental colors: "I stand or fall as a man and a magistrate with the rise or fall in history of the 54th Massachusetts regiment."[17]

Once the first Confederate shot hit Fort Sumter, according to one contemporary observer, the representatives of pre-Civil War Massachusetts conservatism quickly took refuge in "the Democratic party, in historical societies, and in benevolent corporations," all of which offered them shelter from the impending revolutionary storm. Of those who had cast ballots for the Constitutional Unionist gubernatorial candidate in 1860, virtually none was found in the Republican column in 1861. They either voted for Isaac Davis, the Democratic gubernatorial candidate, or they abstained from voting altogether (see Table 3.2). A remarkably high 70 percent of those who voted the Constitutional Union ticket stayed away from the polling places in 1861. Even former Whig Senator Edward Everett, John Bell's running mate, abstained, feeling it his duty to stand aloof from all party associations.[18]

To some extent the apathy of the former Constitutional Unionists resulted from their party's bankrupt position caused by the secession crisis and the outbreak of war. Just before hostilities erupted in April 1861, John Bell advised the citizens of his home state of Tennessee to form military leagues with other southern states against their common northern enemies. The reaction in conservative quarters in Massachusetts was predictable: "Is it possible that our 'Constitutional Union' leader is giving aid and comfort to traitors," wrote an outraged Amos A. Lawrence, the Constitutional Union gubernatorial candidate in 1860, "while the Democrat Andrew Johnson . . . is suffering obloquy at the hands of a mob? God forbid." Clearly, Bell's behavior was in sharp contrast to his pledge the previous year to maintain the Union and the Constitution inviolable. The secession crisis also caused Everett to reject the principles of the Constitutional Union party. After Lincoln's victory Everett was convinced that the only way to avoid civil war "would be for congress, by a joint Resolution, to create General [Winfield] Scott dictator for six months." Everett knew that Congress had no such power, but the impending crisis demanded, in his opinion, an extreme solution. As dictator, Scott would "wind up the clock and set it going again," and thus, according to Everett, precious time would be gained for the application of legal remedies.[19]

Bay State Democrats formulated a more realistic strategy. During the secession crisis and throughout the war, they constantly tried to split Republican ranks by driving a wedge between the radicals and Lincoln. Their best chance came in March 1862, when Lincoln urged Congress to adopt a joint resolution expressing the government's willingness to provide financial assistance to any state adopting a grad-

TABLE 3.2
Estimated Relationships Between Voting Patterns in the 1860 and 1861 Gubernatorial Elections
(by percent of 1861 electorate)

Candidate in 1861	Candidate in 1860						
	Erasmus D. Beach (Dem.)	John A. Andrew (Rep.)	Amos A. Lawrence (C.U.)	Benjamin F. Butler (Breck.Dem.)	Not Voting for Governor 1860	Not Eligible 1860	Percent of 1861 Electorate
Isaac Davis (Dem.)	9	1	3	1	0	0	14
John A. Andrew (Rep.)	2	25	0	1	1	0	29
Not Voting for Governor 1861	5	19	7	1	23	2	57
Percent of 1861 Electorate	15	46	10	3	24	2	100

Note: Actual N = 331.

ual plan to abolish slavery. William D. Northend, a prominent Democratic state senator, speaking in favor of Lincoln's proposal, claimed that those who advocated a different policy "not only place themselves in opposition to the Administration, but initiate a partisan conflict."[20] In addition, some moderate and conservative elements within the Republican party saw in the difference between the radicals and the president an opportunity to oust Sumner and the Bird Club from political power.

In a bold move to outflank their enemies, Bird and his associates forced the Republican state convention to take unprecedented action, namely, to endorse Sumner's bid for reelection to the Senate. In protecting Sumner's position, they left nothing to chance. As early as April they alerted Sumner to the importance of organizing the federal government agents in the state who were to be appointed as assessors and collectors under the new tax bill. In August, with the aid of George S. Boutwell, whom Lincoln had made commissioner of revenue, Sumner and his allies looked after the appointments under the tax act. When the inspectors, clerks, and watchmen from the Boston Custom House were added to the delegates who received appointments as assessors and collectors, the radicals easily managed the convention.[21]

When the motion endorsing Sumner carried, Republican conservatives led by Joel Parker, a Harvard law professor and former Whig, formed a new "People's" party convention at which a schismatic ticket was nominated on a platform of unconditional support for Lincoln. "For the first time in our political history," Horace Greeley observed of Bay State politics, "a party has been organized and a state ticket nominated for the sole purpose of defeating the re-election of one who is not a State official, and never aspired to be." Former Free-Soiler Charles Francis Adams, then absent as Lincoln's minister to the Court of St. James, was chosen by the allegedly nonpartisan People's party to replace Sumner in the Senate. Adams was unwelcome in radical circles after his concessions to southern demands on behalf of slavery while he was a member of Congress during the secession crisis. As a political ally of William H. Seward, Lincoln's secretary of state, Adams was opposed to the radicals but in 1862 he did not feel that differences were great enough to call for an open break with the Sumner wing of his party in his home state. Therefore, he refused to be a candidate for the Senate.[22]

Critical of Sumner for harassing Lincoln by repeatedly urging emancipation, the formal call for delegates to the People's party convention declared against the government's issuance of any "impotent proclamations" on slavery. The day after this manifesto appeared, however, Lincoln issued his preliminary Emancipation Proclamation, which undercut the very basis of the anti-Sumner movement. "Warrington" wrote gloatingly that he hoped that People's party leader Parker "had finished his coffee and muffins before he read the morning papers."[23]

With its position of loyalty to Lincoln and opposition to emancipation rendered inconsistent, if not ridiculous, the People's party switched the focus of its attack from Sumner to Andrew for his part in the allegedly anti-Lincoln Altoona Conference, a gathering of governors of the loyal states called when the North was threatened with invasion. When it became obvious that the Democrats were interested in using the People's party for their own purposes, the threat of massive Republican defections ended. But for those conservative Republicans who felt Lincoln had capitulated to the pressure of fanaticism, there was no hope for reconciliation. "These men of the people's party are going to unite with us hereafter," explained a Democratic party politician, "there *is nowhere else* they can go."[24]

When Democrats formally endorsed the slate of candidates nominated by the People's party, many of the conservative Republican "bolters" who had initiated the anti-Sumner movement refused to take further part in the campaign. Former Whig Governor John H. Clifford, now president of the state senate, declared that he was "not willing to be sold out to the half-Secession Democracy" and declined a congressional nomination by the People's party in the First District. In refusing to stand as a "People's" candidate, however, Clifford took the opportunity to chastise publicly Sumner's political friends for making support of Lincoln conditional on his adoption of Sumner's policy in the conduct of the war. By the end of the 1862 campaign, only a few prominent Republicans were still part of the anti-Sumner movement. Criticism of Sumner was one thing, but an alliance with the Democrats was farther than most conservative Republicans were willing to go. Even the Springfield *Republican* abandoned its crusade to unseat Sumner, preferring him to any man the Democrats might nominate.[25]

Deciding to let his record in office speak for itself, Andrew took no public part in the 1862 campaign. His opponent, Brigadier General Charles Devens, was a minor hero in the Virginia peninsula operations, but he was also the United States marshal who in 1851 had ordered the fugitive Thomas Sims back to slavery. Absent from the state in the army, Devens naively and reluctantly allowed his name to be used by the People's party against Andrew.

In a private message to his political allies immediately after Lincoln issued the preliminary Emancipation Proclamation, Andrew stated he would "knock the bottom out" of the People's party within ten days. "Republicans must make it *their* business to sustain this act of Lincoln," he wrote. Dropping any pretense of nonpartisanship or reconciliation with the "bolters," he added, "and we will drive the 'conservatism' of a pro-slavery Hunkerism and the reactionaries of despotism into the very caves and holes of the earth. The conquest of the rebels, the emancipation of the slaves, and the restoration of peace founded on liberty and permanent democratic ideas! Let this be our platform."[26]

Andrew was easily reelected governor in 1862, along with an overwhelming Republican legislature pledged beforehand to return Sumner to the Senate. The Republicans elected all ten of the state's congressional representatives, although the vote in the Boston districts (Third and Fourth) was extremely close. On the surface the 1862 election appears to be a classic case of a "maintaining" election: Andrew's capture of 60 percent of the ballots cast matched his command of 62 percent of the total vote in 1860. Similarly, Republican congressional candidates won 63 percent of the ballots cast in 1862, compared with 60 percent in 1860. A more detailed analysis of voting patterns in the 1862 election, however, reveals that there were substantial defections to the People's party from the 1860 Republican camp (see Table 3.3).

The Republicans anticipated that in 1862 voter concern over a purely local issue would cost Andrew some support. Boston and an entire string of western towns on the Troy and Greenfield Railroad route in Berkshire and Franklin counties had a vital interest in the completion of the Hoosac Tunnel. Work had started in 1856 and many believed that, when finished, the tunnel would usher in an economic "millennium" by linking Boston directly to the Hudson River. Soon after taking office, however, Andrew removed the state engineer engaged for the job. When a new engineer subsequently halted work on the project in summer 1861, it was charged that Andrew looked unfavorably on the tunnel's completion. In the 1861 gubernatorial contest an

TABLE 3.3
Who Voted for the "People's" Party in 1862?
Crossover Voting Between the 1860 and 1862 General Elections
(by percent of 1862 electorate)

A. Estimated Relationships Between Voting Patterns in the 1860 and 1862 Congressional Elections
(Actual $\underline{N}$ = 254)

Party in 1862[a]	Party in 1860				
	Anti-Republican	Republican	Not Voting 1862 Congressional Election	Not Eligible 1860	Percent of 1862 Electorate
"People's" Party	13	7	0	0	20
Republican	0	32	2	0	34
All Others	0	0	0	0	0
Not Voting 1862 Congressional Election	14	6	22	4	46
Percent of 1862 Electorate	27	45	24	4	100

B. Estimated Relationships Between Voting Patterns in the 1860 and 1862 Gubernatorial Elections
(Actual $\underline{N}$ = 331)

Candidate in 1862	Candidate in 1860						
	Erasmus D. Beach (Dem.)	John A. Andrew (Rep.)	Amos A. Lawrence (C.U.)	Benjamin F. Butler (Breck.Dem.)	Not Voting for Governor 1860	Not Eligible 1860	Percent of 1862 Electorate
Charles Devens ("People's" party)	12	2	7	2	0	0	23
John A. Andrew (Rep.)	0	32	1	0	2	0	34
Not Voting for Governor 1862	3	11	2	1	21	4	42
Percent of 1862 Electorate	15	45	10	3	23	4	100

[a]Voting returns from the Ninth Congressional District (where the Republican congressional candidate, William B. Washburn, was unopposed) were omitted from the analysis.

anti-Republican protest vote occurred in towns such as Shelburne, Buckland, Hawley, and Rowe, where "the great bore" was a vital issue. Bird, who was known to be hostile to the tunnel project, worked assiduously in the legislature to defuse the issue politically before the 1862 election. His efforts were moderately successful.[27]

A glance at voting returns from the string of twenty-two towns located on the railroad route from the northern tip of Berkshire County to the town of Gardner in Worcester County reveals that displeasure with Andrew in these areas culminated in 1861 (see Table 3.4). By 1862 the twenty-two towns were more Republican and less anti-Republican than the state as a whole, an outcome that had not been the case in 1861. Nevertheless, the decline in Andrew's percentage of the electorate between the 1860 presidential election and the "off-year" 1862 congressional election was greater in the towns located on the railroad route than in the state-at-large. This suggests that there was still some lingering disaffection with Andrew in the twenty-two towns in

1862. The People's party, however, was unable to capitalize on this voter disaffection, because Devens fared no better in these same towns than predictable, given the normal drop-off in the anti-Republican vote in the entire state between 1860 and 1862. Eventually, presidential politics pushed the tunnel issue into oblivion; in 1864 Andrew ran better in the western tunnel towns than he had in 1860. His opposition polled slightly less than had been the case in the first Lincoln election. Such an interpretation of the impact of the Hoosac Tunnel issue on wartime politics is compatible with the more general statewide voting patterns that shaped the 1862 election outcome.

Except for the handful of Constitutional Unionists who voted for Andrew, the movement across party lines in 1862 was entirely in one direction: although virtually none of the 1860 Democrats, whether "regular" Democrats or "Breckinridge Democrats," subsequently voted Republican, almost one-sixth of the 1860 Republican vote went to People's party congressional candidates (see Table 3.3). The Republican defections accounted for about 35 percent of the 1862 anti-Republican congressional vote, but in the gubernatorial race less than 10 percent of Devens's total vote came from those who had voted in 1860 for Andrew and the Republicans. Former Constitutional Unionists, who were politically stranded in 1861, found a temporarily congenial home in the ranks of the People's party in 1862 (see Tables 3.2 and 3.3.B). About 70 percent of those who cast ballots for Lawrence, the Constitutional Union candidate, voted for Devens and the People's party. In net results, however, the strength of the Republican voter coalition vis-à-vis its adversaries remained basically unchanged between 1860 and 1862.

The relatively high abstention rate in 1862 among those who had opposed Republican congressional candidates in 1860 was due, in part, to the absence of a regular Democratic ticket and the lack of enthusiasm of many Democrats for the People's party ticket, which was laden with conservative Republicans, many of them former Whigs. The same circumstances help explain the Republican crossover vote between the 1860 and 1862 congressional elections. The People's party ticket, tailored to attract disaffected Republicans, presumably was more suitable to 1860 Republicans who might otherwise have balked at voting a regular Democratic ticket. While the 1862 election witnessed some split-ticket voting, there was no unusual amount of "scratching" Andrew from Republican ballots or voting for Devens along with Republican congressional candidates. Thus, there was no indication of voter disaffection directed only at Andrew (see Table 3.5).

Did, however, the 1862 Republican "bolters" vote for People's party congressional candidates to protest the Lincoln administration's eman-

TABLE 3.4
The Effects of the Hoosac Tunnel Issue on Andrew and the
Republicans in 1862: Voting Behavior in a String of Towns
from Gardner to Williamstown
(by percent of electorate)

	Gardner to Williamstown[a]		Entire State	
Gubernatorial Election Year	Republican	Anti-Republican	Republican	Anti-Republican
1860	55.8%	19.8%	46.7%	22.4%
1861	28.6	17.7	28.6	13.7
1862	36.6	19.7	34.3	23.3
1863	33.4	12.8	29.7	12.3
1864	57.9	16.6	51.8	20.3

[a]Williamstown, Adams, Florida, Rowe, Charlemont, Buckland, North Adams, Hawley, Shelburne, Conway, Deerfield, Greenfield, Montague, Wendell, Orange, Royalston, Athol, Templeton, Winchendon, Erving, Phillipstown, Gardner.

TABLE 3.5
Estimates of Split-Ticket Voting in the 1862 General Election
(by percent of 1862 electorate)

Party in 1862 Congressional Election[a]

Gubernatorial Candidate in 1862	"People's" Party	Republican	Others	Not Voting 1862 Congressional Election	Percent of 1862 Electorate
Charles Devens ("People's" party)	18	1	0	4	23
John A. Andrew (Rep.)	2	32	0	0	34
Not Voting for Governor 1862	0	1	0	42	43
Percent of 1862 Electorate	20	34	0	46	100

Note: Actual <u>N</u> = 252.

[a]Voting returns from the Ninth Congressional District (where the Republican congressional candidate, William B. Washburn, was unopposed) were omitted from the analysis.

cipation policy? While historians can never know all they would like to know about voter motivation, the subsequent behavior of the 1862 Republican bolters is revealing. The Republican disaffection in 1862 did not carry over into 1864, but was confined largely to voting the People's party ticket in 1862 (see Table 3.6). In the three congressional elections held in 1860, 1862, and 1864, about 16 percent of the 1860 Republicans voted for the People's party in 1862, but only about 2 percent of them voted Democratic in 1864 (see Tables 3.3 and 3.6). If the Republicans who voted for the People's party ticket had genuinely believed that Lincoln's preliminary Emancipation Proclamation signaled only further strife, destruction, and anarchy, and the advent of a mongrelized American Republic, it follows that they would have voted with the Bay State Democracy, which shared their fears about the implications of emancipation.

TABLE 3.6
Crossover Voting Between the 1860 and 1864 Congressional Elections
(by percent of 1864 electorate)

| Party in 1864 | Party in 1860 | | | | |
	Anti-Republican	Republican	Not Voting 1860 Congressional Election	Not Eligible 1860	Percent of 1864 Electorate
Democratic	19	1	0	0	20
Republican	3	38	9	3	52
Not Voting 1864 Congressional Election	5	4	14	4	27
Percent of 1864 Electorate	27	43	23	7	100

Note: Actual N = 332.

In the North many states that had supported Lincoln in 1860 turned against the Republicans in the 1862 elections. The Democrats gained seats in the House of Representatives and would have controlled it had not the New England states along with Michigan, Iowa, California, and the border states supported the Lincoln administration. Andrew felt that, outside of Massachusetts, the results of the 1862 elections were attributable to a belief in the ineffectiveness of the Union army's military operations against the Confederacy. Among members of the Bird Club the general prescription for victory at the polls was larger doses of radicalism and abandonment of what the radicals derogatorily referred to as Lincoln's conservative "border state" policy.[28]

The 1863 Republican party platform reflected the effort of the radicals to sharpen public awareness of the purpose of the war. The Republicans called the Emancipation Proclamation "a guaranty to the world that the contest is for civilization and Christianity" and deprecated the idea that permanent peace was possible as long as slavery existed. They considered enemies those who would make peace with the rebellious states on any basis short of the destruction of the Confederacy and its submission to federal authority. To this end, the Republicans approved the use of black troops based on "perfect equality" as to rights and compensation with white soldiers. In contrast, the Democratic state convention, which included "Peace" and "War" Democrats, many former "Cotton" Whigs, and even a contingent of former Know-Nothings led by former Governor Henry J. Gardner, placed the Bay State Democracy firmly in opposition to the onsweeping revolutionary implications of emancipation. The Democrats declared against all interference by the national government in local and state affairs, against the exercise of any "implied powers" by any department of the federal government, against continuance of the war for reasons of subjugation or emancipation, and against any extension of martial law over states not in the southern rebellion.[29]

In Massachusetts, 1863 was a watershed. The gestures of certain politicians early in the war to abandon partisan politics, and the rhetoric surrounding the People's party movement in 1862, had fostered the illusion among voters that the war against the South was a "popular-front" undertaking waged in defense of the Union. By 1863, however, Republicans and Democrats were diametrically opposed in their views of the war. The increasing radicalism of the Republicans and the deepening fear of revolutionary change on the part of the Democrats resulted in an ideological polarization of the two parties. The moderate center of opinion eroded and party lines remained unbroken for the duration of the war (see Table 3.1).

The anger of the radicals at Lincoln's moderate war and Reconstruction policies, and especially at his pocket veto of the Wade-Davis Bill, resulted in a Republican intraparty struggle over the 1864 presidential nomination. In Lincoln's cabinet, Secretary of the Treasury Salmon P. Chase was the strongest friend of the Massachusetts radicals, and a powerful movement to nominate him instead of Lincoln developed in the Boston Custom House with the blessing of the Bird Club. When the Chase boom collapsed, a Frémont movement began; it quickly ran into difficulty when it appeared that, after Lincoln received the Republican nomination, Frémont's managers were flirting with the pro-Confederate, "Copperhead" element in the Democratic party. To complicate matters, in the summer of 1864 defeatism almost overcame some Republican politicians. With Ulysses S. Grant stalemated in Virginia and William Tecumseh Sherman stymied before Atlanta, Bird and his allies were anxious to pressure Lincoln to withdraw in favor of another candidate who would have a better chance of winning. Sumner and Andrew were sympathetic to the movement to make Lincoln step down, but Bird did not trust Wilson, who was on good terms with Lincoln, with knowledge of his anti-Lincoln schemes. When Sherman took Atlanta, plans for a new Republican convention were abandoned and the Massachusetts radicals rallied to Lincoln's candidacy. "We have knocked down and stamped out the last Copperhead ghost in Massachusetts," proclaimed a jubilant Governor Andrew after Lincoln carried the state with an overwhelming majority in the 1864 presidential election.[30]

An analysis of the relationships between voting patterns in the 1860 and 1864 presidential contests offers no support for the hypothesis that the use of the "Union," rather than "Republican" party, label facilitated the transition of an 1860 Democrat to a war Democrat to a Republican (see Table 3.7.B).[31] If the Union designation was substituted in order to attract the votes of former Democrats, then it proved a total failure—at least in Massachusetts—as a political tactic. However, some Constitutional Unionists and many 1860 abstainers may have been roped into the Republican party by the Union lasso, because Lincoln won the votes of about one-third of those who had supported John Bell in 1860. Perhaps the Republicans were helped by Edward Everett's acceptance of the Republican nomination for presidential elector-at-large, although it is impossible to gauge the extent to which former Bell-Everett men took their cue from Everett's declaration of support for Lincoln. Everett's place on the Republican ballot was balanced by the acceptance of Robert C. Winthrop, a former Whig party leader and supporter of Bell's candidacy in 1860, of the same position on the Democratic ballot. In this battle for former Constitutional Unionists, the Democrats fared better than the Republicans. George B. McClellan, the Democratic presidential candidate in 1864, captured over 40 percent of the Bell-Everett men, winning, in effect, four for every three won by Lincoln. The breaking up of the Constitutional Union constituency accounted for all of the crossover voting in 1864, if the votes for John C. Breckinridge are lumped together with the votes for Stephen A. Douglas to equal the 1860 Democratic vote. Virtually all who voted the Breckinridge Democratic ticket and over 90 percent of the regular Douglas Democrats subsequently voted for McClellan.

Unfortunately, there were no popular referenda in Massachusetts on the manner in which Lincoln and the Republican party conducted the war—specifically, on the operation of the conscription law, on the suspension of the writ of habeas corpus, on the centralized control of banking, on increased measures of national taxation, and on the establishment of military rule in states not in rebellion. Nor were any public opinion polls taken to discover the attitudes of ordinary citizens toward the desirability of a thorough reconstruction of the economic, political, and social structure of the South. Yet the absence of quantifiable data does not indicate that these issues were unimportant to the voters, for the best evidence is not always the most easily quantifiable. To overlook more traditional evidence is to run the risk of forgetting how incomparably divisive the war years were, not just across the firing line, but within northern society as well.

Events moved so rapidly during the war years that what at one time was perceived as radical policy, such as emancipation or the use of black troops, became largely acceptable as a means to defeat the South. Thus, the men "who [once] abhorred the thought of abolition," wrote George Bancroft early in 1865, "are now unanimous for it." In urging passage of the Thirteenth Amendment, the scholarly statesman declared that times can arise "when the most radical measure is the most

TABLE 3.7
Crossover Voting Between Presidential Elections from 1856 to 1864
(by percent of 1864 electorate)

A. The 1856 and 1864 Presidential Elections
(Actual N = 324)

Candidate in 1864	Candidate in 1856			Not Voting for President 1856	Not Eligible 1856	Percent of 1864 Electorate
	Buchanan	Fremont	Fillmore			
McClellan	16	0	2	0	2	20
Lincoln	0	35	5	5	7	52
Not Voting for President 1864	1	9	1	10	6	27
Percent of 1864 Electorate	16	45	8	16	15	100

B. The 1860 and 1864 Presidential Elections
(Actual N = 332)

Candidate in 1864	Candidate in 1860				Not Voting for President 1860	Not Eligible 1860	Percent of 1864 Electorate
	Douglas	Lincoln	Bell	Breckinridge			
McClellan	13	0	4	3	0	1	20
Lincoln	0	39	3	0	7	3	52
Not Voting for President 1864	1	5	3	0	15	3	27
Percent of 1864 Electorate	14	44	9	3	22	7	100

conservative: such a time is come." At the end of the war, John Lathrop Motley realized that the nation was still in the midst of an unresolved crisis because the southern black could not be left "a pariah without right to testify . . . to hold land, to be educated or to vote." And consequently, Motley found it natural to conclude: "We are in a revolution and we are responsible to all coming generations for our use of the victory which the God of battles has given to us."[32] This basic insight, which was so obvious to Motley writing from his distant diplomatic post in Vienna, by the end of the war had become second nature to the citizens of his own state who back home experienced more directly the trauma of the war years. To lose sight of how sharply divided were Bay State voters on the issues arising directly from the war and to overlook how that division formed the basic demarcation between Republicans and Democrats, is to ignore altogether what was axiomatic in the minds of the people of Massachusetts who had lived through the most disruptive period of American history.

Chapter 4
The Civil War Years:
Geography, Social Contexts, and
Voting Behavior

The money power has joined hands with the slavery power.
Selfish, grasping, subtle, tyrannical. Like its ally, it will brook
no opposition.—*Charles Sumner quoted in Edward L. Pierce,*
Memoir and Letters of Charles Sumner

Although the railroads built in Massachusetts in the 1840s and 1850s
had linked communities and conquered distances, different regions retained unique cultural characteristics. From the sandy beaches
of Cape Cod to the jagged peaks of the Berkshire Mountains localism
conflicted with the onslaught of rapid modernization. On the eve of the
Civil War a distinctive local culture was claimed by almost every city
and town in the Commonwealth. Community life ranged from the
working-class consciousness of shoemakers in Lynn to the conservative provincialism of residents in Lenox, and from the irrepressible
radicalism of reformers in Worcester to the intellectual smugness of
professors in Cambridge. Despite the cosmopolitan diversity of the
Boston area and the often overdrawn picturesque quaintness of local
histories, the most salient demographic fact about mid-nineteenth century Massachusetts was the concentration of population and wealth in
thirty-two towns in the immediate vicinity of Boston. In 1865 over half
the population of the Commonwealth, about 70 percent of the value of
personal property, and approximately two-thirds of the real estate
value were located within a radius of just twenty-five miles from the
State House and the Boston Common.[1]

Boston was not only the ancient capital and largest city, it also
represented a frame of mind. "There is something in the power of
Boston," declared Frank Bird, "something in the power of wealth concentrated there which creates sentiment somewhat different from that

of the country."[2] In the antebellum period the city's business and banking magnates exercised a disproportionate influence in state politics through their control of the Whig party. Many Bay Staters had automatically deferred to the Hub's entrepreneurial elites, believing that whatever contributed to the growth of industry and commerce improved the welfare of all citizens. As long as the Whig party projected an image of steady economic progress and high-minded moral superiority, the Boston Whigs were able to rule Massachusetts politics. However, when the slavery issue made the Whigs appear to place economic self-interest and personal gain above moral precepts, their opponents lost no time in exploiting the resulting hypocrisy. The "Cotton" Whigs, in particular, were charged with having grown morally indifferent to the question of slavery in direct proportion to the amount of money they made through their commercial dealings with the South.[3]

During the 1840s and 1850s the antislavery sentiment of the countryside continually threatened the alliance between the state's manufacturing, commercial, and maritime interests, on one hand, and the southern slave states, on the other. The conservatism of communities like Hull and Lowell differed from that of Boston, in the words of antislavery intellectual Thomas Wentworth Higginson, "as a rope's end differs from a rapier."[4] The antagonists of the conservative Whigs argued that bankers and manufacturers preferred bales of cotton to the dictates of their conscience and that shipowners and sea captains chose invoices and bills of lading over liberty and justice. The claim that the "lords of the loom," the wealthy owners of the new cotton mills in towns around Boston, were locked into an unholy alliance with the "lords of the lash," the wealthy owners of slave plantations in the South, was a common political charge against the Boston textile magnates by the so-called "Conscience" Whigs, and later by the Free-Soilers and Republicans.[5]

This accusatory political rhetoric appealed to many in the Massachusetts hinterland who questioned the claims of Boston Whigs that their leadership had brought prosperity to hard-working and independent common men throughout the state. Under antebellum Whig tutelage industrialization had proceeded at a dazzling pace, achieving a rate of economic growth that one state official called "without parallel in the history of the world."[6] But with industrialization also had come a host of problems. The developments in transportation left farmers in central and western Massachusetts unable to compete with the influx of cheaper agricultural products from as far away as Illinois. By the eve of the Civil War over half of the beef consumed in Massachusetts came from the Midwest. The state's production of wheat and cereals became of relatively minor economic importance, and the Massachusetts sheep herds were less than a third of what they had been in 1840. Of those who gave up farming altogether, most sought jobs in the new industrial towns that sprang up along the Merrimac and Connecticut rivers.[7]

Young rural men who flocked to the factory towns encountered a variety of problems. The newcomers faced competition for jobs from impoverished Irish immigrants. More importantly, the realities of factory life and the unsanitary conditions, poverty, slums, and limited chances for advancement in the cities challenged the Yankee notion of the sturdy, independent, hard-working small businessman, artisan, or laborer—a man responsible for his own destiny and free of dependent relationships. On the eve of the Civil War the Springfield *Republican* warned young rural people that their chances of success in the city were less than one in a hundred. Many in the countryside believed that the monied aristocracy had deliberately created a large, permanent, servile working force comprised of Irish peasants. Early in the 1850s, Henry Wilson, then a Free-Soil party leader, attacked the wealthy Whig manufacturers for suggesting that their employees should vote, not according to their convictions, but according to the interests of their employers.[8]

Contemporaries of the period and historians alike have assumed that the Republicans drew their strongest support from the middle-class voters of the small towns and countryside or from areas where the ideal of the sturdy and independent farmer, mechanic, or small businessman endured.[9] The egalitarian ideology of the Republican party held little importance for city dwellers, particularly Irish immigrants, nor did it appeal to the very wealthy urbanites. Before the Civil War antislavery agitation, according to one contemporary observer, "drew a line of cleavage through all Boston society, leaving most of the more powerful or wealthy families on the conservative side."[10] Throughout the war and Reconstruction period the Democrats captured the fashionable areas of Beacon Hill and Back Bay, verifying the assumption that the most affluent men in Massachusetts were Democrats. John Murray Forbes, a rare Republican among Boston's prominent businessmen, claimed that the monied leisure classes identified themselves with the southern planters. "'Club men' who live by wine, cards, tobacco and billiards . . . gravitate very strongly to secesh sympathies," wrote Forbes. For such reasons, Forbes was convinced that Abraham Lincoln and the Republicans could not depend upon the wealthy classes, nor upon Boston, but would have to appeal to "the hardhanded people of the country."[11]

In trying to identify who, in social and economic terms, voted for the

Republicans or their opponents, one must combine literacy and impressionistic evidence with a quantitative analysis of voting returns. An examination of voting statistics is a prerequisite step to making inferences about voter motivation. For example, based on an analysis of voting returns in the 1864 presidential election, it would be a mistake to conclude that support for George B. McClellan and the Democrats came primarily from the state's largest cities and that the Democratic ticket drew poorly in small towns.[12] Compared to the 183 smallest towns in the state, Boston was only 4 percentage points more Democratic, and the next 47 largest cities were no more Democratic than were the smallest towns (see Table 4.1.A). Also, Lincoln's candidacy appealed to both small-town and city dwellers. Lincoln's percentage of the electorate in the largest cities excluding Boston was only 4 percentage points below his percentage in the state's 183 smallest towns, and only 2 percentage points less than his percentage in the state's medium-sized towns (between 2,000 and 5,000 inhabitants). But he fared dismally at the hands of the Hub's voters. In Boston Lincoln ran 12 percentage points below his statewide average.

Lincoln fared best in predominantly rural and agrarian Hampshire County and worst in urban Suffolk County, which included Boston (see Table 4.1.B). But voting returns in the counties sandwiched between Hampshire and Suffolk counties prevent a conclusion that the Republican ticket ran strongest in areas least affected by new developments in transportation and industry, and ran weakest in places most affected by rapid modernization and concomitant developments such as immigration and urbanization. Lincoln drew less than his statewide average on Cape Cod (Barnstable County), on one of the two Islands (Dukes County), and in Berkshire County—areas relatively untouched by rapid economic and social change. He fared better than average in counties such as Middlesex and Worcester where substantive economic and social changes were occurring. On the other hand, McClellan fared best in remote Berkshire County and in rapidly growing Norfolk County, thus further frustrating the generalization that a simple urban-rural cleavage shaped the partisan vote.[13]

Many contemporary political pundits and later-day historians have generalized about the voting behavior of "shoe," "cotton," and "woolen" towns.[14] In 1865 roughly a quarter of the state's towns were either boot and shoe manufacturing towns or cotton textile mill towns, classifications based rather arbitrarily on the industry employing the largest work force in each community. Because the Massachusetts textile industry depended on the South for supplies of raw cotton, the cotton towns were assumed to be less Republican than the shoe or woolen towns. Abolitionist Wendell Phillips, for example, believed in 1861 that

TABLE 4.1
The 1864 Presidential Vote in Selected Cities and Towns Grouped by Size, Counties, and Major Industries
(by percent of 1864 electorate)

Description of Voting Units	Number of Cases	Vote in 1864 Presidential Election		
		Republican	Democratic	Abstained
A. By Town Size				
Towns under 2,000	183	57%	20%	23%
Towns between 2,000 and 5,000	99	55	18	27
Towns over 5,000 (excluding Boston)	47	53	20	27
Boston	1	40	24	36
B. By County				
Hampshire	23	66	11	23
Franklin	26	60	18	22
Worcester	57	56	18	26
Nantucket	1	56	4	40
Middlesex	51	55	23	22
Essex	34	53	18	29
Bristol	18	53	12	35
Hampden	21	53	24	23
Norfolk	23	53	26	21
Plymouth	25	52	17	31
Berkshire	31	51	32	17
Barnstable	13	48	9	43
Dukes	3	43	13	44
Suffolk	4	42	24	34
C. By Major Industry				
Iron	12	58	21	21
Straw and rattan goods	13	57	16	27
Furniture or woodenware	15	56	20	24
Woolens	34	56	21	23
Boots and shoes	51	53	20	27
Cottons	36	52	20	28
Fishing, whaling, and navigation	28	50	9	41
Lumber, paper, and charcoal	10	49	33	18
All Cities and Towns	330	52%	20%	27%

Sources: The size of a city or town was determined by its population as reported in the 1865 state census. The major industry was determined by the industry that employed the largest work force in 1865. The classification of the cities and towns by major industry was derived from Massachusetts, Secretary of the Commonwealth, Statistical Information Relating to Certain Branches of Industry in Massachusetts, for the Year Ending May 1, 1865. The above means were calculated by first adding all votes together and then dividing by the number of potentially eligible voters; thus the means were, in effect, "weighted" by voting population.

Massachusetts was too "choked with cotton-dust" to mobilize for war with the rebellious slave states. On the other hand, it was axiomatic during the 1850s that "radicalism went with the smell of leather" and that shoe towns "were usually anti-slavery."[15]

But in 1864 Lincoln and the Republicans did not fare unusually well in the state's major boot and shoe cities and towns (see Table 4.1.C). Moreover, cotton towns were as ardent in their support for Lincoln as were shoe towns. In the 1850s the Free-Soil ticket had run decidedly well in the shoe towns.[16] But by 1864, as a result of divided feelings of the shoemakers toward the Republicans and changes in the social structure of the shoe towns, there was little connection between the vote for Lincoln and the relative rank of towns as manufacturers of shoes, cotton goods, or woolens (see Table 4.1.C).

The contemporary influence and historical significance of the boot and shoe towns cannot be adequately measured from their voting record alone. The shoe and leather industry became one of the Commonwealth's most important industries during the 1850s and was destined during the Civil War years to become important in state politics. Although Lynn and Abington were the acknowledged centers of trade, the boot and shoe industry brought growth and prosperity to such towns as North Brookfield, Natick, Weymouth, Stoughton, and Danvers. Many boot and shoe factory owners held positions of leadership in the Republican party. In 1860 roughly 10 percent of the members of the state legislature were shoe manufacturers and the majority of these were Republicans. From the time that Henry Wilson, the "Natick cobbler," began making antislavery stump-speeches, to the 1868 election to the governorship of his close friend William Claflin, one of the state's leading shoe manufacturers, boot and shoe towns grew in political power.[17]

Contemporaries acknowledged both the political importance and volatility of the shoe towns. In the 1850s, the cordwainers took great pride in their status as skilled workers, were quick to protest any perceived injustice, aspired to become factory owners, and formed stable communities. The gradual displacement of craft skills by machines, the growing rate of absentee ownership, and the resulting emphasis on low costs and high production soon transformed the work patterns and life-styles of the shoemakers. By the end of the decade the Irish immigrants had become a new social element among them, accelerating the decline of their status and income. Early in 1860, in response to a series of hardships, the shoemakers staged the largest strike ever. Only the unity forged by the war against the Confederacy snuffed out the smoldering conflict between the Bay State shoemakers and their employers.[18]

Any quantitative analysis of voting must be truly multivariate in design if it is to determine the influence of a variety of factors on voting decisions. A multiple regression analysis was used here to detail Massachusetts voting in the 1860 and 1864 elections. The analysis statistically disentangles the effects of a large array of demographic variables in order to ascertain what weight ought to be attached to each to explain voting behavior. The results identify political, economic, social, and religious factors that account for variations in voting in different parts of the state. These variations are explained statistically when, for example, the reason one city or town is heavily Republican is shown to depend on the presence or absence of certain variables. The amplified description, mean, and standard deviation of each variable are presented in Table 4.2. A matrix of the intercorrelations between

TABLE 4.2
Descriptions, Means, and Standard Deviations of Variables Selected for Stepwise Regression Analysis

Variable Name	Amplified Description	Mean	Standard Deviation
Douglas	Percent of electorate voting Democratic in 1860 presidential race	15.4	7.9
Lincoln 1860	Percent of electorate voting Republican in 1860 presidential race	47.7	10.1
Bell	Percent of electorate voting Constitutional Union in 1860 presidential race	10.0	7.6
Breckinridge	Percent of electorate voting as Breckinridge Democrat in 1860 presidential race	2.8	2.6
Abstaining 1860	Percent of electorate not voting in 1860 presidential race	24.1	13.0
Lincoln 1864	Percent of electorate voting Republican in 1864 presidential race	52.4	9.7
McClellan	Percent of electorate voting Democratic in 1864 presidential race	20.2	8.4
Abstaining 1864	Percent of electorate not voting in 1864 presidential race	27.4	9.8
Congregational	Church seating accommodations, Congregational Trinitarian, 1860, divided by population, 1860	20.4	20.4
Unitarian & Universalist	Church seating accommodations, Congregational Unitarian and Universalist, 1860, divided by population, 1860	10.9	10.6
Baptist	Church seating accommodations, Baptist, 1860, divided by population, 1860	9.2	8.4
Episcopalian	Church seating accommodations, Episcopalian, 1860, divided by population, 1860	2.5	3.8
Quaker	Church seating accommodations, Society of Friends, 1860, divided by population, 1860	.1	2.9
Methodist	Church seating accommodations, Methodist, 1860, divided by population, 1860	8.8	9.4
Catholic	Church seating accommodations, Roman Catholic, 1860, divided by population, 1860	5.7	6.7
Other churches	Church seating accommodations, all other churches, 1860, divided by population, 1860	3.8	7.8
Foreign-born	Percent of population born in foreign countries, 1865	20.5	10.7
Out-of-state	Percent of population born in states other than Massachusetts, 1865	13.9	6.2
Foreign growth rate	The average annual growth rate (in percentage terms) of the foreign-born population between 1855 and 1865	.6	4.4
Native growth rate	The average annual growth rate (in percentage terms) of the native-born population between 1855 and 1865	1.5	1.8
Valuation per capita 1860	Value of taxable real and personal property, 1860, divided by population, 1860	733.7	486.6
Valuation per capita 1865	Value of taxable real and personal property, 1865, divided by population, 1865	808.7	562.8
Manufacturing	Percent of occupied males engaged in manufacturing, 1865	24.1	16.2
Agriculture	Percent of occupied males engaged in agriculture, 1865	11.4	14.5
Fishing	Percent of occupied males engaged in fishing, 1865	4.4	12.3

TABLE 4.2 Continued

Variable Name	Amplified Description	Mean	Standard Deviation
Voters of polls	Percentage of "ratable" polls, 1860, who were "legal" voters, 1860	75.3	11.2
For "two-year" amendment	Percent of electorate favoring restrictions on immigrant voting, 1859	9.9	5.7
Against "two-year" amendment	Percent of electorate against restrictions on immigrant voting, 1859	6.9	4.5
Poll-tax voters	Percentage of legal voters assessed for a poll tax only in 1869	43.3	16.6

Sources: Voting returns for the 1864 election and the 1859 referendum are the official totals. The 1860 presidential returns were supplemented by unofficial tallies in instances where the votes from certain cities or towns were excluded from the official record because of a mere technicality, such as the failure of the report of votes to arrive at the State House before a certain deadline. The source for the number of church seating accommodations is the manuscript "Social Statistics" schedule of the 1860 federal census, which is deposited in the State Library, State House, Boston. The source for the valuation of the state in 1860 is Massachusetts, General Court, Journal of the Senate, S.Doc. 33 (1861), pp. 4-11. The source of the 1865 valuation is Massachusetts, General Court, Manual for the Use of the General Court (Boston: 1866), pp. 113-21. The sources for all remaining variables are Massachusetts, Secretary of the Commonwealth, Abstract of the Census of the Commonwealth of Massachusetts, 1855, pp. 2-63, and Abstract of the Census of Massachusetts, 1865, pp. 56-81, 144-67; and Massachusetts, General Court, Journal of the House of Representatives, H.Doc. 82 (February 1870), pp. 1-11.

the independent or explanatory variables is displayed in Table 4.3. The regression results are presented in Tables 4.4 and 4.5.[19]

Preliminary insights into the relationship between the average voter turnout for Lincoln in 1864 and the independent variables may be discovered by examining the simple correlation coefficients between the Republican vote and each explanatory variable (see Table 4.5). The Republican vote was both positively and slightly correlated with occupied males engaged in agriculture, and with Congregational church seating accommodations. The Republican vote was both significantly and negatively associated with the per capita valuation, the population born in foreign countries, and voters who paid no tax other than the required poll tax. There is an important difference in the signs of the correlation and regression coefficients in the case of the growth rate of the native-born population. Whereas the association of the native-born growth rate with the percentage Republican was negative according to the correlation coefficient, it became positive after the effects of the other variables were controlled. In other words, the average vote for Lincoln was lower in communities with high growth rates of native-born inhabitants, but not because of this characterization of the communities. The vote for Lincoln was relatively low because these same communities also tended to have large per capita valuations and large concentrations of immigrants and "poll-tax voters" (see Table 4.3). Once the effects of these and other variables were controlled, the association of the Republican vote with the native-born growth rate actually became positive (see Table 4.5).

TABLE 4.3
Correlation Matrix of Explanatory Variables Selected for Stepwise Regression Analysis

	Congregational	Unitarian & Universalist	Baptist	Episcopalian	Quaker	Methodist	Catholic	Other churches	Foreign-born	Out-of-state
Congregational	1.00									
Unitarian & Universalist	-.23	1.00								
Baptist	-.01	-.03	1.00							
Episcopalian	-.15	.01	.04	1.00						
Quaker	-.07	.05	-.02	.01	1.00					
Methodist	.13	-.14	-.03	-.16	.06	1.00				
Catholic	-.31	.00	-.04	.21	-.04	-.15	1.00			
Other churches	-.15	-.03	-.06	.01	.21	.04	.04	1.00		
Foreign-born	-.38	-.06	-.14	.26	-.13	-.32	.57	-.08	1.00	
Out-of-state	-.20	-.17	-.01	.18	-.11	-.13	.16	-.03	.39	1.00
Foreign growth rate	.03	-.06	-.11	.04	-.04	.02	.03	-.04	.23	.14
Native growth rate	-.26	.01	-.11	.18	-.14	-.20	.35	-.10	.56	.31
Valuation per capita 1860	-.29	.15	-.14	.25	.00	-.23	.39	.02	.60	.11
Valuation per capita 1865	-.27	.15	-.13	.28	-.05	-.24	.40	-.02	.62	.11
Manufacturing	-.16	-.16	-.10	.01	-.01	-.06	.22	-.02	.26	.33
Agriculture	.43	-.04	.19	-.21	.02	.15	-.41	-.03	-.56	-.23
Fishing	-.09	.05	-.11	-.07	.05	.21	-.03	.08	-.06	-.27
Voters of polls	.27	-.04	.03	-.21	.07	.32	-.38	.16	-.71	-.29
For "two-year" amendment	-.34	.12	-.07	.15	-.02	-.30	.36	-.02	.49	.25
Against "two-year" amendment	-.03	-.18	-.01	.01	-.07	.00	.21	-.15	.40	.22
Poll-tax voters	-.38	.00	-.18	.24	.03	-.24	.47	-.01	.66	.28

	Foreign growth rate	Native growth rate	Valuation per capita 1860	Valuation per capita 1865	Manufacturing	Agriculture	Fishing	Voters of polls	For "two-year" amendment	Against "two-year" amendment	Poll-tax voters
Foreign growth rate	1.00										
Native growth rate	.41	1.00									
Valuation per capita 1860	.03	.36	1.00								
Valuation per capita 1865	.00	.35	.99	1.00							
Manufacturing	.17	.31	-.17	-.19	1.00						
Agriculture	-.11	-.53	-.39	-.40	-.33	1.00					
Fishing	.07	-.04	.10	.08	-.29	-.19	1.00				
Voters of polls	-.13	-.46	-.33	-.36	-.28	.37	.20	1.00			
For "two-year" amendment	-.04	.30	.34	.35	.14	-.44	-.12	-.50	1.00		
Against "two-year" amendment	.09	.12	.21	.24	.05	.02	-.14	-.22	.13	1.00	
Poll-tax voters	-.01	.36	.60	.62	.24	-.63	-.04	-.42	.47	.23	1.00

TABLE 4.4
Influence of Explanatory Variables on Voting Patterns in the 1860 Presidential Election

Dependent Variable	Explanatory Variables	Simple r	Regression Coefficients	Adjusted Standard Errors of Reg. Coef.	Beta Coefficients	Change in R^2
Douglas [R^2=.40]	Out-of-state	.43	.28	.08	.22	.18
	Voters of polls	-.42	-.17	.05	-.23	.09
	Fishing	-.34	-.12	.05	-.18	.04
	Quaker	-.23	-.45	.14	-.16	.03
	Against "two-year" amendment	.31	.28	.09	.16	.02
	Manufacturing	.34	.06	.05	.13	.02
	Congregational	-.20	-.05	.02	-.12	.01
	For "two-year" amendment	.19	-.14	.09	-.11	.01
	Foreign growth rate	.04	-.00	.00	-.04	.00
	Catholic	.24	.06	.08	.05	.00
	Episcopalian	.08	-.06	.11	-.03	.00
	Other churches	-.14	-.03	.05	-.03	.00
	Valuation per capita 1860	.08	-.00	.00	-.02	.00
	Unitarian & Universalist	-.06	.02	.03	.03	.00
	Methodist	-.14	.02	.03	.02	.00
	Foreign-born	.39	.04	.09	.06	.00
	Agriculture	-.13	.01	.04	.02	.00
	Native growth rate	.23	-.00	.00	-.02	.00
	Baptist	.03	.01	.04	.01	.00
	Poll-tax voters	.23	-.01	.05	-.02	.00
Lincoln [R^2=.51]	Valuation per capita 1860	-.48	-.00	.00	-.37	.23
	Fishing	-.42	-.18	.06	-.22	.14
	Congregational	.34	.11	.02	.22	.04
	Voters of Polls	-.10	-.30	.06	-.34	.06
	Agriculture	.34	.09	.04	.14	.01
	Out-of-state	.14	.20	.09	.13	.01
	Foreign-born	-.22	-.17	.10	-.18	.01
	Foreign growth rate	.05	.00	.00	.10	.00
	For "two-year" amendment	-.05	.13	.11	.08	.00
	Catholic	-.23	-.09	.11	-.06	.00
	Methodist	-.04	-.05	.04	-.05	.00
	Native growth rate	-.15	-.00	.00	-.05	.00
	Manufacturing	.16	.02	.06	.03	.00
	Against "two-year" amendment	.01	.06	.10	.03	.00
	Other churches	-.10	.03	.06	.03	.00
	Quaker	-.06	-.07	.16	-.02	.00
	Baptist	.12	.02	.04	.02	.00
	Poll-tax voters	-.29	.02	.05	.03	.00
	Episcopalian	-.09	-.02	.12	-.01	.00
	Unitarian & Universalist	-.12	.01	.04	.01	.00
Bell [R^2=.65]	Valuation per capita 1860	.59	.00	.00	.35	.35
	For "two-year" amendment	.47	.30	.06	.23	.08
	Against "two-year" amendment	-.10	-.40	.06	-.23	.06
	Unitarian & Universalist	.34	.10	.02	.15	.03
	Native growth rate	.42	.01	.00	.16	.03
	Out-of-state	-.04	-.25	.05	-.20	.02
	Other churches	-.12	-.11	.03	-.11	.02
	Quaker	-.13	-.27	.09	-.10	.01
	Foreign-born	.45	.09	.06	.09	.01
	Manufacturing	-.10	-.08	.03	-.17	.01
	Fishing	.01	-.07	.03	-.12	.01
	Episcopalian	.24	.13	.07	.06	.00
	Agriculture	-.41	-.05	.02	-.09	.00
	Congregational	-.29	-.02	.01	-.06	.00
	Baptist	-.12	-.05	.02	-.05	.00
	Voters of polls	-.39	-.04	.03	-.06	.00
	Poll-tax voters	.40	-.02	.03	-.04	.00
	Catholic	.29	-.02	.05	-.02	.00
	Methodist	-.29	-.02	.02	-.02	.00
	Foreign growth rate	.07	.00	.00	.01	.00
Breckinridge [R^2=.19]	Manufacturing	-.30	-.04	.02	-.27	.09
	Against "two-year" amendment	.15	.10	.04	.18	.03
	Voters of polls	.17	.02	.02	.08	.02
	Out-of-state	.05	.08	.03	.20	.02
	Quaker	.05	.04	.06	.04	.00
	Methodist	.11	.01	.01	.04	.00
	Poll-tax voters	-.02	.01	.02	.07	.00
	Foreign-born	-.11	-.06	.04	-.26	.01
	Valuation per capita 1860	.10	.00	.00	.12	.01

TABLE 4.4 Continued

Dependent Variable	Explanatory Variables	Simple r	Regression Coefficients	Adjusted Standard Errors of Reg. Coef.	Beta Coefficients	Change in R²
	Catholic	-.03	.03	.04	.08	.00
	Unitarian & Universalist	-.06	-.01	.01	-.05	.00
	Fishing	.10	.01	.02	.06	.00
	Other churches	-.02	-.01	.02	-.04	.00
	Congregational	.09	.01	.01	.05	.00
	Baptist	.06	.01	.02	.04	.00
	Episcopalian	.02	.01	.05	.02	.00
	Native growth rate	-.13	-.00	.00	-.04	.00
	Agriculture	.11	-.01	.02	-.04	.00
	Foreign growth rate	-.05	.00	.00	.03	.00
	For "two-year" amendment	-.06	.01	.04	.01	.00
Abstaining [R²=.55]	Voters of polls	.54	.49	.06	.42	.29
	Fishing	.51	.36	.06	.34	.16
	Quaker	.26	.77	.18	.17	.04
	Out-of-state	-.36	-.32	.10	-.15	.01
	Foreign-born	-.32	.10	.11	.08	.01
	Other churches	.23	.12	.06	.07	.01
	For "two-year" amendment	-.34	-.30	.11	-.13	.01
	Foreign growth rate	-.10	-.00	.00	-.07	.01
	Unitarian & Universalist	-.06	-.12	.04	-.10	.00
	Congregational	.01	-.05	.03	-.07	.01
	Agriculture	.03	-.05	.04	-.06	.00
	Valuation per capita 1860	-.05	.00	.00	.08	.00
	Manufacturing	-.21	.04	.06	.05	.00
	Methodist	.26	.03	.04	.03	.00
	Native growth rate	-.25	-.00	.00	-.03	.00
	Episcopalian	-.12	-.05	.13	-.02	.00
	Against "two-year" amendment	-.17	-.04	.11	-.01	.00
	Catholic	-.13	.02	.12	.01	.00
	Baptist	-.05	-.00	.05	-.00	.00
	Poll-tax voters	-.14	-.00	.06	-.00	.00

Note: Actual N = 314. Voting units are "weighted" by population in order to ensure that smaller towns are not overrepresented in the analysis. Standard errors, however, are computed according to the original, unweighted number of cities and towns.

The regression results suggest that communities that voted heavily Republican in 1864 had higher percentages of Congregationalists, Unitarians, and Universalists; lower concentrations of fishermen and industrial workers; lower per capita valuations; and had experienced significant increases, presumably due to internal migration, in their native-born populations (see Table 4.5). Among all the independent variables, the per capita valuation of a town had the greatest relative impact, albeit a negative impact, on the Republican vote. Roughly half the percent of the variation in the 1864 Lincoln vote was explained by per capita valuation. This had also been the case in the first Lincoln election (see Table 4.4).

The wealth of Massachusetts was concentrated largely in the areas around Boston, including the cities and towns in the Merrimac River Valley. The communities tied to Boston by trade, transportation, and investment capital reflected the conservative political views of the Hub's businessmen and bankers. Towns with high ratios of the value of tax-assessed property to their total population were also the same maritime and commercial areas that had been most eager not to offend the southern slave states in 1860. The per capita valuation in that year

TABLE 4.5
Influence of Explanatory Variables on Voting Patterns in the 1864 Presidential Election

Dependent Variable	Explanatory Variables	Simple r	Regression Coefficients	Adjusted Standard Errors of Reg. Coef.	Beta Coefficients	Change in R²
McClellan [R²=.34]	Foreign-born	.35	.06	.10	.08	.12
	Fishing	-.29	-.16	.06	-.23	.07
	Quaker	-.30	-.79	.16	-.26	.06
	Manufacturing	.03	-.06	.06	-.12	.02
	Congregational	-.18	-.06	.02	-.15	.02
	Against "two-year" amendment	.28	.24	.10	.13	.02
	Voters of polls	-.35	-.14	.06	-.18	.01
	Episcopalian	.17	.15	.13	.06	.00
	Agriculture	-.04	.06	.04	.11	.00
	Out-of-state	.25	.12	.09	.09	.00
	Catholic	.22	.09	.11	.07	.00
	Unitarian & Universalist	.04	.04	.04	.05	.00
	Valuation per capita 1865	.25	.00	.00	.05	.00
	For "two-year" amendment	.20	-.05	.10	-.04	.00
	Native growth rate	.17	-.00	.00	-.03	.00
	Methodist	-.15	.03	.04	.03	.00
	Foreign growth rate	-.00	-.00	.00	-.02	.00
	Other churches	-.11	-.02	.06	-.01	.00
	Poll-tax voters	.20	.00	.05	.01	.00
	Baptist	.04	-.00	.04	-.00	.00
Lincoln [R²=.41]	Valuation per capita 1865	-.46	-.00	.00	-.42	.22
	Congregational	.36	.11	.02	.23	.06
	Unitarian & Universalist	.04	.12	.04	.12	.03
	Fishing	-.18	-.12	.05	-.15	.02
	Manufacturing	-.09	-.13	.05	-.21	.02
	Native growth rate	-.12	.01	.00	.19	.03
	Quaker	.06	.27	.16	.08	.01
	Agriculture	.37	.06	.04	.09	.00
	Against "two-year" amendment	-.19	-.14	.10	-.06	.01
	Out-of-state	-.05	.15	.09	.10	.01
	Episcopalian	-.08	.15	.13	.06	.00
	Foreign growth rate	.08	.00	.00	.05	.00
	Foreign-born	-.41	-.14	.10	-.15	.00
	Voters of polls	.18	-.08	.06	-.09	.00
	Baptist	.06	-.05	.04	-.04	.00
	Methodist	.05	-.05	.04	-.04	.00
	Poll-tax voters	-.43	-.02	.05	-.03	.00
	Other churches	-.02	.02	.06	.02	.00
	For "two-year" amendment	-.23	-.03	.10	-.01	.00
	Catholic	-.30	.01	.09	.01	.00
Abstaining [R²=.46]	Fishing	.43	.27	.05	.34	.18
	Poll-tax voters	.26	.01	.05	.03	.07
	Quaker	.19	.52	.14	.15	.03
	Voters of polls	.12	.21	.05	.24	.02
	Manufacturing	.07	.19	.05	.31	.03
	Valuation per capita 1865	.25	.00	.00	.37	.04
	Out-of-state	-.16	-.27	.08	-.17	.02
	Unitarian & Universalist	-.08	-.16	.03	-.17	.02
	Native growth rate	-.03	-.01	.00	-.16	.01
	Agriculture	-.33	-.12	.04	-.18	.02
	Episcopalian	-.07	-.30	.11	-.11	.01
	Congregational	-.20	-.04	.02	-.09	.01
	Foreign growth rate	-.07	-.00	.00	-.05	.00
	Catholic	.10	-.10	.10	-.07	.00
	Baptist	-.09	.06	.04	.05	.00
	For "two-year" amendment	.06	.09	.09	.05	.00
	Against "two-year" amendment	-.06	-.10	.09	-.05	.00
	Foreign-born	.10	.08	.09	.08	.00
	Methodist	.08	.02	.03	.02	.00
	Other churches	.12	-.01	.05	-.01	.00

Note: Actual N = 314.

was both positively and strongly associated with the support received by the Constitutional Union party, suggesting that Unionist sentiment was strongest in communities that had the most to lose economically if the nation were to become wracked by civil war (see Table 4.4).

In 1864 the Democratic ticket did not necessarily draw heavier support in areas with higher aggregate values of real and personal property. Although the vote for McClellan correlated positively and slightly with per capita valuation, this relationship became insignificant when the effects of all other explanatory variables were controlled (see Table 4.5). In terms of the relative ability of all the explanatory variables to account for the differences in the average rate at which town electorates supported the Democrats in 1864, the population born in foreign countries was the most important. McClellan also ran well in communities where voters in 1859 had expressed strong opposition to the "two-year" amendment that restricted immigrant voting. He fared poorly in localities with large proportions of fishermen, Quakers, industrial workers, and Congregationalists. Clearly, the ethnic factor was important in accounting for the variations in McClellan's support. However, the relative importance of cultural and noncultural predictors of the partisan vote demands further analysis, especially because apparently economic variables were as important as religious and ethnic variables in explaining the vote for Lincoln.

The results in Table 4.6 suggest that ethnic or religious identifications of voters were less important than economic predictors in explaining the support for Lincoln in 1864. The set of religious variables (the ratios of church seating accommodations to population held by the eight major religious denominations and by all other churches) explained only a paltry 5 percent more of the variance in the Republican vote than was accounted for by three major occupational aggregates, namely, the percentages of occupied males engaged in agriculture, manufacturing, and fishing. Per capita valuation explained slightly more of the variance in the Republican vote than did the entire set of religious variables (see Tables 4.5 and 4.6). It explained almost as much as seven major social aggregates, namely, the percentages of the population born in Ireland, Germany, England, Scotland, British America, Massachusetts, and states other than Massachusetts. In accounting for the differences in the average rate at which town electorates supported Lincoln, the combined explanatory power of per capita wealth and the percentage of "legal" voters assessed both property and poll taxes was slightly greater than either the set of place-of-birth variables or the set of religious variables.

Republican voter strongholds were communities of predominantly

TABLE 4.6
Total Variance Explained in the 1864 Presidential Vote by
Selected Sets of Social, Economic, and Political Variables

Variables	Number of Cases	Percentage of Variance Explained		
		Republican	Democratic	Abstained
Valuation and tax category[a]	329	23%	6%	6%
Place of birth[b]	329	22	27	12
Religious[c]	327	20	19	13
Occupational[d]	326	15	11	24
Town size and growth rate[e]	329	3	0	2
Competitiveness[f]	320	--	--	5

Note: The percentage of variance explained (R^2) was computed by running separate regressions with each set of variables.

[a]Per capita valuation in 1865 and the percentage of "legal" voters assessed both property and poll taxes in 1869.

[b]Percentages of the 1865 population born in Ireland, Germany, England, Scotland, British America (Canada and other British territorial possessions in the Western Hemisphere), Massachusetts, and states other than Massachusetts.

[c]Percentages of church seating accommodations of the total population belonging in 1860 to the following denominations: Congregational Trinitarian, Unitarian, Universalist, Baptist, Methodist, Episcopalian, Quaker, Roman Catholic, and all other churches.

[d]Percentages of occupied males in 1865 engaged in manufacturing, agriculture, and fishing.

[e]Population in 1865 and population growth rate between 1855 and 1865.

[f]David Index of party competition in the 1864 presidential election.

"middling" wealth. In the antebellum period Free-Soilers and Republicans had celebrated the virtues of the "middling-interest class" as being vital to the northern way of life. When Massachusetts Republicans stressed the importance of maintaining the chance for all men to share equitably in the distribution of wealth, they voiced not a campaign promise but a living reality. Because per capita valuation was positively and strongly associated with the percentage of poll-tax voters (see Table 4.3), the lower aggregate wealth of Republican areas was, in fact, associated with a more equitable distribution of wealth. In the absence of wealthy family dynasties coexisting with working classes, an independent or radical stance was more safely undertaken. But where the poor depended on the rich for sustenance, the Republicans fared poorly, and political participation, if not the democratic process itself, was adversely affected, especially in the absence of a secret ballot.[20]

Areas of low turnout in the 1864 election were those stratified by wealth, areas that had been bastions of Whiggery in the 1840s and 1850s, and that had disproportionally voted the Constitutional Union ticket in 1860. Many well-to-do former Whigs and Constitutional Unionists did not turn out to vote in 1864, and those who did participate did not throw the weight of money and influence behind their electoral efforts to the same extent as they had in former years. Although the presence of Quakers in a community tended to suppress turnout in 1864, the bulk of the variation in the rate of nonvoting was accounted for primarily by the joint influence of economic variables (see Tables 4.5 and 4.6). Voter participation was lower in areas with large concentrations of fishermen, industrial workers, and poll-tax voters, and in communities with high per capita valuations. It is of special interest that there was no significant relationship between the degree of competition between the Republican and Democratic tickets and the rate of voter turnout (see Table 4.6). The perception that the vote in a locality might be extremely close did not stimulate voter interest or participation in the 1864 election.[21]

The most important reservation to the conclusion that noncultural variables were more important than ethnocultural ones in explaining voting patterns arises from the variance explained in the McClellan vote by the sets of social and religious variables (see Table 4.6). The total variance explained in the Democratic vote by the set of seven place-of-birth variables equaled over three-fourths of the total variance explained by all variables used in the multiple regression analysis (see Tables 4.5 and 4.6). Moreover, the relationship between the sets of social and religious variables and the vote for McClellan was not a spurious relationship that vanished when economic variables were brought into the analysis (see Table 4.7). The results indicate that ethnic-group consciousness contributed more to the forging of loyalties to the Democratic party than either the interaction between shared taxpayer status and per capita valuation or the shared familiarization with an occupational grouping.

On the other hand, in explaining the variance in the Republican vote, the sets of religious variables and place-of-birth variables were comparatively less important than taxpayer status, per capita valuation, and three groupings of employed males (see Table 4.7). Nor was the relationship between these five economic variables and the vote for Lincoln a spurious relationship that disappeared once cultural variables were brought into the analysis. Even when the effects of the sets of cultural variables were controlled, the incremental variance explained by the addition of the set of economic variables was greater than that caused by the addition of the sets of cultural variables when the effects of the set of economic variables were controlled. These results suggest that economic considerations were more important than ethnocultural factors in explaining the vote for Lincoln.

Partisan divisions in Massachusetts during the Civil War thus re-

TABLE 4.7
Religious, Ethnic, or Economic Variables?
A Comparative Evaluation of Effects on Republican and Democratic Voting, 1864

A. Economic Versus Religious Variables

	Effects of Economic Variables on the Partisan Vote with Religious Variables Controlled	
	Lincoln	McClellan
Percent variance due to religious variables	20%	19%
Percent incremental variance due to economic variables	16	10
Percent Total Variance	36	29

	Effects of Religious Variables on the Partisan Vote with Economic Variables Controlled	
	Lincoln	McClellan
Percent variance due to economic variables	28%	15%
Percent incremental variance due to religious variables	8	14
Percent Total Variance	36	29

B. Economic Versus Ethnic Variables

	Effects of Economic Variables on the Partisan Vote with Ethnic Variables Controlled	
	Lincoln	McClellan
Percent variance due to ethnic variables	22%	27%
Percent incremental variance due to economic variables	9	3
Percent Total Variance	31	30

	Effects of Ethnic Variables on the Partisan Vote with Economic Variables Controlled	
	Lincoln	McClellan
Percent variance due to economic variables	28%	15%
Percent incremental variance due to ethnic variables	3	15
Percent Total Variance	31	30

Note: Economic Variables = percentages of occupied males engaged in fishing, agriculture, and manufacturing in 1865, percentages of "legal" voters assessed both property and poll taxes in 1869, and valuation per capita in 1865. Religious Variables = percentages of church seating accommodations of the total population in 1860 belonging to the following denominations: Congregational Trinitarian, Unitarian, Universalist, Methodist, Baptist, Quaker, Episcopalian, Roman Catholic, and all other churches. Ethnic Variables = percentages of total population in 1865 born in Ireland, Germany, England, Scotland, British America (Canada and other British territorial possessions in the Western Hemisphere), Massachusetts, and states other than Massachusetts.

flected more than conflicting values rooted in ethnocultural subgroupings of the electorate. Although there was a significant foreign-born vote in the Democratic column, no Protestant bloc shaped the contours of support for the Republicans. The religious composition of a community did not serve as a useful predictor of support for the Republicans. In studying voting patterns in other northern states during the nineteenth-century, historians have presented strong evidence that the most important determinants of voting have usually been the religious identifications of citizens.[22] Clearly, the extent to which religious differences determined voting patterns in Massachusetts in the 1860s demands further investigation.

There was no dearth of religious conflict during the antebellum period. The Whigs had maneuvered cautiously, although not always successfully, among antagonistic religious denominations and an aggressive evangelical Protestantism. In the early nineteenth century, disaffection between Unitarians and Congregationalists was often very bitter and constantly threatened to spill over into the political arena. In 1833 a constitutional amendment ended the connection between church and state that for two centuries had made Massachusetts ostensibly a homogeneous Congregationalist commonwealth. To generalize, the Calvinist Congregationalists (formerly Unitarian allies in the old Federalist party) joined forces with members of "dissenting" religious denominations (mostly Democrats) to disestablish religion. Disestablishment was not a strictly partisan victory, however, because Trinitarian Congregationalists, Universalists, and Baptists—all seeking reform—were themselves politically divided. The Democratic and Whig leaderships avoided any explosive religious issue having the potential to split their rank and file; they were acutely aware that religious beliefs were important social and intellectual factors to be taken carefully into account in any political decision.[23]

The political cooperation between the Massachusetts Unitarian Whig establishment and its orthodox Congregationalist brethren was repeatedly jeopardized by the long-standing conflict between two polarized religious perspectives, the evangelical and the ritualistic. In general, the evangelical outlook stressed a strong personal faith in God and emphasized "correct" or moral standards of behavior. At times, evangelical denominations sought to convert sinners through a variety of missionary activities. On the other hand, the ritualistic religious orientation accentuated belief in elaborate and unchanging creeds and ceremonies, and emphasized adherence to sacramental or doctrinal standards. The Roman Catholic church was the most ritualistic, followed by descendants of national European churches with lingering Roman practices, namely, the Episcopalian church and some Lutheran churches.

Examples of how the clash of these two polarized religious views generated political differences in the 1830s and 1840s are numerous. The evangelical crusade to eradicate sin and bring the kingdom of God to earth by enforcing prohibition, banning Sunday mail, and inculcating Protestant morality in the public schools had compelled the Boston Unitarians in the 1820s to open up their Whig party caucuses to zealous pietists. Trinitarian Congregationalists secured from the state legislature a charter allowing orthodox-supported Amherst College to share public funds previously monopolized by Harvard College, a bastion of Unitarianism. However, when in 1839 a Whig governor supported evangelical demands for a temperance measure banning the retailing of liquor in any quantity less than fifteen gallons, he was defeated dramatically by a coalition of antievangelical Democrats and dissident Unitarian Whigs.[24]

During the political crisis of the 1850s, evangelical Protestantism helped to form both the Know-Nothing and Republican parties. But pietism, nativism, and antislavery were neither identical nor mutually exclusive. The anxieties of native-born Protestant workmen in the industrial towns and the antislavery sentiment of predominantly Congregationalist rural areas represented different kinds of voter concerns. During the Civil War years, Republican voter sentiment did not flow through the state along the same channels as had either the revivalist enthusiasm or the anti-Catholic, Know-Nothing phenomenon. The last of the great religious revivals of the antebellum period, which swept through Massachusetts in the winter of 1857–58, was not confined to Republican or antislavery strongholds. Know-Nothings and northern evangelists were not united on the slavery issue; they varied from extreme abolitionists to cautious "doughfaces." It was the Republican party, not the sermons of the preachers or the propaganda of the nativists, that mobilized Bay Staters against slavery expansionism.[25]

Precisely how, then, was evangelical Protestantism related to Republican party allegiance? Estimates of voting preferences of individuals comprising the state's eight largest religious denominations were derived by using the number of seating accommodations of each denomination as a measure of the religious composition of the electorate: the number of seats each denomination had in 1860 was divided by the total population to create dichotomous variables. These were used as the independent variables on which the partisan vote was regressed (see Tables 4.8 and 4.9).

Admittedly, the use of church seating accommodations is an unrefined measure of church membership and of the percentage of legal voters who were formally affiliated with a specific church. Its use here may have resulted in inflating the number of male members for all Protestant denominations. In the nineteenth century, at least 60 percent of church members, especially in the Protestant denominations, were women.[26] Conversely, because Roman Catholic masses often

TABLE 4.8
Estimated Relationships Between Religious Affiliation and Voting in the 1860 Presidential Election
(by percent)

Denomination	% for Lincoln	% for Douglas	% for Bell	% for Breckinridge	% Against Lincoln	% Not Voting
Congregational	62	11	5	3	19	20
Baptist	59	17	0	4	21	20
Unitarian	47	9	32	1	42	10
"Nothingarian"	47	19	11	2	32	22
Others	42	6	0	2	8	51
Episcopalian	37	21	36	5	62	2
Methodist	35	11	0[a]	5	16	50
Universalist	31	15	20	1	35	33
Quaker	30	0[a]	0[a]	7	7	100[a]
Roman Catholic	26	39	31	2	72	3
Actual Vote	48	15	10	3	28	24

Note: Actual N = 329.

[a]Logically impossible estimates have been set at the 0 or 100 percent limits.

TABLE 4.9
Estimated Relationships Between Religious Affiliation
and Voting in the 1864 Presidential Election
(by percent)

Denomination	% for Lincoln	% for McClellan	% Not Voting
Quaker	72	0[a]	96
Congregational	65	15	20
Unitarian	65	24	11
Baptist	55	23	22
Others	52	13	35
"Nothingarian"	49	22	29
Universalist	49	14	37
Methodist	46	16	38
Episcopalian	45	44	11
Roman Catholic	22	40	38
Actual Vote	52	20	27

Note: Actual N = 327.

[a]Logically impossible estimates have been set at the 0 or 100
percent limits.

served four or five groups of parishioners, Catholics were underrepresented by just counting seats. Yet, in the regression analysis, systematic underrenumeration or overrenumeration would not affect the regression estimates if, for example, Catholic accommodations were doubled and all other church seatings were left unchanged, or if Protestant accommodations were slightly reduced and Catholic accommodations were unchanged. The imprecision of seating accommodation data cannot vitiate the analysis if actual male membership correlated highly with comparable data on seating accommodations.

Church membership records indicate that in Massachusetts, as elsewhere in the nineteenth century, the number of men unaffiliated with a church was high. A survey conducted in 1869 and 1870 found that most Protestant workingmen did not attend church. Their decisions were affected by the snobbishness of middle-class churchgoers and, in some cases, the cost of pews. A Boston newspaper, in an effort to refute statements about the existence of "unchurched thousands" in the state's cities, reported that in Lowell one-third of the city's residents attended church on a pleasant Easter Sunday in 1872. Probably well over a third of the state's eligible voters were nonchurchgoers.[27]

The unaffiliated remain a major social, if not religious and intellectual, grouping about which little is known. In the history of religion they have often been ignored. The "Nothingarians" or nonchurchgoers, because they were less visible than the affiliated, have been neglected in recent historical studies focusing on religious affiliation as a powerful determinant of voting behavior. Although they were clearly excluded from party allegiance based upon church membership, their impact on voting patterns, nevertheless, must be taken into account.[28]

The distribution of the Nothingarian vote was roughly analogous to the voting patterns in the state-at-large in both the 1860 and 1864 presidential elections (see Tables 4.8 and 4.9).[29] One could reasonably assume that many of the unaffiliated were strongly hostile to any Protestant political reform impulse that threatened to dictate "correct" personal behavior to them. If a crusading evangelicalism advocating temperance, nativism, and antislavery resulted in "a cultural unity for the Republican party,"[30] there is no evidence, at least in the case of Massachusetts, of a Nothingarian disapprobation expressed by votes against Lincoln and the Republicans. In both the 1860 and 1864 elections, however, Lincoln fared the worst at the hands of those opposed to government regulation of morality, namely, Catholic and Episcopalian voters. Lincoln's opponents in 1860 and McClellan in 1864 ran the best among these same liturgical and antirevival Christians (see Tables 4.8 and 4.9).

Until the outbreak of the Civil War, both Catholic and Episcopal churches were practically silent on the slavery question. Both had hesitated to take any stand for fear of antagonizing their coreligionists in the South. Contemporary antislavery opinion in Massachusetts often commented on the affinity of Catholicism for the South's "peculiar institution." In 1854 Catholics were conspicuously absent among the 3,050 New England clergymen who signed a remonstrance against the prosouthern Kansas-Nebraska Bill. The Boston *Pilot*, the influential Irish immigrant newspaper, took pride in reporting that not a single Catholic priest had signed the anti-Nebraska petition.[31]

Historians have accounted for the conservatism of the Catholic church on the slavery issue with reasons ranging from the philosophic implications of the Papacy's counter-revolutionary stance to the concrete fact that American Catholics—most of them unskilled Irish workers—took comfort in knowing that at least one social class in their adopted nation was below them. But any explanation must entail an understanding of Irish immigration history. Driven in the 1840s from their native land by the terrible potato famine, the Irish arrived in Massachusetts impoverished and, consequently, were often trapped in Boston where they disembarked. By the 1850s the Irish immigrants were the primary source of manpower for Boston's recently organized clothing industry. Gradually, they moved out of the Hub into suburban areas and by the end of the Civil War they lived in factory towns and cities throughout the eastern part of the state and in the Connecticut River Valley. It was not so much the fear of job competition from emancipated slaves that caused Irish antipathy toward blacks as it was the ingrained belief that only by strict obedience to the Constitution and laws of their adopted land could the Irish demonstrate that they were full-fledged American citizens. Not surprisingly, Irish Catholics in the southern states were often found among the ranks of the anti-secessionists. Senator John Slidell of Louisiana remarked that the Irish of New Orleans were "at heart abolitionists" because of their strong support in the 1860 election for Stephen A. Douglas, who competed with John Bell for the city's Unionist vote.[32]

In 1860 the leaders of the newly formed Constitutional Union party were anxious to secure Irish Catholic support to prevent Lincoln and the Republicans from carrying Massachusetts.[33] There was no statewide anti-Republican fusion ticket in Massachusetts, but Lincoln's opposition did unite behind Constitutional Unionists in three of its eleven congressional races. The John Bell-Edward Everett ticket thus could have attracted a substantial number of Irish Catholic votes. Estimates of the relationships between religious affiliation and voting in 1860 indicate that Catholics voted against Lincoln at the rate of almost three to one. Although Douglas won the Catholic vote, a substantial number of Catholics voted for Bell (see Table 4.8).

Curiously, on a political spectrum stretching from radical abolitionism to conservative unionism, the positions of nativist Know-Nothings and Irish Catholic Democrats were not far apart. Both felt that equality under the law should be limited either to native-born men or to white men. Preoccupied by the fear of disunion and war, many Know-Nothings sought refuge in the patriotic Constitutional Union party. Irish-Americans also sought refuge in extreme patriotism, but it was the nativist movement of the mid-1850s that had pushed them to the defense of American values and institutions. To both Irish Catholic Democrats and Constitutional Unionists, the Republicans threatened national unity by putting their personal beliefs about the immorality of slavery above the Constitution. Thus, at the 1863 Democratic state convention, former Know-Nothing Governor Henry J. Gardner voted with the Irish delegates surrounding him to support the American union as it existed before the war and to oppose the revolutionary implications of President Lincoln's Emancipation Proclamation.[34]

Because of their support for the Union and their contribution to the war effort, the Bay State Irish were able to obtain additional civic rights. The radical Republican establishment, moreover, led in demolishing the legal barriers separating the Irish from native-born Protestants. The radicals worked to repeal the amendment restricting immigrant voting and helped to abolish the state law requiring the King James version of the Bible to be read in the public schools. In addition, the notorious "pro-Catholicism" of the burly and popular war Governor John Andrew served to lessen remaining religious and ethnic antagonisms. In one instance, Andrew discharged a reform-school superintendent for destroying the Catholic newspapers sent by friends and relatives of the recalcitrant youths.[35]

When the war to preserve the Union became a war to free the slaves, the Massachusetts Irish felt betrayed by the Lincoln administration. In the spring of 1863, the Boston *Pilot* lamented that the issue was no longer unity but slavery. In the wake of the bloody New York City draft riots, Boston experienced disturbances in the Irish North End. In the interest of preserving law and order the *Pilot* strongly condemned the rioting; but when the 1864 election approached, the newspaper increasingly relied on religious and ethnic appeals to rally Irish Catholic support for McClellan. It wrote: "the Democratic party . . . has been . . . the only hope and refuge to which the oppressed of Ireland could flee. . . . [T]he opposition, on the other hand, whether known by the name, Federalist, Know-Nothing, Free Soil, or Republican . . . has distinguished itself by . . . its narrow bigotry . . . and its open hatred for the rights of the poor and laboring classes."[36]

Irish-Americans preferred McClellan to Lincoln at a rate of nine to one (see Table 4.10). Assuming that in 1864 Irish-born eligible voters equaled at least 10 percent of the electorate, approximately 37 percent of McClellan's total was composed of Irish-born voters, whereas Irishmen constituted only about 2 percent of the vote cast for Lincoln. German-born voters, who represented a small fraction of the electorate, were overwhelmingly identified with the vote for McClellan (see Table 4.10). Karl Heinzen, the militant abolitionist editor of Boston's German immigrant paper *Der Pioneer*, apparently exercised more influence on Americans like Wendell Phillips and William Lloyd Garrison than he did upon his fellow German-Americans. Bay State Germans ignored the advice of Heinzen and voted for McClellan and the Democrats in 1864, as they evidently did in many other northern states during the Civil War.[37]

McClellan ran best among Episcopalians and Catholics, and Irish and German-Americans, and fared worst among Quakers, Scottish, English-Americans, and voters born in British America, including Canadians of French descent (see Tables 4.9 and 4.10). But the comparatively small proportion of foreign-born, Catholic, Episcopalian, or Quaker voters sharply limits the extent to which voting patterns in either 1860 or 1864 can be explained by transplanted Old World antagonisms or by conflicts between pietistic and antirevival Christians. Moreover, the voting behavior of the Methodists, one of the most intensely evangelistic of the major Protestant denominations, challenges the notion that the more evangelical the religious orientation of a group, the more likely it was to support the Republican party.[38]

The Massachusetts Methodist clergy adopted a semiofficial antislavery position in the late antebellum period. They publicly supported Charles Sumner's first election to the Senate, openly opposed the enforcement of the Fugitive Slave Law, and in 1856 held prayer meetings for Republican presidential candidate John C. Frémont. The Methodist *Zion's Herald*, under the editorship of Daniel Wise, took a clearly antislavery stand by the late 1850s. The paper's editor in the 1860s, Gilbert Haven, was a dedicated opponent of slavery who had grown to prominence by preaching antisouthern "political sermons" to his parishioners.[39] The Methodist clergy, however, had difficulty conveying their antislavery enthusiasm to their flocks.

In both the 1860 and 1864 elections, Lincoln ran better among the

TABLE 4.10
Estimated Relationships Between Birthplace and Voting
in the 1864 Presidential Election
(by percent)

Place of Birth	% for Lincoln	% for McClellan	% Not Voting
Scotland	100[a]	0[a]	0[a]
Canada	69	0[a]	44
Out-of-state	59	32	9
In-state	56	12	32
British America	46	0[a]	75
England	42	0[a]	92
In-town[b]	40	16	44
Ireland	8	73	19
Germany	7	95	0[a]
Other foreign-born	0[a]	0[a]	100[a]
Actual Vote	52	20	27

Sources: The breakdown of the electorate by place of birth was accomplished by interpolations from data on the nativities of voters in each city and town in 1875. See Massachusetts, Bureau of Statistics of Labor, Thirteenth Annual Report of the Bureau of Statistics of Labor, Public Doc. 15 (Boston: 1882), table 1, pp. 97-168. On the multiple regression procedure used, see my "'Irish Vote' and Party Politics," p. 123. The 1865 state census did not report the number of "legal" voters born in-town, in-state, and out-of-state. The percentages of eligibles in these categories were estimated by extrapolations from census data on the nativities of males in each voting unit in 1875. See Massachusetts, Bureau of Statistics of Labor, The Census of Massachusetts: 1875, table 1, pp. 273-84.

Note: Actual N = 329. The small numbers of voters born in Scotland, Canada, British America, and Germany do not permit safe generalizations about their voting behavior. The ignoring of other possible determinants of the vote, such as occupation or religious affiliation, could have biased all the above estimates.

[a]Logically impossible estimates have been set at the 0 or 100 percent limits.

[b]Born in the city or town in which voting.

electorate-at-large than among Methodist voters (see Tables 4.8 and 4.9). Both Methodist and Baptist voting patterns in 1864 were roughly analogous to those of nonchurchgoers. A pietistic crusade for individual improvement through self-denial and moral legislation was perhaps easily channeled into votes for nativist or prohibitionist candidates, but the notion of Republicanism as an exclusive function of evangelicalism during the Civil War, at least in Massachusetts, is not supported by the quantitative evidence.

The estimate that 72 percent of the Quakers voted for Lincoln in 1864 is suspect since the Society of Friends was over-identified with nonvoting in both 1860 and 1864 (see Tables 4.8 and 4.9). These illogical, but not statistically impossible, estimates suggest that Quakers apparently voted Republican or they did not vote at all. The estimated high rate of abstention among them might be explained by a schism in the denomination in the late 1830s. A majority of the Friends passed through a period of "quietism," in which they withdrew from worldly activities and established a rigorous supervision of the private lives of their members. Nevertheless, by the outbreak of the Civil War, other more evangelical Quakers regarded the abolition of slavery as more important than the blessings of peace between the states.[40]

In both 1860 and 1864, Lincoln ran the best among the Congregationalists. If the Congregationalists on the eve of the Civil War were not abolitionists, they were, perhaps, the next closest thing. From the time of the first New England Puritan settlements, religious concerns in the Congregational churches were intermingled with political and social issues. The annual "election sermons" preached by every minister before election day often directly related public questions to religious obligations. Congregationalist pastors were concerned with the condition of the southern slaves and many of them actively promoted the abolition movement. Hoping to spare Christianity from the evils of caste, polygamy, and slaveholding, the Congregationalists were the driving force behind the founding of the nondenominational American Missionary Association, which founded antislavery churches in the western states before the war. During and after the war the Missionary Association opened and staffed schools to teach southern blacks of all ages how to read and write.[41]

Roughly three out of every four Congregationalists who voted in 1860 cast ballots for Lincoln. In 1864 the Congregationalists were even more emphatically in the Republican column (see Tables 8 and 9). One would expect to find similar voting patterns among the two Congregational splinter-groups, the Unitarians and Universalists, but the evidence suggests a strong conservative tendency in the political outlook of these religious groupings, especially in the first Lincoln election. The majority of Universalists voting in 1860 cast their ballots against the Republicans. In 1864 Lincoln ran behind his statewide percentage among the Universalists, although he did much better than McClellan. In 1860 Unitarian voters were sharply divided between Lincoln and his opponents, but in 1864 their voting preferences shifted dramatically in favor of Lincoln.

The substantial anti-Republican vote cast by Unitarians and Universalists in 1860 is explained by their attraction to the Constitutional Union ticket. They were joined in their support for Bell by many Episcopalians who disapproved of the crusading moralism of the antislavery forces. A quick perusal of the religious affiliations of the leaders of the Constitutional Union party reveals its connection with wealthy Episcopalians and Unitarians in and around Boston. Edward Everett, who reluctantly became the party's vice-presidential candidate, was a representative par excellence of the old Bay State Unitarian Whig establishment. He had once been a Unitarian minister at the prestigious Brattle Street Church in Cambridge, and was also an accomplished Greek scholar, editor, and author. He had served in both houses of Congress and briefly as secretary of state in Millard Fillmore's cabinet. During the Civil War Everett became a staunch Unionist, although he favored reconciliation with the Confederacy and, by instinct, distrusted the radical Republicans. In 1864 he allowed the Massachusetts Republicans to place his name at the head of the list of electors on their state ballot. Perhaps because of Everett's support, Lincoln ran much better among both Unitarian and Universalist voters than he had in 1860 (see Tables 8 and 9). The war itself did much to unite Unitarians behind the Republican cause, for the war destroyed irrevocably much of the cultural outlook that characterized the widespread influence of the Unitarians in the antebellum period.[42]

Since the 1820s Unitarianism had been a vehicle for the expression of a socially, economically, and culturally privileged class centered in the eastern part of the state, especially in and around Boston. Unitarians were on the average much wealthier than their fellow citizens, and everywhere they were at the upper end of the job ladder. Their cultural influence was extensive: they maintained such institutions as the Boston Athenaeum, the Lowell Institute, and the Boston Public Library. They controlled Harvard College and sustained numerous learned societies, charitable organizations, publishing houses, and magazines. Believing that patterns of social deference should be honored and that political affairs should be monopolized by an educated and wealthy elite, Unitarians had a deep-seated tendency to view political parties as obnoxious religious sects constantly disturbing dispassionate inquiry and mutual tolerance. These notions were often mixed with intense party loyalty, because the Unitarians had exercised their political power through the old Whig party. Considering themselves defenders of republican institutions, protectors of intellectual freedom, and champions of social decorum, their social outlook was often a mere rationalization for the comfortable status quo. They distrusted any social change, including abolition, that might bring uncertainty. For the Unitarians, in the words of Henry Adams, "difficulties might be ignored; doubts were waste of thought; nothing exacted solution: Boston had solved the universe."[43]

In the late antebellum period Unitarians had been largely unwilling to gird themselves for ideological battle with the South over slavery. Instead, they tended to align themselves against every movement that threatened to destroy the Union, and even defended slavery against abolitionist attacks. Everett, like Daniel Webster before him, as a spokesman for the Hub's Unitarian merchant elite had claimed that slavery was "a condition of life, as well as any other to be justified by morality, religion, and international law."[44] The reaction of the anti-slavery forces was predictable: Unitarians, concluded abolitionist Samuel May, Jr., "were preeminently guilty on the subject of enslavement of millions in our land." May noted, however, that some Unitarian clergymen abandoned this position during the war. But most Unitarians believed that partisan politics had prevented a speedy end to the war, and that the North had more to fear from internal dissensions than from Confederate armies. Everett shared this point of view, even though he declared for Lincoln's reelection and became a popular speaker for the Union cause. Everett confessed "it went a little hard" with him to withhold his support for McClellan for whom he cherished "a sincere personal regard."[45] The substantial increase in Unitarian support for Lincoln in 1864 should not obscure the finding that McClellan ran better among Unitarian voters than he did at large (see Table 4.9).

The voting behavior of Unitarians cautions against imposing on voting patterns a rigid model that ignores the variety of factors that shaped or influenced voting decisions. Theoretical parsimony has been eloquently served by suggesting that in the North "the primary cleavage line of party oppositions during the second half of the nineteenth century pitted evangelical pietistic against ritualistic religious groups."[46] To suggest, however, that political differences reflected the clash of two identifiable types of religious values, when applied to Massachusetts voting in the 1860s, simplifies voting behavior to a dangerous extent. Ordering the major religious denominations by both Republican and anti-Republican support in either 1860 or 1864 produces two different lists and not a single continuum (see Tables 4.8 and 4.9). Therefore, except for Catholics and Congregationalists at opposite ends of the continuum, the relative support of a religious grouping for Lincoln was a decidedly poor predictor of that denomination's support for either Lincoln's opponents in 1860 or McClellan in 1864. The pietistic-liturgical typology must be expanded along another dimension before it can take into account the limited political involvement of some evangelical religious groups.[47]

The interrelations between the Massachusetts electoral system during the Civil War years and the larger social context defy a clear-cut, all-encompassing interpretation of voting. Categorization, in social and religious terms of the individuals who behaved politically as a voting bloc reveals that Irish Catholic and German-born voters cast their ballots overwhelmingly against the Republicans, whereas Scottish-Americans and Congregationalists decidedly favored the Republicans. The Republicans also ran exceedingly well among Quakers, English-Americans, and colonial British American-born citizens who bothered to vote. Yet in trying to account for the different levels of partisan support and for the rate of voter abstention using a wide variety of socio-economic variables, the results consistently revealed the greater importance of economic, rather than ethnoreligious indicators to explain Republican voting and nonvoting patterns. Not only support for Lincoln but also voter turnout generally was higher in areas with the fewest, although more equitably distributed, economic resources, measured in terms of the per capita value of taxable real and personal property. The conclusion is inescapable that voter turnout and political conflict in Massachusetts during the Civil War years were largely determined by the economic milieu in which men lived and worked, and by an antislavery commitment that transcended religious considerations as the primary basis for partisan identification and political participation.

Chapter 5
The Radical Republicans versus Andrew Johnson: The Congressional Elections of 1866

The president's dreadful folly and blunder are fastened upon all those who dare dissent from the Radicalism of the opposite faction and I see no help.—*James S. Amory to Thomas C. Amory, 26 September 1866*

The assassination of Abraham Lincoln in April 1865 elevated Andrew Johnson to the presidency. Massachusetts Republicans accepted Johnson's succession without trepidation. Johnson had been the only senator from the seceded states not to resign his seat during 1860–61. Although he was a slaveholder and states-rights Democrat before the war, he subsequently proved to be an ardent Unionist. His ties with some of the Bay State's leading Republicans helped win him acceptance among the radicals. George L. Stearns had developed a close association with Johnson while recruiting black soldiers in Tennessee. Stearns's favorable reports to the Bird Club were reinforced by word from Senator Charles Sumner that the new president had not, despite rumors to the contrary, fallen under the influence of Montgomery Blair, the conservative former postmaster general. Personal conversations with the president convinced Sumner that Johnson could be expected to give radical reconstruction proposals a fair hearing. Most importantly, Sumner claimed that Johnson was not adverse to the principle of black suffrage.[1]

For the Bird Club, genuine reconstruction of the South depended on the freedman's full participation in the reorganized state governments. This meant enfranchising the former slaves. The argument for equal suffrage was based not only on the fear that without black political power emancipation would be a sham, but also on the practical grounds of self-interest. The Bird Club radicals wanted national political power to remain within the Republican party. Assuming President Johnson, like Lincoln, could be influenced by public opinion, in the spring of 1865 the Bird Club with Sumner's approval mounted a propaganda effort on behalf of equal suffrage. Because Massachusetts was one of the five northern states allowing blacks to vote on an equal basis with whites, the radicals were spared the additional task of doing battle on this issue in their own state.[2]

Radical confidence in Johnson proved short-lived, however. Distrust of the new president rose sharply when he pursued a policy of extending pardons to rebels and issued a reconstruction proclamation for Mississippi, which, like a previous edict for North Carolina, made no provision for black suffrage as a prerequisite to readmission to the Union. Ben: Perley Poore, the clerk of Sumner's Committee on Foreign Relations and a Boston newspaper correspondent, concluded privately what most other radicals were beginning to dread: Johnson was firmly in the hands of corrupt Democratic politicians who intended to use him to restore their party to power. Yet in the summer of 1865 the Bird Club radicals clung to the slim hope that Johnson's actions did not constitute a fixed and final policy, and they refrained from criticizing him publicly. Although Sumner had not foreclosed the possibility of reaching an understanding with Johnson, in September he narrowly avoided an open assault on the president at the state Republican convention where he gave an elaborate black suffrage speech. The convention applauded Sumner's remarks, but refused to condemn the president or support Sumner's position in any resolutions.[3]

Reconciliation between Johnson and the radicals proved impossible. In addressing the first session of the Thirty-ninth Congress in December, Johnson reiterated his contention that he had no authority to dictate suffrage qualifications to any of the southern states. Furthermore, he claimed that the restored state governments already provided sufficient protection for the freedmen. It was clear to the radicals that Johnson desired a restoration and not a reconstruction of the white South. Thus, by the end of 1865 Johnson and the Massachusetts radicals were already involved in the bitter public debate that dominated national politics throughout the following year.[4]

The events leading up to Johnson's break with the party that elected him to the vice-presidency in 1864 coincided with divisions within Republican ranks at the close of the Civil War. With the war no longer imposing a necessary unity, widespread factionalism beset the Republican party in state after state. These intraparty intrigues and factional rivalries confirmed the diagnosis of many contemporaries that a realignment of the electorate, even to the extent of producing entirely new parties, would be inevitable once the war ended. This sentiment served to bolster Johnson's hope to forge a new coalition of voters, composed in the North chiefly of War Democrats and conservative Republicans, to sustain his reconstruction policies against radical objections. Long-standing ideological cleavages in the Republican party's leadership made Massachusetts a promising arena for such maneuverings.[5]

Before the war the radical Bird Club had battled the conservative Banks Club for control of the Bay State Republican party. The Banks Club, launched in 1857 when Nathaniel P. Banks was a Republican congressman, reflected Banks's own political posture before the war. The club was antislavery, but not concerned with abolition, and was in favor of sundry state reforms, but not willing to eschew nativism or any other illiberal sentiment to win votes. The group included Congressman Anson Burlingame, Charles Hale of the Boston *Daily Advertiser*, Charles O. Rogers of the Boston *Daily Journal*, and Congressman Henry L. Dawes. After 1860 the Banks Club continued to represent the "compromising" wing of the Republican party, precisely the "time servers" whom the radicals feared might "outweigh the earnest men" after the war.[6]

Conflict between the two factions erupted over the contract labor system instituted in Louisiana during the war by General Banks in his position as commander of the Department of the Gulf. Banks's labor system, as viewed by the Massachusetts radicals, was indistinguishable from slavery. It required blacks to sign year-long contracts with their employers and to secure passes from provost marshals in order to travel from one place to another. Furthermore, the Bird Club was convinced that Banks's support for the moderate Republican faction in Louisiana reconstruction politics constituted a sellout of the Louisiana radicals. When in 1864 President Lincoln had appeared to subscribe to Banks's plan to build the Louisiana Republican party on white suffrage alone, Sumner and his allies were placed squarely on the defensive. At the end of the war Banks's old political associates, believing that the Sumner clique was rapidly losing support among voters who favored a moderate approach to Reconstruction, pleaded with him to return to Massachusetts and reenter the arena of state politics.[7]

Long-term Congressman Henry Dawes could be counted on to side with Banks and the conservative wing of his party in any showdown with the Sumner radicals. Early in the Thirty-ninth Congress Dawes had been urged by his Democratic colleagues to seize the initiative in forging a new conservative pro-Johnson coalition in the House. Dawes, an admirer of Lincoln, displayed such an annoying inclination to compare Johnson's southern policies with Lincoln's own, that Pennsylvania

Congressman Thaddeus Stevens considered it necessary to "reconstruct" Dawes off any committee assignment dealing with Reconstruction policy in the next Congress.[8]

The ideological division between the Banks-Dawes faction on one side and the Sumner radicals on the other thus provided President Johnson an excellent opportunity to find ready allies in Massachusetts. But it was another, less predictable rift in state Republican ranks that greatly enhanced Johnson's chances of taking the control of the party machinery away from the Bird Club radicals. The most serious split in the Bay State Republican party at the end of the war was between Sumner and Governor John Andrew, both of them Free-Soilers "from the start" and among the original members of the Bird Club.[9]

Andrew's radicalism had subsided during his last three years in the governor's chair. In the summer of 1863 he seemed ready to accept a Union defeat. With northern morale at its lowest point of the war, Andrew anticipated further military setbacks, and at times seemed to adjust his political course accordingly. By 1864 he had established contacts with conservative politicians in both parties. Having resolved to step down from the governorship once the war ended, Andrew decided to test the political waters after Lincoln's reelection. To Andrew's disappointment, his prospects for a post in Lincoln's cabinet were quashed by Sumner, who desired the "Massachusetts cabinet position" for himself. Such rivalry did not improve relations between the two men. Those close to Andrew knew that he resented Sumner's greater stature in the party. The challenge made by Andrew's friends in the legislature in his behalf against Henry Wilson's reelection to the senatorship in early 1865 was more symbolic than serious; had their opposition to Wilson been known in advance, few, if any, Republicans would have been nominated by their party to run for the legislature in the first place. But Andrew's frustration was real: all paths to higher office seemed closed to him.[10]

In the fall of 1865 Andrew undercut Sumner by publicly supporting President Johnson's lenient policies toward the South. Andrew attacked Sumner's "state suicide" theory of Reconstruction and refused an invitation to speak at a meeting called to protest a hasty readmission of the southern states before they had demonstrated their loyalty. At a meeting in Boston, Andrew defended the provisional governor of Alabama, Lewis E. Parsons, who remarked that he would rather move away from Alabama than allow former slaves to vote. Parsons, who was soliciting investment funds for his state, was assailed by Sumner, who warned would-be investors in the audience of Parsons's questionable intentions to secure any political or civil rights for Alabama blacks. Later Andrew rebuked Sumner in a letter: "[T]he right position for New England," he wrote, "is one of friendliness, not of antagonism." In a terse reply Sumner declared that "justice to the oppressed [blacks]" had to be the first order of business in any reconstruction program, and that no "[N]egro-hater, with his sympathizers" should convince the governor of Massachusetts that anything short of that would be acceptable. The rift between Sumner and Andrew was complete and irrevocable.[11]

In his valedictory address to the Massachusetts legislature in January 1866, Andrew presented his own theory of how the southern states ought to be brought into the Union. While pleading for the goodwill and cooperation of North and South to solve the problems of Reconstruction, Andrew discounted black enfranchisement as a prerequisite to reorganizing former rebel states and rejected the idea of alloting congressmen based on the number of legal or qualified voters. The latter point was significant, for it attacked a constitutional amendment introduced by Sumner to make congressional representation proportional to the number of legal voters rather than to the total population. Sumner had failed to foresee that his amendment, if enacted, would reduce the number of representatives from Massachusetts, which had a disproportionate percentage of women and aliens who would no longer be counted in the apportionment of congressmen. Andrew not only capitalized on the unpopularity of Sumner's proposal but, more importantly, he insinuated that, unlike Sumner, he would act toward settling the complex problems of the South with unselfish principle. In response, Sumner denounced the proposed Fourteenth Amendment in a long speech in the Senate, a tactic that exasperated his Republican colleagues who earnestly wanted the amendment passed and who had no sympathy for Sumner's political difficulties in his home state. But in opposing the amendment, Sumner freed himself of Andrew's charge of political expediency to avoid a direct stand on the question of black suffrage.[12]

At the end of the war, Andrew enjoyed tremendous popularity, especially among local politicians, returning soldiers, and Boston's business community. It is questionable, however, whether he embodied the sentiment of the "real" Massachusetts.[13] Whereas the overwhelming majority of Bay State Republicans, including most abolitionists and radicals, advocated fairness for former Confederate leaders, few considered the economic difficulties of the former slaveholders as important an issue as the continued oppression of the blacks. Yet Andrew not only advocated that the South should return to the Union under the leadership of the old planter elites—the only natural leaders, Andrew believed, that the South possessed—but he also tried to put himself in touch with the planters to learn their plight at first hand. His concern was consistent with his belief that the problem of Reconstruction was primarily economic. His emphasis on the financial rehabilitation of the South with the assistance of northern capital explained his convoluted conclusion regarding Reconstruction in his valedictory address: "We want the popular vote," he declared, "and the rebel vote is better than a loyal one, if on the right side."[14]

Of the entire Massachusetts Republican congressional delegation, only Dawes subscribed to Andrew's plan. The remaining members would have nothing to do with it. They realized, as did most Republican politicians, that the retiring Civil War governor's speech was a bold move to try to wrest the mantle of party leadership in state politics away from the Sumner radicals. They also were aware of the appeal of Andrew's speech, for at the beginning of 1866 there still existed a sentimental desire among many Massachusetts voters to put behind them the horrible years of conflict on the battlefield and move ahead with the business of reuniting the nation with the least amount of confusion. Since the end of the war, the Springfield *Republican* had editorialized repeatedly on this theme: "We want true union and concord in the quickest possible time," declared editor Samuel Bowles's influential paper, "and by such means as will make these blessings perpetual."[15]

The Sumner radicals, however, feared that a conciliatory attitude toward the South would necessarily fail to protect the freedmen from discrimination and violence. Any policy based on reconciliation, the radicals believed, was impractical, for it would allow the white South to be an equal partner in the Reconstruction process with the power to withhold political rights from blacks. Hasty restoration procedures, the radicals argued, were leaving the antebellum southern social structure completely intact and, thus, the fruits of the hard-won Union victory were being given away. The Massachusetts radicals saw an unrepentant South that would have to be reformed by placing the new freedom of the blacks on a lasting foundation. They thus wanted to reverse the counterrevolutionary policies initiated by Johnson, set new terms for reunion, and implement them coercively—without Confederate participation or approval.[16]

The irreparable breach between Johnson and all but the most conservative Republicans occurred when the president, in February 1866, vetoed a moderate measure to continue federal aid for the newly freed slaves through the agency of the Freedmen's Bureau. Johnson followed his veto message with accusations against radical leaders—Sumner, in particular—of treason and plots of assassination. Johnson's attack on Sumner had a profound impact on Massachusetts politics, for it rallied popular opinion to Sumner's defense and, in effect, destroyed the budding movement to replace him with Andrew as the leader of the state party. The retired Civil War governor, sensing that the president's intemperate remarks had unified Bay State Republicans, abandoned the challenge to Sumner and informed the president's allies that he would henceforth not "act at all, in *political*, still less, partisan ways."[17] After Johnson's verbal assault on Sumner, few Republicans were willing to resuscitate the movement to drive the radicals out of the party.

Leadership of the anti-Sumner cause fell to the eldest son of Charles Francis Adams, John Quincy Adams, Jr., formerly a military aide to Governor Andrew. In 1866, as a new member of the state legislature, J. Q. Adams was clearly identified with the Andrew faction of the party and with his father's endorsement of Johnson's policies. Moreover, J. Q. Adams had absorbed some of the pessimism that overcame Andrew as governor. For example, he had constantly predicted defeat, destruction, and death during the war—all much to the annoyance of his brother, Charles Francis Adams, Jr., who had fought at Antietam and Gettysburg and had served part of the war under General Ulysses S. Grant. J. Q. Adams represented the aspirations of conservative Republicans who supported the Thirteenth Amendment, but sought to stem the revolutionary policies of the radicals that looked beyond emancipation to broad changes in southern society. The Sumner radicals, Adams believed, wanted to tear up the Constitution; thus the necessity for calm, rational, and patriotic men to defend it.[18]

Despite the resentment against Johnson caused by his attack on Sumner, the radicals' prospects for getting through the state legislature a strong resolution excoriating the president were not good. Henry Wilson, desiring to maintain the pretense that Republicans in Congress were not divided, had urged moderation. Hoping to drive a wedge between Wilson and Sumner, J. Q. Adams introduced a resolution approving Wilson's attempt to mitigate the acrimony between Johnson and his party. The strategy failed, however, as the radicals obtained an overwhelming majority against it. The result was a sharp rebuke to Adams, who now appeared to be trying to fracture the party. With his effectiveness among Republicans destroyed, Adams turned to the National Union movement organized specifically to elect congressmen in the coming fall elections who would support Johnson's Reconstruction policy.[19]

The National Unionist state convention was attended mostly by Democratic party regulars and a segment of the 1862 Democratic converts from the old Constitutional Union and Know-Nothing parties. Conspicuously absent were any prominent Republicans, with the notable exception of J. Q. Adams who presided over the convention. When the National Unionists met in Philadelphia in August, the presence of such infamous Copperheads as Fernando Wood of New York and Clement Vallandigham of Ohio discredited the pro-Johnson movement among all but the most conservative Massachusetts Republicans. Opposition to Sumner and the radicals was one thing, but few Republicans were willing "to go to bed with Copperheads and rebels." When the Massachusetts and South Carolina delegates entered the convention arm-in-arm, Bird Club member William S. Robinson wondered if they had been handcuffed together. The alliance between the National Unionists and the Massachusetts Democratic party was consummated in a Boston meeting in October, when the Democrats made support for the National Unionist platform and candidates unanimous, finding it "inexpedient" to make separate nominations. In reality, the National Union movement in Massachusetts was a Democratic party front.[20]

No facade, however, could cover up the crippled condition of the Bay State Democratic organization in 1866. The Democrats never recovered from the debate over slavery that had wracked their party a generation earlier. Overlooking some temporary Democratic defections in the four-way presidential race of 1860, the rebuilt coalition initially put together by James Buchanan's candidacy in 1856 had stayed intact for the next eight years, although the party subsequently fared poorly— in contrast to the Republicans—in attracting previous nonvoters or "new" voters.[21] After the war, the Democratic party was identified with disloyalty and antiblack prejudice. In the fall election campaign of 1865, the Democratic press upheld the banner of white supremacy, claiming the nation must continue to "live by the will of white, patriotic men, whether of the Anglo-Saxon, the Norman, the Celt, the Teuton, or of some other *Caucasian* race who have cast their lot among us." The radical Republicans were depicted as "gaunt, hungry, fiery fanatics" desiring to "trample down all that is fair and beautiful to secure the phantom of [N]egro freedom" and "[to elevate] the degraded African to the *status* of the white *Caucasian* citizen."[22] The notions that the government at all levels was constituted only for white men, that God had created blacks as an inferior or subhuman species, and that at no time in civilized history had the African race demonstrated any capacity for self-government were standard tenets of Democratic ideology. The Confederate States of America had been established on these same propositions.

Virulent antiblack sentiment, prevalent among many Irish immigrants, had profound consequences for the Massachusetts party system. The state's Irish-American citizens did not alter their party commitments or even temporarily shift their partisan allegiances during the realignment of the 1850s. Hostile to both the antislavery cause and the nativist movement, the Irish had remained loyal to the Democratic party. During the war they were among Bay Staters who, in general, disliked Lincoln, despised the blacks, and were hostile to emancipation. They had cast over one-third of the Democratic ballots in the 1864 presidential election and were unquestionably the party's most important constituents (see Table 5.1). In 1866 they instinctively sympathized with Johnson's attempts to restore the white South to power.[23]

Despite their importance to the Democratic party, the Irish were not represented in its leadership ranks in proportion to their actual numbers. At the end of the war a small group of old-line Yankees continued to exercise leadership by the forces of deference and habit. Josiah G. Abbott, a lawyer with close ties to railroad and manufacturing interests, exemplified this type of leadership. Many of the party's most capable leaders, including Benjamin F. Butler, George S. Boutwell, and George L. Loring, had previously joined the Republicans. The National Union movement got off to a poor start in Boston by failing to include any of the city's Irish politicians among its keynote speakers.[24]

The difficulties of the National Unionists were complicated by the Fenian issue. The Fenian Brotherhood, formed as a secret society in the United States in 1858, grew to about 50,000 members by the end of the Civil War. Aiming for Irish independence from Great Britain by armed force, the Fenians supplanted the parliamentary reformist movement of Daniel O'Connell, the great Irish leader who had agitated first for Catholic emancipation and later for repeal of the Act of Union. While central direction of the Fenian movement remained in the United States, its influence extended widely in both Great Britain and Ireland. A spectacular rise of Fenian groups occurred within the Union army during the Civil War. The Fenians regarded every soldier of Irish descent as a potential recruit for the eventual war with England. Such activities received the approval of the Lincoln administration, which was convinced that the Fenians would dissipate the Democratic party's influence among the Irish troops.[25]

Anti-British sentiment was not confined to Irish-Americans but was widespread throughout the North during the war and immediate postwar period. Although Great Britain had declared its neutrality, it recognized the Confederate States of America as a belligerent and had permitted southern privateers to be fitted out and built in her ports.

TABLE 5.1
Estimated Relationships Between Birthplace and Voting in Massachusetts Presidential Elections, 1864-1876
(by percent)

Presidential Election Year	Actual Number of Cases	Ireland			Massachusetts			Other U.S.A.			(All)[a]		
		Dem.	Rep.	Not Voting	Dem.	Rep.	Not Voting	Dem.	Rep.	Not Voting	Dem.	Rep.	Not Voting
1864	327	73	8	19	12	56	32	32	59	9	(20)	(52)	(27)
1868	328	61	32	8	9	54	37	40	70	0[b]	(23)	(53)	(24)
1872	328	62[c]	34	4[c]	5[a]	44	50	35[c]	60	5	(20)[c]	(44)	(37)
1876	341	71	17	11	19	52	29	43	39	18	(30)	(42)	(28)

Sources: The estimate that 73 percent of the Irish-born eligible voters cast ballots for the Democratic presidential candidate in 1864 was derived by running a multiple regression with the 1864 Democratic percentage as dependent and the percentages of the electorate born in Ireland, other foreign countries, the Massachusetts town or city in which they were living in 1864, and other towns or cities in Massachusetts as independent variables. The percentage of the electorate born in the United States but not in Massachusetts was not used to avoid multicollinearity. The breakdown of the electorate by place of birth was accomplished by extrapolations from data on the nativities of voters and males in each city and town in 1875. See Massachusetts, Bureau of Statistics of Labor, Thirteenth Annual Report of the Bureau of Statistics of Labor, Public Doc. 15 (Boston: 1882), table 1, pp. 97-168, and The Census of Massachusetts: 1875, 1:273-84. It was necessary to make the artificial assumption that the ratio of Irish-born eligible voters to the naturalized voter population in each voting unit remained constant throughout the Civil War and Reconstruction era. The source for the number of naturalized voters in 1865 is Massachusetts, General Court, Journal of the House of Representatives, H.Doc. 82 (February 1870), pp. 1-11. In 1875 there were 86,056 Irish-born males of voting age in Massachusetts. Of these, 38,498 were aliens and, therefore, were unable to vote. The remaining 47,108 were "legal" or eligible voters; they constituted the full potential voting power of the Irish-born in 1875. Because there were 351,113 eligible voters in 1875, the Irish-born constituted 13.4 percent of the potential electorate. Among the foreign-born groups the Irish had the highest percentage (54.7%) of eligible voters. The sources for the number of eligible voters are Massachusetts, Manual for the Use of the General Court (Boston: 1858), pp. 115-23; and Massachusetts, General Court, Journal of the House of Representatives, H.Doc. 82 (February 1870), pp. 1-11, and H.Doc. 65 (February 1876), pp. 4-8. Because of the impact of the Civil War years on the population growth rate, it was necessary to use an interpolative procedure that assumed a curvilinear pattern of both growth and decline in order to estimate the voting population when registration data were not readily available. For the actual formulas used, see Dollar and Jensen, Historian's Guide to Statistics, pp. 130-32.

[a]Actual, not estimated, statewide voting preferences of all eligible voters.

[b]Logically impossible estimates have been set at the 0 or 100 percent limits.

[c]Liberal Republican.

Supplying the South with armed ships violated both British neutrality laws and international law, and the strong protests of the Lincoln administration had encouraged Irish-American hopes for a United States declaration of war on England. While one group of American Fenians schemed to capture Canada and use it as a hostage for British concessions in Ireland, another group favored fomenting revolution directly in the Emerald Isle. The Fenian movement was a tremendous source of pride to the Massachusetts Irish. Many Fenian headquarters flying the flag of the harp and sunburst operated in Boston after the war. In Lawrence both a Fenian Hall and a Fenian Sisterhood revealed the popularity of the movement among the city's large Irish population. By the summer of 1865, Patrick A. Collins, the future political leader of the Boston Irish, had helped launch seventy-five Fenian "circles" in the eastern industrial cities and towns of the state.[26]

Because it had flourished in spite of ecclesiastical disapproval, the

Fenian movement demonstrated convincingly that the influence of the Catholic church over its Irish-born parishioners was limited. For the first time the parish priest was no longer the foremost spokesman for the Irish immigrant community. Moreover, by rallying progressive forces against the conservative tendency of Irish life, the Fenian movement threatened the allegiance between the Irish and the Democratic party. The legacy of the struggle against the secessionist slaveholders and their English sympathizers gave Republicans a chance to make inroads among Irish-American voters. Many Republicans were convinced that Irish war veterans who had learned the political lessons of the Civil War first-hand on the battlefield would subsequently find their way into Republican ranks. They pointed to the career of Colonel Patrick R. Guiney, a Douglas Democrat who returned home a war hero and a Republican with sympathy for the Sumner faction of the party and for the Fenians.[27]

Significantly, the delicate task of enforcing the neutrality laws against the Fenian-launched invasions of Canada fell upon the Johnson administration. Trapped by their endorsement of the National Unionist party, the Massachusetts Democrats were compelled to apologize for the president's actions against the Fenian invaders. The threat of large-scale Irish defections at the polls worried Democratic party chieftains. The pro-Democratic Boston *Pilot* confessed its concern with inroads made on Irish voters by "political adventurers" trying to take advantage of the Fenian issue, and the Boston *Post* quipped that Republicans regarded Fenianism "as a big fish," which they were "toiling to draw into their net."[28]

Naturally, in 1866 Republicans took the opportunity to fish in Democratic waters. *The Right Way*, a black suffragist Boston weekly, appealed to the Irish to act with the Republican party in "fighting the desperate battle against social classes, which under another form has weighted down Irishmen for ages." Some Fenians viewed Republicans like Butler and Banks as the only instruments through which they could achieve their goals. Butler advocated the annexation of Canada, and Banks called upon the Johnson administration to recognize a lawful state of war between Ireland and England. By August rumors spread among President Johnson's allies that the Republicans had reached an agreement with Colonel William B. Roberts, the president of the militant branch of the American Fenians. Addressing a Fenian picnic, Senator Wilson appeared on the speaker's platform with Roberts. Quoting Roberts's definition of the Fenian cause as "the cause of liberty everywhere," Wilson proclaimed: "Well, if that be Fenianism, then I am a Fenian."[29]

In the summer of 1866 the pro-Democratic press stepped up its effort to counter what it called Republican attempts to "blarney" the Irish-American vote with the Fenian issue. The Boston *Pilot* claimed that the primary goal of the state's radical Republican establishment was to put the ballot in the hands of the former slaves; to achieve this, the Republicans needed Irish votes "to kill off Johnson." The *Pilot* declared that the radical Republicans and the principles they represented were the natural enemies of everything the Irish cherished and that the radicals believed that a black man was superior to an Irishman. Nevertheless, the paper was clearly concerned about erosion of support for the president because of the Fenian question. In September, an Irish citizen delegation visiting the White House indicated the Democratic party's fear that Republicans, "by honeyed phrases and high sounding promises," were dissuading Irish voters from their duty to support the president. The Democrats were able to persuade Johnson to issue a directive to Secretary of State William H. Seward, asking the Canadian government for clemency for Fenians who had been captured, convicted, and sentenced to execution. Gradually, it appeared that Irish voters might be held in line in the coming November elections.[30]

Neither the Republican gubernatorial candidate nor the party's congressional candidates, including Butler and Banks, made significant inroads into the Irish vote in the 1866 election (see Tables 5.2, 5.3, and 5.4). What happened to the Irish vote is best explained by the "cross-pressure-withdrawal" theory of voting behavior; that is, if a group is torn between conflicting stimuli of loyalty to one particular party and support for a cause championed by another party, the group is likely to resolve the conflict by not voting.[31] The Irish were caught between their traditional allegiance to the Democrats, on one hand, and the Republican defense of the Fenians held in Canadian and British jails, on the other. The number of Irish-born eligible voters abstaining in 1866 was unusually large: over one-third stayed away from the polling places (see Tables 5.2 and 5.3). Of the Irish-Americans who participated, the majority voted Republican in both the congressional and gubernatorial contests. Due to the heavy one-sided voter abstentions of the Irish in 1866, however, the Republicans won the Irish vote without the votes of 1864 Irish Democrats (see Table 5.4). The strong stand taken by Republicans on the Fenian issue, including hints of modifying the neutrality laws in the next session of Congress, did not produce significant Irish Democratic defections into Republican ranks, but it did keep from the polls many Irish voters who could not bring themselves to cast a Republican ballot.[32]

TABLE 5.2
Estimated Voting Preferences of Irish-Born and Massachusetts-Born Eligible Voters in Massachusetts Congressional Elections, 1864-1876
(by percent)

Congressional Election Year	Actual Number of Cases	Ireland				Massachusetts				(All)[a]			
		Dem.	Rep.	Other	Not Voting	Dem.	Rep.	Other	Not Voting	Dem.	Rep.	Other	Not Voting
1864	326	78	32	0	0[b]	12	55	0	32	(20)	(53)	(0)	(27)
1866	326	29	34	1[c]	36	4	34	0[c]	62	(11)	(36)	(0)[c]	(53)
1868	326	64	36	0[b]	2	9	52	1	38	(23)	(51)	(1)	(25)
1870	326	45	23	7[d]	24	9	30	5[d]	55	(18)	(32)	(4)[d]	(47)
1872	327	49[e]	38	1	12	7[e]	44	0	48	(21)[e]	(43)	(0)	(35)
1874	328	68	18	0[b]	17	14	28	3	55	(27)	(27)	(1)	(45)
1876	340	72	21	0[b]	8	20	50	0	30	(31)	(40)	(1)	(29)

[a]Actual, not estimated, statewide voting preferences of all eligible voters.

[b]Logically impossible estimates slightly below the 0 percent limit have been set at 0 percent.

[c]Patrick R. Guiney ran on a Workingman's party ticket in the Third District.

[d]The Labor Reform party endorsed regular Democratic congressional candidates in the Third, Ninth, and Tenth districts, but the only Republican congressional candidate endorsed was Nathaniel P. Banks in the Sixth District.

[e]Liberal Republican.

TABLE 5.3
Estimated Voting Preferences of Irish-Born and Massachusetts-Born Eligible Voters in Selected Gubernatorial Elections
(by percent)

Gubernatorial Election Year	Actual Number of Cases	Ireland				Massachusetts				(All)[a]			
		Dem.	Rep.	Other	Not Voting	Dem.	Rep.	Other	Not Voting	Dem.	Rep.	Other	Not Voting
1864	328	73	28	--	0[b]	12	55	--	33	(20)	(52)	(0)	(28)
1866	328	30	33	--	37	5	34	--	61	(11)	(37)	(0)	(53)
1868	327	63	27	--	10	10	52	--	37	(25)	(51)	(0)	(24)
1870	328	33	19	25[d]	23	9	29	7[d]	55	(18)	(29)	(8)[d]	(45)
1872	328	63[c]	38	--	0[b]	6[c]	45	--	49	(20)[c]	(44)	(0)	(36)
1874	328	69	14	--	17	15	30	--	55	(29)	(27)	(0)	(44)
1876	341	67	21	0[e]	13	19	45	7[e]	29	(30)	(38)	(3)[e]	(29)

[a]Actual, not estimated, statewide voting preferences of all eligible voters.

[b]Logically impossible estimates of Irish-born eligible voters have been set at the 0 percent limit.

[c]Liberal Republican.

[d]Labor Reform & Prohibition.

[e]Prohibition & Suffragist.

TABLE 5.4
Voting Stability in Massachusetts Congressional Elections,
1860-1876
(by percent of electorate)

Election Pair	Actual Number of Cases	Percent Switching Parties	Percent Behaving Stably[a]	Gross Change in Turnout[b]
1860-1862[c]	254[d]	7%	71%	22%
1862-1864	254[d]	4	75	21
1864-1866	327	0	76	24
1866-1868[e]	329	0	68	32
1868-1870	329	8	69	24
1870-1872	328	6	77	17
1872-1874	326	13	57	29
1874-1876	328	19	60	22

Note: The figures above are estimates of the behavior of all eligible voters in the second election in each pair of elections. Rounding procedures occasionally produce totals greater or less than 100 percent.

[a] Those voting for the same party twice or not voting in both elections.

[b] Previous voters who dropped out of the active electorate in the second election plus previous nonvoters and new voters who cast ballots in the second election.

[c] The entire anti-Republican congressional vote in 1860 is treated as the Democratic party vote.

[d] The 1862 congressional vote cast in the Ninth District where the Republican incumbent ran unopposed has been omitted from the analysis.

[e] The National Unionist congressional vote is treated as the Democratic party vote.

The pro-Johnson forces failed to assemble a new coalition of Democrats and Republican conservatives. Given that the National Union party was the Democratic party under another name, virtually no voters switched parties between the 1864 and 1866 congressional elections (see Table 5.4). Not only did party lines remain unbroken in 1866 but, as would be expected, virtually no split-ticket voting occurred in the gubernatorial and congressional races, although a tiny percentage of voters managed to "scratch" a Republican congressional candidate off their Republican ballots (see Table 5.5).

Even though party lines remained unbroken between 1864 and 1866, the possibility remains that in the immediate postwar years Republican candidates could have attracted the votes of many industrial workers voting for the first time. Not only was the revival of the labor movement a result of the Civil War, but the debates arising from the war provided the intellectual scaffolding of the workingmen's own protest. Many labor reformers compared their crusade against "wage slavery" with the Republican battle against chattel slavery.[33] Republican Governor Alexander H. Bullock, a proven friend of labor, swept

TABLE 5.5
Estimates of Split-Ticket Voting in the 1866 General Election
(by percent of 1866 electorate)

Party in 1866 Congressional Election	Party in 1866 Gubernatorial Election				
	Democratic	Republican	All Others	Not Voting for Governor 1866	Percent of 1866 Electorate
Democratic	11	0	0	0	11
Republican	0	36	0	0	36
All Others	0	0	0	0	0
Not Voting 1866 Congressional election	0	1	0	53	53
Percent of 1866 Electorate	11	37	0	53	100

Note: Actual N = 333. To adjust for the varying populations of cities and towns, variables used in regression equations are "weighted" by the potential voting population. Rounding procedures occasionally produce totals greater or less than 100 percent.

the labor vote in both the 1865 and 1866 elections, each time receiving over 80 percent of the votes cast by factory workers (see Table 5.6). At first glance, the voting returns suggest that the Republicans benefited from working-class support in the immediate postwar period, precisely when the labor movement and radicalism were functioning harmoniously in many quarters of the state. However, the percentages of workers voting Democratic in 1865 and 1866 were substantially below normal, thus accounting for Bullock's lopsided sweep of the ballots cast by workers. The turnout of workingmen for the Republicans in these elections was roughly equal to the average worker turnout from 1864 to 1876 for all Republican gubernatorial candidates (see Table 5.6).

If the labor issue had an impact in 1866 on voting patterns anywhere, it would have been in the Boston congressional districts where labor reformers had formed a new political party. Claiming that the time had arrived for "the so-called common, plain sort of people" to have representation in Congress, Patrick Guiney campaigned on the Workingman's party ticket in the Third District, including parts of South Boston, Roxbury, and Brookline. "[T]he rich sort of people, the wealthy merchants and the great monopolies," he asserted, had manipulated the nomination process in the party caucuses long enough. The issue, according to Guiney, was "capital against labor." The same "brutal thirst for gain" that had caused men to enslave their fellow beings in the South now caused the factory owners in the North to declare higher dividends to their stockholders without "one cent increase in the wages of those out of whose life-essence it was made."[34]

Guiney was not the first choice of the Boston laborites. The Workingman's party had initially hoped to influence the Republican congressional nomination in the Third District. When the incumbent Alex-

TABLE 5.6
Estimated Partisan Preferences of Industrial Workers in Gubernatorial Elections, 1864-1876
(by percent)

Gubernatorial Election Year	Actual Number of Cases	Percent of Workers Favoring:		Republican Share of Labor Vote	(Republican Share of Total Vote)[a]
		Democratic Candidates	Republican Candidates		
1864	328	18	51	73	(72)
1865	328	7	30	81	(77)
1866	328	10	43	81	(77)
1867	323	39	56	59	(58)
1868	323	28	57	67	(68)
1869	323	11	32	30	(54)
1870	323	16	27	37	(53)
1871	323	23	27	39	(55)
1872	323	33	59	64	(69)
1873	323	33	32	49	(55)
1874	339	40	51	56	(48)
1875	340	28	23	39	(48)
1876	341	27	41	51	(54)
Mean for All Elections		24	41	56	(61)

Sources: Estimation of the percentages of eligible voters engaged in manufacturing in each voting unit in these years was made from interpolations from data contained in the 1865 and 1875 state censuses on the number of occupied males employed in factories. The regression equations included similar estimates of the percentage of males engaged in fishing and agricultural pursuits. The percentage engaged in all other categories was omitted to avoid multicollinearity problems. The variables were "weighted" by the number of potentially eligible voters.

[a]Actual, not estimated, Republican percentage of the total vote cast for governor between 1864 and 1876.

ander H. Rice, a spokesman for Boston's conservative business elite and a member of the Banks Club, announced his intention to retire from Congress, the laborites had proposed abolitionist Wendell Phillips for consideration as Rice's successor. Phillips, however, declined a formal nomination for Congress tendered to him by the Workingman's party, and it is doubtful that he would have secured the Republican nomination even if he had wanted it. Phillips, who had eschewed politics altogether until 1864 when he tried to replace Lincoln with John C. Frémont on the national Republican ticket, highly valued his role as an independent reformer. It had allowed him to criticize freely the Republican party without ever having to compromise his principles for the sake of party expedience. The Workingman's party selected Guiney to replace Phillips as its nominee for Congress.[35]

To nobody's surprise Republicans in the Third District settled on Ginery Twitchell, president of the Worcester Railroad and a member of the American Emigrant Company, to replace Rice. Although Twitchell, admittedly, "walked in Rice's footsteps and was the very archetype of the candidate 'radical only for Louisiana,'"[36] the traditional conservatism of Republican candidates running in the Third District reflected the strength of the Democrats in Boston's congressional districts. No seat there was considered "safe" for Republicans. The Boston districts had sent to Congress such conservative Republicans as Anson Burlingame, who was made minister to China after his defeat for reelection in 1860, and Charles Francis Adams, whom Lincoln appointed minister to Great Britain in 1861. Anyone running against the Democrats in the Boston districts, according to former Whig and former Know-Nothing Amos A. Lawrence, "must be what we call 'right,' but he must be something of a hunker to be elected." The Boston districts, therefore, demonstrated that Bay State Republican congressmen elected from districts in which there was consistently high Democratic voter support tended not to belong to the radical faction of their party.[37]

The Workingman's party thus failed to influence the Republican decision to nominate Twitchell. Nor did Guiney's candidacy have an impact on the outcome of the vote in the Third District in the 1866 election. Guiney received a meager 463 out of 9,152 votes cast. The real contest was between Twitchell and William Aspinwall, the Democratic nominee with little to recommend him for public office except his aristocratic family name. Twitchell won rather easily with 66 percent of the total ballots cast. The Republicans also won the congressional race in the Fourth District (including Boston's North End, East Boston, and Chelsea) where the Workingman's party endorsed Democratic candidate Joseph M. Wrightman, a former mayor of Boston. Wrightman ran on a platform favoring an eight-hour workday, which pleased labor reformers, but the Democratic planks calling for the preservation of a white man's government in the South and support of President Johnson alienated many pro-Phillips laborites. (Guiney told his working-class audiences that southern blacks should have the ballot; however, he rationalized this as a means of keeping them from flocking to the North.) Wrightman was defeated by over a two-to-one margin by Samuel Hooper, the Republican incumbent, who had publicly opposed legislation to shorten the workday. Thus, endorsement by the Democrats of the eight-hour day and the independent Workingman's party had not taken Republican votes away from the Third and Fourth districts where presumably, if the labor issue were to have had an impact on voting patterns anywhere, it would have been in the Boston area where the labor reformers and the Eight Hour Leagues were most influential.[38]

Nor were Republicans in 1866 able to capitalize on the labor issue in congressional districts where they ran candidates sympathetic to the demands of labor reformers. Banks enjoyed the support and confidence of many workingmen in the Sixth District, especially workers in the Charlestown Navy Yard who regularly petitioned him to correct labor injustices at the shipyard. Yet initially Banks had refused to endorse the eight-hour movement, only changing his position on the eve of his successful bid for Congress in a special election in 1865. Given Banks's chameleonic political stands on the issue, many labor leaders were not impressed with the onetime Waltham "bobbin boy." "[T]he fact that he was a workingman, has no more significance to us, than the fact that Benedict Arnold was an American," commented Ira Steward, an influential labor leader in Cambridge, located in the eastern part of Banks's district. Steward had reason to be cynical about Banks's appeal to the labor vote because Banks had never hesitated to use his influence on behalf of business interests whenever it benefited him personally or politically. In running for reelection in the Sixth District in 1866, however, Banks fully appreciated the potential vote-getting power of the labor reform issue.[39]

Labor reformers believed they had a long-proven friend in Butler, who in 1866 was running for Congress from the Fifth District or the Essex County district. In the 1850s, in his conservative hometown of Lowell, Butler had helped to organize the Democratic and Free-Soil coalition, which successfully challenged the Whigs and the textile owners by championing the drive for a secret ballot and the ten-hour workday.[40] It appeared that Butler and Banks, because of their stands on the labor issue and their strong pro-Fenian positions, would most likely capture a significant number of Democratic votes in their respective districts. Both Butler and Banks actively sought the Democratic vote. In Butler's case some of his old Democratic party associates were prominent in organizing his campaign. The stage was thus set in the Fifth and Sixth Districts for a genuine reshuffling of voters across party lines. But no significant realignment occurred. The political warfare between President Johnson and the Republicans over Reconstruction drove local issues, such as the eight-hour agitation, far into the political background (see Table 5.4).

The Massachusetts Republicans, therefore, had not needed the vote of a single worker or Fenian who had voted for the Democrats in 1864 to roll up their impressive victory against Andrew Johnson in 1866. They could have ignored both the labor issue and the Fenian question, for attention was focused on events in the South where a struggle was developing between black survival and white supremacy. While the Democrats were placed on the defensive by their endorsement of Johnson's policies, the Republicans had rallied behind the proposed Fourteenth Amendment to the Constitution, letting it provide a platform upon which conservatives, centrists, and radicals could unite. Because the amendment avoided the delicate question of black suffrage, historians have interpreted Republican victories in the congressional elections nationwide as having demonstrated popular support of the Reconstruction program envisioned by moderate Republicans.[41] Perhaps in other states the radicals stayed in the background in order to let the conservatives and centrists carry the election, but in 1866 such was not the case in Massachusetts where there was no retreat from radicalism.

In retrospect, Johnson's intemperate remarks about Sumner foiled efforts to drive the Bird Club radicals from power, for Massachusetts Republicans closed ranks behind their senator, and Johnson lost the trust of most of those who had previously approved of his handling of Reconstruction. Andrew, it will be recalled, took note of the shift in political opinion and gave up his bid for the leadership of the state party. Andrew's supporters, such as Richard Henry Dana, Jr., William Schouler, and John Gorham Palfrey, were rumored to be "waiting for the tornado to subside" before considering any new plans to dislodge Sumner from power. On the other side, Sumner's allies studiously avoided attacking Andrew. Sumner directed Frank Bird to keep in line those seeking to misrepresent his feelings toward Andrew. "What," asked Sumner, "do they seek to accomplish?" In the interests of party unity, Andrew was asked to preside at the Republican state convention, but he declined and managed to be out of Boston when it convened. Andrew took no part in the subsequent campaign, except to deliver a speech in support of Twitchell, the Republican congressional candidate in his home district.[42]

With Andrew retired from politics and the Democrats in disarray, the radicals made black suffrage an issue, denied that the proposed Fourteenth Amendment represented a final settlement of war issues, and paraded the radicalism of the southern loyalists. The Bird Club radicals were anxious to publicize the existence of a viable political element in the South upon which an enduring restructuring of southern society could be based. It was no coincidence that a delegation of southern loyalists visited Boston when the Republican state convention assembled in the city. Resolving itself into a meeting of welcome, the convention enthusiastically greeted the southern delegates who had bravely stood by the Union in the crucible of civil war. The Massachusetts Republicans resolved all questions regarding Reconstruction into one: "Shall we reconstruct the rebels or shall they reconstruct us?"[43]

Presiding over the convention was Benjamin F. Butler, a one-time Jefferson Davis Democrat and now a welcome guest at Bird's dinner table on Saturday afternoons. In a keynote address to the convention, Butler proclaimed that it was the duty of Republicans "to vindicate, to establish, to make certain forever . . . equality of rights and equality of protection under the laws, these great safeguards of human freedom, as a birthright and inheritance indefeasible and inalienable to manhood." The radicals, fully in control of the Republican convention, wrote the party platform, which called for the enfranchisement of the long oppressed blacks and attacked Johnson as a hindrance to progress and a betrayer of the party that elected him. Campaigning in Boston, Sumner declared that emancipation, enfranchisement, equality, land, and education must be secured to the southern blacks before there could be established "a new order of things."[44]

John Quincy Adams, Jr., now in the forefront of the National Union movement, delivered a speech that sharply contrasted with Sumner's address. Adams betrayed fears of congressional usurpation of power, revolutionary changes, prolonged military occupation, and eventual renewal of fighting. While he spoke of the nation as "demoralized by the license of a long war," it was Adams who was demoralized. By his own admission, he noted of his speech: "There was no audience, no applause, no life." J. Q. Adams was the only significant member of the Andrew faction of the state Republican party who broke with his party in 1866. When he ran for reelection to the state legislature from his home in Quincy on the National Union ticket, he found himself isolated from his former associates. Even his own brother, Charles Francis Adams, Jr., was unable to vote against the Republicans. He resolved his dilemma at the polling station by tearing his brother's name off the bottom of the ticket and depositing that name alone in the ballot box, discarding the rest of the Democratic candidates. In justifying this action to his father in London, he wrote: "John's present political associates pretty considerably turn my stomach . . . I am forced to remain a Republican or not vote at all."[45]

Johnson's popularity deteriorated rapidly among northern voters during the 1866 campaign. His use of patronage, which accelerated in September, was counterproductive as he appointed a plethora of well-known Copperheads. Even Congressman Dawes, who privately regretted the split with Johnson, decided not to sacrifice his standing in the Massachusetts Republican party by supporting the president. His chief political lieutenant made it clear to Republican officeholders in the Berkshire district that if they lost their jobs they would just have to pack up "without snivelling." In the wake of the president's "swing around the circle" and the Memphis and New Orleans riots, Samuel Bowles, who had, like Dawes, by his own admission "a little taint of Johnsonism," was forced to admit in the pages of his newspaper that Johnson "sympathizes with and apologizes for violence and outrage in the South." Bowles reassessed his opinion of the president as too "hot, impetuous, violent, and restless" to be the trusted leader of the conservatives. In the minds of many Bay Staters Johnson brought into question his own commitment to states' rights by telling Louisiana voters that he believed military authorities would assist them in dispersing the New Orleans convention composed of pro-Republican forces, including many blacks. The ensuing massacre of the Republican delegates in the streets of the crescent city made a mockery out of Johnson's Reconstruction policy.[46]

Although Johnson remains an enigma to most historians, it is clear that while he occupied the White House he was, in spite of his success, an embittered and lonely man and perhaps, as a consequence, was not equal to the task of forging a viable postwar settlement.[47] But the primary reason for his failure was his mistaken belief that the only way to salvage his political career was to create a new party, an alliance of conservative Republicans, northern Democrats, and conservative southern whites, or some mixture of all three. His threat to purge the radicals meant alienating all but a small group of conservative Republicans. In Massachusetts only a very few members of the Andrew faction ever took the final step of breaking with their party, because there was no middle ground for those opposed to the radicals. Johnson's Reconstruction policies and courtship of the restored white South only served to exacerbate the divisions in the Bay State electorate resulting from the antislavery crusade and the Civil War experience. After the war, as long as fear of a Confederate revival kept party lines firmly intact, the split in Republican ranks that Johnson hoped for could never take place.

On the eve of the 1866 election, the Boston *Daily Journal* summarized the political situation in the Bay State, stating there were no longer two wings of the Republican organization: "We are all radicals in the broadest acceptance of that term." To the staunchly Democratic Boston *Post*, the unrestrained radicalism of the Sumner clique of Republicans demonstrated its insanity: "These wild Robespierres are [becoming] as violent as their French examplares."[48] On election day the Republicans swept the state's congressional seats and Governor Bullock was reelected with over three-fourths of the popular vote. The 1866 election was the most lopsided partisan triumph ever witnessed in Massachusetts in the second half of the nineteenth century.

Chapter 6
The Election of 1867:
A Setback for Radicalism
or Prohibition?

Because men dislike a liquor law and vote to repeal it, [the Democratic party will find] is no reason why they should desert their principles and turn copperheads. — *William Claflin to Charles Sumner, 1 February 1868*

The 1867 state elections were the first to be held after congressional action placed the South under military occupation, partially limited voting and officeholding to loyal Unionists, enfranchised the freedmen, and required ratification of the Fourteenth Amendment. Contemporaries viewed these elections, held in virtually every northern state to fill various state and local offices, as an indirect popular referendum on Republican national policies. Recent works by historians have interpreted the Republican reverses at the polls in nearly every one of these "off-year" elections as evidence of weaknesses in Republican voting strength, disapproval of the advanced position taken by the radical Republicans on Reconstruction issues, and the impracticality of radicalism as a political ideology during the postwar period. The Republican setbacks in the 1867 elections, according to one authority, "led to the defeat of radical hopes to impeach Andrew Johnson, stiffen the Reconstruction laws, and elect a radical president upon a radical platform in 1868."[1]

The nation's pro-Democratic press interpreted the rout of Republican candidates as the beginning of a "counter-revolution" against the "radical program of reconstruction." Strictly speaking, the congressional Reconstruction policy embodied in the First Reconstruction Act of 1867 appealed more to moderate and conservative Republicans than to the radical wing of the party. What Democrats called "radical" reconstruction was actually a compromise plan worked out among conservative, moderate, and radical Republicans. Truly radical legislation would have guaranteed freedom, justice, and safety to every former slave in the South, a situation that would be realized, in the words of former abolitionist Wendell Phillips, only when the black man had "40 acres under his feet, a schoolhouse behind him, a ballot in his right hand, the sceptre of the Federal Government over his head, and no State Government to interfere with him, until more than one-half of the white men of the Southern states are in their graves."[2]

Although congressional reconstruction never embodied the complete program of the radicals, the ideas and aspirations of the radicals caused consternation among Democrats. The Democratic New York *Times*, for example, claimed the elections were a reaction against "unqualified suffrage," "the menace of confiscation," and "the bullying influences" of men like Senator Benjamin F. Wade of Ohio. While many Democratic party chieftains were careful to state that the victories at the polls belonged to their party and not to President Andrew Johnson, others proclaimed that the results were the outcome of "a struggle on the part of the defenders of constitutional liberty" to save the president "from the assaults of Radical leaders" who were determined to oust him from the presidency in order to put "their Ohio champion" in his place. The reference to Wade was clear.[3]

The Democratic gains in Massachusetts in 1867 were tantamount to a victory and were celebrated accordingly. Republican reverses were quite dramatic. Republican gubernatorial candidate Alexander H. Bullock received over 77 percent of the popular vote in 1866; yet in running for a third term in 1867 Bullock was reelected with only 58 percent of the total vote cast. The entire thrust of postwar politics in Massachusetts appeared to have been checkmated. The state was "no longer bound hand and foot to the Radical chariotwheels," concluded the archconservative Robert C. Winthrop. The Democratic gubernatorial vote in 1867 was the largest vote that the party had ever polled. While Bullock received some 6,000 more votes in 1867 than he had in 1866, the Democrats increased their vote from 26,671 in 1866 to 70,360 in 1867. This was a remarkable increase of more than 21,000 over the vote George B. McClellan had attracted in the state as the 1864 Democratic presidential candidate.[4]

Some Republican conservatives welcomed the defeats and setbacks of their party in 1867, hoping this would result in more satisfactory ideological adjustments in 1868. To Republican John H. Clifford, a former Whig governor, the results could not fail to have "a salutary influence." Similarly, the Springfield *Republican* asserted that the results would have a sobering effect, "like a bucket of cold water on the head of a drunken man, and the inclination now will be to moderate and reasonable counsels." The paper interpreted the Democratic gains nationwide to mean that the voters had started to doubt the wisdom of disfranchising southern whites in order to build Republican majorities with black votes. Republican Congressman Nathaniel P. Banks, the long-standing rival of the Sumner radicals, gloated that Washington politicians looked upon the election "as a crusher for the wild men."[5]

Nowhere had radical hopes flown higher than in Massachusetts before the 1867 elections. At the state convention the Republicans had declared themselves in favor of checking the president, should the necessity arise, to the extent of exercising the power of impeachment. Some speeches by individual radical leaders, especially by Congressman Benjamin F. Butler, were more extreme than the resolutions. Butler had pressed on the floor of Congress for confiscation and land redistribution in the former rebel states. Sumner had demanded that Congress pass a law requiring racially nondiscriminatory voting qualifications within every state of the Union, and he had urged that southern states be required to support a system of free public education to all children regardless of race.[6]

The implications of the radical Republican position on the issues of race and Reconstruction were not lost on conservative Republicans. After Butler expostulated about the undesirability of a permanent landed aristocracy in the South, the Boston *Daily Advertiser* asked: "Why a landed aristocracy? This mode of argument is two edged. For there are socialists who hold that *any* aristocracy is 'fatal to the advance of the cause of liberty and equal rights'—socialists who would not hesitate to say that General Butler's large income places him in the ranks of an aristocracy." The *Daily Advertiser*, controlled by Peleg W. Chandler, a close associate of former Civil War Governor John Andrew, was sympathetic to Boston's business and banking community. The paper found Butler's views on financial questions and labor issues more disturbing than his southern policy.[7]

Although Sumner, who stayed aloof of these newer issues, escaped similar criticism in the conservative Republican press, he was fair game in the elegant parlors of upper-class Boston society which had never held him in high esteem. The respect that Sumner enjoyed from conservative Republicans was a sore point with the Charles Francis Adams family, whose eldest son John Quincy had been the only prominent Republican in 1866 to join the National Union movement in support of Johnson. Henry Adams, who had accompanied his father to London, complained that Andrew, Richard H. Dana, Jr., and John G. Palfrey, along with the entire "conservative liberalism of New England," had allowed themselves to be "whipped and kicked like a mangy spaniel by Sumner and his party, and had cowered under the flogging without a growl or even a whine."[8]

In 1867 J. Q. Adams, perceiving the radical blueprint for Reconstruction as more revolutionary than it had been the year before, joined the Democrats. He equated radical proposals with "reckless political debauchery," which would result inevitably "in delirium if not death" of democratic constitutionalism. It was a bitter disappointment to Charles F. Adams, Jr., however, to see his brother take the irrevocable plunge into Democratic ranks. Although he did not sympathize with the radical Republicans, he could not abide the Democrats whom he described as "Copperheads and curs,—their ideas are low and Irish. . . . [T]hey foam at the mouth as they talk about Sumner and say openly that he desired his 'flogging' from Brooks, though they will not sustain Brooks in his outrage. . . . [T]he [N]egro they seem to go crazy over—they wish to hand him over to his old master to be dealt with. . . . [T]hey dare not denounce the war, so they expatiate on the national disgrace when we were 'three to one' that we had to call in the 'niggar' to finish it." C. F. Adams believed that the "most radical Republican," on the other hand, at least "has some intelligent, philanthropic or loyal end in view,—he may be revengeful, unscrupulous, and revolutionary, but he generally wishes for that which he thinks will improve his race or his country."[9]

In states where the white voter backlash from the black suffrage question played a role in the 1867 elections, Republican setbacks were clear signals that northern conservatism on the race question would limit radical reform efforts. The issue of black political equality played a part in Republican losses in Pennsylvania, New Jersey, and New York. Black suffrage amendments on the ballots in Ohio, Kansas, and Minnesota were rejected by the voters in all three states, although there were some complicating—and therefore to many Republicans, mitigating—circumstances such as in Ohio, where the impartial suffrage proposal was coupled with a proposition disfranchising thousands of discreditably discharged Ohio soldiers. The results proved politically injurious to the Republicans everywhere the question of race entered the campaign.[10]

Nevertheless, the election results did not totally represent a repudiation of congressional Reconstruction. In Massachusetts, at least, Republican policy toward the South was not the controlling issue in the 1867 election. National issues stemming from the war and its settlement were temporarily eclipsed by a purely local issue that dominated political commentary and cost Republicans many votes. On the eve of the balloting, the Springfield *Republican* editorialized that it was "well understood that in this election we are acting upon local questions and interest, as it is certainly our right and duty to do." Voter concerns in 1867 focused on the state's liquor law.[11]

In 1852 a State House coalition of Free-Soilers, Whigs, and a sizable number of Democrats had passed a prohibitory law, called the "Maine Liquor Law" after the state inaugurating the policy. The antiimmigrant and anti-Catholic Know-Nothings who dominated the 1855 legislature amended the law after parts of it were invalidated by the courts. The revised law prohibited sales of all intoxicating beverages, including beer, wine, and cider, and forbade their sale for medical purposes unless sold by state-appointed agents, but did not restrict the manufacture of liquor and its export and sale in large quantities. This 1855 temperance law was still in effect in 1867.[12]

The "cold-water" campaign that succeeded in imposing total prohibition upon Massachusetts in the 1850s had drawn from a reservoir of popular support. In the antebellum period the temperance movement sprang up in urban industrialized areas, where it received disproportional support among entrepreneurs alarmed at the amount of accidents and lost time caused by their inebriated employees. The factory workers who shared their employer's progressive vision of a future shaped by moral and material progress were sharply distinguishable from their incorrigible counterparts who believed that drink was an essential aid to physical labor. The temperance movement also struck a responsive chord among religious denominations that stressed a strong personal faith in God and emphasized "correct" moral standards of behavior. Conversely, nonevangelical or liturgical denominations, which accentuated right belief in traditional creeds, such as Catholics and Episcopalians, were generally unsympathetic with the temperance movement. But the religious affiliations of Massachusetts citizens were not always reliable determinants of temperance commitment in the antebellum period. Evangelicals—even if they favored voluntary temperance—were sharply divided over the prospect of state-imposed prohibition.[13]

In Massachusetts, as in England in the second half of the nineteenth century, the temperance crusade cut across both class and religious lines, had deep roots in the working classes, and appealed to aspirations for self-improvement and social betterment. The temperance movement was not merely a vehicle for native American Protestants to exert cultural dominance over immigrant Irish Catholics. In the postwar period Catholics were not categorically opposed to prohibition. The Father Matthew Total Abstinence Society—named after

Theobald Matthew, a Capuchin priest from Ireland who had crusaded against intemperance in Boston—was one of the most influential temperance groups among Bay State Catholics. Nor were Catholics totally supportive of prohibition laws. While temperance societies affiliated with Catholic church parishes often did more to cope with the problem of drunkenness and alcoholism than did public authorities, Catholic priests favored a liberalization in the liquor law. In the heat of the debates over the liquor question, Catholics drew a distinction between unworkable, total prohibition with its secret "rum holes" and bootleggers, on one hand, and a license system that could control the irrepressible saloons with regulations, taxes, and fines, on the other.[14]

The relationship between the Republican party, which after 1858 controlled both the governorship and the legislature, and the Massachusetts temperance crusaders was complex. The Republicans renominated Andrew, the popular Civil War governor, in spite of his well-known hostility to the State Temperance Alliance, the most powerful antiliquor organization in the state. The temperance cause, by admission of the antiliquor forces, lost considerable ground during the Civil War years. The campaign against the Confederacy took precedence over the fight against liquor, and with Andrew in the governor's chair the 1855 prohibitory law became a "dead letter" in most cities and towns. Andrew opposed further efforts to enforce the liquor law and crippled the operations of the state constabulary authorized to enforce liquor, gambling, and prostitution statutes. Even the Republican-controlled federal government seemed tacitly to approve the traffic in liquor, for during the Civil War Congress passed a revenue law requiring brewers to pay a license fee.[15]

But under Governor Bullock, Andrew's successor, the state constabulary began to enforce the liquor law in earnest. The years during Bullock's administration marked the high point of attempts to enforce prohibition in nineteenth-century Massachusetts. In 1866, in Suffolk County alone, 3,307 arrests were made for "Liquor Nuisances," 2,240 for "Common Selling," 134 for "Single Sales," and 56 for "Keeping, Intent to Sell"; in 1867, the state police seized nearly 100,000 gallons of liquor. Opponents of prohibition protested vehemently; in 1866 and 1867 Democrats in the state legislature submitted bills to liberalize the law, but their attempts were defeated by large margins. Bullock, a supporter of the State Temperance Alliance, defended the work of the state constabulary and even praised its controversial chief, Major Edward J. Jones, claiming that the organization had obtained results that municipal police forces, "embarrassed by local influences and association," had failed to achieve.[16]

The attempt to enforce the liquor law in Boston almost provoked a riot in the spring of 1867 when Jones's constables seized a liquor dealer's stock. The Boston *Pilot* pleaded with its Irish immigrant readers to avoid participating in any disorderly demonstration against the state police. Opponents of strict enforcement organized and took the offensive. Former Governor Andrew, acting as an attorney for Boston innkeepers, argued before a legislative committee that alcohol was a food, not a poison. His arguments for a license system received extensive press coverage throughout the Commonwealth, although his recommendations went unheeded. The *Pilot* called his performance before the legislative committee "one of the most masterly efforts that has ever proceeded from a Massachusetts jurist," while the German immigrant press congratulated him for having "the courage to combat the tendencies of Puritanism."[17]

Failing to obtain repeal of the prohibition law in the courts or in the legislature, an influential lobby of liquor dealers organized for political action in the 1867 local and state elections. They formed an alliance of Republicans and Democrats called the Personal Liberty League (PLL). The efforts of the many secret organizations spawned by the PLL to combat the unpopular sumptuary law were comparable to the methods used in the 1850s by anti-Catholic and antiimmigrant Know-Nothings. At one time, the prolicense Boston *Pilot* favored the creation of a "no-party" for the sole purpose of electing men pledged for repeal. From his supporters in Lowell Congressman Butler learned that the "only visible movement in state politics is the formation of the Secret Rum Societies which are said to be on the increase." In Boston small posters with "P.L.L." printed on them, along with cabalistic numbers that changed from time to time, began to appear by later summer. Republican Congressman Nathaniel P. Banks, always sensitive to grass-roots political movements, predicted that "Half a Revolution" would occur at the polling places in November.[18]

Legislative debates on the liquor issue focused on the desirability of a license law, but the issue was more complex than either side would admit. Public intoxication and its treatment were different problems than the prohibition of liquor sales in saloons, bars, and hotels, but rarely were they separated. The arguments presented by interested parties, moreover, were often underpinned by a confusing set of motives, and never did the debates follow partisan lines. The prohibitionist forces were a vocal minority within the Republican party; the majority of Republicans were never zealous teetotalers, not even in Boston. The city's Republican mayor, Otis Norcross, had campaigned without making promises to temperance advocates, and once in office he came out for licensing as the most effective way of dealing with the problems of intemperance. Thus, the liquor issue, although it dominated political discussion in Boston during 1867, never became a clearly partisan test.[19]

Endorsement of the 1855 prohibition law was an individual, not a party, matter. The candidates running for election to the state legislature stated their own position on the liquor issue without respect to party affiliation. The overwhelming majority of voters, perhaps as high as 70 percent, cast ballots in 1867 for candidates favoring a repeal of the prohibitory law and advocating the enactment of a liquor license law in its place. Only the strong ties of party loyalty gave Republican prohibitionists many votes, which in the absence of a partisan election—such as in a popular referendum—would certainly have been cast for repeal. Nevertheless, the prohibitionists suffered a crushing defeat. Two-thirds of the legislators who had opposed licensing in the previous legislative session failed to win reelection. In the state senate, the proponents of the prohibitory law were reduced to 9 and in the lower house to 50, whereas 31 senators and 184 delegates to the lower house were pledged to support a license law.[20]

The Democratic Boston *Post* linked both the defeat of Republican prohibitionists in the legislature and Governor Bullock's reduced majority to "a dissatisfaction with . . . the coercive and oppressive measures adopted to produce acquiescence in the sumptuary laws that burden the people." The paper interpreted the Democratic gains as a defeat for the state's radical Republicans, equating the zealousness of those who would enforce an unworkable liquor law with the fanaticism of radicals who would impose a harsh and unrealistic settlement on the postwar South. "The seal of fanaticism was broken" by the voters in the recent election, it argued, and the result "may be taken for a fatal blow to Radicalism."[21]

The leadership of the Massachusetts radical Republican establishment had never formed a united front on the liquor issue. Frank Bird had lashed out at the State Temperance Alliance as early as 1865, when one of its officials charged that Governor Andrew had liquor furnished to himself at public expense. Bird countercharged that he knew well "the power of the compact cabal" that had turned the State Alliance into "an unholy alliance for deeds of envy and slander and all uncharitableness." Bird Club members in the legislature, James M. Stone, the speaker of the house, and William S. Robinson, the clerk of the house, joined Bird in attacking the State Alliance. Robinson claimed that the prohibitory faction in state politics had managed to mesmerize the legislature by intrigue since 1855 while never once having had a majority of the votes on its side. The prohibitionists, according to Robinson, had never done anything more constructive than organizing "ridiculous orders of sons and daughters and babies" and packing local Republican caucuses in order to nominate prohibitionists for the legislature.[22]

On the other hand, George L. Stearns supported the movement among members of Congress to form a congressional temperance society. Other prominent radicals, although not members of the Bird Club, also supported prohibition. Gilbert Haven, the veteran antislavery Methodist minister, accused former Governor Andrew of having arrayed himself against the cause of morality by taking an antiprohibitionist stand before the legislative committee. Another conspicuous link between antislavery radicalism and state-imposed prohibition was Wendell Phillips, who called upon God to "dash the Republican party to pieces if it could not fully embrace the temperance cause." Senator Henry Wilson, perhaps more than any other individual, caused many voters to connect the radical Republicans with the temperance crusade. Many Republican party leaders blamed him for unnecessarily politicizing the liquor issue with his protemperance speeches during the summer of 1867.[23]

Although Wilson had urged his fellow Republicans to avoid the liquor issue, his individual pronouncements favoring prohibition were so strong as to render his advice meaningless. Wilson's protemperance remarks were quoted by the Democratic press as proof of the connection between the fanaticism of radical Republicans and the overzealousness of the "cold-water" crusaders. Telling his audiences he would rather license men to sell Africans into slavery than license men in Massachusetts to sell liquor, Wilson declared it was his duty to speak out against the "monster proposition to license men and put the cup of intoxication to the lips of the people." Wilson had a facility for mixing the issue of intemperance with slavery and rebellion but, as the Boston *Commonwealth* pointed out, national issues unfortunately had little relevance in the selection of representatives to the state legislature.[24]

In 1867 the majority of Republicans, including Wilson, were determined to avoid taking an official stand on the liquor issue. They had difficulty, however, holding in line the prohibitionists and license advocates within their ranks. At one crucial point at the state convention a resolution was introduced disclaiming all party responsibility for the liquor law, signifying that support of the present law was not an essential duty of any Republican. The resolution was voted down, but in the process the license men were reassured that, because historically the Massachusetts Republican party had never committed itself to prohibition, no disclaimer was necessary. On the other hand, the prohibitionists were reminded that the party had never required a man to be a prohibitionist before he could "march on Richmond." Governor Bullock promised the license men that he would not veto the repeal of the prohibition law if the legislature enacted a license law, a pledge that constituted an important concession to the antiprohibitionist forces. At the same time, Bullock gave the State Temperance Alliance such assurances of his support for prohibition in principle that some of its leaders publicly endorsed his reelection.[25]

Democratic strategy in the 1867 campaign aimed at avoiding national issues and instead concentrating on the liquor-license issue. Under the slogan "Adams and Liberty" (rather than "Adams and Freedom," which had been derisively transformed into "Adams and Free Rum"), the Democrats proclaimed that the rights and liberties of Massachusetts voters were directly affected by the liquor question and not by the reconstruction of the southern states. Yet there was considerable truth in the Republican countercharge that every Democrat in the state cared ten times as much about defeating the Republicans in the next presidential election as they did about any aspect of the liquor question. J. Q. Adams privately acknowledged that he could not vote for any license law that a Republican-dominated legislature might pass because, as a politician, he saw the advantages to the Democrats of retaining the prohibition law and having Republicans take responsibility for enforcing it.[26]

Adams's adjustment to Democratic strategy proved difficult; his major commitment was to Reconstruction issues and he personally cared nothing about the liquor question. In his widely circulated letter accepting the Democratic nomination and endorsing the movement for repeal of total prohibition, Adams stated the necessity of rescuing "from unmerited obloquy" the doctrine of states' rights as understood "by the founders of our Commonwealth and by the fathers of our national Union." Yet the Democrats were most vulnerable on Reconstruction issues because Republicans adroitly exploited the specter of the Copperhead Democracy and the former secessionists.[27]

Undoubtedly, in 1867 the Massachusetts Democrats hoped that the Adams name, with its roots deep in American history, would help to expunge the taint of disloyalty attached to their party because of its Civil War record. In many localities Democrats distributed ballots with only "Adams and Liberty" printed at the top, leaving off any mention of Democratic endorsement. The Adams name entailed liabilities as well as advantages. The Fenians, who were disturbed by Johnson's efforts to thwart their attempts to liberate Canada, accused Adams's father, the American minister to Great Britain, of helping English authorities jail American Fenians working to liberate Ireland. Adams, nevertheless, enjoyed the endorsement of the Irish immigrant press and the support of the Personal Liberty League. The impact of early out-of-state election returns gave a sharp impetus to his candidacy. As election day drew nearer, most contemporary observers concluded that his candidacy would divert many votes that otherwise would go to Bullock. Few predicted an Adams victory, but the closeness of the election was a matter of lively speculation.[28]

If the 1867 Massachusetts gubernatorial elections were to be considered as a referendum on congressional reconstruction, then it could be hypothesized that Republican defections occurred at higher rates in congressional districts represented by radicals, and, conversely, that the least amount of Republican voter disaffection took place in districts represented by conservative Republicans. A Republican who voted for Adams and the Democrats in 1867 could have been registering his disapproval of the advanced position on the issues of race and Reconstruction taken by his representative in Congress.

Thomas D. Eliot, Benjamin F. Butler, George S. Boutwell, and John D. Baldwin represented the First, Fifth, Seventh, and Eighth districts, respectively, in the first session of the Fortieth Congress. Most historians agree that Eliot, Butler, Boutwell, and Baldwin were decidedly in the radical camp. All except Butler had been members of the lame-duck session of the Thirty-ninth Congress. Baldwin, a former Congregationalist minister and antislavery newspaper editor, consistently supported the radical position in the first session of the Thirty-ninth Congress but began voting frequently with the opposition in the second session. Nevertheless, he maintained a radical position. Historian David Donald classifies Baldwin as an "independent radical," and he elevates both Eliot and Boutwell to the status of "Thaddeus Stevens-type" radicals.[29]

Ginery Twitchell, Samuel Hooper, Nathaniel P. Banks, and Henry L. Dawes represented the Third, Fourth, Sixth, and Tenth Districts, respectively, in the first session of the Fortieth Congress. With the exception of Twitchell, all had been members of the Thirty-ninth Congress in which they maintained a moderate or centrist position in regard to congressional control over Reconstruction. Dawes and Banks had even shown signs of moving toward the conservative wing of the Republican party. Donald classifies Banks as a "conservative," but he describes Dawes and Hooper as "moderates." Twitchell, the president of the Worcester Railroad, had replaced the retiring Alexander H. Rice in the Third District (including parts of South Boston, Roxbury, and Brookline). Rice maintained a middle position through both sessions of the Thirty-ninth Congress and Twitchell in practically every respect was Rice's political counterpart.[30]

In the congressional districts represented by Republican moderates or conservatives, Adams managed to capture 26 percent of those who had voted for Bullock and the Republicans in 1866 (see Table 6.1). In the First, Fifth, Seventh, and Eighth districts, which were represented by radicals, Adams made the identical inroad into the ranks of 1866 Republicans. Bullock actually fared better in 1867 than in 1866 in the radical-represented districts, but the districts sending moderate and conservative Republicans to Congress in 1866 were less Republican in 1867. Therefore, there is insufficient quantitative evidence to support the notion that 1866 Republicans, by voting for Adams and the Democrats in 1867, were punishing congressional radicals.

A sharp voting cleavage between urban and rural areas would have had special significance in 1867. Because rural areas were presumed to be prohibitionist strongholds, contemporaries of the period often believed that Democratic gains attributable to the liquor issue would come primarily from the cities and larger towns. The Boston *Pilot*, for example, angrily chided country members of the legislature for clinging "with a stupid persistency to the idea of prohibition." But more astute and objective observers realized that the issue was not as clear-cut as this. Surveying the actual voting returns reported by cities and towns, at least one newspaper concluded that larger cities did not swamp "the sober opinion" of rural areas, thus laying to final rest "the superstition" that the country districts were solid for the prohibitory law. Democratic gains in towns with a population of less than 5,000 almost equaled the Democratic increases in the larger communities (see Table 6.1). One reason why the rural areas were not immune to the general disaffection with the Republicans in 1867 was the prohibition on selling cider. Under the law, farmers could be compelled to post exorbitantly high bonds to turn apples into cider and were technically subject to imprisonment if they sold a single gill of cider to their neighbors.[31]

In general, the areas that traditionally voted lopsidedly Republican, such as Worcester County and Cape Cod, came to Bullock's support in greater numbers in 1867 than in 1866. But there is no support for the notion that the political tornado of 1867 stopped short of Bristol County. Although the gap between Democratic and Republican increases was relatively narrow in the southeast third of the state, including Cape Cod and the Islands, hidden in the aggregated voting statistics was a large Republican crossover vote for Adams and the Democrats (see Table 6.1). Large Republican defection rates also occurred in Essex,

TABLE 6.1
An Anatomy of Democratic Gains in the 1867 Gubernatorial Election, by Selected Geographic Regions

Description of Voting Units	Number of Cases	Republican Increase[a]	Democratic Increase[b]	Republican Defections[c]	Democratic Repeaters[d]	Previous Non-voter Support for Adams[e]
Radical-represented districts (1, 5, 7 & 8)	142	4%	17%	26%	100%	10%
Nonradical-represented districts (3, 4, 6 & 10)	86	-3	17	26	98	17
Cities (populations greater than 5,000)	48	-1	18	27	100	14
Towns (populations less than 5,000)	286	5	15	16	100	15
Western Massachusetts	101	2	13	6	100	38
Worcester County	58	8	19	7	100	29
Bristol and Plymouth counties and Cape Cod and the Islands	62	8	13	24	100	3
Essex, Middlesex, Suffolk and Norfolk counties	113	-2	18	27	100	12
Statewide	334	2	17	25	100	15

[a]Percentage of the electorate voting for Alexander H. Bullock in 1867 minus the percentage of the electorate who voted for him in 1866.

[b]Percentage of the electorate voting for John Quincy Adams in 1867 minus the percentage of the electorate who voted for Theodore H. Sweetser in 1866.

[c]Estimated percentage of 1866 Republicans who subsequently voted Democratic in 1867.

[d]Estimated percentage of 1866 Democrats who repeated a Democratic vote in 1867.

[e]Estimated percentage of 1866 nonvoters (including those not yet eligible) who subsequently voted for John Quincy Adams in 1867.

Middlesex, Suffolk, and Norfolk counties, areas where political contests were more competitive, suggesting that Republicans were especially vulnerable where competition between the parties was keenest.

A regression of the Democratic increase in the gubernatorial vote between 1866 and 1867 upon a large array of explanatory variables reveals that Adams ran disproportionately well among factory workers (see Table 6.2). The dramatic Democratic gains in industrial areas suggest that economic issues may have shaped the 1867 outcome. Although both parties took antiinflationist positions on the national financial question, the government's deflationary monetary policy was one cause of the fall in prices and the resulting economic slump that the nation as a whole experienced beginning in the winter of 1866–67 and lasting into 1868. Because there is evidence that Republican setbacks in the 1867 elections in other states were attributable, at least to some degree, to the general business recession, it would be reasonable to speculate that Democratic gains in Massachusetts would be greater in the predominantly manufacturing cities and towns. A serious reservation to the conclusion that economic factors helped Adams's candidacy, however, remains: the issue of the state's economic health did not receive much emphasis during the 1867 campaign.[32]

An alternative explanation for the Democratic increase among industrial workers focuses squarely on the impact of the liquor issue. The saloon-infested industrial areas and factory towns had been the main arenas for repeated clashes over temperance in the antebellum period. (Not until the 1880s and 1890s did antiliquor sentiment in Massachusetts become more of a rural than an urban movement.) Before Bullock became governor, the prohibition issue was resolved, according to one historian, "by letting one side have the law and the other the liquor." When the state constabulary refrained from marching through the dining rooms of reputable hotels and searching the cellars of rural farmhouses, and concentrated its efforts on shutting down the worst "rum holes" in working-class neighborhoods, protest in the manufacturing cities and towns took the form of an increased anti-Republican vote.[33]

Democratic gains were also significantly higher in areas that in 1860 had voted disproportionately for the Constitutional Union party (see Table 6.2). Commenting on the 1867 gubernatorial campaign in Massachusetts, the New York *Times* had predicted that "'Old Time Whigs'" would "give Bullock the go-by and vote for Adams." The basis for this assumption was a widely reprinted letter endorsing Adams signed by Thomas Aspinwall, Leverett Saltonstall, and 271 other citizens, most of whose signatures had been omitted "for want of space." Letters such as this were frequently believed to have a bearing on elections, but most signers of this particular letter were never thoroughly identified with the Republicans. Many, such as Saltonstall, had been Constitutional Unionists in 1860. Although at the time there were few, if any, indications that the letter endorsing Adams would change many votes, the quantitative evidence suggests that many former John Bell supporters voted for Adams in 1867.[34]

Republican reverses in the North in the 1867 elections helped dash radical hopes to impeach and convict President Johnson. The acquittal of Johnson, it is argued, signaled the eclipse of emotional battles over Reconstruction and the beginning of a return to more mundane concerns. The effect was registered immediately in the voting alignments in Congress, where an increasing number of radical Republicans became more conservative. Sumner expressed the disappointment of the Massachusetts radicals with the turn of events: "Alas for that race so long oppressed, but at last redeemed from bondage, now plunged back into another hell of torment!" For Sumner and the Bird Club radicals, the success of Reconstruction had hinged on Johnson's removal.[35]

TABLE 6.2
Influence of Explanatory Variables on the Increase in the Democratic Gubernatorial Vote Between 1866 and 1867

Dependent Variable	Explanatory Variables	Simple r	Regression Coefficients	Adjusted Standard Errors of Reg. Coef.	Beta Coefficients	Change in R^2
Democratic	Manufacturing	.30	.08	.05	.16	.09
Increase	Bell	.16	.22	.09	.23	.04
1866-1867	Valuation per capita 1865	-.15	-.00	.00	-.40	.07
[R^2=.32]	Competitiveness[a]	.22	.09	.03	.23	.04
	Native growth rate	.23	.01	.00	.16	.02
	Fishing	-.26	-.09	.05	-.15	.02
	Out-of-state	.05	-.11	.09	-.09	.01
	Methodist	-.16	-.06	.04	-.06	.01
	Poll-tax voters	-.03	-.07	.05	-.14	.01
	Baptist	-.05	-.06	.04	-.06	.01
	Voters of polls	-.23	-.05	.06	-.05	.00
	Other churches	-.03	.08	.06	.08	.00
	Episcopalian	-.03	-.13	.12	-.06	.00
	Unitarian & Universalist	.07	.05	.04	.07	.00
	Foreign-born	.13	.06	.10	.09	.00
	Congregational	-.05	.02	.02	.06	.00
	Agriculture	-.09	-.02	.04	-.04	.00
	Foreign growth rate	.09	-.00	.00	-.02	.00
	Catholic	.09	.01	.10	.01	.00
	Quaker	-.12	-.01	.16	-.00	.00

Note: Actual N = 320. Voting units are "weighted" by population in order to ensure that smaller towns are not overrepresented in the analysis. Standard errors, however, are computed according to the original, unweighted number of cities and towns.

[a]David Index of party competition in the 1864 presidential election. For descriptions of all other explanatory variables, see Table 4.2.

The reverses of 1867 encouraged Sumner's political enemies to try to deny him another term in the Senate. At a Boston dinner party in honor of Senator William P. Fessenden of Maine, there emerged a consensus that Charles F. Adams would be a strong contender for Sumner's seat. Sumner accepted with alacrity the challenge from the Republican conservatives: "If this is the beginning of an issue with me,—very well! I think the people of Massachusetts are not for A. J. or for any of the 'quibbles' by which he was saved." In public Sumner always revealed little concern for the prospect of losing a political battle, but behind the scenes he worked with the help of his allies in the Bird Club to slash away at his opponents. The elements uniting behind Adams were, according to Charles Slack, the editor of the Boston *Commonwealth*, "diverse & very bad" and threatened to give Sumner more opposition than he had experienced in 1863. Because the eldest son in the Adams family, John Quincy, was the ostensible leader of the state Democratic party, Bird Club members feared that Charles F. Adams might be able to draw on considerable Democratic support in the legislature. Both the Boston *Post* and the Boston *Herald* endorsed Adams as a possible Democratic candidate for the vice-presidency in 1868. Thus Democratic support for Adams's candidacy could not be ruled out.[36]

Adams was an old adversary of Sumner. Any friendship between the two had ended in 1861 when Adams, as a member of the Massachusetts congressional delegation, turned up a compromiser during the secession crisis. When his son, John Quincy, defected from Republican ranks to join the National Unionist movement, the Bird Club radicals did not hesitate publicly to insult the Adams family. When Adams returned home in mid-summer 1868 from his distinguished diplomatic career in London, he was studiously snubbed by the radicals who ignored a public reception in his honor. Charles Slack in the Boston *Commonwealth* and "Warrington" in the Springfield *Republican* attacked Adams's career. Meanwhile, Sumner tried assiduously to mend political fences with the influential Boston conservative community. He gave his attention to legislation desired by Massachusetts merchants and shippers, voted against the eight-hour workday for laborers in government arsenals and shipyards, and delivered speeches favoring the resumption of specie payments to demonstrate that he was a fiscal conservative.[37]

To complicate matters for Sumner's allies, early in 1868 Governor Bullock embarked on an effort to forge an antiradical coalition. His first overt act was to nominate Benjamin F. Thomas to be chief justice to the Massachusetts Supreme Court. Thomas had been almost unanimously elected to the Thirty-seventh Congress as a "Conservative Unionist" to fill the vacancy created by the resignation of Charles F. Adams when he was appointed minister to England. If Thomas had been reelected to Congress in 1862, he would have been brought forward by the Boston conservatives as a challenger to Sumner in the 1863 senatorial contest. Sumner used his influence among members of the Governor's Council to have Thomas's nomination squashed and worked at destroying Bullock's chances for reelection. After the Thomas incident Bullock's relations with Sumner and the Bird Club radicals deteriorated sharply.[38]

In the spring of 1868 Bullock decided not to seek another term as governor and let it be known that he favored Dawes as his successor. Dawes had acquired perhaps the most conservative voting record of all the Massachusetts congressmen in the Thirty-ninth Congress. At the time of his renomination for a sixth consecutive term, Dawes was silent on Reconstruction issues. This strategy of avoiding the southern question appealed to his constituents in the Tenth District (Berkshire County) where Democrats traditionally ran well. Even the local Republican press defended Dawes against the charge of radicalism, pointing out that in Congress he had "not taken the extreme views and denunciatory course of Thad. Stevens and Co." Although Dawes would have accepted an unequivocal call from the Republicans to run for governor, he did not seek the office because of inhibitions against "self-electioneering." Only Dr. George B. Loring, a long-time associate of Butler, campaigned aggressively among the party's leaders for the Republican nomination. At one point Loring secretly offered to sign a guarantee that he would keep the governorship for only two years in exchange for supporting Dawes in 1870.[39]

Dawes, who had no choice but to oppose Andrew Johnson in 1866, privately abhorred the tactics of the radicals. His possible candidacy for the governorship was unacceptable to the Sumner-Bird faction of the party. While the radicals admired the radicalism of Loring, they feared that he walked in Butler's footsteps and, consequently, they distrusted him. The Bird Club radicals were determined to place William Claflin, the chairman of the Republican National Committee and a close friend of Henry Wilson, in the governor's chair. By actively working behind the scenes to secure Claflin's nomination, Bird and his associates blocked any chances Dawes or Loring had of obtaining the nomination.[40]

Harmony prevailed at the 1868 Republican state convention when Butler withdrew Loring's name as a possible candidate for governor and moved for the nomination of Claflin by acclamation. Bird's supporters then inserted in the resolutions a statement praising Sumner's "devotion to the cause of human rights" and calling for his reelection. The convention approved the endorsement of Sumner with three rousing cheers. To further ensure Sumner's reelection, the convention ignored the prohibition issue, but made an important concession to the prohibitionists in order to silence them during the campaign. The basis for selecting the number of delegates to future state conventions would be determined by the number of Republican votes in a locality. (The prohibitionists believed that the new representation plan would guarantee that more prohibitionists attended the next Republican convention.) When the legislature elected in 1868 assembled in early 1869, some Republicans may have preferred someone other than Sumner to represent Massachusetts in the Senate, but according to the Springfield *Republican*, "very few of them will care to say so, for no political sin is remembered so long, or punished so severely, as a vote against Mr. Sumner."[41]

The Massachusetts Democrats in 1868 renominated J. Q. Adams for the governorship. President Johnson praised Adams's identification of the major campaign issue in Adams's letter of acceptance: "That the battle is between the Constitution and Congress, and thank God! you have taken your stand for the Constitution." In a speech delivered in Charleston, South Carolina, which received national attention, Adams denounced the Reconstruction policies of the Congress led on by an im-

patient and vindictive Charles Sumner. The response of William Lloyd
Garrison to Adams's denunciation of the radical Republicans was typi-
cal of many Massachusetts citizens. Garrison was amused that Adams
was "constrained to utter encomiums and make confessions that must
have tried his rebel auditors," but he was convinced that Adams, "in
going with the rebel and copperhead party, and for its line of policy,
. . . is as bad as the worst practically."[42]

Democratic leaders realized that their party was not going to win
votes on the Reconstruction issue upon which Adams, somewhat stubbornly, desired to campaign. The Massachusetts Democratic party's
orientation was changing, and Adams adjusted uncomfortably to its
new course. Although the Democrats called congressional Reconstruction unconstitutional and revolutionary, they resolved to make the liquor question the most important issue in the coming election. They
denied responsibility, however, for the poorly drawn (and extremely
liberal) license law passed by the 1868 legislature and permitted by
Governor Bullock to become law without his signature. Convinced of
the need for some system of regulating the sale of alcoholic beverages
and confident that the majority of voters disagreed with the principle
of total prohibition, the Democratic press predicted that the large
Democratic gains of 1867 would be retained because the zealous antiliquor forces were again working to reimpose the old prohibitory law.[43]

But in 1868 the liquor question was not the most important issue in
the minds of the voters, not even among Democrats. Behind Democratic campaign rhetoric that the presidential election was a choice
between a free system of government and the capricious rule of a
sectional oligarchy lurked the question of race and Reconstruction.
The Boston *Pilot* reduced the campaign to a battle between the friends
and foes of Irish-Americans and charged that "five-sixths" of all Republicans believed that a black man was superior to an Irishman.
Moses Bates, a long-time member of the Democratic State Central
Committee, wrote that while he had risked his life in the army to preserve the Union, "I did not seek to uphold the American flag that igno-
rant [N]egroes may rule over white man." Even J. Q. Adams believed
that blacks could not be artificially elevated from their subordinate
position in southern society. As his brother, Charles, explained, John
believed that "the Negro must go back to his proper position & it's a
very low one."[44]

Just as in 1866 when many Republican conservatives opposed the
radicals but could not bring themselves to join the Copperhead Democracy, in 1868 the Republican opponents of Sumner were unable to swal-
low the Democratic presidential candidacy of Horatio Seymour. To

Samuel Bowles, a persistent admirer of William Seward and Charles F. Adams, the Seymour nomination meant that the Democrats had not purged the reactionaries from their ranks: "Vallandigham, the Jonas of the Democratic party from '61 to '66, is still its prophet, still its ruler, still its gravedigger."[45]

The early election returns from around the nation in 1868 forced the Democrats to realize that 1867 had not inaugurated a shift of support to their party because of any substantial disaffection with congressional Reconstruction. The Republican victory in Vermont in September could be dismissed as "the Dutch taking Holland," but not the results that followed in other states. In October the Republicans swept Ohio, Indiana, and Pennsylvania. The Republican setbacks in 1867 were being reversed in all parts of the country.[46]

In Massachusetts, the Democratic gains of the previous year were erased as 1866 Republicans who had defected to Adams in 1867 returned to the Republican fold (see Table 6.3). The analyses of 1866, 1867, and 1868 gubernatorial election returns show, first, that the crossing of party lines in the 1867 election consisted only of Republicans switching to the Democratic ticket, and second, that all Republican defectors returned to their party in 1868. In 1867 Adams had captured approximately 25 percent of the 1866 Republicans or about 23,000 former supporters of Governor Bullock (see Table 6.3.A). As a consequence, in 1867 about 33 percent of Adams's total vote (and not half his total, as contemporary opinion suspected) was comprised of Republicans.[47] Whereas about 75 percent of the 1866 Republicans repeated a Republican vote in 1867, virtually all of them voted Republican in 1868 (see Tables 6.3.A and 6.3.C). Claflin, the Republican gubernatorial candidate in 1868, took into his column about one-third of the 1867 Democrats—approximately 23,000 voters—virtually all of whom were Republican defectors to Adams in 1867 (see Table 6.3.B).

Thus, the 1867 governor's race was a deviating election for both Republicans and Democrats because the crossing of party lines was merely temporary and not permanent. The 1868 election can be characterized as a reinstating election because it reestablished the pre-1867 voter coalitions (see Tables 6.3, 6.4, and 6.5.B). What had occurred in Massachusetts in 1867 was summed up best by the Boston *Daily Journal*, which claimed the results showed that "party lines were forgotten, the local [prohibition] issue dissolving temporarily the political affiliations of the voters."[48] The intense polarization of the two major parties on the central issues of the 1860s underscores the deviant nature of a campaign, such as the campaign of 1867, that turned on the issue of prohibition.

Nationwide, Grant's majority exceeded by over 100,000 votes the to-

TABLE 6.3
The 1867 Governor's Race Was a Deviating Election for Both Republicans and Democrats
(by percent of 1867 and 1868 electorates)

A. The 1866 and 1867 Gubernatorial Elections
(Actual <u>N</u> = 334)

	Candidate in 1866				
Candidate in 1867	Theodore H. Sweetser	Alexander H. Bullock	Not Voting for Governor 1866	Not Eligible 1866	Percent of 1867 Electorate
John Q. Adams	10	9	8	0	28
Alexander H. Bullock	0	27	12	0	39
Not Voting for Governor 1867	0	0	32	2	34
Percent of 1867 Electorate	10	36	52	2	100

B. The 1867 and 1868 Gubernatorial Elections
(Actual <u>N</u> = 332)

	Candidate in 1867				
Candidate in 1868	John Q. Adams	Alexander H. Bullock	Not Voting for Governor 1867	Not Eligible 1867	Percent of 1868 Electorate
John Q. Adams	18	0	6	1	25
William Claflin	9	33	9	0	51
Not Voting for Governor 1868	0	5	18	1	24
Percent of 1868 Electorate	27	38	33	2	100

C. The 1866 and 1868 Gubernatorial Elections
(Actual <u>N</u> = 332)

	Candidate in 1866				
Candidate in 1868	Theodore H. Sweetser	Alexander H. Bullock	Not Voting for Governor 1866	Not Eligible 1866	Percent of 1868 Electorate
John Q. Adams	10	0	14	1	25
William Claflin	0	36	15	0	51
Not Voting for Governor 1868	0	0	22	2	24
Percent of 1868 Electorate	10	36	51	3	100

<u>Note:</u> Rounding procedures occasionally produce totals greater or less than 100 percent.

tals of candidates running on Republican state tickets. One historian interprets this as evidence that many who backed President Johnson's Reconstruction policies were subsequently attracted to Grant in 1868.[49] In Massachusetts Grant ran 4,268 votes ahead of Claflin while Adams ran 4,163 votes ahead of Seymour. Most of Adams's tally over Seymour's total did come from those who also had voted for Grant, despite the limited number of split tickets that circulated at the polling places (see Table 6.6).

At his home in Quincy, Charles F. Adams had carefully prepared his

TABLE 6.4
Influence of Explanatory Variables on Voting Patterns in the 1868 Presidential Election

Dependent Variable	Explanatory Variables	Simple r	Regression Coefficients	Adjusted Standard Errors of Reg. Coef.	Beta Coefficients	Change in R²
Seymour [R²=.47]	Foreign-born	.61	.37	.11	.39	.37
	Quaker	-.25	-.67	.17	-.17	.03
	Fishing	-.20	-.12	.06	-.15	.03
	Congregational	-.30	-.06	.03	-.12	.01
	Out-of-state	.37	.22	.10	.13	.01
	Foreign growth rate	.04	-.00	.00	-.07	.00
	Valuation per capita 1865	.38	.00	.00	.06	.00
	Against "two-year" amendment	.32	.11	.11	.05	.00
	Voters of polls	-.47	-.07	.06	-.07	.00
	Methodist	-.20	.05	.04	.04	.00
	Manufacturing	.15	-.03	.06	-.05	.00
	Catholic	.37	.06	.12	.04	.00
	Baptist	-.05	-.04	.04	-.03	.00
	Episcopalian	.16	-.07	.13	-.03	.00
	Other churches	-.10	-.03	.06	-.02	.00
	Native growth rate	.34	.00	.00	.03	.00
	Agriculture	-.31	.02	.04	.03	.00
	Unitarian & Universalist	-.02	.01	.04	.01	.00
	Poll-tax voters	.41	.01	.06	.01	.00
	For "two-year" amendment	.34	.00	.11	.00	.00
Grant [R²=.34]	Valuation per capita 1865	-.52	-.00	.00	-.51	.27
	Congregational	.26	.07	.03	.13	.02
	Methodist	.01	-.15	.05	-.13	.02
	Native growth rate	-.08	.01	.01	.19	.01
	Foreign-born	-.35	-.05	.13	-.05	.01
	Fishing	-.16	-.06	.07	-.07	.01
	Out-of-state	.01	.14	.11	.08	.00
	Episcopalian	-.17	-.15	.16	-.05	.00
	Quaker	.04	.22	.20	05	.00
	Agriculture	.26	.08	.05	.10	.00
	Poll-tax voters	-.33	.06	.07	09	.00
	Against "two-year" amendment	-.17	-.14	.13	-.06	.00
	Voters of polls	.20	.07	.08	.07	.00
	Unitarian & Universalist	-.07	.04	.05	.04	.00
	Manufacturing	.12	-.02	.07	-.04	.00
	Baptist	.05	-.03	.05	-.03	.00
	Catholic	-.25	-.03	.14	-.02	.00
	For "two-year" amendment	-.20	-.03	.13	-.02	.00
	Other churches	-.02	-.01	.08	-.01	.00
	Foreign growth rate	.05	.00	.00	.00	.00
Abstaining [R²=.33]	Out-of-state	-.35	-.36	.12	-.20	.12
	Fishing	.33	.18	.08	.20	.06
	Native growth rate	-.23	-.01	.01	-.21	.02
	Valuation per capita 1865	.13	.00	.00	.43	.04
	Foreign-born	-.23	-.33	.13	-.31	.04
	Quaker	.19	.45	.22	.10	.02
	Methodist	.17	.10	.05	.08	.01
	Episcopalian	.01	.22	.17	.07	.01
	Agriculture	.04	-.10	.06	-.12	.00
	Foreign growth rate	-.09	.00	.00	.06	.00
	Baptist	.01	.07	.06	.05	.00
	Manufacturing	-.25	.05	.08	.08	.00
	Poll-tax voters	-.07	-.07	.07	-.10	.00
	Unitarian & Universalist	.08	-.05	.05	-.04	.00
	Other churches	.11	.05	.08	.03	.00
	Catholic	-.11	-.03	.15	-.02	.00
	For "two-year" amendment	-.12	.03	.14	.01	.00
	Congregational	.04	-.01	.03	-.01	.00
	Against "two-year" amendment	-.13	.02	.14	.01	.00
	Voters of polls	.24	-.00	.08	-.00	.00

Note: Actual N = 315. For descriptions of explanatory variables, see Table 4.2.

TABLE 6.5
Crossover Voting Between Presidential Elections from 1860 to 1868
(by percent of 1868 electorate)

A. The 1860 and 1868 Presidential Elections

Candidate in 1868	Candidate in 1860						
	Douglas	Lincoln	Bell	Breckinridge	Not Voting for President 1860	Not Eligible 1860	Percent of 1868 Electorate
Seymour	13	0	5	2	2	1	23
Grant	0	37	4	0	7	5	53
Not Voting for President 1868	0	4	0	0	12	8	24
Percent of 1868 Electorate	13	41	9	2	21	13	100

B. The 1864 and 1868 Presidential Elections

Candidate in 1868	Candidate in 1864				
	McClellan	Lincoln	Not Voting for President 1864	Not Eligible 1864	Percent of 1868 Electorate
Seymour	19	0	4	0	23
Grant	0	46	6	1	53
Not Voting for President 1868	0	3	16	5	24
Percent of 1868 Electorate	19	49	26	6	100

Note: Actual N = 332.

TABLE 6.6
Estimates of Split-Ticket Voting in the 1868 General Election:
The Presidential and Gubernatorial Contests
(by percent of 1868 electorate)

Gubernatorial Election	Presidential Election			
	Seymour	Grant	Not Voting for President 1868	Percent of 1868 Electorate
John Q. Adams	23	1	0	25
William Claflin	0	51	0	51
Not Voting for Governor 1868	0	1	24	24
Percent of 1868 Electorate	23	53	24	100

Note: Actual N = 332.

own ballot in order to vote both for Grant for president and for his eldest son for governor, but he put a sales receipt into the ballot box instead of his handwritten ballot. Realizing his mistake he returned to the polling place and embarrassingly looked on while an examination of the contents of the ballot box produced his receipt. About three thousand other voters also managed to split their tickets, presumably with less difficulty than Adams. Moreover, the chances are that former Republican voters comprised most of the split-ticket voters in 1868, suggesting that Grant did not benefit from an inflated Republican vote, but that Adams took votes that otherwise would have gone to Claflin.[50]

"The great contest . . . has resulted disastrously to the Democracy," admitted the staunchly Democratic Pittsfield *Sun.* When Charles F. Adams took the pulse of the influential and wealthy Boston conservative community after the election, he found most "prepared to have the radical wave roll over them, just as the higher classes did in the French Revolution." The radical wing of the Massachusetts Republican party had successfully met the challenge of the 1867 election results by regaining the allegiances of voters who had defected to the Democracy because of the liquor issue. The constituencies of both the Republican and Democratic parties had not changed from what they had been in 1864 (see Table 6.5.B). The Massachusetts results were not unique: nationwide, the similarity of the partisan vote in 1868 to what it had been in 1864 was the most compelling result of the 1868 presidential election.[51]

Chapter 7
The Transition from Ideological to Pragmatic Politics, 1869–1871

The elections . . . teach that the Republican Party,
having fought through the great questions of the war and
Reconstruction, ought not any longer to look back or stand
still; but with the same vigor as of old, to take up the
questions which affect the welfare of the masses at the
present time. —*Boston* Daily Journal, *12 November 1870*

The election of Ulysses S. Grant to the presidency in 1868 dashed the hopes of many Massachusetts radicals for a further reconstruction of southern society. The conservative drift nationwide that had compelled the Republicans to choose Grant as their presidential nominee meant that Reconstruction increasingly would have to depend upon the radicals' major accomplishment: securing the ballot to the freedmen. Although President Andrew Johnson had killed radical hopes for land redistribution, the Bird Club members still wanted to enact a nationally enforced education policy, end racial segregation, and impose a strict probation period on any readmitted state. They feared, however, that Congress's power over the South at the war's end would be checked in the future by the traditional doctrine of states' rights and the old dogma that black Africans belonged to an inferior race.

Diverse interests and values within the northern Republican coalition also served to blunt the force of radicalism. Even though the Massachusetts Republican party seemed invincible, new issues unrelated to southern affairs were potential causes of turmoil and dissension in the party's ranks. Consequently, the radical leadership avoided strong stands on purely state and local issues. Even among the members of the Bird Club there was no consensus on support for the new demands of workers, prohibitionists, women, and business leaders. Whether the Republican party could deal pragmatically with the new social and political realities of the day, rather than with outmoded ideological slogans, remained to be seen.

In 1869 a major political blunder by the Republican-dominated state legislature led many workingmen to split from the Republicans. The Knights of St. Crispin (KOSC), the largest labor union in the state, had appealed for a charter to establish producing and marketing cooperatives, but the legislature rejected its petition. The lawmakers' action reflected pervasive antilabor sentiment. Critics of trade unions depicted them as coercive organizations bent on promoting the special interests of their members. Manufacturers claimed that the KOSC called into question the employer's control of his property and meddled in the affairs of workers who were not its members. A few radical Republicans distrusted the union because it challenged their party's egalitarian notion of a classless society. But Bird Club member and House Clerk William S. Robinson vehemently protested that the KOSC was no different from other societies and business groups that routinely got the lawmakers' approval. In a last-minute, conciliatory gesture toward the angry Crispins, the legislature voted to establish a Bureau of Statistics of Labor to report on the state's labor conditions.[1]

The Crispins were not dissuaded from launching an independent Labor Reform party, which fielded a large slate of candidates in the "off-year" November election. For governor, the new Labor Reform party nominated the pious and well-to-do Edwin N. Chamberlain, a former commander of a GAR post. Chamberlain was identified with the Boston-centered Workingman's party, but was wholly unknown to laborites outside the Hub and was not himself a worker. For lieutenant governor the delegates chose James Cattaway, a machinist in the Springfield Armory. The Labor Reformers demanded a ten-hour workday and the creation of a Department of Labor in Washington to help protect the interests of America's wage earners.[2]

Although the anti-Republican tone of the labor convention delighted many Democrats, not all welcomed a third-party movement. It is true that most Boston labor leaders were Republicans, and Boston's influential labor paper, the *Daily Evening Voice*, was sympathetic to the radical Republicans' Reconstruction goals. However, not all Massachusetts labor reformers, organizations, and papers were pro-Republican. Many Democrats recognized that the new labor party threatened to draw votes away from their party as well. Labor's move into politics in 1869 took both Democrats and Republicans by surprise.[3]

The problems plaguing Republicans led many to question whether the incumbent Governor William Claflin could beat John Quincy Adams, Jr., the perennial Democratic challenger. In 1866 the radical Republicans had been in firm command because of their coherent program to secure the goals the North had fought for in the Civil War. By 1869, however, the radicals had no comprehensive program to deal with the welter of new issues ranging from national monetary policy to town boundary lines. The hypocrisy of the legislature that reinstated the old prohibition law but exempted cider, the railroad lobbies' influence over the lawmakers, and the KOSC disaffection that triggered the third-party movement, threatened to cost the Republicans many votes, if not the election itself. When the Bird Club radicals fell back upon their time-tested strategy of subordinating state issues to national concerns, the Boston *Post* chided them for "raking over [their] negro embers to find warmth in them."[4]

The Massachusetts "new departure" Democrats tried to overcome their image as Confederate sympathizers by dropping their opposition to the "settled results" of the Civil War. They endorsed black suffrage and formulated shrewd resolutions on labor, prohibition, poll-tax, and railroad lobbying issues. They condemned the Republicans for failing to grant the Crispins their charter, for increasing the state debt by extravagant grants, and for thwarting majority sentiment over the liquor question. The Democrats were confident that voter interest in purely local and state issues would be translated into large gains for their party.[5]

The Labor Reformers were also optimistic, and the election results justified their expectations. Their new party, which was effectively organized, captured 10 percent of the ballots cast for governor and elected twenty-two representatives and one senator to the state legislature. Voters in "boot and shoe" cities or towns (a classification based on the largest industrial employer) were over three times more likely to cast ballots for Chamberlain than voters in the state-at-large. In accounting for the differences in the level of support for Chamberlain, the most important factor in an array of explanatory variables was whether a locality was a boot and shoe city or town, with the percentage of employed males engaged in manufacturing close behind (see Tables 7.1 and 7.2). The conclusion is inescapable that the KOSC, the 40,000 member-strong shoemakers' union, furnished the party with the bulk of its supporters. In spite of the KOSC's rule against engaging in political activity, the union and its Labor Reform party threatened to upset the political status quo in Massachusetts in the coming decade.[6]

House Clerk Robinson estimated that two-thirds of Chamberlain's vote was cast by 1868 Republicans. An analysis of voting patterns in

TABLE 7.1
Descriptions, Means, and Standard Deviations of Variables Selected for Stepwise Regression Analysis

Variable Name	Amplified Description	Mean	Standard Deviation
Chamberlain 1869	Percent of electorate voting for the Labor Reform gubernatorial candidate, 1869	5.2	7.6
Phillips	Percent of electorate voting for Wendell Phillips for governor, 1870	8.0	6.8
Pitman	Percent of electorate voting for the Temperance party gubernatorial candidate, 1871	2.3	2.2
Chamberlain 1871	Percent of electorate voting for the Labor Reform gubernatorial candidate, 1871	2.4	3.1
Manufacturing	Percent of occupied males engaged in manufacturing, 1875	29.1	10.1
Agriculture	Estimated percentage of occupied males engaged in agriculture, 1875	10.3	13.2
Fishing	Estimated percentage of occupied males engaged in fishing, 1875	4.2	12.0
"Boot and shoe" towns	Dummy variables for largest industrial employer, 1865: 1 if boot and shoe town; 0 if otherwise	.2	.4
Poll-tax voters	Percent of "legal" voters assessed for a poll tax only in 1869	43.3	16.6
Voters of polls	Percent of "ratable" polls, 1875, who were legal voters, 1875	78.7	9.8
Sex ratio	The number of males in the population divided by the number of females, 1875 (multiplied by 100 to clear the decimal point)	93.2	7.5
Valuation per capita	Value of taxable real and personal property, 1875, divided by population, 1875	1086.5	727.7
Native growth rate	The average annual growth rate (in percentage terms) of the native-born population between 1865 and 1875	2.6	2.8
Foreign growth rate	The average annual growth rate (in percentage terms) of the foreign-born population between 1865 and 1875	5.1	4.1
In-town	Percent of population born in the Massachusetts city or town in which they resided, 1875	37.3	11.5
In-state	Percent of population born in Massachusetts cities or towns other than those in which they resided, 1875	22.8	8.2
Out-of-state	Percent of population born in states other than Massachusetts, 1875	14.7	5.8
Ireland	Percent of population born in Ireland, 1875	13.7	6.7
England & Scotland	Percent of population born in England or Scotland, 1875	4.3	3.7
Canada	Percent of population born in Canada, 1875	5.0	3.7
Germany	Percent of population born in Germany, 1875	1.0	1.2

Sources: Estimations for "Agriculture" and "Fishing" in 1875 are based on extrapolations from the 1865 and 1875 censuses. Voting returns for Chamberlain, Phillips, and Pitman are the official totals. Sources for all other variables are Massachusetts, Bureau of Statistics of Labor, The Census of Massachusetts: 1875, 1:3-8, 273-84, 2:454-77, and Thirteenth Annual Report of the Bureau of Statistics of Labor, Public Doc. 15 (Boston: 1882), pp. 93-192; Massachusetts, General Court, Journal of the House of Representatives, H.Doc. 82 (February 1870), pp. 1-11, and Manual for the Use of the General Court (1876), pp. 183-91; Massachusetts, Secretary of the Commonwealth, Abstract of the Census of Massachusetts, 1865, pp. 56-81, 144-67; U.S. Census Office, The Statistics of the Population of the United States: Ninth Census (1872), 1:165-67. The use of 1870 data on church seating accommodations could have served as a measure of church membership. Unfortunately, the manuscript "Social Statistics" schedules of the 1870 federal census for Massachusetts are incomplete: the reports for all but a dozen towns have been lost or misplaced.

TABLE 7.2
Influence of Explanatory Variables on Support for Labor Reform and Prohibition Endorsed
Gubernatorial Candidates, 1869-1871

Dependent Variable	Explanatory Variables	Simple r	Regression Coefficients	Adjusted Standard Errors of Reg. Coef.	Beta Coefficients	Change in R^2
Chamberlain	"Boot and shoe" towns	.64	.06	.01	.32	.41
(L.Ref.1869)	Manufacturing	.57	.43	.05	.57	.11
[R^2=.61]	England & Scotland	-.18	-.24	.37	-.12	.04
	In-town	.16	.15	.34	.22	.02
	Sex ratio	.18	.00	.00	.13	.01
	Poll-tax voters	.05	.05	.03	.11	.01
	Foreign growth rate	-.16	-.00	.00	-.10	.00
	Ireland	-.10	-.05	.35	-.05	.00
	Canada	.04	.20	.34	.10	.00
	Valuation per capita	-.28	.00	.00	.11	.00
	Native growth rate	-.14	-.00	.00	-.05	.00
	Voters of polls	.15	-.04	.05	-.05	.00
	Germany	-.25	-.12	.45	-.02	.00
	Agriculture	-.13	.02	.03	.03	.00
	Fishing	-.17	-.00	.04	-.00	.00
	Out-of-state	-.07	.09	.35	.07	.00
	In-state	.03	.08	.34	.09	.00
Pitman	Manufacturing	.33	.10	.02	.44	.11
(Pro.1871)	In-town	.21	.19	.14	.98	.09
[R^2=.30]	Fishing	.14	.04	.02	.24	.03
	"Boot and shoe" towns	.31	.01	.00	.11	.02
	Voters of polls	.15	.01	.01	.02	.01
	Valuation per capita	-.15	.00	.00	.23	.01
	Sex ratio	.10	.00	.00	.12	.01
	Native growth rate	-.12	-.00	.00	-.28	.01
	Foreign growth rate	.02	.00	.00	.14	.01
	Agriculture	-.18	-.03	.01	-.17	.00
	Ireland	-.11	.13	.14	.39	.00
	Canada	-.02	.12	.14	.21	.00
	England & Scotland	.01	.20	.15	.34	.00
	In-state	-.05	.17	.14	.65	.00
	Out-of-state	-.16	.17	.14	.44	.00
	Germany	-.18	.18	.18	.10	.00
	Poll-tax voters	.01	-.00	.01	-.00	.00
Phillips	Manufacturing	.59	.33	.04	.49	.35
(L.Ref.&Pro.)	"Boot and shoe" towns	.55	.05	.01	.29	.11
[R^2=.54]	Ireland	-.09	-.06	.31	-.06	.03
	In-state	-.06	.19	.30	.23	.01
	Germany	-.27	-.35	.40	-.06	.01
	Agriculture	-.22	-.07	.03	-.14	.01
	Sex ratio	.11	.00	.00	.12	.01
	Valuation per capita	-.28	.00	.00	.11	.00
	Foreign growth rate	-.02	-.00	.00	-.06	.00
	Voters of polls	.06	-.06	.04	-.08	.00
	Native growth rate	-.06	-.00	.00	-.09	.00
	Poll-tax voters	.06	.03	.03	.06	.00
	Canada	.13	.31	.30	.17	.00
	England & Scotland	.02	.31	.33	.17	.00
	Fishing	-.07	.02	.04	.04	.00
	Out-of-state	-.02	.27	.31	.23	.00
	In-town	.10	.25	.30	.42	.00
Chamberlain	Manufacturing	.49	.11	.02	.35	.24
(L.Ref.1871)	"Boot and shoe" towns	.48	.03	.00	.34	.09
[R^2=.38]	Foreign growth rate	-.10	-.00	.00	-.06	.01
	Poll-tax voters	-.03	-.02	.02	-.09	.01
	Out-of-state	.09	.14	.15	.27	.01
	Voters of polls	.05	-.04	.02	-.13	.00
	England & Scotland	-.06	.02	.16	.02	.00
	Sex ratio	-.00	-.00	.00	-.09	.00
	Valuation per capita	-.28	-.00	.00	-.07	.00
	Native growth rate	-.07	-.00	.00	-.08	.00
	Germany	-.15	.18	.20	.07	.00
	In-town	-.03	.10	.15	.38	.00
	Ireland	-.02	.11	.15	.24	.00
	In-state	.05	.11	.15	.29	.00
	Canada	.05	.11	.15	.13	.00
	Fishing	-.20	.01	.02	.02	.00
	Agriculture	-.10	-.00	.02	-.01	.00

Note: Actual N = 328. Voting units are "weighted" by population in order to ensure that smaller towns are not overrepresented in the analysis. Standard errors, however, are computed according to the original, unweighted number of cities and towns.

the 1868 and 1869 gubernatorial races suggests that approximately 10,500 former Claflin supporters—slightly more than Robinson suspected—had bolted Republican ranks and voted for Chamberlain and the Labor Reform party (see Table 7.3). The remainder of Chamberlain's total came from former Democrats. Altogether, 8 percent of the Massachusetts electorate switched parties between 1868 and 1869. The Boston *Post* congratulated these "independent voters" who had the courage to break from "the paralyzing persuasions of party." In general, the Democrats were pleased with the 1869 results, because Claflin's margin over Adams dropped from a comfortable 68,855 in the 1868 Grant sweep to only 23,371 votes.[7]

Believing that the new Labor Reform party would soon hold the balance of power in state politics, Massachusetts Democrats began to calculate their strategy accordingly. Early in 1870, Democrats in the lower house promised to join in "any arrangement" with the Labor Reformers that would "take power from the Sumner ultraists in the state." Their primary goal was to deny Henry Wilson reelection to the Senate in 1871. The Democrats wanted to unite with the laborites behind a conservative Republican, particularly an old foe of the Bird Club. Nathaniel P. Banks's conversion to the cause of the eight-hour workday made him an ideal leader of an anti-Wilson movement. For the 1870 governor's race, the Democrats were willing to merge ranks with the Labor Reformers if an acceptable "bolting" Republican would take Chamberlain for lieutenant governor on an anti-Republican ticket.[8]

The calculus of Democratic strategy, however, had overlooked a new variable. Encouraged by the success of the laborites in 1869, the prohibitionists decided in 1870 to form their own separate party. At a well-attended convention the antiliquor delegates—described by the Boston *Post* as "primed and cocked, and ready to go off at the least provocation, like a collection of hair-triggers"—agreed to discontinue supporting the Republicans, whom they saw as unable to adopt any firm policy on the liquor issue. The goal of the teetotalers was "the extinction of the entire dram shop system," but they refused to endorse any special statute or law. Wendell Phillips, a temperance advocate for nearly forty years, received their gubernatorial nomination, while Eliphalet Trask, a former Know-Nothing, was their choice for lieutenant governor. Phillips hesitated to accept because he still considered protection of the southern blacks a more important issue than prohibition. Eventually, however, he accepted the Prohibitionist nomination.[9]

Phillips also accepted the Labor Reform party's gubernatorial nomination. Crispin leader S. P. Cummings, an ally of Republican Congressman Benjamin F. Butler and national committee chairman of the

TABLE 7.3
Estimated Relationships Between Voting Patterns in the 1868 and 1869 Gubernatorial Races
(by percent of 1869 electorate)

Candidate in 1869	Candidate in 1868				
	John Q. Adams	William Claflin	Not Voting for Governor 1868	Not Eligible 1868	Percent of 1869 Electorate
John Q. Adams	17	2	0	0	19
William Claflin	1	28	0	0	28
Edwin M. Chamberlain	1	4	0	0	5
Not Voting for Governor 1869	5	17	24	1	47
Percent of 1869 Electorate	24	50	24	2	100

Note: Actual $\underline{N}$ = 332. Rounding procedures occasionally produce totals greater or less than 100 percent.

newly formed National Labor Reform party, explained that, because laboring men were divided or indifferent on the question of prohibition, the Labor Reform party could ignore the liquor issue and nominate Phillips on his record as a proven friend of labor. According to Cummings, the Labor Reformers did not care what other nominations Phillips had received because they were convinced that the crusade for workers' rights commanded his strongest sympathies. Phillips himself resolved his temperance and labor reform goals by affirming that, while intemperance was a cause of poverty, poverty was also a cause of intemperance: "Crowd a man with fourteen hours' work a day and you crowd him down to a mere animal life." [10]

The reactions to Phillips's candidacy among the old abolitionist guard were divided. Lining up behind him were those who thought antislavery organizations still had important work to do after emancipation, but less sympathetic were those who considered the goals of the antislavery movement fulfilled. The latter, led by William Lloyd Garrison, were unable to see any connection between the plights of southern blacks and northern laborers, and they regarded Phillips as a perennial reformer who needed to latch onto a cause. Samuel May, for one, considered the Labor Reformers "idle & noisy men & women, whose maxims are of the most selfish and monopolizing sort & undeserving of respect." Phillips, in May's estimation, was "stirring the workers up to measures wholly at variance with his earlier principles." [11]

Men who had spent so much of their careers fighting slavery did not automatically respond enthusiastically to the claims of workers that they were victims of "wage slavery." Behind the demands of labor reformers lurked the specter of class warfare and special legislation. For both Republicans and Democrats, class consciousness and class action ran counter to an ideal of shared goals between employers and employees. Virtually no prominent Republican or Democrat approved of strikes. Phillips himself shared the view that capital and labor were friends, not foes: "[T]hey are the two parts of one scissors—each useless without the other." Phillips, like most partisans, believed that in any fair economic system there could be no antagonism between employer and wage earner.[12]

Because Phillips had shunned all political involvement in the past, the Democratic Boston *Post* concluded that there was a hidden motive for his sudden leap into politics. Phillips, the newspaper charged, "is consciously, if not deliberately, cooperating with General Butler in shaping the next Legislature on the Senatorial election." The *Post* was correct. Although Phillips did not fully trust Butler, they had collaborated closely after the war. Phillips once stated that he was ready, when "struggling with savage forces" to utilize Butler, "whose original nature is a little like that of the enemy." Furthermore, Phillips's association with Butler was natural because each was trying to bring about a realignment in state politics. As Robinson explained, Phillips was "trying to kill the Republican party from the outside, Butler, from the inside." During the course of the 1870 campaign, Phillips left little doubt that he was paving the way for Butler. In his last speech before the election Phillips exhorted: "Do your duty tomorrow and in another year some of us will get out of the way, and give you the opportunity to elect a real governor."[13]

During the campaign the Bird Club radicals alleged that Crispin leader Cummings was a conduit for bribe money offered by the Hartford and Erie lobby to Labor Reformers in the legislature. Cummings issued a weak retort to the charges. Claiming the railroad operated in the best interest of the working classes that he represented, he swore that he never received a dollar from the lobby, but then admitted that money had been offered for successful passage of bills committing more public funds to the railroad. In effect, only Governor Claflin's dramatic veto of the Hartford and Erie Bill prevented Cummings from collecting his payoff.[14]

Phillips retaliated by equating the Bird Club members with the railroad magnates who influenced state legislatures: If Vanderbilt and Drew ran New York, then "Mr. Bird of Walpole" was the "one great commander-in-chief for the last twenty years of the lobby forces" in Massachusetts. According to Phillips, during meetings at a "grogshop" (Young's Hotel in Boston) on Saturday afternoons, Bird and his associates had determined who would be the state's governor and representatives in Congress and had even drawn up the agenda for the legislature a year in advance. Because Phillips had not responded to the basic issue of Cummings's dealings with the railroad lobby, his attack on the Bird Club seemed pathetic to those who understood the reasons behind it.[15]

Republican party chieftains, however, did not underestimate the impact of Phillips's speech. While they reassured each other that Phillips "knocked some of the moss off the calves of our legs but did not break the skin," they feared his vote-getting power. Even Bird Club member Robinson admitted that no one equaled Phillips on the speaking platform. People liked to hear and see him. His candidacy threatened to attract friends of woman suffrage as well as those of labor reform and prohibition. Many predicted that Phillips would win the support of many Irish-Americans because of his eloquent eulogy of Daniel O'Connell, the great Irish leader who had agitated for Catholic emancipation and repeal of the Act of Union.[16]

At their 1870 state convention the Republicans cautiously straddled the labor reform and liquor issues. The delegates resolved that the Republican party had achieved more for "the laborers of America" than had anyone since 1789, and they registered their "surprise and indignation" that any other party dared claim the title "labor party." They handled the liquor issue by adopting a harmless resolution favoring laws "wisely calculated to prevent tippling and drunkenness." Although they seated Lucy Stone and another suffragist as delegates, the attempt to pass a woman suffrage resolution failed. Robinson's resolution praising Sumner for attempting to eliminate the word "white" from the naturalization laws only tried the patience of the resolutions committee. The party could not afford to further alienate the KOSC, which was already outraged over the importation of Chinese "coolies" to break a strike at a shoe factory in North Adams.[17]

At their convention the Democrats pledged themselves against state-imposed prohibition; against taxes and tariffs levied for any purpose besides revenue; against grants of land, money, or credit by federal or state governments to private groups or corporations; and against stimulating "by artificial means" the introduction into America of "swarms of mongolians." They blamed the "unjust currency system," "arbitrary and excessive taxation," and "great monopolies" for the high cost of living and low wages of workers, and they asserted that workers' best interests resided in their party. They demanded removal of the poll tax as a requirement of voting, but snubbed the advocates of woman suffrage.[18]

The Democratic convention was completely controlled by the so-called "Young Democracy"—Democrats eager to remove from their party the taint of disloyalty acquired during the Civil War. They had mobilized in reaction against the Boston *Post*'s support of Theodore H. Sweetser for governor. Sweetser, a Whig before the war and a southern sympathizer during it, had been in 1866 the National Unionist gubernatorial candidate. He had annoyed his working-class constituents in Lowell by voting against the ten-hour bill and by allegedly taking a bribe from the railroad lobby. The Young Democracy preferred J. Q. Adams who, despite his sincere declination before the convention, was nominated for the fourth consecutive time. Cattaway, the Labor Reform party's candidate for lieutenant governor, was selected for the same position by the Democrats. When Cattaway accepted the Democratic nomination, the Labor Reformers removed his name from their ticket, thus rejecting any move toward collaborating with the Democrats.[19]

In spite of his support by the Young Democracy, Adams was out of step with Democratic positions on the new issues. His private correspondence reveals that he had no conviction whatsoever on the liquor question and had contempt for most labor reformers. Rumors that he failed to appreciate the importance of the Chinese experiment in North Adams led to repeated challenges on the issue. Adams responded by stating that he would be happy if another "heathen Chinee [sic]" never set foot on American soil, because the country already had "a sufficient puzzling race-problem" without adding to it. Turning to philosophical differences between the parties, he equated Republican hegemony with majority usurpation, arguing that the radical Republicans were the Hamiltonian "much government-men" who mistakenly believed that government could "create and bestow positive blessings" upon its citizens. Adams had only disdainful words for the Prohibitionists who would compel men to be abstemious. He claimed, however, that the Labor Reformers belonged in the Democratic party, which stood for freedom of trade, absence of monopolies, and a fair division of profits. Workers, according to Adams, needed the Democratic party to help them accomplish what they could never accomplish by strikes or factory legislation.[20]

The Democrats expected to win as many as 65,100 votes in the 1870 gubernatorial contest, about 6,000 more than Horatio Seymour had polled in the state in the 1868 presidential election. Even the Boston *Commonwealth*, the organ of the Bird Club, conceded nearly this number to Adams. The Springfield *Republican* predicted that Phillips, whose name was on both Labor Reform and Prohibitionist ballots, would receive between 25,000 and 30,000 votes and that two-thirds of this total would be cast by Republicans.[21]

Phillips's vote fell just short of 22,000. As expected, he captured the bulk of the 1869 Labor Reformers (see Table 7.4). The rest of his total came from 1869 Republicans, from previously ineligible voters, and from those who in 1869 had sat out the balloting for governor. Labor Reformers who did not vote for Phillips preferred Adams to Claflin. Adams polled a respectable 48,680 votes, but fell far short of most expectations.

Because Claflin ran behind the Republican candidate for lieutenant governor and over 8,000 votes behind Republican congressional candidates, the unavoidable conclusion was that he had been "scratched" from Republican ballots in areas upset over his Hartford and Erie veto (see Table 7.5). Claflin's 53 percent of the popular vote represented the worst showing ever by a Republican gubernatorial candidate in a congressional election year. Although Republicans managed to win every congressional race, many were close, and they lost ground in almost all ten districts. Roughly one-eighth of the 1868 Republican congressional vote went to Democrats or Labor Reformers in 1870 (see Table 7.6). The combination of reduced Republican majorities and increased display of voter independence, as evidenced by the number of split tickets in the gubernatorial and congressional races, was an ominous sign for the Republicans.[22]

Among explanatory variables having a relatively large positive impact on the average level of turnout for Phillips were, in order of significance, the percentage of males engaged in manufacturing and knowledge of whether a community's largest employer was the boot and shoe industry (see Table 7.2). Phillips, it is estimated, ran better among industrial workers than did either Adams or Claflin (see Table 7.7). His strong showing in the boot and shoe towns was directly attributable to the appeal of his candidacy among 1869 Labor Reform party supporters (see Table 7.4). The estimates suggest that Phillips's total vote could easily have been drawn entirely from the support he received from workingmen.

Because Phillips received 40 percent of his total vote from those who cast "straight" Prohibitionist party ballots, the votes of factory workers, although not necessarily ballots cast by shoemakers, reflected to some degree Prohibitionist support for Phillips's candidacy.[23] Many industrial workers presumably voted the Prohibitionist ticket as a way of demonstrating their endorsement of their employer's argument that intemperance militated against factory discipline. Workingmen who supported temperance reform societies launched by their employers often found themselves estranged from their counterparts who went on periodic binges, expected rum rations on the job, and had lackadai-

TABLE 7.4
Estimated Relationships Between Voting Patterns in the 1869 and 1870 Gubernatorial Races
(by percent of 1870 electorate)

| Candidate in 1870 | Candidate in 1869 | | | | | |
	John Q. Adams	William Claflin	Edwin M. Chamberlain	Not Voting for Governor 1869	Not Eligible 1869	Percent of 1870 Electorate
John Q. Adams	14	0	1	2	1	18
William Claflin	1	20	0	7	1	29
Wendell Phillips	0	3	3	1	1	8
Not Voting for Governor 1870	3	4	1	35	2	45
Percent of 1870 Electorate	18	27	5	45	5	100

Note: Actual N = 332.

TABLE 7.5
Estimates of Split-Ticket Voting in the 1870 General Election:
The Gubernatorial and Congressional Races
(by percent of 1870 electorate)

| Party in 1870 Congressional Election | Party in 1870 Gubernatorial Election | | | | |
	Democratic	Republican	Labor Reform	Not Voting for Governor 1870	Percent of 1870 Electorate
Democratic	16	0	2	0	18
Republican	2	26	2	2	32
Labor Reform	0	1	3	0	4
Not Voting in 1870 Congressional election	0	2	1	43	47
Percent of 1870 Electorate	18	29	8	45	100

Note: Actual N = 333.

sical attitudes toward work. Phillips, moreover, had been perceived as a "stand-in" candidate for Butler, who demanded impartial enforcement of the state's prohibitory law and postured increasingly as a friend of the Bay State workingman.[24]

In the summer of 1871, Butler, in an unprecedented manner, publicly announced his intention to seek the Republican gubernatorial nomination. He denounced Governor Claflin and called for reform in the legislature, changes in the laws, and revitalization of his party. Very few voting blocs escaped Butler's attention. He used sharp class rhetoric to denounce capitalists who exploited the labor of honest workingmen. He promised to enforce prohibition laws. He championed woman suffrage. Radicals were attracted by his support of federal laws to protect southern black voters and to outlaw the Ku Klux Klan. The Irish ap-

TABLE 7.6
Estimated Relationships between Voting Patterns in the 1868 and 1870 Congressional Races
(by percent of 1870 electorate)

| Party in 1870 | Party in 1868 | | | | | |
	Democratic	Republican	All Others	Not Voting 1868 Congressional Election	Not Eligible 1868	Percent of 1870 Electorate
Democratic	15	3	0	0	0	18
Republican	2	28	0	1	1	32
Labor Reform	0	3	0	1	0	4
Not Voting in 1870 Congressional Election	5	15	1	21	5	47
Percent of 1870 Electorate	22	48	1	23	6	100

Note: Actual N = 329.

TABLE 7.7
Estimated Voting Preferences of Industrial Workers in the 1870
Gubernatorial Election
(by percent)

Percent of Industrial Workers Favoring:

Wendell Phillips (Lab. Ref. & Pro.)	31%
William Claflin (Rep.)	27
John Q. Adams (Dem.)	16
Not voting for governor in 1870	26
Total	100

Note: Actual N = 329. Estimation of the percentage of occupied males engaged in manufacturing in 1870 was based on extrapolations from the 1865 and 1875 state censuses. The regression equations included similar estimates of the percentage of males engaged in fishing and agricultural pursuits. The percentage engaged in all other categories was omitted to avoid multicollinearity problems.

preciated his belligerent stand toward England, Civil War veterans knew they could always count on his support, and fishermen were attracted by his hard line toward Canada. Common people liked his gutsy, flamboyant, combative style of debate and his refusal to straddle a controversial issue. Even his enemies acknowledged that few could match Butler's quick wit and skillful repartee as a stump-speaker.[25]

By actively campaigning for the nomination, Butler broke the unwritten rule decreeing that openly seeking office demonstrated unsuitability for any position of public trust. A would-be candidate, according to custom, discreetly told his friends of his goals and then feigned indifference to possible advancement. Butler's lack of inhibition against "self-electioneering" led his opponents to denounce him as a powerful machine politician. But Butler's putative "machine" was never more than a derisive label for his unorthodox campaign style. As

Butler's popularity grew among the people and as his influence increased in Washington, so did the specious allegations about his political ethics.[26]

The Butler canvass in 1871 shook the Bay State Republican party to its depths. Controversy between President Grant and Sumner over Santo Domingo had increased Sumner's political isolation and Butler, to the surprise of many, had enhanced his power by acquiring a strong influence over Grant. Few Republicans could ignore the rapidly forming battle lines with Butler and Grant on one side, and Sumner and his allies in the Bird Club on the other, especially after Sumner lost the chairmanship of the Senate Foreign Relations Committee. In response to the allegation that he was recklessly breaking up the state party, Butler retorted that the current leadership had already driven away the reform element led by Phillips. Butler explained his alienation from the Sumner radicals by claiming that the Bird Club members—or the "State House Ring" as he called them—had always held him at arm's length when he dined in their company because of personal jealousy and spite.[27]

Conservative Republicans who had once felt the sting of attack from Sumner's political allies watched the unfolding confrontation between Butler and Sumner with unconcealed delight. Although the Republican Boston *Daily Advertiser* sought to discredit Butler's career and character, the paper's editor, Peleg W. Chandler, admitted privately that Butler was just the man to destroy "those scoundrels at Young's Hotel." Chandler predicted that one of Bird's frequent dinner guests, Governor Claflin, could not possibly survive Butler's attack: "Poor Claflin—a dead Ass." Banks confided that he was also glad that it was Butler, "the man—who[m] they [Bird and Sumner] built up to destroy other men—who now beats their brains out." Sumner's friends, who in the past had valued Butler for his radicalism, were among those whom Banks declared "had been, with so much insincerity, so long praising him" and who now "have to eat their words."[28]

The Democratic leadership had a very low opinion of Butler, regarding him as "a renegade politician and a party adventurer." Yet Butler's unprecedented canvass gave the Democrats plenty of ammunition. The 1871 Democratic platform reiterated many of Butler's charges against Governor Claflin. The pro-Democratic press gave Butler credit for revealing how the conclave at Bird's dinner table had governed the Commonwealth through an expensive machinery of boards, bureaus, and commissions. Surely Butler had known, the Democrats pointed out, what transpired at Young's Hotel on Saturday afternoons.[29]

The leadership of both the Democratic and Republican parties, the state's respectable citizenry, and almost every newspaper in the state opposed Butler. With Grant's help, however, Butler moved ahead, lining up delegates behind his candidacy. He controlled most federal appointments, and his willingness to take an unequivocal stand on issues won him strong popular support. He believed that the Fourteenth and Fifteenth amendments had robbed Republicans of their distinctive position on equal rights, leaving no single issue to keep their supporters together. Therefore, in his quest for the nomination, he felt justified in making special appeals to many different segments of the electorate. Had Butler abided by the rules of the game and acceded to the traditional politics of deference and detachment, he never would have had a chance for the Republican nomination.[30]

Historians have assumed that Butler's supporters included Irish-Americans, factory workers, veterans, fishermen, inflationists, woman suffragists, blacks, and even "members of the politically dispossessed" and many "who sought in politics a personal reward."[31] Some of these groups formed significant voting blocs which, to some degree, can be measured. Therefore, the bases of support for Butler and Republican congressional candidates-at-large can be compared (see Table 7.8). In 1870 about 30 percent of the eligible voters in the Fifth Congressional District (Essex County) cast ballots for Butler, compared with a similar percentage of voter support for Republican congressional candidates statewide. Butler fared slightly better than average among Irish-Americans, fishermen, and those living in the town where they were born, but ran no better than average among workers, farmers, and poll-tax voters. The largest discrepancy between the profiles of support for Butler and all Republican candidates occurred among former Democrats. For every 1868 Democrat captured in 1870 by Republicans statewide, Butler attracted three former Democrats in his district.[32] Yet these minor differences should not be allowed to obscure the remarkable similarity of Butler's support to that of his party. Butler was perceived as different only after he began his campaign for the governorship, with its appeals to different constituencies.

The Sumner wing of the Republican party anxiously sought allies for the inevitable showdown with Butler at the 1871 state convention. The Bird Club knew that the positions of influential Grant supporters, such as George F. Hoar and Henry L. Dawes, would be crucial in a movement to stop Butler. The decision was easy for Hoar. His brother, Ebenezer Rockwood Hoar, was dismissed as attorney general because of Butler's influence with Grant. Dawes, however, was not eager to be used by the Bird Club to check Butler's growing power. He informed Edward L. Pierce, a close friend of Sumner, that he would not consent

TABLE 7.8
Comparative Estimated Support in 1870 for Butler
and All Republican Congressional Candidates

	Percentage Turnout in 1870 for:	
Description of Voters	Benjamin F. Butler	All Republican Congressional Candidates
Poll-tax voters	20%	25%
Irish-born	27	23
English-born	100[a]	91
Other foreign-born	0[a]	0[a]
Born in town in which residing in 1870	29	22
Born in Massachusetts, but not in town in which residing in 1870	20	41
Born in United States, but outside Massachusetts	43	50
Engaged in manufacturing	36	36
Engaged in agriculture	42	48
Engaged in fishing	24	12
Engaged in all other occupations	22	24
Those who voted for Democratic congressional candidates in 1868	33	10
Those who voted for Republican congressional candidates in 1868	37	57
1868 eligibles who did not vote for any congressional candidate in 1868	13	3
"New" or previously ineligible voters	10	22
Among All Voters	29%[b]	32%[b]

Note: For the Fifth Congressional District (Essex County),
actual $\underline{N}$ = 26; for the state-at-large, actual $\underline{N}$ = 328.

[a]Logically impossible estimates of voting have been set at
the 0 or 100 percent limits.

[b]Actual, not estimated, voting preferences of all potentially
eligible voters.

to having his name circulated as a possible gubernatorial candidate. In spite of a clash with Butler in Congress over federal spending, Dawes sought early in 1871 to establish peaceful relations with Butler. Sumner's friends would not be able to take Dawes's support for granted.[33]

Nevertheless, Dawes was reluctantly drawn into the "stop-Butler" movement. Pressure on Dawes came primarily from Samuel Bowles, his long-time personal friend and editor of the Springfield *Republican*. Bowles believed that Dr. George B. Loring, Claflin's chief rival for the party's gubernatorial nomination in past years, was supporting Butler's bid for the governorship in return for assistance in securing the Essex County congressional seat. Bowles threatened that he would never forgive Dawes if Butler became governor and Loring took Butler's place in Congress. If Dawes failed either to seek the nomination himself or to lead the stop-Butler movement, then Bowles would advise Dawes to place his "order for a political coffin" before leaving again for Washington. When Dawes finally agreed to lead the anti-Butler forces at the convention, many heaved a sigh of relief. Pierce wrote Claflin that Dawes's decision was "worth one or two hundred votes."[34]

Sumner personally convinced Wilson to join in a public statement announcing that both Massachusetts senators "deeply regret and deplore the extraordinary canvass which Gen. Butler has precipitated upon the Commonwealth . . . and that in their opinion, his name as governor would be hostile to the best intersts of the Commonwealth and the Republican party." Wilson, Sumner, and Claflin timidly stayed away from the Republican convention, leaving Hoar and Dawes to engineer the gubernatorial nomination of William B. Washburn, a conservative congressman from the western part of the state. The vote was close and, as Wendell Phillips remarked, Butler supporters were the only delegates "whose knees did not tremble" during the balloting.[35]

Contrary to some delegates' expectations, Butler submitted gracefully to his defeat and the Republicans remained ostensibly united. But the damage was done: the party leadership had split wide open. Sumner and Butler were now open enemies. The focus of power in the party had shifted from Sumner and his allies to Hoar and Dawes. Wilson, however, sought to avoid further war with Butler. Emphatically denying that he once referred to Butler's followers as "scum," Wilson told Butler that had he let the governorship seek him and not vice versa, and had he only refrained from attacking Claflin, he would have received the nomination. Wilson urged Butler to make amends for past mistakes: "Now you can right this,—silence assaults,—disarm opposition,—do good,—win influence and power & make—not a sensation— but a high character. Now do it General." In the future Wilson would play the role of chief conciliator between warring factions in the state party.[36]

There was speculation that many Butler men, rather than voting the Democratic ticket, would simply sit out the 1871 election, thus greatly reducing the Republican vote. Some of Butler's supporters indicated that they would register their disappointment by voting the Labor Reform party ticket.[37] Neither of these predictions materialized. About one-fourth of the 1870 Republicans sat out the balloting in 1871, but this was normal for an off-year election. Chamberlain, running on the Labor Reform party ticket, failed to attract any significant number of 1870 Republicans (see Table 7.9).

The constituency of the Labor Reform party in 1871 dwindled to less

TABLE 7.9
Estimated Relationships Between Voting Patterns in the 1870 and 1871 Gubernatorial Races
(by percent of 1871 electorate)

Candidate in 1871[a]	Candidate in 1870					
	John Q. Adams	William Claflin	Wendell Phillips	Not Voting for Governor 1870	Not Eligible 1870	Percent of 1871 Electorate
John Q. Adams	13	2	1	0	1	17
William B. Washburn	4	18	1	1	1	26
Edwin M. Chamberlain	0	0	2	0	0	2
Robert C. Pitman	0	0	2	0	0	2
Not Voting for Governor 1871	0	7	2	42	3	53
Percent of 1871 Electorate	17	28	8	43	5	100

Note: Actual N = 332.

[a]Benjamin F. Butler received an inconsequential 157 votes for governor in 1871.

than half of its 1869 size, although the party's socioeconomic basis of support had not changed significantly from the year of its electoral debut (see Table 7.2). The weak political clout of the Prohibitionists was also exposed in 1871 when, without the benefit of fusion with the Labor Reformers, the "Temperance party" ran Judge Robert C. Pitman of New Bedford for the governorship. Although the percentage of males employed in manufacturing was the best single predictor of the differences in levels of support for Pitman, the percentage of people living in the same city or town in which they were born also had a significant positive impact on Pitman's vote. This suggests that the political movement for total prohibition struck a responsive chord among local long-term residents who were perhaps more aware than comparative newcomers of the profound changes that had occurred in their hometowns over the years. In the midst of problems caused by rapid social and economic change, the temperance movement often sought to create a greater sense of community by enforcing total prohibition. On the other hand, towns with small proportions of long-term residents and high levels of relative newcomers may have been less receptive to the temperance movement because they lacked members of an old, permanent class with established social ties.[38]

Neither the subsequent shredding of the coalition of voters assembled by Phillips nor the waning of third-party efforts accounted for all the electoral volatility in 1871. Surprisingly, Washburn and the Republicans ran very well among former Democrats, capturing almost one-fourth of the 1870 Democrats and approximately one-sixth of the 1869 Democrats (see Tables 7.9 and 7.10). These Democratic losses were offset, to some extent, by Adams's capture of some former Claflin

TABLE 7.10
Estimated Relationships Between Voting Patterns in the 1869 and 1871 Gubernatorial Races
(by percent of 1871 electorate)

Candidate in 1871[a]	Candidate in 1869					
	John Q. Adams	William Claflin	Edwin M. Chamberlain	Not Voting for Governor 1869	Not Eligible 1869	Percent of 1871 Electorate
John Q. Adams	11	2	1	1	2	17
William B. Washburn	3	16	1	4	1	26
Edwin M. Chamberlain	1	1	1	0	0	2
Robert C. Pitman	0	1	1	1	0	2
Not Voting for Governor 1871	3	6	1	37	6	53
Percent of 1871 Electorate	18	26	5	43	9	100

Note: Actual N = 332.

[a]Benjamin F. Butler received an inconsequential 157 votes for governor in 1871.

supporters. Altogether, roughly 11 percent of the Massachusetts electorate crossed party lines between the off-year gubernatorial elections of 1869 and 1871, attesting to the new unpredictability in Bay State electoral politics.

It was not a coincidence that the Bird Club's influence and the electoral stability of the 1860s ended during Grant's first term. The former consensus among radicals on Reconstruction issues was shattered by intraparty factionalism. The Bird Club members allowed their dislike of Grant and Butler to influence their positions on the southern question. Sumner's allies interpreted the controversy between Grant and Sumner, not as an isolated personal conflict, but as one with far-reaching implications. For example, they considered Sumner's removal from the chairmanship of the Foreign Relations Committee as an alarming display of executive power to crush senatorial independence. Some Bird Club members even regarded Ku Klux Klan outrages in the South as far less dangerous than what they perceived as a trend toward personal government. Bird feared that legislation against the Klan would perpetuate the Grant administration and Robinson spoke openly of forming a new political party to oppose Grant. The fabric of Massachusetts politics was fast unraveling.[39]

Chapter 8
The Liberal Republican Movement and the Eclipse of Radicalism

I cannot name in public the name of Charles Sumner and the words of eulogy not spring, unbidden, to the lips. . . . But we cannot give up our judgment even to his. . . . Mr. Sumner in a recent speech and letters has done a great wrong to the President, has done a great wrong to you, and a greater wrong than all to himself.—*George F. Hoar, Address to the Grant and Wilson Club of Worcester, 13 August 1872*

"In another form, and with another feeling," wrote an elated Samuel Bowles, the influential editor of the Springfield *Republican*, the Liberal Republican movement "is a know-nothing movement over again." Bowles, an early champion of the 1872 Cincinnati convention, understandably might exaggerate the extent to which the anti-Grant movement had reached the people. In Massachusetts, however, it was definitely not a grass-roots movement comparable to the Know-Nothing excitement that took the old parties by surprise in 1854. The Liberal Republican movement was, in contrast, a classic example of elites trying to generate enthusiasm for reform "from the top down."[1]

The "Liberals" represented a consolidation of prominent men with varied motives for opposing Grant's reelection. Many disaffected Republicans in 1872 stood for any one or any combination of the following: tariff reduction, free trade, civil service reform, efficient and honest government, and sectional harmony or "conciliation" between the northern and southern states, which meant amnesty for former Confederates and abandonment of continued federal support for the Republican governments in the South. The Liberals rationalized their position on these issues by drawing on the tenets of nineteenth-century Manchester liberalism that stressed laissez-faire economics and limited government, giving the entire movement the semblance of a common philosophical scaffolding. Few Liberal Republicans were concerned with the plight of immigrants in the urban slums or with the grim daily lot of factory workers. Bowles, for one, was hostile to the labor movement, believing it to be nothing more than a conspiracy of men wrongfully attempting to impose its own terms on employers. This suggests that a few self-styled Liberals might have found in the Liberal Republican movement a refuge from such unwelcomed consequences of radical Republican ideology as the revitalization of the labor movement, which threatened to overthrow the status quo in their own communities after the Civil War.[2]

Sorting out the motives of individual Liberal Republicans is a complicated task. Many Liberals advocated that government at all levels should be controlled by men of ancient Yankee ancestry or by "respectable" men who were honest, disinterested, and incorruptible—presumably men like themselves. In their view Republican Congressman Benjamin F. Butler was the embodiment of the ambitious "spoilsman" they self-righteously denounced. The same men doubted that the Republican "carpetbag" regimes entrenched in the former Confederacy were in the hands of the "best men." An aversion to Butler's brand of politics and a suspicion of the quality of the southern Republican governments, combined with a disgust with corruption in the Grant administration, were shared by virtually all Liberals. But not all had acquired these sensitivities through reading the works of John Stuart Mill, or through fear of unchecked egalitarianism as manifested by the increasing class-consciousness of industrial workers, or even through a crotchety aristocratic disgruntlement with the nouveau riche.[3]

In Massachusetts, the Liberal Republican movement grew out of the political infighting among Republican leaders following the 1868 presidential election. Frank Bird believed in free trade and was lukewarm in his support for labor reform measures, but his decision to bolt from the Republican party stemmed from his refusal to overlook the unjust treatment that Charles Sumner received from the Grant administration after his opposition to Santo Domingo annexation. Bird initially was followed into the Liberal Republican movement by most of his political allies, including William S. Robinson, Franklin B. Sanborn, Elizur Wright, and Charles G. Davis. Robinson, who with Bird called for a convention of Liberals, reasoned that an end had to be put to Grant's attempt to saddle Republicans with a "personal party" even if it meant risking a Democratic capture of the White House. Not all of the surviving original members of the Bird Club, however, joined the call for a new party after it became clear in the spring of 1872 that the Republicans would renominate Grant. Sumner himself refused to participate in the Liberal Republican convention; also conspicuously absent from Bird's side were Samuel Gridley Howe and Charles Wesley Slack.[4]

The Liberals believed that unless Sumner publicly pronounced against Grant's reelection the movement for a new party would collapse in Massachusetts and elsewhere. Pressure on Sumner came from Bowles, David A. Wells, and his long-time allies in the Bird Club. Bird expressed most cogently the exasperation of the Liberals with Sumner's silence. Sumner's continued failure to openly denounce Grant, according to Bird, was an inexcusable political blunder because the battle against him organized by Butler and Grant was nothing less than "one of extermination."[5]

At the same time Bird was pleading with Sumner to lead the Liberal Republicans, he was trying to undercut a movement to nominate Charles Francis Adams, Sumner's old antagonist, for the presidency on a Liberal Republican ticket. The torch for Adams was carried by Bowles, who turned his influential newspaper into a vehicle for promoting Adams as a presidential candidate. The mere mention of Adams as presidential timber elicited caustic comments from members of the old abolitionist leadership. The majority of surviving abolitionists were extremely critical of the Liberal movement. In 1872, most of them endorsed Grant's reelection because they feared that Liberal rhetoric about conciliation of the South meant abandonment of federal protection of the freedmen.[6]

Although Adams led all others on the first ballot at the Cincinnati convention, the assiduous efforts of Whitelaw Reid and Theodore Tilton on behalf of Horace Greeley, plus the political engineering on the convention floor by the Blair family, Reuben Fenton, Samuel McClure, and B. Gratz Brown, gave Greeley the nomination on the sixth ballot. Greeley's nomination came as a mild surprise but brought a sense of relief to many Massachusetts Republican party regulars; a Greeley candidacy posed no serious threat to Grant and presented far less of a threat in their districts than an Adams candidacy. "The whole thing, convention, platform, and nomination," concluded a political operative of Congressman Henry L. Dawes, "is simply a broad farce." Indeed, any consideration of Greeley for the presidency would have been written off as ridiculous in Massachusetts in any year before 1872. But Greeley benefited considerably from the Liberal consensus on reconciliation with the South, a cause his New York *Tribune* had championed after Grant's election.[7]

In accepting the Liberal Republican nomination, Greeley proclaimed that he would make Grant's "repressive Southern policy" the main issue in the campaign, believing "that the masses of our countrymen,

North and South, are eager to clasp hands across the bloody chasm which has too long divided them." Greeley argued that universal amnesty would prevent partisan divisions in the South from forming along strictly racial lines and would encourage the growth of a southern Republican party led by wealthy whites. With the spotlight on Greeley and sectional reconciliation, issues such as tariff reduction and civil service reform faded into the background. Greeley himself was an exponent of protectionism and was relatively indifferent to the alleged abuses in the dispensing of patronage. Textile manufacturer Edward Atkinson, who supported a lobbying effort in Washington to push a tariff reform bill through Congress, was bitterly disappointed over the selection of Greeley. Atkinson, whether nobly or foolishly, had resisted the offer of the secretaryship of the treasury in exchange for his support of Gratz Brown for president. To many original Liberals like Atkinson, it appeared that their reform movement had been raided by professional politicians. Atkinson subsequently voted for Grant because he believed the tariff reduction issue had been traded away at Cincinnati.[8]

Greater disillusionment with Greeley was generated by his emphasis on amnesty and home rule as the primary focuses of Liberal Republicanism. After the Democratic national convention endorsed him, some Liberals believed that their movement was a stalking horse for a Democratic party takeover of the presidency. Robinson, who with Bird had cast his fate with the Cincinnati convention, became convinced that Greeley's election would usher in a successful white conservative counterrevolution against Reconstruction. The pro-Grant press repeatedly played on the suspicion of many voters that Liberal Republican collusion with the Democrats meant a betrayal of the freedmen. What else, implied the Boston *Daily Evening Transcript*, could "reconciliation" really mean?[9]

Even though the sectional issue proved to be a liability for Liberal Republicanism in Massachusetts, Bird had set his course and was determined to continue the crusade against "Grantism." Nor did Bird recoil from clasping hands with the Democrats—a strategy he termed "our old coalitional tactics," in reference to Free-Soil party collaboration with the Democrats against the dominant Whigs in the early 1850s. He also liked to compare the 1872 revolt in Republican ranks with his own bolt in 1848 from the Whig party into the new Free-Soil party. The prospect of Greeley being thoroughly beaten was of small consequence to Bird if the Liberal Republican crusade against "personal politics" eventually emerged victorious. As in the past, the cause and not the party was everything. In 1854, 1856, and 1857, Bird had been on the losing side, a member of the most dismal electoral minorities; but still he had managed to emerge triumphant without having to compromise his principles.[10]

Under pressure from Bird and others, Sumner finally announced publicly his support for Greeley's candidacy. His endorsement came in a reply to an open letter written to him by a group of blacks in the District of Columbia asking for his opinion of Grant and Greeley. Sumner rationalized his position by writing that Grant's southern policy was too repressive because it alienated southern whites and too lax because it allowed civil disorder and violence to occur. Sumner also claimed that Greeley was a better friend of the freedmen because he had been an earlier convert to the antislavery cause than Grant. Although inconsistencies in his arguments must have troubled Sumner himself, this was the utterance that the Liberals had been waiting for. With Sumner on their side, it would be easier to counter the charge that all Republicans supporting Greeley had deserted the fight to secure justice for southern blacks.[11]

To nullify the impact of Sumner's endorsement of Greeley, the Republican Boston *Daily Journal* asked former abolitionist William Lloyd Garrison to write a review of Sumner's letter to the Washington blacks. Garrison charged that Sumner had abandoned the great struggle for equality, and that Greeley's Democratic allies "have *not* become converts to the principles of the Republican party—they are simply in masquerade!" Privately, Garrison believed that Sumner had stained his entire career "beyond eradication" by attacking Grant and giving aid and comfort to former rebels and Copperheads. The pro-Grant forces also enlisted Wendell Phillips. Responding to a group of Boston blacks on the conflicting positions of Sumner and Garrison, Phillips proclaimed that Greeley's election would mean "the constitutional amendment neutralized by a copperhead Congress" and "the [N]egro surrendered to the hate of the Southern states." He took the opportunity to counsel the freedmen: "Vote, every one of you for Grant, if you value property, life, wife, or child. If Greeley is elected, arm, concentrate, conceal your property, but organize for defense. You will need it."[12]

One of the puzzling events in the 1872 campaign was Republican Congressman Nathaniel P. Banks's declaration for Greeley. In the 1850s, Banks had led the conservative and nativist wing of the Republican party, and during the Civil War he had never concurred with radical opinion. By the spring of 1871, Banks concluded that six more years of Grant would be fatal to the Republican party; but he hesitated to join the ranks of the Liberals, perhaps because of his antipathy to his old political enemies, Bird and his associates. Thus, Banks's decision to join Sumner and Bird in support of Greeley took many by surprise. In a public letter announcing his break with the Republican party, Banks declared that Greeley's candidacy represented the "unity of the masses of the people of all parties, sections, and races, in support of the grand results of the war." Bird immediately hailed Banks's letter as a "timely and effective utterance."[13]

While Banks's course of action in 1872 was consistent with his conservative views on Reconstruction issues, other factors propelled him into the Liberal Republican camp. Since the end of the Civil War his political career had been stagnating. Grant had not offered him a position in his cabinet, had circumvented him as chairman of the House Foreign Affairs Committee in foreign policy matters, and had failed to work with him in making political appointments. In bolting for Greeley, Banks again was at the center of attention. He was soon talking to Sumner of "carrying Massachusetts." His initial optimism waned, however, as the November election drew closer.[14]

Another surprise, in the summer of 1872, came when Butler refused to be a candidate for the Republican gubernatorial nomination. Because he had made a strong bid for the nomination the previous year, many assumed Butler would redouble his efforts in 1872, especially when the Liberals who had opposed him previously now stayed away from the "regular" Republican caucuses. Although Butler stated that his candidacy would only further split the Republican party, there were other reasons for his decision not to run again. Butler's allies could not unconditionally guarantee that they could secure the Republican nomination for him in a presidential election year. Rather than risk another defeat, he declined the candidacy. Butler later claimed that if he had tried he would have won, but in the higher interest of party unity he had decided not to try at all. He also faced the problem of finding an issue upon which to run against an incumbent governor who belonged to the same party and who had done nothing to offend leading Liberal Republicans like Sumner, Banks, Bird, Adams, and Bowles. Under William B. Washburn's administration, $3 million of the funded debt had been paid off and few could charge, as they did the previous administration, that the state's finances had been inefficiently and uneconomically managed.[15]

Washburn was easily renominated at the Republican state convention, which also declared for Grant and his running mate, Henry Wilson of Massachusetts. The convention recognized few new issues; instead, most of its time was consumed by speakers who glorified the party's past accomplishments. Developments at the Liberal Republican and Democratic conventions were less predictable. The Liberals and Democrats held separate conventions in Worcester, but a committee from both conferred and agreed on a joint slate of candidates that both conventions accepted enthusiastically. Then, a combined convention of the Liberals and Democrats supported the principles that had been framed at Cincinnati and approved by the Democratic national convention, attacked the Grant administration, and endorsed Greeley.[16]

In a surprise move Sumner was nominated for the governorship. Many observers believed that, because of the ill-feelings between Sumner and Adams, both of them had been dismissed from consideration beforehand. Speculation quickly arose that outside pressure had forced Sumner's nomination in an attempt to give "some sort of éclat" to the Greeley cause in other states. Sumner heard the news of his nomination while he was out of the country, and immediately wired Bird his formal declination statement. Privately, he chastised Bird for consenting to such a ploy, and told Bird he would rely on him to withdraw his name; only by continuing as senator, he explained, could he maintain the political independence needed to fight the battle against Grant and Butler.[17]

Only the most imaginative minds in 1871 could have predicted that a radical Republican would be the gubernatorial candidate of the Massachusetts Democratic party in 1872. Upon Sumner's refusal to be a candidate, Bird received the "Liberal Republican and Democratic" nomination for the governorship. Bird was selected at a joint meeting of the state committees empowered to fill any vacancies on the ticket that might open up. Former Republican George H. Monroe, a long-time friend of Bird, was also on the Liberal Republican and Democratic ticket as the nominee for secretary of state. Admittedly, the ticket was a disappointment to many Democratic politicians, who were keenly aware of the disproportionate numerical strength of their party in the coalition. Bird was not a favorite among the Democratic rank and file or with many Liberal Republicans, including Adams, Bowles, and William Schouler. Bird, it will be recalled, had helped to engineer the "slaughter" of Adams at Cincinnati. Consequently, Bowles could not bring himself to support Bird in the pages of the Springfield *Republican*. Nor was his newspaper interested in avenging Sumner. The *Republican* championed the Liberal Republican movement because, according to its editor, it wanted to protest against a party turned into a mere political machine.[18]

The Liberal Republican/Democratic and regular Republican ballots were the only two passed out at the polling places. The "straight" Democratic ticket appeared in 23 of the 37 states, but it was not circulated in Massachusetts even though John Quincy Adams, Jr., received the vice-presidential nomination of the Louisville convention of Democratic bolters. Nor was there a Prohibitionist party ballot. There was considerable disenchantment with the national Prohibition party ticket among Massachusetts teetotalers, and Governor Washburn consistently had expressed his support of prohibition. Thus, the state Prohibitionist party decided not to endorse a slate of candidates. Because the machinations of presidential politics had destroyed the National Labor Reform party, the state Labor Reform party did not field a separate ticket. At their convention in Charlestown the Massachusetts laborites endorsed Leopold Morse, a Jewish clothing merchant, for Congress from the Fourth District and Banks from the Fifth District. In addition, a few nominations were made for the state senate in Essex and Middlesex counties and for state representatives in Suffolk County.[19]

The chief labor issue in the 1872 campaign was the laxity in the enforcement of the national eight-hour law limiting the workday of laborers employed by the federal government. Although enforced in the Charlestown Navy Yard and at the Springfield Armory, the law was ignored by public officials in many cities where large government buildings, such as post offices, were under construction. In the spring and summer of 1872 there was considerable labor unrest. Numerous small strikes and lockouts occurred throughout the state, but the building trades were the most active. Having reorganized their unions, they seemed on the verge of striking for the eight-hour system. The Liberal Republicans touted Greeley's prolabor credentials and claimed that the workingmen would instinctively recognize him as a proven friend. The Republicans responded by presenting Wilson, Grant's running mate, as "the father of the Eight Hour Labor Bill." Wilson's and Greeley's positions on the liquor question tended to cancel out any clear advantage one of the parties might have had among the Prohibitionist voting bloc: both repeatedly had expressed their support of total prohibition by the enactment and enforcement of law.[20]

At first glance, Grant's decisive, if not overwhelming, victory over Greeley seems to indicate that an insignificant number of Republicans defected to the opposition in 1872, certainly less than the number who would bolt in 1884 in the famous Mugwump revolt against their party's nomination of James G. Blaine. Consequently, historians have interpreted the results of 1872 as a victory for the status quo, implying that party lines held firm as the electorate failed to respond to any of the newer issues. Such an interpretation assumes that, beyond the small group that withdrew from the original Bird Club, Sumner had virtually no following. Sumner himself, it appears, even accepted the postelection judgment of Republican "Stalwarts" that his quarrel with the president never affected the rank-and-file members of his party.[21]

At the top of the Republican party pyramid, relatively few influential Republicans bolted for Greeley. Many Mugwumps, or Independent Republicans, who deserted their party in 1884 were not even lukewarm in their support of Greeley in 1872. Boston businessman John Murray Forbes was such an individual. The "newer" issues, such as corruption in Grant's administration, civil service reform, tariff reform, or even "Butlerism," never took precedence in Forbes's mind over the need for continued federal protection of the freedmen. While traveling in the South immediately after the war, Forbes witnessed at first hand the rise of the Ku Klux Klan, along with its grotesque symbols of resistance: the skulls and crossbones and the knives dripping with blood. He believed that the Klan was a guerrilla military organization determined, in his own prophetic words, "to eventually control the Southern elections by intimidation and actual violence against the Union or Republican voters, white or black." Any sympathies Forbes had for the views of the Liberals were submerged by his belief that what the Liberal Republicans were calling "conciliation" was a codeword for a "sell-out" of the southern blacks. If Greeley were elected with Democratic votes, Forbes warned, the new president would be inexorably drawn into "the reactionary vortex."[22]

Such considerations prevented many of Sumner's old antislavery friends from voting for Greeley. The original Bird Club members who sided with Grant gave Sumner the greatest sorrow, for Sumner believed that the "good men who loved truth and justice" should have stood by him on the strength of friendship. The apostasy of his old friend Samuel Gridley Howe, who privately stated that Sumner had succumbed to "personal hate and envy," and of Charles Slack and Edward L. Pierce, greatly upset him. Sumner called Pierce's decision "reckless," but assured himself that Slack regretted his course and had acted only under pressure of economic self-preservation.[23]

Neither Sumner's inability to convince even some of his closest friends to vote for Greeley, nor Grant's overwhelming reelection victory among the voters-at-large, should conceal the substantial amount of shifting across party lines that occurred in 1872.[24] According to the estimates of relationships between voting patterns in 1868 and 1872, approximately 11 percent of the 1868 Republicans—about 15,170 voters—cast ballots for Greeley, thus directly repudiating the man they helped to elect to the presidency four years earlier (see Table 8.1). The Liberal Republican movement had an even greater impact on the congressional races: about 16 percent of the 1868 Grant men, approximately 21,240 voters, voted for Liberal/Democratic candidates for Congress. Bird, however, fared no better among 1868 Republicans than Greeley. Nevertheless, about one-fourth of the vote received by Greeley and Bird was comprised of 1868 Republicans, and approximately one-third of the votes received by Liberal Republican congressional candidates were cast by former Grant men.

Compared with other states, Massachusetts demonstrated substantial Republican disaffection with Grant in 1872 (see Table 8.2). In five midwestern states (Illinois, Indiana, Michigan, Ohio, Wisconsin) less than 3 percent of the 1868 Grant voters switched to Greeley. In the Midwest the major desertion of the 1872 election was not from Grant to Greeley, but rather from 1868 Democrats to Grant. Results of the 1872 election in the mid-Atlantic states (Delaware, Maryland, New Jersey, New York, Pennsylvania) were more analogous to the outcome in Massachusetts in that the crossing of party lines favored Greeley rather than Grant. Greeley captured almost 6 percent of the 1868 Republicans in the mid-Atlantic states. In sharp contrast to the Midwest, the abstention rate of 1868 Democrats was relatively high in the mid-Atlantic states: over one-fifth of those who voted for Horatio Seymour in New York, New Jersey, Pennsylvania, Delaware, and Maryland subsequently sat out the 1872 election. In Massachusetts, about 30 percent of the Seymour voters stayed away from the polls in 1872. Thus, in Massachusetts and in the mid-Atlantic states, Republican defections to Greeley and the poor showing by Greeley among former Seymour voters were obscured by the impressive lopsided Grant victory expressed by the percentage of the number of ballots cast.

The comparatively small number of Democratic defections to Grant in Massachusetts was significant, for the rate of Democratic defection to the Republican opposition was higher in 1872 than in the two previous presidential contests. About 3,000 former Seymour voters reversed themselves and voted to reelect Grant, marking the first crack in twelve years in an otherwise solid Bay State Democratic voter coalition. A clue to the identities of those Democratic "bolters" lies in the behavior of some prominent former Whigs who, after the outbreak of the Civil War, protested radical Republican policies by joining the Democrats and then bolted from Democratic ranks in 1872 to vote for Grant. Former Whig party leader and Boston Brahmin Robert C. Winthrop, for one, felt that only "discord and confusion" would have resulted from the success of "so unnatural a combination as Greeley and the Democrats," and, accordingly, he voted Republican for the first time in his life. Similarly, old-line Whig George S. Hillard looked

TABLE 8.1
Republican Defections to the Democrats in the 1872 Election
(by percent of 1872 electorate)

A. The 1868 and 1872 Presidential Elections
(Actual N = 334)

Candidate in 1868

Candidate in 1872	Seymour	Grant	Not Voting for President 1868	Not Eligible 1868	Percent of 1872 Electorate
Greeley	13	5	0	2	20
Grant	1	37	0	6	44
Not Voting for President 1872	6	3	21	6	36
Percent of 1872 Electorate	20	45	21	14	100

B. The 1868 Presidential Election and the 1872 Congressional Races
(Actual N = 331)

Presidential Candidate in 1868

Party in 1872 Congressional Race	Seymour	Grant	Not Voting for President 1868	Not Eligible 1868	Percent of 1872 Electorate
Democrats	12	7	0	2	21
Republicans	1	36	0	6	43
Not Voting in 1872 Congressional Election	7	1	21	6	35
Percent of 1872 Electorate	20	45	21	14	100

C. The 1868 Presidential Election and the 1872 Gubernatorial Race
(Actual N = 332)

Presidential Candidate in 1868

Gubernatorial Candidate in 1872	Seymour	Grant	Not Voting for President 1868	Not Eligible 1868	Percent of 1872 Electorate
Francis W. Bird	13	5	0	2	20
William B. Washburn	1	37	0	6	44
Not Voting for Governor 1872	6	3	21	6	36
Percent of 1872 Electorate	20	45	21	14	100

Note: To adjust for the varying populations of cities and towns, variables used in regression equations are "weighted" by the potential voting population. Rounding procedures occasionally produce totals greater or less than 100 percent.

upon Democratic endorsement of Greeley as a renewal on a large scale of the "unprincipled" Free-Soil and Democratic coalition of 1850; he indicated he would vote for Grant or, if unable to bring himself to vote Republican, would sit out the balloting.[25]

The nature of the areas of the state where Greeley's candidacy either helped or hurt the Democrats can be gleaned from the results of a

TABLE 8.2
Extent of Republican Defections to Greeley in the Midwestern and Mid-Atlantic States
(by percent of 1872 electorate)

A. Crossover Voting Between the 1868 and 1872 Presidential Elections in Illinois, Indiana,
Michigan, Ohio, and Wisconsin
(Actual $\underline{N}$ = 393)

Candidate in 1872	Candidate in 1868		Not Voting for President 1868	Not Eligible 1868	Percent of 1872 Electorate
	Seymour	Grant			
Greeley	30	1	0	1	32
Grant	3	32	1	4	40
All Others	0	0	0	0	1
Not Voting for President 1872	0	6	15	6	27
Percent of 1872 Electorate	33	40	16	10	100

B. Crossover Voting Between the 1868 and 1872 Presidential Elections in Delaware,
Maryland, New Jersey, New York, and Pennsylvania
(Actual $\underline{N}$ = 170)

Candidate in 1872	Candidate in 1868		Not Voting for President 1868	Not Eligible 1868	Percent of 1872 Electorate
	Seymour	Grant			
Greeley	27	2	0	0	29
Grant	0	29	8	0	37
All Others	0	0	0	0	0
Not Voting for President 1872	8	3	15	8	34
Percent of 1872 Electorate	35	34	23	8	100

Source: Political Science Data Archives, University of Minnesota, Minneapolis. The
county election returns for the midwestern and mid-Atlantic states were supplied by W.
Phillips Shively of the Department of Political Science, University of Minnesota.

Note: In 1872, there were approximately 2,582,055 eligible voters in the above
mid-Atlantic states compared with about 2,345,810 in the midwestern region.

multiple regression analysis in which the decline in the Democratic
presidential vote between 1868 and 1872 was regressed upon a large
number of independent variables, measuring social and economic characteristics of the state's cities and towns (see Table 8.3). In accounting
for the average Democratic decline in 1872, again in terms of the difference in the percentages of the electorate turning out to support
Seymour or Greeley, the per capita valuation of a community was the
most important. Greeley thus ran farthest behind Seymour in the
wealthier areas where Republicans traditionally fared poorly. In areas
where there were large concentrations of immigrant and working-class
populations, however, the Democratic drop-off was either nonexistent
or very small. This is noteworthy because high aggregate wealth often
coexisted with a high level of income inequality. Yet when controlling

for the effects of variables measuring the number of "poll-tax voters," immigrant groups, and workingmen in each locality, the influence of the per capita valuation of each city or town still had the greatest relative positive impact in explaining the Democratic decline between 1868 and 1872.

Estimates of the relationships between a voter's place of birth and his voting preferences in 1868 and 1872 suggest that Greeley's support among those born in Ireland, in Massachusetts, and in states other than Massachusetts did not differ sharply from the support Seymour received from these same voters (see Table 8.4). In particular, the results suggest that Irish-Americans were divided between Grant and Greeley in much the same way as they had been between Grant and Seymour four years earlier. Although there is evidence to suggest that the Irish "scratched" the names of some Liberal Republican congressional candidates, the Irish vote was unquestionably in the Greeley column.[26] Workingmen, farmers, and fishermen were also found in the Grant and Greeley columns much the same as they were previously distributed in the Grant and Seymour columns (see Table 8.5).

The estimated relationships between a voter's occupation or place of birth and his voting behavior in 1868 and 1872 pinpoint segments of the active electorate in 1868 that subsequently sat out the 1872 election (see Tables 8.4 and 8.5). Only recently have historians considered participation rates of different groupings of voters in more than a perfunctory fashion, yet turnout is the key to understanding what happened in the 1872 presidential election in Massachusetts. First, the sharp increase in abstentions between 1868 and 1872 hurt the Democrats more than it did the Republicans. Approximately 30 percent of the 1868 Seymour voters did not cast ballots for president in 1872, whereas only about 7 percent of the 1868 Republicans sat out the balloting (see Table 8.1.A). Second, because the Democratic decline was largest in wealthier areas and there was no falloff of support for the Liberal Republican ticket among Irish-Americans or factory workers, presumably many former Whigs and Constitutional Unionists who subsequently joined the Democrats were among those Greeley was unable to mobilize (see Tables 8.3, 8.4, and 8.5). Finally, it appears that Grant's support slipped among farmers and native-born voters (see Tables 8.4 and 8.5). Because the Republicans traditionally drew heavy support from agricultural regions containing few immigrants, many Republican bolters and abstainers presumably were native-born farmers.

Many of the Republican bolters and abstainers also were part of the large Republican "reserve" vote that was mobilized only during presidential years (see Tables 8.1.A and 8.6). The "dependable" Republican

TABLE 8.3
Regression Results: Determinants of the Decline in the Democratic Presidential Vote Between 1868 and 1872

Dependent Variable	Explanatory Variables	Simple r	Regression Coefficients	Adjusted Standard Errors of Reg. Coef.	Beta Coefficients	Change in R^2
Democratic Decline[a] [R^2=.28]	Valuation per capita	.39	.00	.00	.32	.15
	Agriculture	-.01	.04	.06	.08	.03
	In-state	-.11	-1.51	.53	-1.69	.02
	Canada	-.09	-1.43	.52	-.73	.01
	"Boot and shoe" towns	-.24	-.03	.02	-.17	.01
	Fishing	-.06	-.21	.06	-.34	.01
	Manufacturing	-.28	-.10	.06	-.13	.01
	Germany	.13	-2.13	.70	-.34	.01
	Sex ratio	-.06	.00	.00	.09	.01
	Ireland	.17	-1.44	.54	-1.30	.00
	Poll-tax voters	.21	.03	.05	.06	.00
	Native growth rate	.15	.00	.00	.15	.00
	Foreign growth rate	.01	-.00	.00	-.07	.00
	Out-of-state	.05	-1.37	.54	-1.07	.00
	In-town	-.04	-1.32	.53	-2.06	.00
	England & Scotland	.00	-1.35	.57	-.68	.00
	Voters of polls	-.08	.05	.07	.06	.00

[a]The Democratic decline between 1868 and 1872 equals the percentage of the electorate in 1868 voting for Horatio Seymour minus the percentage of the 1872 electorate voting for Horace Greeley.

Note: Actual N = 328. For a description of the explanatory variables selected for the stepwise regression, see Table 7.1. Voting units are "weighted" by population in order to ensure that smaller towns are not overrepresented in the analysis. Standard errors, however, are computed according to the original, unweighted number of cities and towns.

TABLE 8.4
Estimated Relationships Between Birthplace and Voting in the 1868 and 1872 Presidential Elections (by percent)

Presidential Election Year	Actual Number of Cases	Ireland Dem.	Rep.	Not Voting	Massachusetts Dem.	Rep.	Not Voting	Other U.S.A. Dem.	Rep.	Not Voting	(All)[a] Dem.	Rep.	Not Voting
1868	328	61	32	8	9	54	37	40	70	0[b]	(23)	(53)	(24)
1872	328	62[c]	34	4	5[c]	44	50	35[c]	60	5	(20)[c]	(44)	(36)

Sources: The estimate that 61 percent of the Irish-born eligible voters cast ballots for Seymour in 1868 was derived by running a multiple regression with the Seymour percentage as dependent and the percentages of the electorate born in Ireland, other foreign countries, the Massachusetts town or city in which they were living in 1868, and other towns or cities in Massachusetts as independent variables. The percentage of the electorate born in the United States but not in Massachusetts was not used to avoid multicollinearity. The breakdown of the electorate by place of birth was accomplished by extrapolations from data on the nativities of voters and males in each city and town in 1875. See Massachusetts, Bureau of Statistics of Labor, Thirteenth Annual Report of the Bureau of Statistics of Labor, Public Doc. 15 (Boston: 1882), table 1, pp. 97-168, and The Census of Massachusetts: 1875, 1:273-84. It was necessary to make the artificial assumption that the ratio of Irish-born eligible voters to the naturalized voter population in each voting unit remained constant throughout the period from 1865 to 1875. The source for the number of naturalized voters in 1865 is Massachusetts, General Court, Journal of the House of Representatives, H.Doc. 82 (February 1870), p. 1-11.

[a]Actual, not estimated, statewide voting preferences of all eligible voters.

[b]Logically impossible estimates have been set at the 0 percent limit.

[c]Liberal Republican.

TABLE 8.5
Estimated Relationships Between Occupation and Voting in the 1868 and 1872 Presidential Elections
(by percent)

Election Year	Actual Number of Cases	Manufacturing			Agriculture			Fishing			(All)[a]		
		Dem.	Rep.	Not Voting	Dem.	Rep.	Not Voting	Dem.	Rep.	Not Voting	Dem.	Rep.	Not Voting
1868	328	26	62	12	8	82	10	0	27	73	(23)	(53)	(24)
1872	328	33[b]	57	9	3[b]	65	31	6[b]	22	72	(20)[b]	(44)	(36)

Source: The breakdown of the male population by occupation--i.e., into groups engaged in manufacturing, agriculture, fishing, and all other occupations--was derived from interpolations from data contained in the 1865 and 1875 state censuses. Ignoring other possible determinants of the vote, such as religious and ethnic identities of voters, could have biased the estimates of occupational voting presented above. Therefore, the results are perhaps more valuable for comparative purposes than for generalizations about the actual voting behavior of workers, farmers, or fishermen.

[a]Actual, not estimated, statewide voting preferences of all eligible voters.

[b]Liberal Republican.

voters cast ballots with regularity in "off-year" gubernatorial elections. Virtually all of those who cast ballots for Republicans in 1870 and 1871 turned out for the Greeley-Grant contest in 1872 (see Table 8.6). Grant, as was usual for a Republican presidential candidate, won the overwhelming majority of votes cast by those who chose to sit out the balloting in 1870 and 1871. The Democrats, by comparison, were not able to rely on a large reserve vote.

Neither Grant nor Greeley monopolized the votes cast for Wendell Phillips in the 1870 gubernatorial election (see Table 8.6.A). Phillips's constituency was evenly split between Greeley and Grant, although the "persistent" Prohibitionists, those voting for the 1871 temperance candidate, studiously avoided the Greeley column (see Table 8.6.B). Phillips himself was also "rummy" enough to vote for Grant in 1872. Greeley, however, attracted the bulk of the die-hard laborites, those voting in 1871 for Chamberlain on the Labor Reform ticket. Moreover, many of the approximately 5,780 former Washburn voters who subsequently voted for Greeley were former Republicans who voted for Phillips. The evidence strongly suggests, therefore, that not all the 1872 Republican bolters were found among the large Republican reserve vote.

Crossover voting and the decision of previously active voters to stay away from the polls in 1872 were breaches in party regularity. The number of split tickets cast in the 1872 election was a further measure of "independent" voting (see Table 8.7). In 1864 the probability of voters splitting their tickets when voting for president, governor, and congressman was insignificant. In 1868 a few "otherwise Republican" ballots with John Quincy Adams's name substituted for William Claflin's name for governor accounted for most of the split tickets cast. How-

TABLE 8.6
Relationships Between Voting Patterns in the 1870 and 1871 Gubernatorial Races and the 1872
Presidential Election
(by percent of 1872 electorate)

A. The 1870 Gubernatorial Race and the 1872 Presidential Election

| | Candidate in 1870 | | | | | |
Candidate in 1872	John Q. Adams	William Claflin	Wendell Phillips	Not Voting for Governor 1870	Not Eligible 1870	Percent of 1872 Electorate
Greeley	13	0	4	0	3	20
Grant	2	26	4	7	4	44
Not Voting for President 1872	1	0	0	34	2	37
Percent of 1872 Electorate	16	26	7	41	9	100

B. The 1871 Gubernatorial Race and the 1872 Presidential Election

| | Candidate in 1871 | | | | | | |
Candidate in 1872	John Q. Adams	William Washburn	Robert Pitman	Edwin M. Chamberlain	Not Voting for Governor 1871	Not Eligible 1871	Percent of 1872 Electorate
Greeley	12	2	0	2	2	2	20
Grant	2	23	2	1	13	3	44
Not Voting for President 1872	2	0	0	0	35	0	37
Percent of 1872 Electorate	16	25	2	2	50	5	100

Note: Actual N = 334.

ever, in 1872 there occurred a rash of split tickets involving every possible combination save one: virtually nobody voted for both Greeley and Washburn. Ballots cast for both Grant and a Liberal Republican congressional candidate constituted the largest number of split tickets. Consequently, the Liberal/Democratic congressional candidates as a group ran slightly ahead of both Greeley and Bird in the balloting (see Table 8.1).

Results in the Fifth District where Banks, elected in 1870 as a Republican, sought reelection with Liberal/Democratic and Labor Reform endorsements, accounted for many of the split tickets. Although he lost the election to Daniel W. Gooch, the regular Republican candidate, Banks ran considerably ahead of his own ticket throughout his district. Because of the difficulties of splitting one's ticket, it was no small accomplishment that approximately 1,770 voters managed to vote for both Grant and Banks. In one town the ballot distributors came prepared with Banks's name printed on small slips of paper with glued backs to stick over Gooch's name on regular Republican ballots.[27]

In the Second Congressional District, including parts of Bristol and

TABLE 8.7
Estimated Number of Split Tickets Cast in the 1864, 1868, and
1872 General Elections

Combinations of Possible Split Tickets	Election Year		
	1864	1868	1872
Republican presidential and Democratic congressional	0[b]	774	5,733
Republican presidential and Democratic gubernatorial	0[a]	3,097	1,274
Democratic presidential and Republican congressional	0[a]	0[a]	1,593
Democratic presidential and Republican gubernatorial	0[a]	0[a]	0[a]
Republican gubernatorial and Democratic congressional	242	0[a]	3,185
Democratic gubernatorial and Republican congressional	483	1,549	3,504
Total Number of Split Tickets	725	5,420	15,289
Total Number of Eligible Voters	241,670	258,085	303,371

Note: The estimate that 774 voters cast ballots in 1868 for
Grant and a Democratic congressional candidate was derived by
running a multiple regression with the Democratic congressional
vote as dependent and the Grant and Seymour percentages as
independent variables. To avoid multicollinearity, the
percentage of 1868 eligibles who did not vote in the
presidential contest was not used. In a hypothetical voting unit
that voted 100 percent for Grant, the predicted percentage of
Grant voters who also cast votes for Democrats in congressional
races was constant plus b_1 coefficient. This sum represented the
estimated proportion of Grant voters statewide who voted for
Democratic congressional candidates. Likewise, constant plus b_2
coefficient gave the estimated proportion of Seymour voters who
also voted for Democrats in congressional races. The constant
was the estimated proportion of those not voting in the
presidential contest who voted for Democratic congressional
candidates. To ensure that the summations of the city and town
voting returns equaled the actual statewide breakdown of the
vote, each voting unit was "weighted" according to the number of
eligibles in its population. In using regression estimation of
cell entries in contingency tables to recover estimates of
split-ticket voting, it is necessary to assume that the internal
cell entries at the city and town level did not vary
systematically with the known marginal proportions. See Cowart,
"A Cautionary Note," pp. 123-26.

[a]Estimates slightly less than 0 percent (logically but not
statistically impossible results) were set at zero.

Plymouth counties, Republican Oakes Ames did not seek a sixth term
because of his involvement in the Union Pacific Railroad and Credit
Mobilier swindle. (Ames had "assigned" to certain members of Congress various shares of Credit Mobilier stock.) The Republican nomination, however, went to Benjamin W. Harris, who was related to the
Ames Family. Extremely high rates of Republican defections to Greeley
occurred in the southeastern part of the state where the Second District was located (see Table 8.8). This suggests that the contest in the
Second District may have been a factor in generating Republican defections to Greeley.[28]

TABLE 8.8
Republican and Democratic Voter Support for Greeley, by Regions
(by percent)

Region	Estimated Percent of 1868 Republicans Voting for Greeley	Estimated Percent of 1868 Democrats Voting for Greeley	Actual Democratic Decrease Between 1868 and 1872[a]
Southeastern Massachusetts[b]	16%	44%	4%
Western Massachusetts[c]	10	63	1
Middlesex, Essex, Suffolk, and Norfolk counties	10	64	5
Worcester County	6	78	0
Statewide	11	65	3

[a]Percentage of 1868 electorate voting for Horatio Seymour minus percentage of 1872 electorate voting for Greeley.

[b]Barnstable, Bristol, Duke, Nantucket, and Plymouth counties.

[c]Berkshire, Franklin, Hampden, and Hampshire counties.

Contemporaries of the period believed that the Liberal Republican movement received strong support in the Berkshire Mountains and Connecticut River Valley. Bowles was not the only prominent Republican who had bolted to Greeley in the western part of the state. In Pittsfield, William F. Bartlett, a Civil War general with a national reputation, and William H. Phillips, an old antislavery Republican, declared against Grant. In North Adams the defections from Republican ranks were led by John L. Arnold, a wealthy cotton manufacturer who received the Liberal/Democratic congressional nomination against Dawes. Part of the strength of the movement might have been attributable to the vitality of the Democratic party, which traditionally received strong support in Berkshire County. Democrats also ran disproportionally well in Suffolk County, but the Liberal Republican movement, by all accounts, had not flourished in Boston.[29] Yet a comparison of voting patterns in the western and northeastern regions of the state reveals similar rates of Republican defection and Democratic repeat voting, despite the discrepancy in the behavior of elites in these regions (see Table 8.8).

The Liberal Republican movement was least successful in attracting former Grant men in Worcester County, traditionally one of the "banner" Republican counties. The rank-and-file Republicans in the center of the state apparently were kept in line by the pro-Grant stands taken by Congressman George F. Hoar and John D. Baldwin of the Worcester *Daily Spy*. Both Hoar and Baldwin felt that, if their party was in need of reform, it should be reformed from within and not by "disloyalty" through collaboration with the Democrats. Hoar addressed the issue troubling many voters in his district: was Charles Sumner right? For many Republicans in Worcester County, Sumner had never once been wrong. Hoar was aware that his constituents shared many of Sumner's suspicions about Grant's administration. In a widely reprinted speech, Hoar told a Worcester audience that he reluctantly was forced to differ with the man with whom, during his entire previous political life, it had been his pleasure to agree on all national issues. Hoar's words reassured the Republicans who were troubled that in voting for Grant they had to part company with Sumner.[30]

The pattern of Democratic and Republican support for Greeley by regions reveals an inverse relationship between Republican bolters and Democratic "repeaters." As the percentage of 1868 Republicans bolting for Greeley increased, the percentage of 1868 Democrats supporting Greeley decreased (see Table 8.8). Thus, the decision within an area that moved one set of voters moved another set as well. This makes sense in Downsian terms: it was rational for former dedicated Democrats to abstain when they perceived their party moving closer, in terms of ideology and constituency, toward the Republicans.[31]

The lack of enthusiasm of Democrats for Greeley and of many Republicans for Grant signaled the end of a political era when knowledge of an individual's stand on issues stemming from the Civil War and its settlement determined his choice at the polls. Neither defeat nor victory of individual congressmen could be translated into defeats or victories for Grant's southern policy. The triumph of Gooch over Banks in the Fifth District, for example, was less a victory for Republican Reconstruction policies than it was a victory for party regularity. Wendell Phillips, who had once claimed Banks plotted with southern rebels to get possession of the national government, declared in 1872 for Banks against Gooch, illustrating the extent to which other concerns had swept aside the older issues. Even Sumner deferred to advice from loyal supporters by acknowledging that voters could no longer be mobilized by Reconstruction issues and that in the future it would be necessary to focus on purely local concerns. Sumner's trusted friend and counselor, Frank Bird, seceded from the original Bird Club, started a new club, and acted with the Democratic party for the rest of his life. The world of Massachusetts politics had moved in 1872 and men and parties had moved with it. Still, the political reconstruction of the Bay State Democratic and Republican parties had only begun.[32]

Chapter 9
The Democratic Resurgence, 1873–1876

No Republican, straight-laced or liberal, denies the bad
character of the Democratic party during the war and
reconstruction period; and no one, if tolerably candid can deny,
that here in Massachusetts at least, . . . it is disposed to be
better now.—*William S. Robinson, quoted in* "Warrington"
Pen-Portraits

Capitalizing on voter discontent caused by the economic depression, scandals in the Ulysses S. Grant administration, disillusionment with Republican southern policy, and a white backlash against
pending civil rights legislation, the Democrats regained control of the
United States House of Representatives in the 1874 congressional elections. No election in the nineteenth century witnessed as great a partisan change from one Congress to the next. Not even Massachusetts,
where the Republicans seemed invincible, escaped the political tidal
wave that rolled over the nation. The Democrats captured the governorship and destroyed the Republican monopoly on congressional
seats. Among the vanquished was the controversial Republican politician, Congressman Benjamin F. Butler, whose defeat attracted nationwide attention, for an ultra radical and a leading supporter of
Grant had been cut down. The 1874 "off-year" election seemed to con-
firm that the readjustment of parties, inevitable with the subordina-
tion of Civil War settlement issues, was finally at hand.[1]

Republican setbacks of 1874 in Massachusetts were foreshadowed by
voting patterns in the 1873 gubernatorial election. Although the Republican incumbent, William B. Washburn, was reelected to a third
term, his margin of votes over his Democratic opponent was unusually
small. There were the usual mitigating circumstances for the Republican decline. For example, the Republican state legislators, elected by

the Grant landslide of 1872, had unwisely reenacted the old liquor law without providing for a licensing system. But the Republicans were also troubled by divisions within their ranks, especially at the leadership level.[2]

The election of Henry Wilson to the vice-presidency in 1872 had given the Massachusetts Republicans the opportunity to select the successor to Wilson's Senate seat. The contest between George S. Boutwell, Grant's secretary of the treasury, and Henry L. Dawes, chairman of the House Ways and Means Committee, brought into focus the conflicting priorities of Republican leaders. Neither Reconstruction issues nor the many newer voter concerns determined the composition of factions among the party leadership. Only the issue of Butler's efforts to influence the election gave some coherence to the struggle between Boutwell and Dawes. To many in the Republican rank and file, the covert maneuvering for Wilson's seat revealed that power and self-interest had replaced idealism and honesty.[3]

Dawes was from western Massachusetts and received almost solid support in the legislature from the four western counties. Dawes was also supported by the Boston *Daily Advertiser* and the Springfield *Republican*. His friendship with Congressman Daniel W. Gooch gave Dawes the backing of the Charleston Navy Yard. Massachusetts Labor Bureau officials favored Dawes and he received strong support from many labor groups. His conservative stand on Reconstruction gave him considerable influence among Democratic members of the legislature. Yet he also had the support of many radical Republicans for his opposition to the legislature's censure of Sumner's vote to return captured Confederate battleflags as a means of punishing Sumner for his attacks on Grant.[4]

On the other side, Boutwell had the advantage of being the "true Blue Union" candidate with excellent radical credentials. He served as a member of the Joint Congressional Committee on Reconstruction, was one of the managers in the impeachment proceedings against Andrew Johnson, and acted as a major force in the passage of the Fifteenth Amendment. Equally important, the railroad lobbies and the Boston Custom House favored Boutwell. He received "early and valuable aid" from William Wayland Clapp and the Boston *Daily Journal*, and won the endorsement of the Boston *Commonwealth*. The Credit Mobilier scandal touched Dawes and thus helped Boutwell's candidacy. Yet Boutwell's friendship with Butler repelled many Republicans who feared that, in return for Butler's support for the senatorship, Boutwell would aid him in his quest for the governorship.[5]

Because Boutwell received the support of Butler, Wilson, and Grant, he was favored to win the Senate seat. There existed, according to one Dawes supporter, "a general feeling that Boutwell is the regular Republican, Custom House, Government candidate and the soundest thing a true man can do is support him." Those critical of the Grant administration and committed to party reform rallied to Dawes as the "liberal" or "independent" candidate. The support Dawes received from Sumner's ally and friend, Henry L. Pierce, reinforced the notion that Dawes was as accessible to the Liberal Republicans as he was to the Custom House gang and the machine politicians. When Butler's allies in Essex County gave Boutwell the necessary margin of votes to win the balloting in the legislature for Wilson's vacant seat, many feared that an alliance between Boutwell and Butler had been consummated.[6]

In 1873 Butler launched another campaign to win the Republican gubernatorial nomination. This time Butler attacked the notion that an aspirant for public office should profess disinterestedness. By charging that it was "more manly, more just, more proper, more everything, to come out openly and boldly and state your case" than to use "tricks," "devices," and "frauds" to deny the voters their "sacred right" to choose the man they wanted, Butler implied that his enemies wanted the voters to defer to the wealthy men and powerful corporate interests who had long exercised control of state politics by a "traditional right."[7]

Butler's opponents, however, were mobilized by more than an aversion to his campaign tactics. His influence with Grant over the dispensing of patronage, his role in securing Boutwell's election to the Senate, and his defense of some Republican officeholders of questionable character also generated hostility to his candidacy. Butler's defense of the "Salary Grab"—a law that raised federal salaries, retroactively, for two years—lent credence to the charge that he was a selfish and ambitious politician. In addition, Butler had to defend his unpopular inflationary monetary policy against the charge that it would undermine the nation's financial structure. Finally, his prolabor utterances and sharp class rhetoric alienated him from conservative Republicans. For many Bay State citizens, "Butlerism," "Grantism," and "Carpetbaggism" were not separate issues but rather manifestations of abuses of political power caused by self-seeking, corrupt, and irresponsible men.[8]

As a consequence, the battle against Butler in 1873 was more bitterly fought than in 1871. Under pressure from Boston businessmen who had quietly led and helped finance the "stop-Butler" movement, Congressman George Frisbie Hoar abandoned his former neutrality. Hoar proclaimed that, even among Butler's supporters, few believed

Butler was "honest, truthful, disinterested, or incapable of using power to gratify both his ambition and his revenge." In a statement that was widely reprinted and quoted, Hoar summed up Butler's career in three words: "Swagger, quarrel, failure."[9]

Butler, of course, had his defenders. Labor reformer Ira Steward wrote Hoar to remind him that the working classes would not be persuaded by attacks on Butler's character. Butler, Steward pointed out, had earned the support of workers. When in 1873 about 15,000 textile workers marched through the streets of Fall River to support a ten-hour workday for women and children, Butler spoke for every one of them when he decried the failure of the legislature to pass this long-overdue labor reform measure. "*Not* to sustain Butler," wrote Steward, "is to please . . . the *class* of men who steadily do Labor injustice." In this group Steward included Governor Washburn, who had been a reluctant supporter of ten-hour legislation.[10]

The Bay State Democratic party leadership made it clear that Butler would receive little Democratic support even if he were to break with the Republicans. Butler's persistent defense of the southern Republican governments and his propensity to wave the "bloody shirt" made him unacceptable to most rank-and-file Democrats. "No man can consistently style himself a Democrat after voting for Butler," declared the staunchly Democratic Boston *Post*. Voting for Republican mavericks and renegades, many Democratic leaders believed, would only lead to the demoralization of their party. In the wake of the Horace Greeley debacle of 1872, the self-styled "Young Democracy," led by Patrick A. Collins, was determined to revitalize its party at the grass-roots level.[11]

At the Democratic state convention, Collins and his supporters worked to secure the gubernatorial nomination for William Gaston, a former Whig who in 1871 had been elected mayor of Boston on a "Citizens and Democratic" ticket. The Boston *Post* and the Democratic party "old guard" favored Leverett Saltonstall, but Gaston, who drew most of his strength from the hostility of Suffolk County voters to the prohibition law, won the nomination. The Democrats openly appealed to all independent and disaffected Republican voters, but Gaston's candidacy created little enthusiasm among nonpartisan "reformers" or "liberals." The Springfield *Republican* dismissed Gaston as incapable of leading the state out of its political "rut."[12]

The Liberal Republicans had intended to issue a statement of their views in 1873, but no meeting was ever held and no address to the voters was ever issued. Among "regular" Republicans there was a great deal of discontent with Governor Washburn because of his support for prohibition. The close political friends of both Dawes and Hoar, along with the editors of the three most influential Republican newspapers in Boston (the *Daily Journal, Daily Advertiser,* and *Daily Evening Transcript*), privately expressed their lack of faith in Washburn, but they had to endorse him or risk a split in anti-Butler ranks, which, in turn, could result in Butler winning the nomination. Thus, fear of Butler gave Washburn the Republican nomination in 1873, just as it had in 1871.[13]

Washburn's narrow margin of victory in the 1873 election led to speculation that Butler supporters had voted for Gaston. Such a crossover of voters, claimed the Springfield *Republican,* was "a fact that is patent on the face of the returns." An analysis of the relationships between voting patterns in the 1873 gubernatorial election and the 1872 presidential race indicates that about 16 percent of Gaston's total vote came from those who had voted for Grant the previous year (see Table 9.1.A). More revealing, however, is that approximately 32 percent of Gaston's support came from 1871 Washburn supporters (see Table 9.1.B). This pattern of Republican support for Gaston suggests that Butler men, who presumably were all in the Grant column in 1872, were not as important to the coalition brought together by Gaston as were former Republicans who did not support Grant in 1872. In short, disgruntled Butlerites were not responsible for Washburn's reduced vote in 1873. The outcome was shaped more by popular indignation with the reimposition of prohibition and widespread impatience with the Grant administration than by any intrigue against Washburn by Butler supporters.[14]

An important result of the 1873 election was the change in the balance between the parties in the legislature. Democratic representation in the lower house more than doubled, and in the state senate the Republican margin over all opposition was slashed to one-sixth of its former spread. The Springfield *Republican* urged the legislature to abandon partisan politics, arguing that there was no longer any need to mix national questions with purely state affairs. The paper claimed that, since it was evident that "the old political organizations" were in the "process of disintegration," all that could be hoped for was that "the best elements of both parties" would unite. The voters, according to the *Republican,* were more interested in the liquor question, the influence of railroad lobbies, extravagant state expenditures, and honest and efficient government than political party labels.[15]

Shortly after the new legislature convened, Republican morale suffered a shocking blow. President Grant appointed William A. Simmons, who managed Butler's unsuccessful campaign for the Republi-

TABLE 9.1
Republican Support for Gaston in 1873
(by percent of 1873 electorate)

A. Estimated Relationships Between Voting Patterns in the 1872 Presidential
and 1873 Gubernatorial Races

	Presidential Candidate in 1872				
Gubernatorial Candidate in 1873	Greeley	Grant	Not Voting for President 1872	Not Eligible 1872	Percent of 1873 Electorate
William Gaston	16	3	0	0	19
William B. Washburn	0	23	0	0	23
All Others[a]	0	0	0	0	0
Not Voting for Governor 1873	3	16	35	5	58
Percent of 1873 Electorate	19	42	35	5	100

B. Estimated Relationships Between Voting Patterns in the 1871 and 1873 Gubernatorial Races

	Candidate in 1871						
Candidate in 1873	John Q. Adams	William B. Washburn	Robert C. Pitman	Edwin M. Chamberlain	Not Voting for Governor 1871	Not Eligible 1871	Percent of 1873 Electorate
William Gaston	12	6	0	1	0	0	19
William B. Washburn	0	16	2	1	4	0	23
All Others[a]	0	0	0	0	0	0	0
Not Voting for Governor 1873	3	2	0	0	44	9	58
Percent of 1873 Electorate	15	24	2	2	48	9	100

Note: Actual $\underline{N}$ = 334. To adjust for the varying populations of cities and towns, variables used in regression equations are "weighted" by the potential voting population. Rounding procedures occasionally produce totals greater or less than 100 percent.

[a]Henry K. Oliver, Benjamin F. Butler, Nathaniel Bartlett and scattered returns.

can gubernatorial nomination, to head the Boston Custom House, the most lucrative and powerful federal office in the state. Talk of a party revolt against Grant made the rounds among regular Republicans. There was speculation that former Governor William Claflin, chairman of the Republican National Committee and a close friend of Vice-President Wilson, would, at the first indication of any growth of a Butler organization in Suffolk County, revolt against Grant, carrying with him all the Boston Republican papers except the pro-Butler *Traveller*. John Murray Forbes, who headed a delegation of merchants to Washington to oppose Simmons's confirmation, believed that Butler was working with the Boston Democrats to divide Republicans for his own selfish motives. The Democratic Boston *Post* labeled Simmons "the most objectionable candidate that could have been presented." Simmons was confirmed despite the opposition of most of Boston's powerful mercantile community, six members of the state's congressional delegation, and both Massachusetts senators. Sumner's negative vote was expected, but Boutwell ignored Butler's request for support and declared against Simmons. It was rumored that Butler subsequently talked in a very "grim suggestive way" whenever Boutwell's name was mentioned to him.[16]

The rift between Grant and the Massachusetts Republican party widened after the Simmons appointment. "We shall have an administration party and a republican party in Massachusetts henceforth," wrote Samuel Bowles. Butler, in Bowles's opinion, was getting desperate in his attempts to win the governorship, and Grant once again had revealed his incompetence. Many observers, including Bowles, feared that Dawes's "neutrality" in the Simmons affair represented a reconciliation between Dawes and Butler that would set the tone of state politics for quite some time. The alliance between Dawes and Butler had been in the making since the Grant and Wilson landslide in 1872. Dawes, having lost the senatorial contest with Boutwell for Wilson's seat, was tired of fighting Butler and receiving no rewards. Subsequently, the bargaining with Butler had begun in earnest.[17]

Butler's pledge to support Dawes for Sumner's seat in the Senate was made before Sumner's death in March 1874. Once again the question of Butler's behind-the-scenes influence was the overriding issue in a senatorial contest. Dawes's supporters in the legislature did not want him to look like the Butler candidate. Nevertheless, the anti-Butler forces rallied to the candidacy of Judge Ebenezer Rockwood Hoar, formerly Grant's attorney general and Butler's long-time political antagonist. Hoar also attracted some support by virtue of his personal friendship with Sumner who, in the last hours of his life, had asked Hoar to "take care of my civil rights bill." The Democrats in the legislature, no longer in a weak minority position, stood behind Benjamin R. Curtis, a dissenting Supreme Court justice in the Dred Scott decision. However, they indicated that they would bargain with "friendly Republicans" on the candidacy of Charles F. Adams or Nathaniel P. Banks in the event of a deadlock between Dawes, Hoar, and Curtis.[18]

Many Republicans believed that the contest between Hoar and Dawes would determine the fate of their party. "If we win it," wrote Hoar supporter Charles Eliot Norton, "the party is safe; if Butler wins it we will break up the party." When the anti-Butler forces created a deadlock between Hoar and Dawes, the Dawes faction, holding a plurality of votes, refused to compromise. After thirty-two ballots, the Hoar faction was ready to form a coalition with the Democrats to elect Charles Francis Adams. At this critical point, Vice-President Wilson, with the support of the Republican State Commitee, intervened and bluntly told the Dawes supporters that Adams's election would destroy the Massachusetts Republican party. On the next ballot Wilson skillfully engineered the election of Governor Washburn, who had received no votes at all on the first ballot.[19]

Although the successful and "unpremeditated" union on the lackluster and conservative Washburn appeared to cement the rift within the Republican leadership, it was interpreted as a victory for the anti-Butler forces. But the unfavorable publicity given to the behind-the-scenes "wirepulling" during the senatorial struggle for Sumner's vacant seat hurt the Republicans at a time when their party was increasingly on the defensive. The apparent plunder of federal money under the cover of the Sanborn contracts, the "back pay grab," and the Credit Mobilier scandal were heavy burdens for the party in a congressional election year. The talk of an unprecedented third term for Grant contributed to the demoralization of the Bay State Republican rank and file. For many it appeared that there was not enough honesty, integrity, and virtue left in their party to hold it together. More than a few Republicans reflected that perhaps it had been a mistake not to listen to Sumner in 1872.[20]

The business depression of 1873 had shattered by the following year the economic equilibrium in Massachusetts. Inventories piled up as the demand for goods fell off; in response, manufacturers cut back production, reduced wages, and laid off workers. Discontent caused by the economic hard times was sure to be registered in the coming congressional elections by a reduced Republican vote. The Democratic press shrewdly linked the economic issue with other issues plaguing the Grant administration. The idle mills and factories were a direct consequence, the pro-Democratic press claimed, of corruption in Congress, "greed for a third term," "salary grabbing," "press gag-laws," and a repressive Reconstruction policy that had created "desolated, bankrupt and downtrodden" states in the South.[21]

In the midst of a rapidly deteriorating political situation, the Republicans mapped out their 1874 campaign strategy. There was little ground upon which they could safely battle the Democrats. Consequently, the Republicans fell back on their past record of accomplishments, hoping that old emotions and loyalties would pull them through in November. In the keynote speech to the state convention, Dawes proclaimed that Massachusetts had an obligation to support the pending congressional civil rights bill, which contained a provision for integrated schools. Massachusetts enjoyed the distinction of being the first state to prohibit racial distinctions in admitting students to any public school, and so the issue of a national civil rights bill was a safe one. That Dawes—once such an enthusiast for President Andrew Johnson's Reconstruction policies that his radical colleagues in the House considered removing him from his committee assignments—now viewed passage of the Senate civil rights bill as the key issue in the 1874 campaign, clearly demonstrated the inability of his party to fight the Democrats on any other issues.[22]

Some issues, such as the integrity and honesty of many of the party's congressional candidates, the Republicans could not easily straddle. In the staunchly Republican Eighth District, George F. Hoar and his political lieutenants grappled with the thorny problem of making reform of the Republican party itself an issue in the campaign. Hoar was urged by his supporters to continue the fight against Butler and to demand the removal of all corrupt officeholders: "No whitewashing of anybody will be tolerated—we care nothing for Dawes, Boutwell, or anybody else except as they concur." Hoar's organization wanted him to quarrel only with Butler, but it was prepared to "meet all comers." There were obvious problems, however, with this course of action. In the first place, Hoar's strategists feared that too many "of our kind of Republicans are so disgusted with the party that they don't care to save it." And secondly, exposing corruption within Republican ranks would only serve to supply the Democrats with campaign propaganda.[23]

To compound problems for the Republicans, the liquor question became an issue in the 1874 campaign when their party nominated Thomas Talbot for the governorship. Talbot, as lieutenant governor, had become acting-governor when Washburn assumed the remainder of Sumner's term in the Senate. While he was acting-governor, Talbot vetoed a bill repealing prohibition and then aggravated his error by also vetoing a bill abolishing the state constabulary. Both vetoes were extremely unpopular, but the influential antiliquor minority within the Republican party—with the help of many of Butler's supporters—was able to secure Talbot's nomination. Although it was understood that Butler supported Talbot, some anti-Butler Republicans feared that Butler might win the nomination if the convention became deadlocked and so joined the Talbot bandwagon.[24]

When Talbot received the nomination of the Prohibitionist party as well, Republicanism and prohibitionism became equated in the 1874 campaign. The Springfield *Republican* declared that the election of Talbot would mean "the continued sham enforcement of an impossible law, to the great injury of the public morals." The paper shared the sentiment of many Republicans who believed that Talbot's nomination ensured a Democratic victory. Republican leaders privately conceded that Talbot would alienate a large portion of the party and that desertions would be heavy at the polling places. His weakness, it was recognized, stemmed solely from his having ignored popular opposition to the liquor law and its enforcement. His personal character and integrity were beyond reproach. To many Republicans, Talbot's possible defeat seemed doubly unfortunate because those who would abandon him in November were sure to forget in their eagerness to secure a license law that a United States senator would be elected by the new legislature.[25]

An important development affecting the outcome of the race occurred in printing shops where ballots for distribution at the polls were prepared on election eve. In the Fifth District, for example, which featured a rematch between Daniel Gooch and Nathaniel P. Banks, no less than 38,000 ballots were printed in all sorts of combinations and sizes. Voters were warned to carefully examine their ballots because "so well and skillfully have the preparations been made to paste and scratch the various nominations." In an orgy of treachery many Republican candidates for Congress and the legislature "sold out" their weaker and endangered fellow Republicans. Talbot, aware of his vulnerability, worked through his political friends to prevent Republican deals with Democrats in state legislative races that left his name off the ballot. The political intrigue was made more interesting, although not less complicated, by the impending senatorial contest to be decided by the legislature elected along with a governor and a congressional delegation.[26]

An analysis of voting returns from throughout the state reveals that the 1874 election was marked by a relatively high degree of split-ticket voting, as measured by the number of "irregular" ballots cast in the gubernatorial and congressional races (see Table 9.2). Not only was there over a fourfold increase in split tickets cast in the gubernatorial and congressional contests between 1872 and 1874, but, because of the lower rate of voter participation in 1874, the relative importance of split tickets was much greater. For example, of those who participated in 1874 in both gubernatorial and congressional elections, about 17 percent did not vote the regular Republican or Democratic ticket; of those who voted in 1872 in both gubernatorial and congressional elections, less than 4 percent managed to cast split tickets.[27]

A large percentage of split tickets combined votes for Talbot and a Democratic congressional candidate (see Table 9.2). This suggests that, although a considerable number of voters vented their distrust of a local Republican congressional candidate, they stopped short of voting for Gaston. And, on the other hand, although the indignation of

TABLE 9.2
Estimated Number of Split Tickets Cast in the 1872, 1874, and
1876 General Elections

Combinations of Possible Split Tickets	Election Year		
	1872	1874	1876
Republican presidential and Democratic congressional	5,733	--	0[a]
Republican presidential and Democratic gubernatorial	1,274	--	0[a]
Democratic presidential and Republican congressional	1,593	--	1,437
Democratic presidential and Republican gubernatorial	0[a]	--	0[a]
Republican gubernatorial and Democratic congressional	3,185	11,705	0[a]
Democratic gubernatorial and Republican congressional	3,504	17,055	1,078
Total Number of Split Tickets	15,289	28,760	2,515
Total Number of Eligible Voters	303,371	334,418	359,339

Note: For the multiple regression procedure used to generate
the above estimates, see Table 8.7.

[a]Negative estimates have been set at zero.

many voters with Talbot's position on the liquor question might have caused them to vote for Gaston, they still managed to vote for a Republican congressional candidate whom they deemed worthy of their support. Moreover, an additional estimate of the number of ballots marked for a Republican congressional candidate, but left blank for governor, reveals that "scratching" did not predominate over the propensity to vote for both Gaston and a Republican congressional candidate. Even in Suffolk County and neighboring Cambridge, where Talbot ran much farther behind his ticket than in the state-at-large, split-ticket voting rather than "scratching" was the rule, and not vice versa, as newspaper reporters at the polls mistakenly believed.[28]

Split-ticket voting was only one indicator of the extent to which the voters exercised their independence. Another measure of voter independence was obliteration of partisan lines in the balloting. Voter crossover between 1872 and 1874 was unusually large in both gubernatorial and congressional contests (see Table 9.3). About 28 percent of those who voted for Republican congressional candidates in 1872 subsequently cast ballots for Democratic or anti-Republican congressional candidates in 1874. The crossing of party lines was not all in one direction, because a small percentage of those who voted for Democratic and Liberal Republicans in 1872 cast ballots for Republicans in 1874. The percentage of the electorate switching parties between the 1872 and 1874 congressional elections was a remarkably high 13 percent; by comparison, the percentage crossing party lines between the 1872 and 1874 gubernatorial elections was approximately 8 percent.

The voting patterns in the 1874 election represented a show of "popular independence of party lines," but the results did not establish a new and lasting realignment of voters (see Tables 9.4 and 9.5). The shuffling of voters across party lines in 1874 proved to be temporary. Although the Democrats hailed the "fresh accessions of strength" to their ranks in 1874, they were aware of the very tenuous hold their party actually had on these voters. John K. Tarbox, one of the sucessful Democratic congressional candidates, believed that the 1874 vote was only "nominally democratic" and that it was "really nonpartisan." According to Tarbox, his party's victory was made possible by the aid of men "who do not call themselves democrats and do not propose to don the old-fashioned democratic livery nor to shout the ancient shibboleths of the party." Whereas about 28 percent of those who voted for Republican congressional candidates in 1872 subsequently voted Democratic in 1874, only about 14 percent of them persisted in voting for Democratic congressional candidates in 1876 (see Tables 9.3, 9.4, and 9.5). From another perspective, slightly less than half of the 1872 Republicans repeated a Republican vote in 1874, but over 80 percent of them voted Republican in 1876. Thus, by 1876 over 30 percent of the 1872 Republicans had returned to the party fold. The 1876 election tended to follow the older party divisions, although it stopped short of completely reassembling them.[29]

The causes of the high amount of unpredictable voting in the 1874 election and the Republican defeats were an endless source of speculation. Clearly, many factors had contributed. The liquor issue, the economic depression, the revelations of scandals in Washington, and the suspicion of Grant's southern policy all played a part. The widespread belief by contemporaries of the period—that the 1874 result represented "Waterloo for the Machine" or "the rejection of Butlerism" and "a moral uprising" by the voters in which only "respectable" candidates nominated by Republicans were elected—bears closer examination. Undeniably, every defeat of a Republican congressional candidate can be explained in part as an aversion to the individual himself and to those who supported him, or to the tactics used to secure his nomination. Wherever "Butlerism" appeared, declared the Democratic Boston *Post*, "the people have put their feet upon the neck of its representative."[30]

Butler's defeat for reelection was not surprising considering the long list of disabilities he had acquired since 1872. His prestige dropped in

TABLE 9.3
Crossover Voting Between the 1872 and 1874 Congressional and Gubernatorial Elections
(by percent of 1874 electorate)

A. The 1872 and 1874 Congressional Races

Party in 1874	Party in 1872		Not Voting 1872 Congressional Election	Not Eligible 1872	Percent of 1874 Electorate
	Democratic	Republican			
Democratic	10	11	4	2	27
Republican	1	19	4	3	27
All Others	0	1	0	0	1
Not Voting 1874 Congressional Election	8	8	25	4	45
Percent of 1874 Electorate	18	39	33	9	100

B. The 1872 and 1874 Gubernatorial Races

Candidate in 1874	Candidate in 1872		Not Voting for Governor 1872	Not Eligible 1872	Percent of 1874 Electorate
	Francis W. Bird	William B. Washburn			
William Gaston	17	7	3	2	29
Thomas Talbot	1	23	3	0	27
Not Voting for Governor 1874	0	10	27	7	44
Percent of 1874 Electorate	18	40	33	9	100

Note: Actual N = 326.

1873 when he failed to capture the Republican gubernatorial nomination. It plummeted after he made his chief campaign worker the collector of the Port of Boston over the objections of both state senators. His reputation was impeached by the conduct of his political allies, such as John D. Sanborn, who received lucrative contracts from the United States Treasury to collect delinquent taxes. He had to defend his support for the "Salary Grab" act and for the greenback inflation bill. In 1874 he was challenged for renomination to Congress and found himself locked in a quarrel with the local Republican leadership in Haverhill and Salem, two important towns in his district. Butler himself became extremely concerned about his chances for reelection as the campaign came to an end.[31]

Those who cheered the defeat of Butler also applauded the voters' rejection of four other Republican congressional candidates: James C. Ayer, J. M. S. Williams, Charles A. Stevens, and Henry Alexander. From the outset, Ayer, a millionaire patent medicine manufacturer, faced an uphill battle to win a congressional seat from the Seventh District (including Lowell and Concord). It was charged that he had pur-

TABLE 9.4
Estimated Relationships Between Voting Patterns in the 1874 and 1876 Elections:
The Congressional and Gubernatorial Races
(by percent of 1876 electorate)

A. The 1874 and 1876 Congressional Elections
(Actual N = 328)

| Party in 1876 | Party in 1874 | | | | | |
	Democratic	Republican	All Others	Not Voting 1874 Congressional Election	Not Eligible 1874	Percent of 1876 Electorate
Democratic	15	7	0	6	3	31
Republican	10	17	1	10	2	40
All Others	1	0	0	0	0	1
Not Voting 1876 Congressional Election	0	1	0	26	2	29
Percent of 1876 Electorate	25	25	1	41	7	100

B. The 1874 and 1876 Gubernatorial Elections
(Actual N = 331)

| Candidate in 1876 | Candidate in 1874 | | | | |
	William Gaston	Thomas Talbot	Not Voting for Governor 1874	Not Eligible 1874	Percent of 1876 Electorate
Charles F. Adams	24	0	6	1	30
Alexander H. Rice	3	24	8	2	38
John I. Baker	0	1	1	1	3
Not Voting for Governor 1876	0	0	26	3	29
Percent of 1876 Electorate	27	25	41	7	100

chased his nomination in a convention in which he encountered strong but divided opposition. In the Eighth District the renomination of Williams aroused public indignation because of his involvement in the Credit Mobilier scandal. Williams also had to defend himself against charges arising from his attempt to ensure that wealthy young men in Cambridge were not drafted during the Civil War. In the Tenth District, opposition to Stevens was intense because many believed he had received his nomination by the behind-the-scenes "wirepulling" of Luke Lyman, reputedly the best convention manager in the western half of the state. In the Eleventh District (including Berkshire County), a similar sentiment existed against Alexander, whom many believed had won the nomination on account of skillful caucus manipulations orchestrated by Dawes's political operative, Edward R. Tinker. Alexander was Bowles's son-in-law, but Bowles supported his opponent, charging that behind his daughter's husband were "the worst men, the worst practices, and the worst tendencies." Bowles referred, in part, to the proliquor forces.[32]

TABLE 9.5
Estimated Relationships Between Voting Patterns in the 1872 and 1876 Elections:
The Congressional and Gubernatorial Races
(by percent of 1876 electorate)

A. The 1872 and 1876 Congressional Elections
(Actual $\underline{N}$ = 326)

Party in 1876	Party in 1872		All Others	Not Voting 1872 Congressional Election	Not Eligible 1872	Percent of 1876 Electorate
	Democratic	Republican				
Democratic	10	5	0	9	6	31
Republican	2	30	0	6	3	40
All Others	0	1	0	0	0	1
Not Voting 1876 Congressional Election	5	1	0	16	7	29
Percent of 1876 Electorate	17	37	0	31	16	100

B. The 1872 and 1876 Gubernatorial Elections
(Actual $\underline{N}$ = 331)

Candidate in 1876	Candidate in 1872		Not Voting for Governor 1872	Not Eligible 1872	Percent of 1876 Electorate
	Francis W. Bird	William B. Washburn			
Charles F. Adams	17	2	6	5	30
Alexander H. Rice	0	28	7	3	38
John I. Baker	0	3	0	0	3
Not Voting for Governor 1876	0	4	17	8	29
Percent of 1876 Electorate	17	37	31	16	100

The Democrats in 1874 neutralized the issues relating to Reconstruction by condemning "the conduct of all those who, under any pretense or guise, disgrace themselves and their country by lawless acts of violence against the colored race in the Southern states." Gaston adhered closely to this position during the campaign, assuring audiences that his party endorsed the three Reconstruction amendments to the Constitution. Butler's Democratic opponent, Charles P. Thompson, a strong Unionist during the war, accepted the notions of racial equality and equal rights, thereby undercutting Butler's campaign emphasis on violations of the rights of southern blacks. Tarbox, who defeated Ayer in the Seventh District, endorsed Grant's Louisiana policy and denounced White League violence. In all the districts where Republicans were defeated, the Democrats had tried to minimize the differences between themselves and their opponents on questions involving civil rights or "Southern outrages." Through this strategy, the Democrats had allowed the Bay State electorate to uphold the Republican party's fourteen-year history of civil rights progress. Thus, the voters were free to defeat a Republican candidate they felt unfit for public office without rejecting the Republican past as well.[33]

Democratic gains in 1874 occurred in both the districts carried and lost by Republicans. In districts where Republican congressional candidates went down to defeat, the Democrats increased their share of the electorate by 10 percentage points over 1872. Even where Republicans won, the Democratic gain between 1872 and 1874 was 15 percentage points. A more detailed analysis of voting patterns in the congressional districts lost by Republicans reveals that a relatively large share of the anti-Republican vote was cast by voters who had sat out the 1872 congressional elections (see Table 9.6). By comparison, previous abstainers represented a very small fraction of those voting for Democrats in districts where Republicans won. Although Republican defections and abstentions were greater where their party's candidates were vanquished, the defection and abstention rates in districts where Republicans won were still relatively high. The pattern of split-ticket voting, moreover, suggests that Talbot's supporters might have done their share of "selling out" their fellow Republicans, especially those acknowledged to have been in trouble, such as Butler, Ayer, Williams, and Alexander. If those who voted for Talbot and Democratic congressional candidates had cast instead the regular Republican ticket, the Massachusetts congressional delegation would most likely have remained solidly Republican. Talbot ran considerably ahead of the Republican ticket where Republican congressional candidates went down to defeat. He even carried Butler's district by over 2,000 votes. On the other hand, if Republican congressional winners had been able to carry Talbot on their coattails, the Republicans would not have lost the governorship.

The 1874 general election forced the Republican caucus in the state legislature to pick a new Massachusetts senator. Large Democratic gains in the legislature meant that a division of Republicans on the senatorial question would make the selection unpredictable. This situation benefited Dawes, who had declined to seek reelection to Congress in order to campaign for the senatorship. If Dawes was not selected, some of his supporters threatened to vote for a "straight-laced" Democrat before supporting any other Republican. Dawes's chief Republican rival, Judge Hoar, had damaged his candidacy among the "Stalwarts" by voting for Tarbox, the Democratic congressional candidate who had defeated Ayer. Hoar also had defended Grant's policies in Louisiana, alienating those critical of federal intervention on behalf of southern Republican governments. As for Dawes, his management of the Pacific Mail investigation improved his image, which had been tar-

TABLE 9.6
A Comparison of Voting Behavior Between Districts Where Republican Congressional Candidates
Lost and Won in 1874
(by percent of electorate)

Description of Voting Behavior	Districts Lost by Republicans	Districts Won by Republicans
Voting for Republican congressional candidates	24%	29%
Voting for Talbot	30	23
Voting for Democratic congressional candidates	32	22
Voting for Gaston	31	27
Voting for Republican congressional candidates in 1872 and for Democratic congressional candidates in 1874	7	4
Voting for Republican congressional candidates in 1872 and not voting in 1874 congressional election	17	10
Voting for Republican congressional candidates in both the 1872 and 1874 congressional elections	16	20
Not voting in 1872 congressional election, but subsequently voting for Democratic congressional candidates in 1874	11	1
Voting for both Talbot and Democratic congressional candidates (split tickets)	9	1
Voting for both Gaston and Republican congressional candidates (split tickets)	5	5
Voting for Talbot, but not voting in congressional elections ("scratching" Republican congressional candidates)	4	0

Note: Congressional districts lost by Republicans in the 1874 election were the Fifth, Sixth, Seventh, Eighth, Tenth, and Eleventh. Districts won by Republicans were the First, Second, Third, Fourth, and Ninth. For the districts lost by Republicans, actual N = 212; for the districts won, actual N = 114.

nished by Credit Mobilier. He still was the candidate of the "neglected" western part of the state. He also had the support of the Butlerites in the legislature, although Collector Simmons ordered the known partisans of Butler to stay far in the background to prevent "anti-Butlerism" from injuring Dawes's chances. Only independent reformers who considered themselves above party concerns were irreconcilably opposed to Dawes.[34]

Dawes's election to the Senate in 1875 for a six-year term was a blow to Charles F. Adams. After voting the straight Democratic ticket in 1874, Adams still hoped that the Republican caucus would offer him the senatorship. The display of voter independence of party lines in the 1874 election justified the selection, Adams believed, of a senator who was above partisan politics. But most anti-Dawes Republicans, including Judge Hoar, preferred Dawes to Adams. Although Adams himself later reflected on the "secret but very determined enmity" to him that showed itself in the senatorial question, his political stock after 1874 was clearly on the rise. The independent voter was becoming a major force in Massachusetts politics and many believed Adams would be the primary beneficiary of the new trend. Accordingly, Vice-President

Wilson, always sensitive to a shift in political currents, worked to effect a reconciliation between himself and Adams. Wilson let it be known that he was considering advocating Adams's nomination for the governorship. Adams, convinced of Wilson's sincerity, agreed to accept a strong universal call, but not a nomination engineered behind-the-scenes. Such "an unequivocal call," however, was unlikely given the opposition to Adams among party leaders in Boston who strongly supported former Congressman Alexander H. Rice. When Rice received Wilson's endorsement and subsequently the Republican gubernatorial nomination, Adams again sensed a deep-seated animosity toward him within the Republican party. When it appeared late in the campaign that Rice's candidacy was not as strong as had been expected, Adams privately gloated that attempts to "crush" him had "backfired" and Republican leaders in the future would be more than ever "at the mercy" of his friends and supporters.[35]

The Republicans felt the pressure of the nonpartisan mood. Some, such as Henry L. Pierce, Charles Codman, and Henry Cabot Lodge, attempted to organize a national independent movement that in 1876 would hold the balance of power between the Grant faction of the Republican party and the southern Democrats. Their leader was Carl Schurz, the Missouri senator who had bolted the Republican party in 1872 to protest Grant's renomination. Bowles believed that in Massachusetts an organized independent reform movement could command one-third of the Republican vote and at least 20 percent of those who had voted for Horace Greeley. Despite the attempts of Bowles and others to stir up enthusiasm for an independent organization, politics in 1875 were, according to the observations of contemporaries, exceedingly dull.[36]

The 1875 campaign was conducted against the grim backdrop of economic hard times. In 1874 and 1875, the city of Holyoke alone housed overnight at public expense 1,225 "tramps" or unemployed men moving from town to town in search of jobs. Reductions in working hours and wages presented as serious a problem for the labor force as did the absence of jobs. Labor leaders appealed to sympathetic politicians for help, often confessing the financial and political weakness of the workers and their unions. But the response of both Republican and Democratic politicians to the economic problems caused by the depression of 1873 was unimaginative and, at times, harmful.[37]

Contemporary understanding of the nature of business cycles held that the panacea for economic depression was retrenchment, a cutback in public spending policies designed to restore the confidence of the business community. Beyond consensus on the need for a general "belt tightening," there were, it was believed, very few things mere mortals could do when caught up in the inexorable working out of immutable economic laws. When an angry crowd of jobless men in Springfield demanded that the government initiate public works projects, they were told by an Irish Democratic city leader that half of the unemployed should go back to the farms they had left. The pro-Democratic Boston *Pilot*, even after shifting its focus from religious and ethnic intolerance to the injustices toward labor, was unable to see the economic marketplace in other than laissez-faire terms. Although Irish Democratic rhetoric seemed at times flamboyant and even populistic, too often it was a cloak for traditional and conservative demands.[38]

The most innovative political response to the depression occurred in Boston in 1876 when a Republican councilman, Halsy J. Boardman, attracted many supporters, including Irish Democrats, by his proposal to employ jobless men on job-creating city projects. Such a scheme was appreciated by business contractors used to doing business with the city and injured by the retrenchment policies of the "nonpartisan" mayor, Samuel J. Cobb. But the Hub's conservative business leadership opposed Boardman and one Boston newspaper charged the councilman with using "communistic" appeals. In the wake of Mayor Cobb's reelection on a nonpartisan "Citizens" ticket, an elated Charles F. Adams recorded in his diary that there was "still some security to property in Boston."[39]

Concerned that many respectable Boston taxpayers were discouraged by the Republican party's refusal to endorse Cobb's reelection, Bowles suggested to Henry Cabot Lodge that the men who had elected Cobb become the nucleus of an independent reform organization, first for Boston and later for the entire state. While Bowles's suggestion revealed the strong conservative bent of many of the self-styled "independents," or "liberals," the Republican revolt against Cobb exposed the superficiality of the city's nonpartisan politics. The spontaneous banding together of supposedly disinterested citizens to secure the election of a nonpartisan mayor may have been more in harmony with the strategy of elites averse to the possibility of lower working-class control of Boston's City Hall.[40]

Both Rice and Gaston, who in 1875 squared off against each other for the governorship, had their careers shaped in the crucible of nonpartisan Boston politics. Rice was essentially a "Republican Mr. Gaston" whose nomination was made "on a low plane by low-plane men." Most Republican party leaders were convinced that Rice would bring back the Republicans who had voted for Gaston in 1874. But the state committee feared that a combination of two things might prevent a Republican victory: a sub-rosa effort by Butler for Gaston and a large vote polled by the Prohibitionists.[41]

The Democrats had their problems, too. Democratic leaders charged that Gaston as governor had not proven bloodthirsty enough in removing Republican officeholders. The state committee's instructions to Gaston to appoint only Democrats to office irritated Tarbox, who despised the old "hunkerism" in his party. Hunkers allegedly dreaded electoral victory because they wanted to keep their party in Massachusetts small in order to monopolize offices in 1877 under a Democratic national administration. The instructions revealed a poor reading of public opinion, according to Tarbox, who believed that the 1875 election would be determined by voters "neither distinctly democratic or republican in a party sense."[42]

The 1875 campaign was conducted feebly and without much spirit. Most Republican party chieftains admitted privately that Gaston had been a respectable governor and that had he been a Republican, they would claim his administration worthy of high praise. To his credit, Gaston had secured a reduced state constabulary and pushed for the enactment of a law to replace prohibition. The legislature responded by passing a local option law giving cities and towns the right to regulate, with certain limitations, the sale of alcoholic beverages. With the liquor issue assuming importance only in the platform of the Prohibitionist party, the contest between Gaston and Rice represented, according to Bowles, "each a mere party organization preparing for mere party triumph." The old campaign rhetoric about parties girding for battle thus seemed quaintly archaic. The Republicans even made the unprecedented assertion that it was a voter's duty to leave his party if it departed from the principles upon which it was founded or proposed candidates unworthy for office.[43]

Many Republicans whose political careers had been forged in the furnace of antislavery radicalism of the 1850s were unable to adjust to the unemotional political world of 1875. For most, it was inconceivable that parties could exist without an underlying ideology to sustain them. For the old antislavery warrior William S. Robinson, the Republican party was "like an old and battered umbrella; of no use for shelter to anybody, and yet *impossible to shut it*." He compared the Republican party in 1875 with the Whig party in 1854: the positions of each were essentially the same because both had forfeited the confidence of the voters. Robinson hoped that the new generation of young men, who were concerned with incompetent officeholders, railroad monopolies, labor reform, and woman suffrage, would take the initiative in reorganizing the party system. It would be a mistake, he argued, to try to graft the new generation of reformers to the old antislavery contro- versy, "especially if we have nothing better to offer them than Grant's bayonets and the Wheeler compromise, based as that is on nothing whatever except partisanship, and a determination to keep power and office for their own sakes."[44]

Relatively few voters in 1875 bothered to go to the polls. Rice won the governorship with a meager 6,000-vote margin over the incumbent Gaston. The days of Republican majorities of 50,000 or even 80,000 seemed gone forever. Because of the relatively low Republican vote and because Rice won with only a plurality of the ballots cast, the Democrats claimed that the outcome had destroyed the prestige of the Republican party "as effectually as a definite defeat."[45]

The Republican leadership was thankful to have avoided defeat and to have won the election with little officeholding interference. Alanson W. Beard, the chairman of the Republican State Central Committee, wrote Dawes that the outcome revealed the tenuousness of the Repub- lican hold on Massachusetts. His formula to strengthen the party was "honest men, honest service to the government and honest money." (Beard had written "civil" before "service" and then scratched it out.) Beard, however, deferred to Dawes and other Republican leaders to interpret Rice's victory, as he was bored with party work and was weary of working on the state committee which, in his words, was "*not* the wisest and most perspective." Beard was also tired of watching the Massachusetts Republicans "who call themselves the best" sit back and complain about "the *Bummers*" in the party. He explained that he occupied his job only because he "did not see who else there was to effectively work the machine." In a period of unemotional politics de- voted to local patronage machines, Beard was uncomfortable controll- ing a purposeless organization for no apparent personal gain.[46]

The fluidity of party lines persisted into the 1875 gubernatorial elec- tion, as evidenced by the degree of crossover voting between the 1875 outcome and the previous off-year gubernatorial election of 1873. Rice captured almost one-fourth of those who had voted for Gaston in 1873 (see Table 9.7). Many of them were former Republicans repulsed by Washburn's support of prohibition. Contributing to the instability in voting patterns between 1873 and 1875 was the large number of Wash- burn Republicans who sat out the balloting in 1875. These abstainers reflected the apathy in the ranks of Republican identifiers who could be expected to vote the party ticket in off years. The bulk of the Prohibi- tionist vote for John I. Baker, as expected, came from former Wash- burn supporters, whereas the "spontaneous" 1,497 votes for Charles F. Adams came exclusively from former Republicans.[47]

TABLE 9.7
Estimated Relationships Between Voting Patterns in the 1873 and 1875 Gubernatorial Races
(by percent of 1875 electorate)

Candidate in 1875	William Gaston	William B. Washburn	Not Voting for Governor 1873	Not Eligible 1873	Percent of 1875 Electorate
William Gaston	13	0	9	0	22
Alexander H. Rice	4	7	12	1	24
John I. Baker	0	2	1	0	3
All Others[a]	0	1	0	0	1
Not Voting for Governor 1875	0	11	31	8	51
Percent of 1875 Electorate	17	21	53	9	100

Note: Actual $\underline{N}$ = 331.

[a]Charles F. Adams, Wendell Phillips and scattered returns.

The organized independent movement was encouraged by the 1875 results. Carl Schurz told Henry Cabot Lodge and others to work within the Massachusetts Republican party with members "of good standing," such as John Murray Forbes and William Gray, and to instruct party delegates to the 1876 national convention to vote for Adams. Perennial Adams supporter Samuel Bowles disagreed with Schurz's strategy, arguing that "the real Adams elements are not in the republican party." Bowles wanted Adams to run as a third-party candidate, but only if the Democrats did not endorse him or somebody else as good for the presidency. On the eve of the delegate selection process, Lodge's "committees of correspondence" elicited many protestations of independent sentiment. Many edged toward the organized independent movement when new scandals in the nation's capital were revealed. In March 1876, when Secretary of War William W. Belknap was proved to have taken bribes from Indian agents, Dawes wrote dolefully that no event since Abraham Lincoln's assassination "caused such universal gloom." The same month witnessed the withdrawal of Richard H. Dana's name for consideration as minister to England. "Haven't we had enough in Massachusetts of Butler's malign influence?" was Beard's terse complaint to the state's Republican congressional delegation.[48]

The nomination of Rutherford B. Hayes for the presidency by the Republicans was interpreted as a victory for the liberal or reform wing of the party and had immediate repercussions for the organized independent movement in Massachusetts. When Schurz decided to endorse Hayes to "gain a decisive influence" in a Hayes administration, he demoralized those who thought they were building the nucleus of a new party. Henry Adams lamented that the formation of an independent party proved "a rope of sand." Many of the Massachusetts "independents" kept the pledges they had made at the Fifth Avenue Conference before the Republican convention and voted Democratic. Hayes's nomination generated little enthusiasm among the ranks of Republican reformers or "Half-breeds." George F. Hoar considered the nomination "respectable and safe," and better than any other proposed "except Bristow or Wheeler."[49]

Most Democrats were extremely sanguine about their party's nomination of Samuel J. Tilden. Patrick A. Collins, for one, regarded Tilden as just the man for the times, but problems arose when Tilden decided he wanted Charles F. Adams on the ticket with him in Massachusetts if only to help his candidacy elsewhere. Pressure had to be placed on Gaston to relinquish his claims to the gubernatorial nomination in order to provide Adams with a convention vote "unequivocally" in his favor. The strong anti-Adams sentiment on the part of many Irish Democrats, including Collins, kept Gaston in the contest until the balloting when Gaston, lacking the votes to win, was forced to withdraw his name from consideration and move that the nomination of Adams be made unanimous. Adams accepted the nomination; he privately stated that for the first time since his return from London public opinion had "testified some measure of sensibility" for his services. Despite Adams's declarations to the contrary, the years of studiously practiced neglect by the Republicans had hurt him deeply.[50]

The Republicans quickly fabricated a deal whereby, in exchange for Adams bestowing some respectability to the Democratic ticket, Tilden, if elected president, would appoint Adams secretary of state. Adams, however, was vulnerable to the charge of having been hostile toward Irish nationalists in the heyday of the Fenian movement. Those who spoke out against Adams used Collins's old denunciations of Adams to prove their point. Democratic chieftains worked hard to keep the Irish in line by enlisting Collins and other leaders of the Boston Irish to campaign for Adams. Collins claimed that Adams, as minister to England, had acted according to instructions from Washington, and that he could hardly be blamed for the statements of his incompetent secretary who wrote lecturing letters to Irish-Americans in British prisons.[51]

On election day Adams "scratched" his own name before depositing the remainder of the regular Democratic ticket into the ballot box. Although Adams feared being elected, he still wanted to run ahead of the rest of the Democratic ticket. To his embarrassment he ran over 4,000 votes behind Tilden. But Irish-American desertions were not injurious to the Democratic ticket as a whole, nor did they cause the defeat of Adams in particular. Only 4 percent of the Irish-born voters either "scratched" Adams from Democratic ballots or managed to split their ticket for Tilden and Rice.[52]

In 1876 there was no continuation of the trend toward split-ticket voting that had characterized the 1874 results (see Table 9.2). The small number of voters who cast split tickets for Republican congressional candidates and for either Adams or Tilden might have been attributable to developments in the Middlesex County district where Butler staged a political comeback by winning the Republican congressional nomination. Butler openly appealed to Tilden supporters and Irish Democrats to vote the straight Democratic ticket with the exception of his name substituted for his opponent's.[53] Butler, an exponent of greenbackism, was convinced that the financial issue was "strong enough to carry the Catholic Church . . . and one-half of the Democratic party." In 1876, however, running as a Republican, he refused to apologize to Irish leaders for waving the "bloody shirt" and asked the Irish to support both his unorthodox financial views and his radical stand on civil rights. But Butler's radicalism, greenbackism, and Republican affiliation were not the reasons the Irish found Butler attractive. His magnetic appeal stemmed from his long record of anti-English and pro-Gaelic stands. The Irish also liked Butler because he was thoroughly despised by the Yankee elites in both the Democratic and Republican parties.[54]

The coalitions established by the Hayes-Tilden contest were slightly more congruent, with divisions separating voters along ethnic groupings geographically distributed throughout the state, than had been the case during the Civil War. In 1864, the nationalities of the inhabitants of all cities and towns in the state, including those born in Ireland, Germany, England, and other foreign countries, along with native-born individuals who were born outside Massachusetts, explains—in a statistical sense—22 percent of the variance in the Republican vote from one locality to the next (see Table 4.8). By 1876, however, the birthplaces of the population accounts for 42 percent of the variation in the Republican vote (see Table 9.8). These same variables also explain a comparatively high percentage of the variance in the vote for Tilden, primarily because of the importance of Irish-born voters in the Democratic coalition.[55]

Contemporaries of the period often attributed the Democratic party resurgence after the Civil War to the increase in the Irish population. While information on the number of second-generation Irish eligible to vote in the 1870s is unavailable, the 1875 state census does list the num-

TABLE 9.8
Total Variance Explained in the 1876 Presidential Vote by
Selected Sets of Social, Economic, and Political Variables

Variables	Number of Cases	Percentage of Variance Explained		
		Republican	Democratic	Abstained
Valuation and tax category[a]	329	44%	7%	18%
Occupational "A"[b]	339	42	29	36
Place of birth[c]	340	42	35	18
Occupational "B"[d]	339	31	13	15
Religious[e]	325	27	21	12
Town size and growth rate[f]	341	5	5	2
Competitiveness[g]	341	--	--	0

Sources: The manuscript "Social Statistics" schedule of the
1870 federal census for Massachusetts is incomplete, making it
necessary to resort to the 1860 data on church seating
accommodations. The source for all other variables is
Massachusetts, Bureau of Statistics of Labor, The Census of
Massachusetts: 1875.

Note: The percentage of variance explained (R^2) was computed
by running separate regressions with each set of variables.

[a]Per capita valuation in 1875 and the percentage of "legal"
voters assessed both property and poll taxes in 1869.

[b]Percentages of occupied males engaged in 1875 in the following
classified occupations: "Government and Professional,"
"Domestic and Personal Office," "Trade and Transportation,"
"Agriculture, Fisheries, etc.," "Manufactures and Mechanical
Industries," and "Indefinite, Nonproductive and Propertied."

[c]Percentages of the 1875 population born in Ireland, Germany,
England, Canada, Scotland, Massachusetts, and states other than
Massachusetts.

[d]Percentages of occupied males in 1875 engaged in
manufacturing, agriculture, and fishing.

[e]Percentages of church seating accommodations of the total
population belonging in 1860 to the following denominations:
Congregational, Unitarian, Universalist, Baptist, Methodist,
Episcopalian, Quaker, Roman Catholic, and all other churches.

[f]Population in 1875 and population growth rate between 1865 and
1875.

[g]David Index of party competition in the 1876 presidential
election.

ber of legal voters in each city and town who were born in Ireland.
This information, however, should have discouraged contemporaries,
especially party canvassers, from exaggerating the importance of both
the Irish vote and the foreign-born vote. In 1875 only 46 percent of the
entire foreign male population of voting age was naturalized, meaning
that less than half of the foreign-born males above the age of twenty-
one were qualified voters. There was great variation in the rate at
which different groups of foreign-born population took out naturalization papers and ultimately became American citizens. Of Irish-born
males of voting age in 1875, 55 percent had become citizens. The com-

parable figures for English-born, German-born, and Canadian-born were 45 percent, 52 percent, and 24 percent, respectively. Naturalized voters comprised about 20 percent of the eligible voters in 1874, whereas they had constituted approximately 13 percent of the voting population in 1865.[56]

The foreign-born vote in Massachusetts was decidedly in Tilden's column in 1876, although this resulted from the heavily Democratic vote cast by Irish-Americans who made up the bulk of foreign-born voters. The small number of English, German, and Canadian voters does not permit safe generalizations about the voting behavior of these groups, but the regression results suggest that the Democrats did not monopolize the loyalties of all foreign-born voters, especially English-born and Scottish-born voters (see Table 9.9).

Compared with the 1864 election, partisan preferences in the 1876 presidential race remained congruent with cleavages splitting voters along economic lines (see Table 4.8 and 9.8). The Republicans continued to run disproportionally well in areas with few economic resources and high proportions of legal voters who paid both poll taxes and property taxes. Conversely, Republicans fared poorly in cities and towns with above-average per capita valuations and higher percentages of voters who paid no tax except the required two-dollar poll tax. The per capita valuation taken in conjunction with the percentage of legal voters paying both property and poll taxes explains—in a statistical sense—44 percent of the average rate at which local electorates supported Hayes. As in the 1864 election, these two variables were slightly better predictors of the Republican vote than other groups of variables measuring religious and social characteristics of the state's cities and towns. In addition, six occupational groupings of employed males in 1875 explained as much of the variance in the vote for Hayes as did the sets of ethnoreligious variables, thus underscoring again the importance of purely economic factors in determining the Republican vote.

The economic basis of the vote had not changed radically since the Civil War because many of the partisan affiliations formed during the first two Lincoln elections endured into the 1870s. Tilden inherited the ballots of over 90 percent of those who had voted for Seymour, and Hayes received the ballots of over 80 percent of the 1868 Republicans (see Table 9.10). Although traces of Civil War voting patterns were still visible in 1876, they were overshadowed by the revitalization of the Democratic party. And although many of the gains made by the Democrats in the off-year 1874 congressional election were temporary, the party underwent a fundamental realignment between 1868 and

TABLE 9.9
Estimated Relationships Between Birthplace and Voting
in the 1876 Presidential Election
(by percent)

Place of Birth	% for Hayes	% for Tilden	% Not Voting
Scotland	100[a]	0[a]	0[a]
England	69	0[a]	49
In-state	52	19	29
Out-of-state	39	44	17
In-town[b]	39	18	42
Ireland	17	71	11
Canada	0[a]	95	28
Germany	0	100[a]	100[a]
Other foreign-born	0[a]	50	100[a]
Actual Vote	42	30	28

Note: Actual N = 341. The 1875 state census data on the
nativities of voters did not divide the total number of
native-born voters into those born in-town, in-state, and
out-of-state. The number of eligible voters born in these
categories was estimated by interpolations from the census
data on the nativities of males in each voting unit. See
Massachusetts, Bureau of Statistics of Labor, The Census of
Massachusetts: 1875, table 1, pp. 273-84.

[a]Logically impossible estimates have been set at the 0 or 100
percent limits.

[b]Born in the city or town in which voting.

1876. One-fifth of Tilden's vote consisted of former Grant supporters, a group that included all the Republicans who had bolted for Greeley in 1872. These Liberal Republicans were joined in the ranks of the Democracy by substantial numbers of new voters. Due to acquisitions of former Republicans and new voters, about one-half of Tilden's supporters did not cast ballots for Seymour in 1868. The Democratic vote in 1876 thus represented more than a mere recovery from the setback of 1872. Tilden and his party were able both to consolidate their hold on anti-Grant Republicans who had defected by way of the Liberal Republican movement and to reap a new harvest of voters who had become eligible to vote after 1872. In net results, the Democratic party climbed up a full seven percentage points higher in its share of the electorate than in any election since 1848 (see Table 1.3). The strong showing made by Tilden's candidacy demonstrated that the Republican hegemony in presidential elections could be challenged.

Whereas the quantitative evidence reveals the emergence of a more competitive party system by the end of the 1870s, the qualitative nature of Bay State politics had also changed. By the second half of the 1870s, the emotional nature of wartime politics had given way to

TABLE 9.10
Republican Disaffection During the Grant Years:
The Effects of Tilden's Candidacy on the 1868 and 1872 Voting Alignments
(by percent of 1876 electorate)

A. Crossover Voting Between the 1868 and 1876 Presidential Elections
(Actual <u>N</u> = 331)

	Candidate in 1868		Not Voting for President 1868	Not Eligible 1868	Percent of 1876 Electorate
Candidate in 1876	Seymour	Grant			
Tilden	15	6	1	8	30
Hayes	0	32	2	8	42
Not Voting for President 1876	1	0	14	12	28
Percent of 1876 Electorate	16	38	17	28	100

B. Crossover Voting Between the 1872 and 1876 Presidential Elections
(Actual <u>N</u> = 338)

	Candidate in 1872		Not Voting for President 1872	Not Eligible 1872	Percent of 1876 Electorate
Candidate in 1876	Greeley	Grant			
Tilden	16	2	6	5	30
Hayes	0	32	7	3	42
Not Voting for President 1876	0	3	17	8	28
Percent of 1876 Electorate	16	37	31	16	100

professionally-managed politics in which party cadres worked diligently to build up local organizations through patronage and careful attention to the needs of constituents. The era when Reconstruction issues could dominate state politics had passed. Although the issue of securing justice for the southern blacks lived on, it was submerged by other issues and concerns that events inevitably pushed upon the Massachusetts electorate. The Republicans failed to stake out positions on the newer issues that would differentiate them from the Democrats. They offered the voters no alternative to the older commitments to racial equality and equal rights. Instead, their energies were completely absorbed in intraparty struggles for the control of a party organization stripped of its old mission and purpose.

Conclusion

How my heart warms as I think of the brave and true men who led the sacramental hosts through the long struggle which placed Massachusetts openly, actively, and perpetually on the side of freedom, and won their final victory in placing John A. Andrew in the chair of Winthrop and Hancock! There were giants on the earth in those days.—*Francis W. Bird, quoted in* "Warrington" Pen-Portraits

---

The centering of power in the radical wing of the Republican party in many ways represented an anomalous event in the political history of Massachusetts. Charles Sumner and his allies in the Bird Club were not true party men, for revolutionary principles regarding human rights, rather than the methodical intricacies of running a party organization, consumed their energies. Their political careers were forged during the antebellum period in the crucible of the national debate over slavery. They had no consistent positions on, and little concern with, economic policy, state issues, and local matters, but rather strove to keep attention rivetted on the evils that lay in the South. Once in command of the most important offices of the Commonwealth, they sought to implement their radical ideas without trying to placate the moderates or conservatives within their own party.

The Bay State Republican party thus owed much to the uncompromising Free-Soil element in its coalition. The dedicated and resourceful radicals in the Bird Club were in the vanguard of those antagonistic to the South and the institution of slavery. They advocated waging total war on the rebellious states, immediate emancipation of slaves, and a basic reorganization of southern society and politics. They were as much concerned with securing full civic and political equality for blacks in the North as they were for blacks in the South.

The rise to power of the Sumner radicals was not just the story of the splitting and hemorrhaging, birth and death, of constituencies and parties in the 1850s. From the time the radical Bird Club gained control of the Republican party in 1860 until power slipped from its grasp in the early 1870s, the political center of Bay State politics was devitalized, and the views held by Republicans and their opponents were diametrically opposed. The majority of Republicans favored the revolutionary ideas espoused by the radicals regarding race relations, the structure of southern society, and the use of federal power. Democrats, on the other hand, advocated a conciliatory policy toward the South based on acceptance of the principle of white supremacy. This ideological polarization between the Republicans and their opponents was institutionalized as the dominant feature of Massachusetts electoral politics during the Civil War and its immediate aftermath.

After the war other controversial topics, such as prohibition, labor reform, women's rights, political corruption, and the currency question, assumed greater importance than before. These issues brought cross-cutting pressures on the Republican majority that triggered third-party movements and produced increasing defections to the Democrats. The mid-1870s witnessed a significant electoral realignment, although by no means of the magnitude of the upheaval that created the Republican party two decades earlier. As a result, a more competitive system emerged in which the ideological differences between the two major parties all but disappeared.

The constituencies of the Republican and Democratic parties differed in social composition as well as in ideology. The Republicans ran best in cities and towns characterized by strong former support for the Free-Soil party, by low levels of relatively equitably distributed aggregate wealth, and by high concentrations of Congregationalists. They did not run particularly well in areas where the antiforeign, anti-Catholic Know-Nothing party received disproportionately high levels of support in the 1850s. Among a large array of explanatory variables, including measures of the ethnic and religious composition of the electorate, the per capita value of taxable personal and real property had the greatest relative impact, although a negative impact, on the Republican presidential vote. Economic factors consistently explained more of the variation in the Republican vote than did religious or ethnic groupings of the electorate. The quantitative and qualitative evidence suggests that Republicans, at least in Massachusetts, were interested in antislavery, not nativism, and were strongest in areas of "middling" wealth.

This statistical portrait is consistent with the party's self image. Republican party leaders were aware of the social levels to which their egalitarian ideology appealed. It was common knowledge that antislavery sentiment was more meaningful in cities and towns located disproportionately in the center of the state, where the idea of a virtuous community peopled by educated and hard-working farmers and mechanics still had validity. Republicans believed that their success at the polls depended on the support of the great "middling-interest" class. "The highest class, aristocratically associated and affiliated," explained Samuel Bowles, the editor of the conservative Springfield *Republican*, were "timid, afraid to change," immobilized because they "held in their hands, the sensitive cords of commerce," while the lowest classes, the poor native and immigrant laborers, were "fed by the rich man's money and led by the rich man's finger."[1]

Because of the variation in voter turnout from one locality to the next, the socioeconomic determinants of support for the Democrats were never the mere inverse of those for the Republicans. Although there was a significant foreign-born voting bloc, composed primarily of Irish-Americans, that shaped in the 1860s the contours of support for the Democrats, there was no comparable pietistic voting bloc. The degree to which a group was evangelical in orientation did not necessarily determine the way its members were likely to vote. Ordering religious denominations by their levels of Republican and Democratic support produced two different lists, not a single underlying continuum demonstrating congruence between religious and political preferences. This conflicts with the position of historians who argue that partisan differences in the nineteenth century reflected the clash of two identifiable types of religious perspectives held by pietists and liturgicals. Until political analysts examine the different levels at which various religious groups and nonchurchgoers turned out and voted and test simultaneously for economic cleavages that might have cut deeply across denominational and "Nothingarian" lines, there is no reason to dismiss the political culture of Massachusetts as an aberration and to believe that no analogies could be found elsewhere in the North.

Recently, historians have offered impressive evidence that in many northern cities and states, prohibition, nativism, and anti-Catholicism were often more important than antislavery extensionism in shaping the political realignment of the 1850s. But such was not the case in Massachusetts where the radical element in the Republican party made no effort to woo teetotalers, nativists, or religious bigots. Not only had the Bird Club radicals been as much at odds with the Know-Nothings as with the Democrats, but they denounced those in Republican ranks who cultivated the virulent anti-Irish sentiment. During the years of Know-Nothing ascendancy, the radicals cheerfully accepted political defeat rather than acquiesce to the denial of equal rights before the law because of religion or nationality.

The quantitative analysis of the movement of voters between parties from election to election in the 1850s reveals that the Bay State American party was a fragile coalition of disparate groups who hoped to use the nativist movement as a vehicle for their own political goals. The short-lived 1856 bargain between the Know-Nothings and the Republicans was engineered by opportunistic and conservative Republicans who drastically underestimated the vote-getting power of the larger issue of slavery. To insist on the importance of antislavery in moving politics from beneath, however, is not to excise nativism or prohibition as surface issues in the 1850s. Nativism, prohibition, and antislavery, moreover, were not mutually exclusive—they overlapped in many ways—but in Massachusetts they were distinct as political forces.

When compelled to choose between nativism and antislavery, most Bay State Republicans chose the latter, although many or even most might have held both values simultaneously. Those who emphasized nativism at the expense of all other concerns increasingly abstained from voting in state gubernatorial elections in the late 1850s and dwindled in size to a small, isolated, and intransigent voting bloc by 1859. The final achievement of Know-Nothingism was the passage of the antiimmigrant "two-year" amendment, which was adopted because the majority of the rump American party constituency voted in favor of it while the overwhelming majority of Republicans and Democrats failed to vote in the referendum. After 1859 what was left of political nativism was confined to the old-line Whigs and the Constitutional Union party, which was ostensibly more interested in unionism than with Know-Nothingism. Nativism never again achieved the considerable influence it exercised at the polls in the mid-1850s. Even then Know-Nothingism represented at most a temporary and abnormal stop for many voters on their way to Republicanism. In their zeal to beat the Whigs and gain power, many antislavery men in 1854 initially joined the Know-Nothings, but the resuscitation of a genuine antislavery party brought them back into the fold, rapidly in 1855 and entirely by 1856. Roughly half of the Massachusetts Whigs on their way into Republican ranks avoided any connection with the anti-Catholic, anti-foreign American party.

After the first Confederate shot hit Fort Sumter, the march of events was so rapid that every month almost seemed to be a new era in the history of the nation. The Democratic party became increasingly identified by its hostility to the measures that the Republican-controlled federal government implemented to crush the rebellion and maintain the national unity. When Bay State Democrats struggled to keep their organizational identity intact by rallying around the "War Democratic" plea for a restoration of "the Constitution as it is and the Union as it was," they exposed their total and absolute disagreement with the Republicans over the character of the war. Depending heavily on the votes of Irish-Americans and on others who feared the revolutionary implications of emancipating slaves, the Democratic party instinctively sympathized with the Confederate determination to maintain white supremacy. Revulsion for the ultraconservative and racist position of the Democrats united conservative, moderate, and radical Republicans.

During the period between the 1864 and 1868 presidential elections, the normal "give and take" of pragmatic politics was suspended and voting patterns reflected an intense and irreconcilable polarization in the beliefs of Massachusetts citizens over the issues arising from the war and Reconstruction. President Andrew Johnson's attempt to unite conservative Republicans in a coalition with Democrats, in order to support his efforts to restore the white South to power in 1866, only exacerbated existing party divisions rather than inaugurating any new alignment of voters. In the "off-year" 1867 gubernatorial election, however, party lines were temporarily ruptured when many Republicans voted with the Democrats to support candidates to the legislature who were pledged to liberalize the liquor law. Prohibition was not a clearly partisan matter and the 1867 outcome was a deviating one. The greatest interest in the election was centered in the manufacturing cities and towns where the temperance crusade had originated and where most violations of the law had occurred. Although the pro-Democratic press tried to equate the radicals with the unpopular prohibitory law, there never existed any consensus among Bird Club members on any aspect of the liquor question.

The election of Ulysses S. Grant to the presidency in 1868 marked the beginning of the end of the era when radicalism, as a powerful political force, sustained by war issues and events in the South, could define political conflict. New controversial issues, including labor reform, temperance legislation, and women's rights, were finally able to loosen party loyalties. Their effects upon the Republicans were first reflected in internal factionalism and then spilled over to the anti-Grant Liberal Republican movement. Because of the lopsided Republican victory in the 1872 presidential race, it has been seductively easy for historians to conclude that few, if any, rank-and-file Republicans bolted to the Liberal Republican and Democratic opposition. Yet estimates of the extent of the movement of voters across party lines reveal that Republican defections were far greater in 1872 than was the case twelve years later with the celebrated Mugwump revolt.

When Charles Sumner and Frank Bird voted for Horace Greeley

and the Democrats, they demonstrated to the Bay State electorate that political independence was not necessarily treasonable. The Democratic party gained a new respectability as it shook off its wartime image as an outright friend of the rebellious South. In 1874 the Democrats electrified the Commonwealth and the nation by capturing the governorship and destroying the Republican monopoly on congressional seats, although Democratic party chieftains were well aware of their party's tenuous hold on many "independent" and nominally Republican voters. Yet the Democrats had skillfully exploited the newer issues and had neutralized those relating to Reconstruction by endorsing equality before the law and equality at the ballot box.

The revival of Democratic party fortunes in Massachusetts presidential politics began with the 1876 election. Bay State Democrats who four years earlier had stayed away from the polls now returned to their party. In addition, in the Democratic column were virtually all the 1868 Republicans who had bolted in 1872 for Greeley. Moreover, the Liberal Republicans were joined in 1876 by a significant number of 1872 Grant men. Not only did the Liberal Republican movement cause a permanent schism in Republican ranks, but when taken in conjunction with the revival of the political fortunes of the Democrats, the period of the 1870s witnessed a gradual or "secular" realignment of state electoral politics, resulting in a more evenly balanced, competitive party system. This finding challenges the standard "critical election" model of voting, which predicts abnormal stability in electoral outcomes in the 1870s and 1880s until a massive reshuffling of voters in the 1890s. Not only was there more permanent shuffling across party lines in Massachusetts presidential contests in the 1870s than in the 1890s, but the 1872 and 1876 elections transformed the public image as well as the anatomy of the Republican and Democratic parties.

The leadership of the Republican party also emerged transformed by the intramural fighting of the 1870s. The radical Sumner wing of the party, along with the Liberals, met with defeat, for their conviction that the party had degenerated into a mere vehicle for the advancement of unprincipled politicians propelled them to make too direct an assault on the party organization. On the other hand, the leading exponent of "Grantism," the colorful Brahmin-baiter Benjamin F. Butler, was also defeated, for his unorthodox campaign style offended the respectable citizenry. With the liberal faction held in check, if not alienated, and "Stalwarts" like Butler held at bay, power in the Republican party shifted to the so-called "Half-breeds." This group included such men as George F. Hoar and Henry L. Dawes, who were willing to curry favor with businessmen and bankers and yet were unwilling to wage intraparty wars on Liberals or Stalwarts.

Although a former radical such as Hoar was able to make the adjustment to the changed political circumstances of the 1870s, he was frustrated by the absence of the old missionary zeal that had sustained his party in the 1850s and 1860s. He reluctantly turned his attention away from Reconstruction issues to less inspiring matters. Even at the grass-roots level, many lamented the passing of the crusading years of a generation earlier. A party worker in Pittsfield waxed nostalgic about "the more active days" of the Republican party when he distributed copies of speeches by Andrew, Sumner, and Wilson by the "hundreds of thousands."[2] The sense of the dissipation of the old zeal was captured by the vapidity of the 1875 gubernatorial election, a contest between Alexander H. Rice, "a Republican Mr. Gaston," and William Gaston, "a Democratic Mr. Rice." The candidates of the two major parties were as indistinguishable as Tweedle-dum and Tweedle-dee. Only a decade earlier it had made all the difference in the world who sat in the chair of Hancock and Winthrop. During the Civil War the future of the nation, not to mention the fate of millions of descendants of black Africans, had hung in the balance when Massachusetts voters went to the polls to choose a governor.

Many predicted in the 1870s that the Republican party, riddled with factionalism, stripped of its old antislavery zeal, and bereft of men of stature at the helm, would fall apart. They, of course, were wrong. As the Boston *Commonwealth* foresaw, the "momentum of the marching" would keep the party alive, and "the breaking up of the Republican organization will be deferred long after the distinctive mission of the party has ended."[3] In a sense, Massachusetts politics had merely resumed a normal condition, returning again to a poltical world devoted increasingly to patronage machines and the routine "business" of making concessions and compromises. The revolutionary phase of the Civil War party system had become history.

Appendix
Decomposition of Variance Analysis
of Electoral Changes in Massachusetts
Presidential, Congressional, and
Gubernatorial Voting Returns,
1852–1896

A detailed technical discussion of the decomposition of variance method of analyzing electoral change is presented by William H. Flanigan and Nancy H. Zingale in their "The Measurement of Electoral Change," pp. 49–82. Consequently, only a brief outline of the technique is included here to enable a lay audience to understand the results that this method produces.

The elements in the array of statistics analyzed by the decomposition of variance model are weighted percentages of the potential electorate who voted for a particular party in a given election in each of Massachusetts's fourteen counties. The "normal" voting pattern of the electorate is defined as the grand mean of the data array or the mean vote of the state as a whole over the series of elections. A two-way analysis of variance design allocates a portion of the total amount of variation in the array to the "county effect" or the sum of the squared deviations from the county means, a portion to the "election effect" or the sum of the squared deviations from the election means, and the remainder to the "interaction effect" or the residual variation not explained by either the county means or the election means. The election effect becomes a measure of "surge" in the vote occurring uniformly across all counties to the benefit or injury of the particular party vote that is being analyzed. The interaction sum of squares is a measure of the amount of nonuniform change in the design. This interaction effect becomes a measure of "interactive" change, which is change due to some compensating shifts in the partisan vote among the counties. The county effect is irrelevant in analyzing each election's contribution to the change in voter support for a particular party. But if, for instance, one were interested in analyzing the socioeconomic characteristics of the counties that contributed more or less to a realignment of voter coalitions, it would be necessary to use the county sum of squares. For an example of correlating county socioeconomic characteristics with county contributions to interactive realigning change, see Nancy H. Zingale, "Third Party Alignments in a Two Party System: The Case of Minnesota," in *The History of American Electoral Behavior*, eds. Joel H. Silbey, Allan G. Bogue, and William H. Flanigan (Princeton, N.J.: Princeton University Press Limited Paperback Editions, 1978), pp. 106–33.

To distinguish between deviating and realigning changes it is necessary to divide up the entire series of elections into overlapping sets of some reasonable number of adjacent elections. This allows measurements of change to be taken for each election when it is compared with elections preceding and following it. If the difference when an election is in the first position in the set of elections is greater than the difference when the election is in the last position, the election has set a new pattern and some realignment has occurred. The specific rules for partitioning surge change and interactive change into their deviating and realigning components are based on the assumption that an election involving some realigning change will more approximate the vote pattern that comes after it than the vote pattern that came before.

The four types of electoral change (deviating and realigning surge, and deviating and realigning interaction) in the Democratic and Republican votes for president, congress, and governor statewide, using the fourteen Massachusetts counties as voting units, are presented in Tables A.1 through A.3 at the end of this appendix. The same types of change in the "party of abstainers" for these same elections are also given. For the presidential series, voting statistics for Democrats and for abstainers include the election of 1844 through the election of 1916, whereas the Republican series begins in 1856. For the congressional series, the Democratic and nonvoting data cover the period from 1848 to 1908; the Republican returns include the period from 1856 to 1908. The gubernatorial series includes the period from 1846 to 1904 for Democrats and abstainers, and from 1855 to 1904 for the Republicans. Three elections were chosen as the number to be included in the moving cross section of presidential elections; five were selected in the cross section of congressional elections and nine for the gubernatorial cross section. This ensures that the results will be comparable to the extent that each cross section covers an eight-year period in the three separate election series. Because the rules for partitioning change into realigning and deviating components require comparing each party's vote with a preceding and succeeding set of elections, the first few and the last few elections in each series cannot be analyzed although they are used in the analysis of other elections.

Two important initial observations should be made about the full range of the results presented in Tables A.1 through A.3. First, most of the changes occurring in the support for the Democratic and Republican candidates for president, congress, and governor during the second half of the nineteenth century are deviating changes. Second, there is a clear dominance of surge over interactive change. This suggests not only that variation was a persistent characteristic of the Civil War party system in Massachusetts, but also that regional considerations did not play as important a role in political realignments as did uniform across-the-board movements of voters away from or into one of the major parties. Over the entire series of elections, a consistent amount of deviating interactive change remains at a fairly constant level. Except in a few instances, most notably in the case of voter abstentions in the 1874 congressional elections, this quantity of change is both small and temporary and can be regarded as idiosyncratic behavior on the part of the county electorates. Realigning interactions, on the other hand, take place very infrequently, and, although usually overshadowed by realigning surges, such changes remain very interesting from the standpoint of trying to explain their occurrences.

The three elections contributing the most to realignments in the Democratic presidential vote were those of 1856, 1876, and 1896 (see Table A.1). Each of these elections was marked by a considerable realigning surge that favored the Democrats only in 1876. A portion of the change that took place in 1856, however, was interactive change, indicative of some counties moving relatively more Democratic, others relatively less Democratic. A minor realignment in the Democratic vote occurred when a small surge vote accured to the party in the 1864 election. Because no new pattern was established for the Republicans in that year, the small, yet permanent, movement of voters into Democratic ranks presumably was due to 1860 Breckinridge Democrats returning to the party fold in 1864. The realigning surge that occurred in 1876 was extremely beneficial to the Democrats. Even though the 1876 presidential election was a two-party contest, Democratic gains were not reflected in Republican losses. The increase in voter turnout apparently affected the realignment process, because the shift to the Democrats in 1876 came about through the entry of new voters and previous apolitical citizens into the active electorate (see Table A.1). A similar process occurred at the end of the nineteenth century when Democratic losses in 1896 were not reflected in any discernible Republican gains.

The presidential elections contributing the most to lasting and realigning changes in the Republican vote were those of 1872, 1884, and 1900 (see Table A.1). In the case of the Republicans it is somewhat misleading to compare the 1870s, 1880s, or any other later period with the 1850s, for there was more than a mere reshuffling of voters in that decade. Both the birth and demise of entire political parties occurred in the 1850s. Thus, the tremendous surge of voters in 1856 into the newly formed Republican party was naturally quite dramatic. Nevertheless, the occurrence of a relatively large realigning interactive change reveals that the Republicans initially drew better in some counties than in others. The presidential elections of 1872, 1884, and 1900 were characterized by uniform losses in voting support for the Republicans. It is of special interest that, while the Democratic party experienced a permanent realignment in its vote in 1896, no parallel realigning change occurred in the Republican vote. The 1896 presidential election apparently was a deviating election for the Republicans.

Except for the Democratic vote, interpretation of the congressional and gubernatorial series is cumbersome and difficult. The two-way analysis of variance technique does not work well over periods of extreme fluctuations in the vote, attributable primarily to the influx of "peripheral voters" in presidential years and their exit from the active electorate in "off-year" elections. This fluctuation caused realignments in opposite directions in elections close together in time in the congressional and gubernatorial series for the Republican and nonvoter coalitions (see Tables A.2 and A.3). Such results, unfortunately, make little sense conceptually. The Democratic congressional and gubernatorial series are both, however, quite interpretable. The realigning surge in the Democratic congressional vote occurring in 1858 was due to the relatively poor performance of Democratic congressional candidates prior to this election. In the post-Civil War period, the 1874 election contributed most to a realigning change in support for Democratic congressional candidates. The 1874 election also marked the largest realigning change in the Democratic gubernatorial vote in the second half of the nineteenth century. In both cases the Democrats benefited from an across-the-board movement of voters into their party. A new and durable pattern was clearly set in Massachusetts in 1874 in the Democratic congressional and gubernatorial vote.

Each Massachusetts county was "weighted" by the number of potential voters or "legal" voters it contained at the time of each election. This ensured that smaller counties would not be overrepresented in the analysis. Because interactive change is compensating, it should be thought of as equal parts of positive and negative change in the tables that follow. The source for the voting returns is the Historical Data Archives of the Inter-University Consortium for Political and Social Research, Ann Arbor, Michigan.

TABLE A.1
Decomposition of Variance Analysis of Electoral Changes in the
Massachusetts Presidential Vote, 1852-1908, Using Counties as
Subunits

Election Year	Deviating Surge	Realigning Surge	Deviating Interaction	Realigning Interaction
Democratic Vote				
1852	-2.77%	0%	2.47%	0%
1856	.84	-7.78	1.94	2.74
1860	-2.83	0	1.15	0
1864	.01	1.98	1.74	0
1868	1.41	0	1.69	0
1872	-1.41	0	1.80	0
1876	1.28	5.46	1.99	0
1880	-.59	0	1.74	0
1884	-.70	0	1.67	0
1888	2.37	0	.97	0
1892	2.50	0	.87	0
1896	-6.17	-5.21	1.58	0
1900	1.45	2.10	1.08	0
1904	.51	0	1.17	0
1908	-1.96	0	1.17	0
Republican Vote				
1856	1.60%	33.37%	2.67%	1.76%
1860	-3.19	0	1.65	0
1864	1.59	0	1.78	1.74
1868	-.18	0	.98	0
1872	.29	-6.19	1.88	0
1876	-.22	0	1.29	1.06
1880	-.08	0	.88	0
1884	-3.22	-2.04	.89	0
1888	1.55	0	.77	0
1892	1.68	0	.62	0
1896	6.72	0	1.07	0
1900	.55	-3.87	1.03	0
1904	-.06	0	1.29	0
1908	-.48	0	.82	0
Abstaining				
1852	7.52%	2.69%	4.80%	0%
1856	-5.46	-1.58	3.10	0
1860	1.09	0	3.39	0
1864	4.37	0	2.63	2.51
1868	1.93	0	1.45	0
1872	7.31	0	2.44	0
1876	-.90	-3.14	2.05	1.67
1880	-.31	0	1.43	0
1884	1.20	0	1.40	0
1888	-.87	0	.81	0
1892	-2.45	0	.58	0
1896	2.18	0	1.85	0
1900	-1.31	4.71	1.14	0
1904	.13	0	1.11	0
1908	1.18	0	1.29	0

TABLE A.2
Decomposition of Variance Analysis of Electoral Changes in the
Massachusetts Congressional Vote, 1856-1896, Using Counties as
Subunits

Election Year	Deviating Surge	Realigning Surge	Deviating Interaction	Realigning Interaction
		Democratic Vote		
1856	2.67%	0%	2.27%	1.55%
1858	-1.64	9.35	4.20	0
1860	9.16	0	3.04	0
1862	1.16	0	3.32	0
1864	.46	0	1.84	0
1866	-8.02	-1.12	2.83	0
1868	1.38	0	3.05	0
1870	-2.12	0	2.52	0
1872	.78	0	2.09	0
1874	.58	7.40	5.27	0
1876	4.38	0	2.05	0
1878	-2.48	-1.94	5.78	1.37
1880	2.24	2.08	1.71	0
1882	-3.06	0	1.99	0
1884	-4.26	0	3.19	0
1886	-.76	0	.93	0
1888	5.84	0	2.04	0
1890	1.68	0	1.43	0
1892	4.04	0	1.81	0
1894	-1.36	-5.22	1.78	0
1896	-2.16	0	1.86	1.23
		Republican Vote		
1856	8.42%	33.58%	7.83%	0%
1858	-7.94	-3.54	3.18	0
1860	2.96	3.00	3.00	0
1862	3.50	-3.44	3.45	0
1864	12.10	0	3.31	0
1866	-.90	-4.40	2.33	0
1868	11.90	0	1.66	0
1870	-4.88	-1.52	1.66	1.76
1872	4.66	2.46	2.98	0
1874	-9.16	-1.98	2.56	0
1876	1.86	2.48	1.94	0
1878	-1.34	0	1.52	0
1880	4.46	0	1.30	0
1882	-.50	-5.24	1.42	0
1884	6.00	0	2.47	0
1886	-5.60	0	1.94	0
1888	2.46	3.54	.66	1.22
1890	-7.82	-1.62	1.37	0
1892	-.06	2.04	.64	0
1894	-.34	-1.12	.50	0
1896	8.36	0	.84	0
		Abstaining		
1856	-11.12%	-2.55%	2.41%	0%
1858	6.46	6.62	3.40	0
1860	-11.24	-3.10	4.84	0
1862	1.38	5.18	2.21	3.74
1864	-13.02	0	3.25	0
1866	13.28	0	1.72	0
1868	-5.28	-5.84	1.34	0
1870	15.32	0	4.24	0
1872	4.02	0	2.18	0
1874	-5.04	-3.94	16.52	0
1876	-1.14	0	2.25	3.72
1878	1.86	0	.86	0
1880	-2.24	0	1.35	0
1882	.78	5.78	.71	0
1884	-5.26	-1.86	1.44	0
1886	8.92	2.02	.85	0
1888	-7.12	-2.36	.92	0
1890	4.92	3.86	1.33	0
1892	-8.66	-1.52	1.11	0
1894	.85	1.99	2.10	0
1896	-3.60	-1.24	1.27	1.14

TABLE A.3
Decomposition of Variance Analysis of Electoral Changes in the
Massachusetts Gubernatorial Vote, 1854-1896, Using Counties as
Subunits

Election Year	Deviating Surge	Realigning Surge	Deviating Interaction	Realigning Interaction
		Democratic Vote		
1854	-9.15%	-2.68%	2.99%	0%
1855	1.11	0	2.90	0
1856	3.29	0	1.74	1.29
1857	-1.11	0	2.20	0
1858	1.64	0	2.30	0
1859	-.05	0	1.81	0
1860	-.42	0	1.36	0
1861	-2.44	0	1.45	0
1862	5.61	1.54	2.08	1.14
1863	-5.36	0	1.93	0
1864	2.67	0	1.46	0
1865	-9.06	0	2.00	0
1866	-7.23	0	1.18	0
1867	5.77	3.16	4.35	0
1868	2.25	0	2.30	0
1869	-2.97	0	2.17	0
1870	-4.34	0	2.00	0
1871	-5.18	0	1.74	0
1872	-1.95	0	1.55	0
1873	-2.69	0	2.57	0
1874	2.66	4.95	3.74	0
1875	-3.47	0	2.52	0
1876	2.77	1.18	1.92	0
1877	-6.03	-1.04	1.73	0
1878	3.15	0	1.39	2.05
1879	2.41	0	1.55	0
1880	2.33	0	1.11	0
1881	-12.40	0	1.46	0
1882	4.68	1.83	.92	0
1883	7.79	0	1.51	0
1884	-1.90	0	2.25	0
1885	-7.35	0	1.04	0
1886	-2.85	0	1.11	0
1887	-2.25	0	1.21	0
1888	4.39	0	1.12	0
1889	.29	-3.27	1.11	0
1890	3.71	0	.87	0
1891	6.48	0	.68	0
1892	11.19	0	.57	0
1893	4.85	0	1.31	0
1894	-1.86	0	1.47	0
1895	-2.81	0	1.41	0
1896	-7.17	-3.86	1.43	0
		Republican Vote		
1855	-13.97%	30.18%	3.11%	1.50%
1856	8.89	3.73	4.56	0
1857	-5.34	-1.83	2.80	0
1858	-2.22	0	2.29	0
1859	-7.34	0	2.06	0
1860	8.81	3.78	1.94	0
1861	-7.00	-2.29	1.54	0
1862	-1.27	0	1.91	1.34
1863	-4.63	-1.25	1.55	0
1864	16.08	1.41	2.46	0
1865	-4.08	-3.31	1.72	0
1866	3.58	0	2.07	0
1867	4.71	0	3.28	0
1868	15.76	0	1.76	0
1869	-2.29	-4.06	2.51	0
1870	-1.35	0	1.22	2.57
1871	-3.74	0	1.73	0
1872	10.49	3.52	3.12	0
1873	-7.80	-2.05	1.38	0
1874	-3.51	0	1.55	0
1875	-6.05	0	2.34	0
1876	4.94	3.50	1.45	0

TABLE A.3 <u>Continued</u>

Election Year	Deviating Surge	Realigning Surge	Deviating Interaction	Realigning Interaction
		Republican Vote		
1877	-7.12	-1.44	2.80	0
1878	3.87	0	1.58	0
1879	-.06	0	1.67	0
1880	9.91	0	1.24	0
1881	-6.45	-1.53	1.87	0
1882	-1.34	0	1.17	0
1883	7.48	0	1.16	0
1884	6.44	0	.77	0
1885	-5.04	0	1.55	0
1886	-3.40	0	1.74	0
1887	-1.09	0	1.49	0
1888	4.23	3.43	1.42	0
1889	-6.58	-1.08	1.84	0
1890	-6.39	0	1.03	0
1891	-3.05	0	.89	0
1892	.76	1.68	.85	0
1893	1.58	0	1.17	0
1894	.13	0	.71	0
1895	-1.21	0	1.29	0
1896	10.77	0	1.25	0
		Abstaining		
1854	2.36%	0%	1.72%	1.92%
1855	1.12	0	3.33	0
1856	-5.87	0	3.53	0
1857	7.15	0	2.66	0
1858	-1.37	13.93	3.74	0
1859	4.42	0	2.48	0
1860	-18.44	-3.35	3.43	0
1861	11.68	3.00	2.35	0
1862	-3.34	0	2.45	3.43
1863	12.26	0	2.93	0
1864	-16.22	-1.66	3.24	0
1865	15.40	3.53	3.50	0
1866	-1.00	0	6.02	0
1867	-9.79	-1.52	6.39	0
1868	-17.35	0	2.12	0
1869	3.71	1.50	3.14	0
1870	1.42	0	2.36	1.40
1871	7.61	0	2.64	0
1872	-2.42	-6.47	4.00	0
1873	16.03	2.47	2.83	0
1874	1.61	0	2.42	0
1875	7.16	0	2.33	0
1876	-8.15	-6.85	1.55	0
1877	10.50	2.68	1.39	1.81
1878	-7.45	0	1.14	0
1879	-2.59	0	1.49	0
1880	-10.96	0	1.03	0
1881	19.80	1.75	1.67	0
1882	-1.14	-2.02	1.29	0
1883	-12.99	0	1.31	0
1884	-9.39	0	1.09	0
1885	13.56	0	1.59	0
1886	7.14	0	.92	0
1887	3.60	0	1.08	0
1888	-8.34	-2.93	.97	0
1889	6.92	2.87	1.80	0
1890	3.69	0	1.51	0
1891	-2.05	0	1.31	0
1892	-11.77	0	.99	0
1893	-7.24	0	1.12	0
1894	-.23	0	1.81	0
1895	2.49	0	2.05	0
1896	-6.41	0	2.02	0

Notes

Chapter 1. Critical Election Theory and the Realities of Massachusetts Presidential Politics, 1848–1908

1. Robinson, *"Warrington" Pen-Portraits*, pp. 109–10.
2. Merriam, *Life and Times of Samuel Bowles*, 2:222.
3. Montgomery, *Beyond Equality*, pp. 45–89.
4. The most influential statement of critical election theory is found in Chambers and Burnham, *American Party Systems*, pp. 289–304. For serious reservations about the existence of a viable party system before the Jacksonian era, see Formisano, "Deferential-Participant Politics," pp. 473–87.
5. The vast literature on critical realignment and party systems begins with the seminal article by Key, "Theory of Critical Elections," pp. 3–18, and culminates in the work of Burnham, *Critical Elections*. The best description of the critical realignment process is contained in Sundquist, *Dynamics of the Party System*. On the connection between voter realignment and public policy, see Clubb, Flanigan, and Zingale, *Partisan Realignment*, especially chapters 5, 6, and 7. Recently, critical election theory has come under attack by scholars who claim that it is plagued with conceptual, descriptive, and measurement problems. See Kousser, "History − Theory = ?" pp. 157–62, and "Key Changes," pp. 23–28; Lichtman, "Critical Election Theory," pp. 317–48, and "End of Realignment Theory?" pp. 170–88.
6. Few historical studies of critical elections treat mobilization of new voters and nonvoting as equal in importance to partisan choice as measures of voter behavior. Exceptions include McCrary, Miller, and Baum, "Class and Party in the Secession Crisis," pp. 429–57; Shortridge, "Voter Realignment in the Midwest," pp. 193–222. See also Anderson, *Creation of a Democratic Majority*, pp. 7–10; and Prindle, "Voter Turnout," pp. 144–70.
7. This point is made by Kousser in his "Ecological Regression," p. 250. See also Anderson, *Creation of a Democratic Majority*, p. 10; Prindle, "Voter Turnout," p. 147.
8. Pole, "Suffrage and Representation in Massachusetts," pp. 562–65, 567–72; Huse, *Financial History of Boston*, pp. 149, 211, 300–301; McCormick, *Second American Party System*, pp. 36–49; Formisano, *Transformation of Political Culture*, pp. 128–48.
9. *Acts and Resolves Passed by the General Court of Massachusetts, 1856–57*, pp. 666–71; *Acts and Resolves Passed by the General Court of Massachusetts in the Years 1858–59*, pp. 442–44; *Acts and Resolves Passed by the General Court of Massachusetts, 1862–1863*, p. 244.
10. Abbott, "Maintaining Hegemony," p. 5.
11. Springfield *Republican*, 23 July 1869; Benton, *Voting in the Field*, pp. 293–304. For a description of how the soldier vote was gathered in the 1864 presidential election, see Diary of Theodore Lyman, Volume XIV, 3 November 1864, p. 1, Lyman Papers.

12. George S. Merrill to Nathaniel P. Banks, 2 February 1866, and Samuel McCleary to Nathaniel P. Banks, 29 January 1866, box 22, Banks Papers.

13. Boston *Daily Advertiser*, 5 November 1872; Blodgett, *Gentle Reformers*, p. 117. See also Thernstrom, *Poverty and Progress*, p. 183.

14. Massachusetts, General Court, *Journal of the House of Representatives*, H.Doc.82 (February 1870), pp. 1–11; Edward Hamilton to Nathaniel P. Banks, 19 February 1870, box 81, Banks Papers; O'Hare, "Public Career of Patrick Andrew Collins," p. 97n.

15. Boston *Commonwealth*, 26 April 1861; Adams, "Oppressive Taxation of the Poor," p. 632. By 1875 over one-half of the state's rural voters and 80 percent of Boston's voters paid only a poll tax—see Massachusetts, House of Representatives, *Report of the Commissioners appointed to Inquire into the Expediency of Revising and Amending the Laws Relating to Taxation and Exemption Therefrom*.

16. Massachusetts, Bureau of Statistics of Labor, *Thirteenth Annual Report*, p. 190; Benjamin F. Butler, "The Mayoralty," a letter [copy] sent to the Boston *Globe*, 10 December 1875, box 214, pp. 474–77, Butler Papers; Huse, *Financial History of Boston*, p. 87; Yearley, *Money Machines*, p. 48.

17. Baltzell, "Social Insulation of the Traditional Elite," in Frazier, p. 92; Yearley, *Money Machines*, pp. 47–49. In 1875 the valuation of personal property in Nahant was over three and a half times the valuation of the town's taxable real estate. By comparison, in Essex County, where Nahant was located, the valuation of real estate was twice the valuation placed on personalty. See Massachusetts, Bureau of Statistics of Labor, *Census of Massachusetts: 1875*, 1:727–31. Voter turnout rates in presidential elections for Nahant and for the state-at-large between 1860 and 1900 were as follows:

	1860	1864	1868	1872	1876	1880	1884	1888	1892	1896	1900
Nahant	86.1%	76.8%	78.3%	52.3%	69.7%	80.9%	91.8%	90.4%	88.5%	89.5%	91.3%
Statewide	75.9	72.6	75.7	63.5	72.2	71.6	70.1	72.4	74.8	70.2	67.5

The above calculations are my own, based on interpolations from lists of "legal" voters and the official returns for presidential electors on file in the Archives Division of the Commonwealth of Massachusetts, State House, Boston.

18. Massachusetts, Bureau of Statistics of Labor, *Thirteenth Annual Report*, pp. 182–86. In the 1876 presidential election the ratio of foreign-born voters to the foreign-born adult male population was insignificantly correlated with the David Index of political party competition ($r = +.08$). The David Index, calculated for every city and town throughout the state, expressed the vote received by the runner-up as a percentage of the vote that would have been needed by the runner-up to have won. See David, *Party Strength in the United States*, pp. 13–14.

19. Boston *Daily Advertiser*, 20 February 1855; Boston *Daily Evening Voice*, 25 September 1866.

20. Joseph Mason to George F. Hoar, 6 June 1870, Hoar Papers. Whether clerks of state or federal courts should receive the fees was often the primary issue in debates over the naturalization laws during the mid-1850s. See Haynes, "Causes of Know-Nothing Success," p. 74n.

21. Richard H. Dana, Jr., quoted in Blodgett, *Gentle Reformers*, p. 115; Rusk, "Effect of the Australian Ballot Reform," p. 1221.

22. Richard H. Dana, Jr., to the Duke of Argyll [undated draft of a letter], "Letterbook, 1853–1880," pp. 58–65, Dana Papers; Charles F. Adams to William H. Hurbbert, 16 September 1870, "Charles F. Adams Letterbook," p. 231, microfilm edition, reel 176, Adams Family Papers. The secrecy of the ballot itself was often an issue in state politics: see Brunet, "Secret Ballot Issue," pp. 354–62.

23. Blodgett, *Gentle Reformers*, pp. 114–17; "Australian Ballot Law," pp. 401–18.

24. On the effects of the Australian ballot on split-ticket voting and "roll-off" in Massachusetts, see Rusk, "Effect of the Australian Ballot Reform," pp. 1220–38, and Burnham, *Critical Elections*, table 2, p. 197. Political scientists debate the impact of the Australian ballot on split-ticket voting and electoral participation in the late nineteenth and early twentieth centuries. See Burnham, "Changing Shape of the American Political Universe," and "Theory and Voting Research," pp. 1002–23; Converse, "Change in the American Electorate," pp. 297–99; Rusk, "Effect of the Australian Ballot Reform"; and an exchange between Rusk and Burnham in the *American Political Science Review* 65 (December 1971): 1149–52.

25. Massachusetts, Bureau of Statistics of Labor, *Thirteenth Annual Report*, p. 186. For lists of the numbers of "legal" voters in each city and town for the years 1851, 1857, 1865, 1869, and 1875, see *Massachusetts Register for the Year 1853*, pp. 323–25; Massachusetts, General Court, *Manual for the Use of the General Court*, pp. 115–23; and *Journal of the House of Representatives*, H.Doc.82 (February 1870), pp. 1–11, and H.Doc.65 (February 1876), pp. 4–8.

26. Burnham, *Critical Elections*, pp. 18–21; Kleppner, *Third Electoral System*, pp. 26–32; Sundquist, *Dynamics of the Party System*, p. 71; Sellers, "Equilibrium Cycle in Two-Party Politics," pp. 16–38; Lipset, "Emergence of the One-Party South," pp. 372–84; Holt, *Political Crisis of the 1850s*, pp. 183–259; McCrary, Miller, and Baum, "Class and Party in the Secession Crisis," p. 439.

27. For descriptions of the third-party system in its post-1874 phase, see Keller, *Affairs of State*; Kleppner, *Third Electoral System*. On the rise of minor parties after the Civil War, see Kleppner, "Greenback and Prohibition Parties," pp. 1549–81. On the Mugwumps, see McFarland, *Mugwumps, Morals, and Politics*.

28. On the realignment of the 1890s, see Bennett and Haltom, "Issues, Voter Choice, and Critical Elections," pp. 379–418; Jensen, *Winning of the Midwest*; Kleppner, *Cross of Culture*; McSeveney, *Politics of Depression*.

29. For example, see Abbott, *Cobbler in Congress*; Bartlett, *Wendell Phillips*; Blodgett, *Gentle Reformers*; Donald, *Charles Sumner and the Rights of Man*; Duberman, *Charles Francis Adams*; Gatell, *John Gorham Palfrey*; Harrington, *Fighting Politician*; Hixon, *Moorfield Storey*; Kirkland, *Charles Francis Adams, Jr.*; O'Connor, *Lords of the Loom*; Pearson, *Life of John A. Andrew*; Shapiro, *Richard Henry Dana, Jr.*; Trefousse, *Ben Butler*; Welch, *George Frisbie Hoar*.

30. For discussions of ecological regression in the historical literature, see Jones, "Ecological Inference and Electoral Analysis," pp. 249–62, and "Using Ecological Regression," pp. 593–96; Kousser, "Ecological Regression," pp. 237–62; Lichtman, "Correlation, Regression, and the Ecological Fallacy," pp. 417–33; Lichtman and Langbein, "Regression vs. Homogeneous Units," pp. 172–93.

31. Incorporation of newly registered or previous nonvoters into the analysis of aggregate voting statistics was initially suggested by Irwin and Meeter in their "Building Voter Transition Models," pp. 545–66. For a brief exposition of the methodology employed here, see Kousser, "The 'New Political History,'" p. 13, n. 11; Langbein and Lichtman, *Ecological Inference*, pp. 54–55.

32. For boundary changes in Massachusetts counties, cities, and towns, see Massachusetts, Secretary of the Commonwealth, *Historical Data* (1975). In a longitudinal analysis of Massachusetts election statistics, it would have been desirable to have used ward-level voting returns for Boston. Throughout the second half of the nineteenth century, ward boundaries in the city were completely redrawn every ten years based on the state censuses. Unfortunately, unlike in Philadelphia and other eastern cities, the new wards bore no resemblance to the old ones.

33. The reliability of all estimates depends on several important assumptions. A check of scattergrams indicated that relationships between the dependent and independent variables were linear, although logarithmic equations could have been used to adjust for curvilinear relations. Three other assumptions involve the relation between each independent variable (x_i) and the stochastic disturbance of error term (e_i). The regression coefficients will be unbiased estimates of individual behavior only if one can assume that the expected value of the mean of the disturbance term equals zero, the error term is normally distributed, and x_i and e_i are statistically independent of one another. The first two assumptions are readily checked by an examination of the residuals from the regression equations. The third, however, is more troublesome. For the regression coefficients to be unbiased estimators, one must assume that the behavior of partisans and abstainers varied randomly when their voting strength or presence in a community changed. For example, Democrats in an overwhelmingly Democratic city or town should behave in similar fashion to Democrats in overwhelmingly Republican cities or towns; or, alternatively, variations in their behavior should be random across all voting units. In tables with a great many cells, such as those generated to produce the estimates in Table 1.3, this assumption is less realistic and less easy to test. See Draper and Smith, *Applied Regression Analysis*, pp. 81–85.

34. Additional evidence reveals that the Democratic decline was not interactive with geographic shifts in the party's support; rather, there was a marked decline in the Democratic vote throughout the state (see the Appendix).

Chapter 2. The Political Realignment of the 1850s: Know-Nothingism and the Emergence of a Republican Majority

In several respects the methodology used in the analysis of voting returns presented in this chapter differs from that employed in my "Know-Nothingism and the Republican Majority in Massachusetts," pp. 959–86. First, the cell entries in the contingency tables presented here were derived by a method of ecological inference suggested by J. Morgan Kousser in his "The 'New Political History,'" p. 13, n. 11. This model, which was designed to account for geographic population shifts between elections, produced some slightly different estimates of voting behavior. Second, the official state election returns were supplemented by unofficial tallies in cases where the official returns did not include votes from cities and towns because of a mere technicality, such as the failure of voting reports to arrive in Boston before a certain deadline. Third, all logically but not statistically impossible estimates of voting behavior that fell slightly outside the 0–100 percent range were arbitrarily set at their respective logical limits; the values of the remaining estimates were then adjusted according to the restraints of the marginal values of the contingency tables. This eliminated illogical estimates of voting from a few tables. Finally, I feel impelled to warn the reader that, in the earlier analysis, the computer program that I used failed at one crucial point. It was unable to collapse some of the Suffolk County voting units into a single voting unit in order to solve the problems caused in the 1860s by the annexation to Boston of several surrounding towns. This resulted in the slight exaggeration of the strength of the nonvoting elements in the county's voting units in 1864 and 1868, and rendered a few of the estimates of voting unreliable. This error has been fully corrected in the analysis presented here.

1. The pioneer work on the movement of voters between parties from election to election in the 1850s is Bean, "Party Transformation." This 1922 Harvard dissertation,

often cited incorrectly in secondary literature, has served as the definitive study of Massachusetts electoral politics in the 1850s for a generation of scholars.

2. Emory Washburn to John H. Clifford, 8 November 1852, Clifford Papers; Daniel Webster quoted in Wilson, "Of Time and the Union," p. 293.

3. Holt, "Democratic Party 1828–1860," p. 525.

4. Blue, *Free Soilers*, p. 254. On the antecedents of 1848 Free-Soilers, see Sweeney, "Rum, Romanism, Representation, and Reform," p. 117.

5. Whig conversions to the Democrats were considerable in the border states. See, for example, Evitts, *A Matter of Allegiances*, pp. 24–53. But the extent of Whig defections to the Democrats in the 1852 election in the deep South has been exaggerated. See McCrary, Miller, and Baum, "Class and Party in the Secession Crisis," table 4, p. 439. On the extent of Whig conversions to the Democrats elsewhere, see Holt, *Political Crisis of the 1850s*, pp. 127–30. On the vote for Webster, see James M. Stone to Charles Sumner, 22 August 1852, Sumner Papers.

6. Anderson, "Slavery Issue as a Factor," p. 118; Bean, "Party Transformation," p. 262.

7. Wilson, *Rise and Fall of the Slave Power*, 2:419–34; Duberman, *Charles Francis Adams*, pp. 194–97; Donald, *Charles Sumner and the Coming of the Civil War*, p. 269.

8. O'Connor, *Lords of the Loom*, 119, 163–64; Handlin, *Boston's Immigrants*, p. 202.

9. Handlin, *Boston's Immigrants*, pp. 178–206; Mulkern, "Know-Nothing Party," pp. 143–45; Formisano, *Transformation of Political Culture*, pp. 332–33.

10. Accounts of the anti-Whig fusion of Free-Soilers and Democrats are found in Blue, *Free-Soilers*, pp. 205–31; Duberman, "Behind the Scenes," pp. 152–60; McKay, "Henry Wilson and the Coalition," pp. 338–57; Sweeney, "Rum, Romanism, Representation, and Reform," pp. 116–37. On the careers of Wilson and Banks during these years, see Abbott, *Cobbler in Congress*, passim; Harrington, *Fighting Politician*, passim.

11. Henry Wilson quoted in Hart, *Commonwealth History of Massachusetts*, 4:99; Duberman, *Charles Francis Adams*, pp. 186–88.

12. Blue, *Free Soilers*, p. 215; Francis W. Bird to Charles Sumner, 15 April 1854, Sumner Papers.

13. Butler, *Butler's Book*, pp. 119–20; Robinson, *"Warrington" Pen-Portraits*, p. 204; Shapiro, "Conservative Dilemma," p. 224; Bean, "Puritan Versus Celt," pp. 78–79; Boston *Commonwealth*, 18 November 1853.

14. Boston *Daily Atlas*, 15 and 17 November 1853; Davis, "Liberty Before Union," p. 28; Donald, *Charles Sumner and the Coming of the Civil War*, p. 248; Sweeney, "Rum, Romanism, Representation, and Reform," p. 136.

15. Harrington, *Fighting Politician*, p. 23; McKay, *Henry Wilson: Practical Radical*, p. 98; Purdy, "Portrait of a Know-Nothing Legislature," passim; Boston *Daily Bee* cited by Haynes, "Causes of Know-Nothing Success," p. 82, n. 1.

16. Hale, *Our Houses Are Our Castles*; Handlin, *Boston's Immigrants*, p. 202; Harrington, *Fighting Politician*, pp. 8–15; Mulkern, "Know-Nothing Party," pp. 136–39, 162–95, and "Scandal Behind the Convent Walls," pp. 22–34.

17. Bean, "Puritan Versus Celt," p. 80; Handlin, *Boston's Immigrants*, p. 204; Hays, "Political Parties and the Community-Society Continuum," p. 158; Silbey, *Transformation of American Politics*, pp. 3–4. See also Sundquist, *Dynamics of the Party System*, pp. 78–80.

18. Foner, *Free Soil, Free Labor, Free Men*, p. 260.

19. Osofsky, "Abolitionists, Irish Immigrants," p. 908; Charles Sumner quoted in Silvia, "Spindle City," p. 123.

20. George W. Richardson quoted in Tyrrell, *Sobering Up*, p. 266.

21. Edward Everett, "Diary," 14 November 1854, microfilm edition, reel 19, Everett Papers; Bean, "Party Transformation," pp. 243–44; Boston *Daily Advertiser*, 15 November and 20 December 1854. See also Charles F. Adams, "Diary," 14 November 1854, microfilm edition, reel 73, Adams Family Papers.

22. Information on individual voters constitutes a rare discovery. A list of the fifty most politically active Know-Nothings in the town of Stoneham reveals that the majority of them were former Whigs and Democrats. See J. P. Gould to Nathaniel P. Banks, 4 December 1855, Banks Papers.

23. Handlin, *Boston's Immigrants*, p. 201. See also Holt, "Politics of Impatience," pp. 311–12; McCabe, "Twilight of the Second Party System," p. 4; Robinson, *"Warrington" Pen-Portraits*, p. 219.

24. Estimated turnout rates for Massachusetts gubernatorial elections from 1850 to 1855 are as follows:

Year:	1850	1851	1852	1853	1854	1855
Turnout:	68.1%	75.0%	73.9%	67.2%	66.1%	67.8%

Cf. Pole, "Suffrage and Representation in Massachusetts," pp. 560–92, who underestimated voter turnout in these elections because he used the number of adult males instead of the number of legal voters as a measure of the size of the potential electorate.

25. On the notion of the Coalition as a progenitor of the Republican party, see Sweeney, "Rum, Romanism, Representation, and Reform," p. 116; Hart, *Commonwealth History of Massachusetts*, 4:99–100. On Know-Nothingism as the successor of the Coalition, see Bean, "Puritan Versus Celt," p. 78; Formisano, *Transformation of Political Culture*, p. 332.

26. Duberman, "Some Notes on the Beginnings of the Republican Party," pp. 364–70; New York *Tribune*, 29 October 1855.

27. George S. Boutwell to Richard H. Dana, Jr., 13 October 1855, Dana Papers.

28. On the Gardner-Frémont deal, see Bean, "Party Transformation," p. 344; Harrington, *Fighting Politician*, pp. 34–38; Mulkern, "Know-Nothing Party," pp. 257–62; Springfield *Republican*, 17 September 1856.

29. For Bird's own account of his role in the "Honest Man's" movement, see his letter dated 6 June 1857 to the Worcester *Daily Spy*, in Robinson, Scrapbook No. 8, "Miscellaneous B," p. 29, Robinson Collection. See also "Warrington" quoted in Robinson, *"Warrington" Pen-Portraits*, p. 64; Daniel W. Alvord to Francis W. Bird, 5 June 1857, Bird Papers.

30. Thomas Drew to Francis W. Bird, 11 September 1857, Bird Papers; Robinson, *"Warrington" Pen-Portraits*, pp. 220–25; Wendell Phillips quoted in Davis, "Liberty Before Union," p. 83; Harrington, *Fighting Politician*, pp. 38–42.

31. Mulkern, "Know-Nothing Party," pp. 283–84, and "Western Massachusetts in the Know-Nothing Years," pp. 23, 25, n. 20; New York *Tribune*, 5 November 1857.

32. Handlin, *Boston's Immigrants*, p. 204.

33. See, for example, Holt, *Political Crisis of the 1850s*, p. 179; Kelley, *Cultural Pattern in American Politics*, pp. 199–200, and "Ideology and Political Culture," p. 544; Potter, *Impending Crisis*, p. 269.

34. New York *Tribune*, 5 November 1857; Boston *Daily Bee*, 31 October 1857; George S. Boutwell to Francis W. Bird, 9 October 1858, Bird Papers; Jonathan Pierce to Amos A. Lawrence, 28 September 1857, Amos A. Lawrence to Lunt and Hillard of the Boston *Courier*, 17 August 1858 [copy], Letterbook No. 4, Amos A. Lawrence to [?], 30 August 1858 [extract of a letter], Letterbook No. 4, James W. Stone to Amos A. Lawrence, 17 September 1858, and Amos A. Lawrence to George N. Briggs, 29 September 1859 [copy], Letterbook No. 4, Lawrence Papers.

35. Massachusetts, General Court, *Journal of the House of Representatives*, H.Doc.34 (1859); Massachusetts, Secretary of the Commonwealth, *Acts and Resolves Passed by the General Court of Massachusetts in the Years 1858–59*, pp. 442–44; Foner, *Free Soil, Free Labor, Free Men*, pp. 250–51; Mulkern, "Know-Nothing Party," pp. 271–74, 294–95; Robinson, "Scrapbook No. 3," pp. 83–95, Robinson Collection.

36. Erastus Hopkins to Edward L. Pierce, 2 April 1859, Pierce Papers [emphasis in the original]; Francis W. Bird to Charles Sumner, 17 April 1859, and Henry L. Pierce to Charles Sumner, 15 April 1859, Sumner Papers; Herriot, "Germans of Iowa and the 'Two Year' Amendment," pp. 202–308; Abraham Lincoln to Theodore Canisius, 17 May 1859, in Lincoln, *Collected Works of Abraham Lincoln*, 3:380; Carl Schurz to Edward L. Pierce, 22 and 26 March, 30 April, and 12 May 1859, in Schurz, *Speeches, Correspondence and Political Papers of Carl Schurz*, 1:41–45, 72–77; Francis W. Bird to Charles Sumner, 17 April 1859, Sumner Papers; Robinson, "Scrapbook No. 3," pp. 91–95, Robinson Collection.

37. Springfield *Republican*, 10 and 12 May 1859. The actual vote was 20,753 to 15,129 in favor of adoption of the "two-year" amendment. Approximately 219,600 were eligible to vote in 1859. The voting returns for the 1859 referendum were obtained from Massachusetts, Secretary of the Commonwealth, *Schedule of Votes Given on the 23rd Article of the Amendment of the Constitution in the Cities and Towns of the Commonwealth, on Monday the 9th Day of May, 1859*. Turnout rates in the 1851, 1852, and 1853 constitutional referenda were 69, 67, and 69 percent, respectively. See Table 2.2 above and Sweeney, "Rum, Romanism, Representation, and Reform," tables VII, XI, XII, pp. 128, 133, 136. At least one newspaper called the low turnout "natural" since the ingredients required to secure a full vote—"the strife, the rivalry, the hot blood of a canvass, inspired by enthusiasm for individuals who are candidates—had been missing." Robinson, "Scrapbook No. 3," p. 91, Robinson Collection.

38. The actual vote was 23,833 to 13,746 in favor of ratification. Massachusetts, Executive Council, *Report of Committee to Council on the Return of Yeas and Nays on Acceptance of the 20, 21, 22 Articles of Amendment to the Constitution, May 16, 1857* does not list the returns received from individual cities and towns. The town-level returns for the 1857 referendum were gathered from newspaper reports published on the days immediately following 1 May 1857. See the Boston *Daily Journal*, 2 May 1857, and the Springfield *Republican*, 2 May 1857.

39. Silbey, *Transformation of American Politics*, pp. 14–15. Results of the analysis of voting in the 1859 referendum support Eric Foner's suspicion that the vote cast in favor of the "two-year" amendment was closely associated with the Suffolk County area where the "Know-Nothings still clung to life." Foner, *Free Soil, Free Labor, Free Men*, p. 252. Suffolk, Middlesex, Norfolk, Plymouth, and Bristol counties—all in the eastern half of the state—gave strong majorities for the amendment. Worcester County voters were divided on the issue. Cape Cod and the Islands and the western counties went against the amendment. See the Boston *Daily Evening Transcript*, 10 May 1859. For Democratic charges of Republican responsibility for the two-year amendment, see the Boston *Pilot*, 3 November 1860.

40. Abbott, *Cobbler in Congress*, pp. 99–100; Henry Wilson to Edward L. Pierce, 12 March 1857, Pierce Papers; Bird, *Review of Gov. Banks' Veto of the Revised Code*, p. 11. Republican leader Charles F. Adams, however, favored passage of the amendment and incurred the displeasure of the Bird Club. See Edward L. Pierce to Charles Sumner, 31 May 1859, Sumner Papers.

41. Schurz, *Speeches, Correspondence and Political Papers of Carl Schurz*, 1:48–72; Edwin Bynner to Francis W. Bird, 23 April 1859, Bird Papers.

42. Francis W. Bird quoted in Davis, "Liberty Before Union," p. 101; Springfield

Republican, 7 April 1863. See also Pearson, *Life of John A. Andrew*, 2:208–09. The actual vote was 10,035 to 6,082 in favor of annulling the "two-year" amendment. See Massachusetts, Secretary of the Commonwealth, *Report of the Committee on Votes of 24th Article of Amendment of Constitution, April 20, 1863*. This report does not list the returns from individual cities and towns.

43. "Warrington" quoted in Robinson, *"Warrington" Pen-Portraits*, p. 92; McPherson, *Struggle for Equality*, p. 7; Mohr, *Radical Republicans in the North*, pp. 3–4.

44. Samuel May, Jr., to Richard Davis Webb, 6 November 1860, Anti-Slavery May Papers; Springfield *Republican*, 30 August 1860; John A. Andrew quoted in Hart, *Commonwealth History of Massachusetts*, 4:496; Boston *Pilot*, 12 October 1860.

45. Boston *Pilot*, 7 July 1860, Boston *Post*, 11 July 1860; Boston *Courier*, 3 July, 29 and 30 September, and 3 October 1860.

46. O'Connor, *Lords of the Loom*, p. 141; Robinson, *"Warrington" Pen-Portraits*, pp. 243–45; Ware, *Political Opinion in Massachusetts*, p. 244n; Henry Wilson quoted in the Boston *Daily Advertiser*, 19 September 1860; Springfield *Republican* quoted in Merriam, *Life and Times of Samuel Bowles*, 1:264; Robert C. Winthrop to [J. P. Kennedy?], 1 October 1860, microfilm edition, section B-14, Winthrop Papers.

47. John J. Crittenden et al., to Edward Everett, 25 May 1860, microfilm edition, reel 17, Everett Papers; Leverett Saltonstall to William C. Endicott, 20 March 1860, box 2, Endicott Papers.

48. Amos A. Lawrence to John J. Crittenden, 21 December 1859 and January 1860 [copies], Letterbook No. 4, Lawrence Papers; Edward Everett, "Diary," 3 November 1857, 2 November 1858, 8 November 1859, microfilm edition, reel 39, Everett Papers.

49. William C. Endicott, part of a draft letter to the *Saturday Review* (Autumn 1861), box 2, Endicott Papers.

50. Holt, *Political Crisis of the 1850s*, pp. 139–81, and *Forging a Majority*, pp. 172–74, 218–19, 263–313; Kremm, "Rise of the Republican Party in Cleveland," pp. 294–95, 297–99, and "Cleveland and the First Lincoln Election," pp. 69–86; Silbey, *Transformation of American Politics*, pp. 1–34.

Chapter 3. The Civil War Years: Ideological Conflict and Political Polarization

1. For a description of the changing of the guard in Bay State politics during this period, see Goodman, "Politics of Industrialism," pp. 161–207.

2. Higginson, *Cheerful Yesterdays*, pp. 144–45; Clarke, "The Anti-Slavery Movement in Boston," pp. 369–400. On Andrew's connections with those associated with John Brown, see Davis, "Liberty Before Union," pp. 53–57.

3. Davis, "Liberty Before Union," p. 151; Pease and Pease, "Confrontation and Abolitionism," pp. 923–37; McPherson, *Struggle for Equality*, p. 7.

4. Abbott, "Maintaining Hegemony," p. 3; McPherson, *Struggle for Equality*, pp. 6–7; Montgomery, *Beyond Equality*, pp. 120–22. For accounts of the Bird Club by contemporaries of the period, see [By his children], *Francis William Bird*, p. 25; Pearson, *Life of John A. Andrew*, 1:58–60; Robinson, *"Warrington" Pen-Portraits*, pp. x, 86–136, 152, 304–5; Stearns, *Cambridge Sketches*, passim, but especially pp. 162–79.

5. Donald, *Charles Sumner and the Rights of Man*, p. 10; Robinson, *"Warrington" Pen-Portraits*, pp. 423, 518.

6. Davis, "Liberty Before Union," pp. 121–49; Schwartz, *Samuel Gridley Howe*, pp. 249–52; Pearson, *Life of John A. Andrew*, 1:152–53.

7. Forbes, *Letters and Recollections of John Murray Forbes*, 1:183; Stearns, *Cambridge Sketches*, pp. 242–61; Robinson, *"Warrington" Pen-Portraits*, pp. 92–107; Montgomery, *Beyond Equality*, pp. 121–22; John A. Andrew to Abraham Lincoln, 20 January 1861, Andrew Papers.

8. Robinson, *"Warrington" Pen-Portraits*, p. 100; John A. Andrew to John M. Forbes, 4 September 1862, quoted in Pearson, *Life of John A. Andrew*, 2:166–67 [emphasis in the original].

9. Richard H. Dana, Jr., to Josiah G. Abbott, 10 October 1861, and Josiah G. Abbott to Henry L. Dawes, 12 October 1861 [draft of a letter], Abbott Papers; Merriam, *Life and Times of Samuel Bowles*, 1:355–56.

10. Ware, *Political Opinion in Massachusetts*, p. 278.

11. Francis W. Bird quoted in State Disunion Convention, *Proceedings*, p. 19.

12. Amasa Walker, "Separation or Emancipation" [undated newspaper clipping, August 1861], *The Independent* (New York), "Amasa Walker articles scrapbook," Walker Papers.

13. The victories (and disappointments) of the Bird Club members during the war are documented in McPherson, *Struggle for Equality*, passim.

14. Curtis, *Memorial of Charles Sumner*, p. 158; John A. Andrew to Benjamin F. Butler, 25 April 1861, quoted in Butler, *Private and Official Correspondence of General Benjamin F. Butler*, 1:37–38; Pearson, *Life of John A. Andrew*, 2:77–79.

15. John A. Andrew to Charles Sumner, 25 December 1862, Sumner Papers; Edward Hamilton to Nathaniel P. Banks, 25 November 1863, box 45, Banks Papers; Charles Sumner quoted in Donald, *Charles Sumner and the Rights of Man*, p. 189.

16. John A. Andrew to William L. Garrison, 7 April 1863 [copy], "Letterbook," Andrew Papers; Caleb Cushing quoted in Davis, "Liberty Before Union," p. 123.

17. *The Liberator* (Boston), 5 June 1863, p. 91; Henry Wadsworth Longfellow quoted in Thomas, *Abraham Lincoln*, p. 364; John A. Andrew quoted in *The Liberator* (Boston), 22 May 1863, p. 83.

18. Congdon, *Reminiscences of a Journalist*, p. 86; Edward Everett, "Diary," 3 November 1863, microfilm edition, reel 40, and Edward Everett to H. R. Low and Benjamin Field, 2 October 1862, "Letterbook," microfilm edition, reel 32, Everett Papers.

19. Amos A. Lawrence to John Bell, 26 April 1861 [copy], "Letters No. 4," Lawrence Papers; Edward Everett to Mrs. Charles Eames, 31 December 1860 [copy], microfilm edition, reel 17, Everett Papers.

20. Northend, *Speeches and Essays upon Political Subjects*, p. 41.

21. John A. Andrew to Charles Sumner, 9 June 1862 [copy], "Letterbook," Andrew Papers; *Appeal to the Republicans of Massachusetts against Gag Resolutions and Forced Pledges, By a Republican*; Donald, *Charles Sumner and the Rights of Man*, pp. 74–75.

22. Horace Greeley, "Charles Sumner as a Statesman," p. 15. The People's party is treated at length in Saunders, "The People's Party in Massachusetts." On Sumner's alienation from Adams, see Duberman, *Charles Francis Adams*, pp. 223–67. On Adams's refusal to be a candidate for the Senate in 1862, see the statement of John Quincy Adams, Jr., in the Boston *Daily Advertiser*, 28 October 1862.

23. Pearson, *Life of John A. Andrew*, 2:54; Robinson, *"Warrington Pen-Portraits*, p. 286.

24. Pearson, *Life of John A. Andrew*, 2:56; Boston *Daily Advertiser*, 10 October 1863 [emphasis in the original].

25. John H. Clifford quoted in Donald, *Charles Sumner and the Rights of Man*, p. 82; John H. Clifford, Letter to the Editor, 23 October 1862 [unidentifiable newspaper clipping], Clifford Papers; Merriam, *Samuel Bowles*, 1:358–59.

26. John A. Andrew quoted in Pearson, *Life of John A. Andrew*, 2:55–56 [emphasis in the original].

27. Kirkland, *Men, Cities, and Transportation*, 1:408–09; Pearson, *Life of John A. Andrew*, 2:241–43; Bird, *Facts vs. Illusions*; Francis W. Bird to John A. Andrew, 15 May 1862, Andrew Papers.

28. John A. Andrew to Francis P. Blair, 8 November 1862 [copy], "Letterbook," Andrew Papers.

29. Boston *Daily Advertiser*, 25 September 1863; Boston *Post*, 4 September 1863; William S. Robinson [undated and unidentified newspaper clippings], "Scrapbook III," p. 143, Robinson Collection.

30. McPherson, *Struggle for Equality*, pp. 262–63; Francis W. Bird to John A. Andrew, 28 August 1864, Andrew Papers; John A. Andrew quoted in Hart, *Commonwealth History of Massachusetts*, 4:592.

31. McKitrick, *Andrew Johnson and Reconstruction*, p. 46; Kleppner, *Third Electoral System*, p. 80.

32. George Bancroft to Samuel A. Cox, 28 January 1865, and George Bancroft to John V. L. Pruyn, 28 January 1865, Bancroft Papers; John L. Motley to Richard H. Dana, Jr., 28 August 1865, Dana Papers.

Chapter 4. The Civil War Years: Geography, Social Contexts, and Voting Behavior

1. Higginson, *Cheerful Yesterdays*; Adams, *Education of Henry Adams*; Massachusetts, Secretary of the Commonwealth, *Abstract of the Census of Massachusetts, 1865*, table 19, p. 278.

2. Francis W. Bird quoted in Goodman, "Politics of Industrialism," p. 190.

3. Davis, "Liberty Before Union," p. 19.

4. Higginson, *Cheerful Yesterdays*, p. 127. Hull was traditionally regarded as the banner conservative town. See the Boston *Post*, 3 November 1869.

5. Brauer, *Cotton Versus Conscience*; Goodman, "Politics of Industrialism"; O'Connor, *Lords of the Loom*.

6. Massachusetts, Secretary of the Commonwealth, *Statistical Information Relating to Certain Branches of Industry in Massachusetts, for the year ending June 1, 1855*, pp. xiii–xiv.

7. Ibid., pp. 640–42; Massachusetts, Secretary of the Commonwealth, *Abstract of the Census of the Commonwealth of Massachusetts, Taken with Reference to Facts Existing on the First Day of June, 1855*, p. 244, and *Abstract of the Census of Massachusetts, 1860, from the Eighth U.S. Census, with Remarks on the Same*, p. 57.

8. Springfield *Republican*, 5 January 1861; Boston *Commonwealth*, 26 April 1851; Siracusa, "A Mechanical People," p. 153.

9. Foner, *Free Soil, Free Labor, Free Men*, pp. 11–40; Goodman, "Politics of Industrialism," pp. 164–65.

10. Higginson, *Cheerful Yesterdays*, pp. 125–26.

11. Forbes, *Letters and Recollections of John Murray Forbes*, 2:80; Ware, *Political Opinion in Massachusetts*, p. 141; Edward Hamilton to Nathaniel P. Banks, 19 February 1870, box 81, Banks Papers; Kirkland, "Boston During the Civil War," pp. 194–203.

12. Technically, cities were communities possessing charters granted to them by the state legislature. For the purpose of analysis, they are considered here to be communities containing 5,000 or more inhabitants.

13. The low turnout on Cape Cod and the Islands and the relatively heavy turnout in Berkshire County were not aberrations peculiar to the 1864 election (see Table 4.1.B). The tendency of Berkshire County to cast the heaviest vote in state and national elections, and the opposite tendency of Barnstable, Dukes, and Nantucket counties to cast the lightest vote continued into the 1870s and 1880s. This contrast in voter participation may have resulted from the lopsided Republican victories on Cape Cod, which possibly inculcated a sense of apathy among many partisans. Whatever its cause, the sharp contrast in voter turnout between these two peripheral areas of the state was recognized by contemporaries as a fundamental characteristic of the state's electoral politics in the second half of the nineteenth century. Massachusetts, Bureau of Statistics of Labor, *Annual Reports*, Report 13 (1881–1882): 186–88. On the unique nature of Berkshire County politics, see the Pittsfield *Sun*, 2 October 1872.

14. Donald, *Charles Sumner and the Coming of the Civil War*, p. 177n; Goodman, "Politics of Industrialism," pp. 161–207; Saunders, "People's Party," pp. 282, 394–413.

15. Wendell Phillips quoted in the Boston *Daily Advertiser*, 22 April 1861; Higginson, *Cheerful Yesterdays*, p. 115; Boutwell, *Reminiscences of Sixty Years in Public Affairs*, 1:119; Hoar, *Autobiography of Seventy Years*, 1:56.

16. In the same fifty-one "boot and shoe" towns analyzed in Table 4.1 above, the 1852 Free-Soil presidential ticket ran ten percentage points ahead of its statewide average. Cf. Goodman, "Politics of Industrialism," table IX, p. 186.

17. Springfield *Republican*, 6 August 1870; Davis, "Occupations of Massachusetts Legislators," p. 94–95.

18. Faler, *Mechanics and Manufacturers*, passim; Dawley, *Class and Community*, pp. 42–96.

19. Unlike bivariate correlation, multiple regression analysis enables the researcher to consider the relative effect of each independent variable on the dependent variable while simultaneously controlling for the effects of the remaining independent variables. The resulting regression coefficients indicate the effect of each of the explanatory variables on the dependent variable, and can be used for computing the expected average party vote in any voting unit based on its socioeconomic characteristics. When the independent variables are measured in different units, however, it is inappropriate to evaluate the relative impact of each variable on the basis of regression coefficients. Instead, it is necessary to calculate standardized regression coefficients (often called "beta weights" to distinguish them from actual "b" coefficients), which provide for each independent variable a measure of its relative importance for the distribution of the vote. Multiple regression analysis is explained in Blalock, *Social Statistics*, pp. 429–70; in Kerlinger, *Foundations of Behavioral Research*, pp. 611–31; and in much greater detail in Theil, *Principles of Econometrics*. The standardized regression coefficients or beta weights for a particular independent variable "indicate *how much change* in the dependent variable is produced by a standardized change in one of the independent variables when the others are controlled" (Blalock, *Social Statistics*, p. 453 [emphasis in the original]). It was necessary to limit the number of variables employed in the multiple regression analysis due to the problem of high correlations among some of the independent variables. Problems of multicollinearity arise when some or all of the explanatory variables are very highly intercorrelated. Extreme multicollinearity prevents coefficients from being calculated, and lesser degrees of high intercorrelations among the independent variables render less reliable the assessment of the relative importance of each independent variable indicated by the partial regression coefficients. Among econometricians a conventional rule of thumb is to eliminate from consideration any variable that is correlated with another at .80 or higher. A more cautious cutoff point was adopted here: whenever two variables were correlated at .725 or

above, one of them was excluded. For example, the percentage of the population in 1865 born in Ireland had to be omitted by this criterion because it was too highly correlated with the percentage of 1860 seating accommodations held by the Catholic church. See Blalock, "Correlated Independent Variables," pp. 233–37; and Farrar and Glauber, "Multicollinearity in Regression Analysis," pp. 92–107. Furthermore, because the relationship between two variables is not always linear, scatterplots for each of the independent variables were examined for nonlinearity in its relationship with the dependent variables. It proved unnecessary, however, to include curvilinear functions in any of the independent variables to make their influence on voting patterns more malleable to analysis by multiple regression. Each voting unit was "weighted" by its population in 1860 or 1865 to ensure that larger voting units would not be underrepresented in the analysis. The procedure used was the SPSS stepwise regression program in which the variables were entered into the equation on the basis of their partial correlation coefficients. See Nie et al., *SPSS: Statistical Package for the Social Sciences,* pp. 342–48; for the weighting procedure, see pp. 129–31.

20. Foner, *Free Soil, Free Labor, Free Men,* pp. 11–39; Hoar, *Autobiography of Seventy Years,* 1:158–59; Merriam, *Life and Times of Samuel Bowles,* 1:158; Goodman, "Politics of Industrialism," pp. 164–65. On the tendency for great wealth to produce even greater wealth and for the gap between rich and poor to widen and harden in the late antebellum period, see Knights, *Plain People of Boston,* pp. 78–102; and Pessen, *Riches, Class, and Power,* pp. 38–40.

21. The David Index of party competition expresses the vote of the runner-up in a voting unit as a percentage of the vote that would have been needed to win. See David, *Party Strength in the United States,* pp. 13–14. The mean David Index for the 1864 election was a low and, therefore, uncompetitive .56 for the entire state. Other useful procedures for measuring electoral competition are suggested by Elkins, "Measurement of Party Competition," pp. 682–700; and Ferejohn and Fioriana, "Paradox of Not Voting," pp. 525–36. A strong relationship between turnout and electorate competition existed for most states during the second-party system. See Chambers and Davis, "Party, Competition, and Mass Participation," pp. 174–97. See also Hofstetter, "Inter-Party Competition and Electoral Turnout," pp. 351–66.

22. Formisano, *Birth of Mass Political Parties,* pp. 102–64; Holt, *Forging a Majority,* p. 311; Jensen, *Winning of the Midwest,* pp. 62–85; Kleppner, *Cross of Culture,* pp. 71–91, and *Third Electoral System,* pp. 144, 363.

23. Darling, *Political Changes in Massachusetts,* pp. 39–43; Formisano, *Transformation of Political Culture,* pp. 149–70; Goodman, "Politics of Industrialism," pp. 167, 178; McLoughlin, *New England Dissent,* 2:1189–1262.

24. Formisano, *Transformation of Political Culture,* pp. 298–99; Goodman, "Politics of Industrialism," pp. 178–79. Studies of nineteenth-century pietistic-liturgical conflict include Hudson, *Religion in America;* Smith, *Revivalism and Social Reform;* Smith, Handy, and Loetscher, *American Christianity.*

25. Cole, *Social Ideas of the Northern Evangelists,* pp. 78–79, 197, 225–26; Smith, *Revivalism and Social Reform,* p. 204.

26. Carroll, *Religious Forces of the United States,* pp. lvi–lix. In the case of the Bay State Congregationalists, for example, there were over twice as many women members as males in 1860. Male members of Congregationalist churches could not have exceeded 10.8 percent of the electorate, but the number of men who were "fellow-travelers" or whose wives or mothers were affiliated with Congregationalist churches could have easily equaled one-fifth of the electorate. The ratio of Congregational seats to total population in 1860 was 20.4 percent (see Table 4.2). *Congregational Quarterly*

3 (January 1861):89. Cf. Goodman, "Guide to American Church Membership Data," table 1, p. 184.

27. Massachusetts, Bureau of Statistics of Labor, *Annual Report, 1871*, p. 606; Boston *Daily Evening Transcript*, 20 April 1872. In the Midwest in 1890, it has been estimated that fully 27 percent of the population was not church-affiliated. See Jensen, *Winning of the Midwest*, p. 88. In Wisconsin and Iowa in the same year similar estimates are as high as 48 percent and 54 percent, respectively. See Wright, "Ethnocultural Model of Voting," p. 662.

28. Stout and Taylor, "Sociology, Religion, and Historians Revisited," p. 33. A "religiosity" index (ratio of church seats to population) can be used to control for the variation in nonchurchgoers across voting units. For an attempt to relate religiosity to party preference, see Formisano, *Birth of Mass Political Parties*, pp. 340–42.

29. Cf. Jensen, "Religious and Occupational Roots of Party Indentification," table 1, p. 326.

30. Hays, "Political Parties and the Community-Society Continuum," pp. 158–59.

31. Bean, "Puritan Versus Celt," pp. 81–83; Boston *Pilot* as reported in the Boston *Commonwealth*, 25 March 1854.

32. Handlin, *Boston's Immigrants*, pp. 43–53, 60, 73–82, 124–50; Walsh, "The *Boston Pilot*," pp. 120–23; John Slidell quoted in McCrary, *Abraham Lincoln and Reconstruction*, p. 56.

33. John J. Crittenden et al. to Edward Everett, 25 May 1860, microfilm edition, reel 17, Everett Papers; Leverett Saltonstall to William C. Endicott, 20 March 1860, box 2, Endicott Papers; Boston *Courier*, 3 July, 29 and 30 September and 3 October 1860; Boston *Pilot*, 7 July 1860.

34. Osofsky, "Abolitionists, Irish Immigrants," p. 900; O'Connor, *Lords of the Loom*, pp. 132–53; Boston *Post*, 4 September 1863; William S. Robinson, [undated and unidentified clippings], "Scrapbook No. 3," p. 143, Robinson Collection.

35. Handlin, *Boston's Immigrants*, pp. 210–11; Pearson, *Life of John A. Andrew*, 2:228.

36. Boston *Pilot*, 30 May 1863; Boston *Pilot* quoted in Walsh, "The *Boston Pilot*," pp. 174–75.

37. Bergquist, "People and Politics in Transition," pp. 196–226; Daniels, "Immigrant Vote in the 1860 Election," pp. 142–62; Kremm, "Cleveland and the First Lincoln Election," pp. 69–86; Kelso, "German-American Vote in the Election of 1860," passim.

38. Formisano, *Birth of Mass Political Parties*, pp. 138, 324, 330; Jensen, *Winning of the Midwest*, p. 69; Kleppner, *Cross of Culture*, p. 71, and *Third Electoral System*, p. 189.

39. Goodman, "Politics of Industrialism," p. 195; Smith, *Revivalism and Social Reform*, p. 205; Mathews, *Slavery and Methodism*, pp. 120ff, 131, 164, 171, 233.

40. Doherty, *Hicksite Separation*, passim.

41. Staiger, "Abolitionism and the Presbyterian Schism," pp. 391–414; Beard, *Crusade of Brotherhood*, pp. 117–18.

42. Ware, *Political Opinion in Massachusetts*, p. 244n; Frothingham, *Edward Everett*. Everett believed his support for Lincoln influenced many voters. See Edward Everett to George Bancroft, 25 October 1864, Bancroft Papers.

43. Formisano, *Transformation of Political Culture*, pp. 290–91; Howe, *Unitarian Conscience*, p. 299; Sykes, "Massachusetts Unitarianism and Social Change," pp. 117–35; Storey, "Class and Culture in Boston," pp. 178–99; Adams, *Education of Henry Adams*, pp. 33–34.

44. Edward Everett quoted in Frothingham, *Boston Unitarianism*, p. 194.

45. Samuel May, Jr., to Samuel Joseph May, 28 September 1868, Anti-Slavery May Papers; Edward Everett to George Bancroft, 17 October 1864, Bancroft Papers.

46. Kleppner, *Third Electoral System*, p. 363.

47. For a reformulation of the pietistic-liturgical typology, see Vandermeer, "Religion, Society, and Politics," pp. 3–24.

Chapter 5. The Radical Republicans versus Andrew Johnson: The Congressional Elections of 1866

1. McPherson, *Struggle for Equality*, pp. 316–17; Charles Sumner to Francis W. Bird, 25 April 1865, Bird Papers.

2. Charles Sumner to George Bancroft, 28 February 1865, Bancroft Papers; Stearns, *Cambridge Sketches*, p. 162; Boston *Commonwealth*, 6 May 1865; Amos A. Lawrence to Andrew Johnson, 1 July 1865 [copy], Lawrence Papers; McPherson, *Struggle for Equality*, p. 319. The Massachusetts radicals in the lower house never hesitated to concentrate their efforts on securing legal justice for blacks for fear of a white voter backlash. In 1865 they led a successful drive to pass the first comprehensive public accommodations law in American history. See Hart, *Commonwealth History of Massachusetts*, 4:58.

3. McPherson, *Struggle for Equality*, pp. 320–22; Ben: Perley Poore to Charles Sumner, 26 June 1865, Sumner Papers; Boston *Commonwealth*, 10 and 17 June 1865; Donald, *Charles Sumner and the Rights of Man*, pp. 226–27; Boston *Daily Advertiser*, 15 September 1865.

4. McPherson, *Struggle for Equality*, p. 341.

5. Benedict, *Compromise of Principle*, p. 69; *Harper's Weekly* 9 (25 February 1865): 114.

6. Harrington, *Fighting Politician*, pp. 41–42; Benjamin F. Butler to Edward L. Pierce, 20 July 1863, Pierce Papers; Boston *Gazette*, 30 November 1873.

7. McCrary, *Abraham Lincoln and Reconstruction*, pp. 135–58, 186–211; Edward Hamilton to Nathaniel P. Banks, 25 November 1863, Banks Papers.

8. John Logan to Henry L. Dawes, 21 November 1865, box 19, Dawes Papers; Thaddeus Stevens to Charles Sumner, 26 August 1865, Sumner Papers.

9. Unlike in New York and Ohio, the prewar partisan affiliations of Massachusetts Republican leaders were not reliable predictors of postwar intraparty divisions. See Mohr, *Radical Republicans in the North*, pp. 66–103 passim.

10. Pearson, *Life of John A. Andrew*, 2:179–92; John Murray Forbes to Edward A. Atkinson, 29 January 1865, Atkinson Papers; Donald, *Charles Sumner and the Rights of Man*, pp. 209–10; McKay, *Henry Wilson*, pp. 190–91; William Claflin to Francis W. Bird, 13 January 1865, Claflin Papers; George Baty Blake to Horatio Woodman, 13 January 1865 [copy], Woodman Papers.

11. Pearson, *Life of John A. Andrew*, 2:261, 263–65, 272–78; McKitrick, *Andrew Johnson and Reconstruction*, p. 229; Donald, *Charles Sumner and the Rights of Man*, 235–36; John A. Andrew to Charles Sumner, 21 November 1865, Sumner Papers; Charles Sumner to John A. Andrew, 22? November 1865, Andrew Papers.

12. Donald, *Charles Sumner and the Rights of Man*, pp. 242–47. Andrew's valedictory address is reprinted in Browne, *Sketch of the Official Life of John A. Andrew*, pp. 167–211, and in Chandler, *Memoir of Governor Andrew*, pp. 239–98.

13. McKitrick, *Andrew Johnson and Reconstruction*, p. 215.

14. Pearson, *Life of John A. Andrew*, 2:266–67. In the fall of 1865 Andrew became

involved in a business and benevolent enterprise that sought to invest northern capital in southern agriculture. See Powell, "American Land Company and Agency," pp. 293–308.

15. Pearson, *Life of John A. Andrew*, 2:286–87; Springfield *Republican*, 10 June 1865.

16. The Sumner radicals saw the legacy of slavery (not individual former slaveholders and ex-Confederates) as the real enemy. See Robinson, *"Warrington" Pen-Portraits*, p. 305. The theme that the radical approach to Reconstruction was more realistic than the moderate policy based on appeasement, compromise, and conciliation is developed in McCrary, *Abraham Lincoln and Reconstruction*, and Perman, *Reunion Without Compromise*.

17. McPherson, *Struggle for Equality*, pp. 347–49; John A. Andrew to Francis P. Blair, Sr., 18 March 1866 [copy], box 18, Andrew Papers.

18. Charles Francis Adams, Jr., to Charles Francis Adams, 12 May 1868, microfilm edition, reel 286, Adams Family Papers; Coleman, *Election of 1868*, pp. 281–82.

19. Mirak, "John Quincy Adams, Jr.," pp. 192–93.

20. Springfield *Republican*, 21 July 1866; "Warrington," Springfield *Republican*, 16 August 1866; Ware, *Political Opinion in Massachusetts*, pp. 359–60.

21. See Table 3.7.

22. Pittsfield *Sun*, 26 October 1865 [emphasis in the original].

23. Handlin, *Boston's Immigrants*, pp. 208–12, 215–16; Baum, "'Irish Vote' and Party Politics," pp. 122–23.

24. Harmond, "Tradition and Change in the Gilded Age," p. 23; Boston *Pilot*, 18 August 1866.

25. Jenkins, *Fenians and Anglo-American Relations*, pp. 23–29; Montgomery, *Beyond Equality*, pp. 129–30. See also D'Arcy, *Fenian Movement*; O'Broin, *Fenian Fever*.

26. Handlin, *Boston's Immigrants*, pp. 206, 298–310; Cole, *Immigrant City*, pp. 45–46; Montgomery, *Beyond Equality*, pp. 130–31.

27. Brown, *Irish-American Nationalism*, p. 36. Guiney was perhaps an exception because, by his own admission, he was in 1864 the only member of his all-Irish, Ninth Massachusetts regiment to vote for Lincoln. See undated newspaper clippings in "Scrapbook of General P. R. Guiney," Guiney Papers.

28. Boston *Pilot*, 14 July 1866; Boston *Post*, 5 September 1866.

29. *The Right Way* (Boston), 1 September 1866; Roda L. White to Benjamin F. Butler, 17 July 1866, series A, box 36, Butler Papers; Harrington, *Fighting Politician*, pp. 178–80; Gambill, "Northern Democrats and Reconstruction," pp. 165–66; Henry Wilson quoted in the Boston *Daily Journal*, 27 August 1866.

30. Boston *Post*, 5 September 1866; Boston *Pilot*, 14 July 1866; Irish Central Executive Committee, *Address of the Central Executive Committee of Irish Citizens*, p. 4; Gambill, "Northern Democrats and Reconstruction," p. 167; Horace H. Day to Benjamin F. Butler, 1 September 1866, series A, box 36, Butler Papers.

31. Lane, *Political Life*, pp. 197–203; Lipset, *Political Man*, pp. 211–26.

32. Boston *Pilot*, 10 November 1866; Neidhardt, *Fenianism in North America*, pp. 93–108. In New York the Fenian newspaper *Irish American* did not endorse the National Union gubernatorial candidate. A regression of the vote received by the 1866 Republican gubernatorial candidate on the vote received in 1864 by Republican and Democratic gubernatorial candidates in the twenty-two wards of New York City produced the estimate that only 4 percent of the former Democratic voters (or about 7,020 voters) switched to the Republicans. Otherwise, in 1866 party lines in the city remained unbroken.

33. Montgomery, *Beyond Equality*, p. 91.
34. Patrick R. Guiney quoted in undated newspaper clippings in "P. R. Guiney Scrapbook," Guiney Papers.
35. Bartlett, *Wendell Phillips*, pp. 268–73.
36. Montgomery, *Beyond Equality*, p. 272.
37. Amos A. Lawrence to Eli Thayer, 24 July 1858 [copy], "Letters No. 4," Lawrence Papers; Donald, *Politics of Reconstruction*, pp. 26–52, especially pp. 43–44. In his analysis of congressional districts, Donald asserts that "the more heavily a district voted Republican, the more surely its Representative would support Radical measures in Congress" (ibid., p. 35). However, his hypothesis has been tested and found wanting by other scholars. See Benedict, *Compromise of Principle*, p. 56, and Swenson, "Midwest and the Abandonment of Radical Reconstruction," p. 92.
38. Montgomery, *Beyond Equality*, pp. 272–75.
39. Henry T. Delano to Nathaniel P. Banks, 18 June 1866, box 62, Banks Papers; Boston *Daily Evening Voice*, 6 November 1865; Ira Steward quoted in ibid., 26 October 1865; Harrington, *Fighting Politician*, pp. 178–80, 197–98.
40. On Butler's career, see Trefousse, *Ben Butler*, and Butler's own account, *Butler's Book*.
41. Benedict, *Compromise of Principle*, p. 257.
42. Charles F. Adams, Jr., to Charles F. Adams, Sr., 20 October 1866, microfilm edition, reel 50, Adams Family Papers; Charles Sumner to Francis W. Bird, 17 August 1866, Bird Papers; John M. S. Williams to John A. Andrew, 7 August 1866, box 19, Andrew Papers; Springfield *Republican*, 14 September 1866, 11 November 1867.
43. Boston *Daily Journal*, 13 September 1866; Springfield *Republican*, 14 and 15 September 1866; Boston *Daily Advertiser*, 14 September 1866. Wilson, wishing to unite the various elements of the Republican party, favored passage of the Fourteenth Amendment and drew the anger of Bird and Robinson. See Boston *Commonwealth*, 16 March and 7 April 1866; Abbott, *Cobbler in Congress*, p. 176.
44. Benjamin F. Butler quoted in the Springfield *Republican*, 14 September 1866; Boston *Daily Advertiser*, 14 September 1866; Charles Sumner quoted in *The Right Way* (Boston), 20 October 1866.
45. John Q. Adams, Jr., quoted in the Boston *Daily Journal*, 12 September 1866, and in Mirak, "John Quincy Adams, Jr.," p. 195; Charles F. Adams, Jr., to Charles F. Adams, Sr., 6 November 1866, microfilm edition, reel 580, Adams Family Papers.
46. Edward R. Tinker to Henry L. Dawes, 30 March 1866, and Samuel Bowles to Henry L. Dawes, 20 April 1869, box 19, Dawes Papers; Arcanti, "To Secure the Party," pp. 33–45; Springfield *Republican*, 17 September 1866; Benedict, *Compromise of Principle*, pp. 206–8.
47. See Castel, *Presidency of Andrew Johnson*.
48. Boston *Daily Journal*, 8 September 1866; Boston *Post*, 1 November 1866.

Chapter 6. The Election of 1867: A Setback for Radicalism or Prohibition?

1. Benedict, "Rout of Radicalism," p. 344; Mantell, *Johnson, Grant, and the Politics of Reconstruction*, pp. 145–46; Trefousse, "Acquittal of Andrew Johnson," p. 150; Benedict, *Compromise of Principle*, quotation on p. 257.
2. New York *Herald*, 10 and 19 October 1867; Wendell Phillips quoted in Benedict, "Rout of Radicalism," p. 336.

3. New York *Times*, 10 October 1867, p. 4; Boston *Post*, 8 November 1867; Horatio Seymour to Andrew Johnson, 9 November 1867, microfilm edition, reel 29, Johnson Papers.

4. Robert C. Winthrop to John H. Clifford, 26 November 1867, microfilm edition, section B-14, Winthrop Papers. The returns for the 1864 presidential election and the 1866 and 1867 gubernatorial contests were as follows:

Year	Republican		Democrat		All Others
1864	Lincoln	126,742	McClellan	48,745	6
1866	Bullock	91,980	Sweetser	26,671	100
1867	Bullock	98,306	Adams	70,360	0

5. John H. Clifford to Robert C. Winthrop, 24 November 1867, Winthrop Papers; Springfield *Republican*, 10 November 1867; Merriam, *Life and Times of Samuel Bowles*, 2:33–34; Nathaniel P. Banks to Mrs. Banks, 13 November 1867, box 3, Banks Papers.

6. *American Annual Cyclopaedia* (1867), p. 482; Boston *Daily Journal*, 12 September 1867; Donald, *Charles Sumner and the Rights of Man*, pp. 297–98.

7. Boston *Daily Advertiser*, 13 June 1867 [emphasis in the original].

8. Henry Adams to Charles F. Adams, Jr., 8 May 1867, microfilm edition, reel 582, Adams Family Papers.

9. John Q. Adams, Jr., quoted in Mirak, "John Quincy Adams, Jr.," p. 197; Charles F. Adams, Jr., to Charles F. Adams, Sr., 12 October 1867, microfilm edition, reel 584, Adams Family Papers.

10. Mohr, *Radical Republicans in the North*, pp. 69, 90; Boston *Daily Advertiser*, 7 November 1867; Boston *Daily Journal*, 10 October 1867.

11. Abbott, "Maintaining Hegemony," pp. 8–9; Springfield *Republican* quoted in the Boston *Post*, 1 November 1867.

12. Lane, *Policing the City*, pp. 39–45, 87–90; Sweeney, "Rum, Romanism, Representation, and Reform," pp. 116–37; Hart, *Commonwealth History of Massachusetts*, 4:608–09; Clark, *History of the Temperance Reform*, pp. 86–94; Tyrrell, *Sobering Up*, pp. 290–91.

13. Studies linking antebellum temperance reform movements with the emergence of a modern industrial system include Dodd, "Working Classes and the Temperance Movement," pp. 510–31; Rorabaugh, "Prohibition as Progress," pp. 425–43; Tyrrell, *Sobering Up*, pp. 3–15, 87–158, and "Temperance and Economic Change," pp. 45–67. On the religious basis of the Prohibitionist crusade, see Formisano, *Transformation of Political Culture*, pp. 291, 297–99; Goodman, "Politics of Industrialism," pp. 167, 174, 178–79, 194–95; Tyrrell, *Sobering Up*, pp. 55–58.

14. Dawley, *Class and Community*, pp. 36–37; Faler, "Cultural Aspects of the Industrial Revolution," pp. 367–94; Harrison, *Drink and the Victorians*; Winsor, *Memorial History of Boston*, 4:529; Green, *Holyoke, Massachusetts*, p. 123; Massachusetts, General Court, *Journal of the House of Representatives*, H.Doc.415 (1867), pp. 865–66.

15. Abbott, "Maintaining Hegemony," pp. 7–8; Kleppner, "Greenback and Prohibition Parties," pp. 1549–81; Pearson, *Life of John A. Andrew*, 2:218–19; Lane, *Policing the City*, pp. 136–37.

16. Edwin Thompson to George F. Hoar, 1 September 1865, Hoar Papers; Lane, *Policing the City*, p. 138; Abbott, "Maintaining Hegemony," p. 8; Alexander H. Bullock quoted in the Boston *Daily Journal*, 4 January 1867.

17. Boston *Pilot*, 13 April 1867; *Staats Zeitung* (New York) [undated newspaper clip-

ping], box 22, Andrew Papers. Andrew's arguments before the legislative committee were published verbatim in a supplement to the Boston *Daily Journal*, 4 April 1867.

18. Amasa Walker [published letter dated "4 November 1867" in an undated and unidentified newspaper clipping], "Amasa Walker Scrapbook," Walker Papers; Boston *Pilot*, 28 September 1867; Tappan Wentworth to Benjamin F. Butler, 8 July 1867, box 41, Butler Papers; Boston *Daily Advertiser*, 16 September 1867; Nathaniel P. Banks to Mrs. Banks, 3 November 1867, box 3, Banks Papers; *Constitution of the P.L.L. of Massachusetts*, "Scrapbook No. 1," p. 180, Robinson Collection.

19. Lane, *Policing the City*, p. 134; Otis Norcross, "Diary," 4 December 1866, Norcross Papers; Boston *Pilot*, 19 January 1867.

20. Springfield *Republican*, 8 November 1867; Abbott, "Maintaining Hegemony," p. 8; *American Annual Cyclopaedia* (1867), pp. 481–83; Hart, *Commonwealth History of Massachusetts*, 4:609.

21. Boston *Post*, 5 November 1867.

22. Francis W. Bird to Rev. William M. Thayer, 15 September 1865 [published letter in undated and unidentified newspaper clipping], "Scrapbook No. 1," pp. 68–70, Robinson Collection; Springfield *Republican*, 3 September 1867.

23. *The Right Way* (Boston), 2 March 1867; Springfield *Republican*, 7 November 1867; Wendell Phillips quoted in the Boston *Pilot*, 19 October 1867; Nathaniel P. Banks to Mrs. Banks, 4 November 1867, box 3, Banks Papers.

24. Henry Wilson quoted in the Boston *Daily Journal*, 23 October 1867; Abbott, "Maintaining Hegemony," p. 8.

25. Boston *Daily Advertiser*, 12 September 1867; Pittsfield *Sun*, 19 September 1867.

26. Boston *Post*, 13 September 1867; Boston *Daily Journal*, 16 September 1867; John Q. Adams to Charles F. Adams, 29 February 1868, microfilm edition, reel 585, Adams Family Papers.

27. John Q. Adams quoted in the Boston *Daily Advertiser*, 11 October 1867.

28. Ballot distributed in 1867 by the Democratic party in Greenfield, Massachusetts Historical Society, Boston; Patrick R. Guiney to Benjamin F. Butler, 25 November 1867, box 41, series A, Butler Papers; Charles F. Adams, Jr., to Charles F. Adams, Sr., 12 October 1867, microfilm edition, reel 584, Adams Family Papers.

29. Brock, *An American Crisis*, pp. 70–73; Benedict, *Compromise of Principle*, pp. 22, 27–28; Donald, *Politics of Reconstruction*, pp. 91–105; McCarthy, "Reconstruction Legislation and Voting Alignments," pp. 198–200; Barnes, *Fortieth Congress of the United States*, 2:539.

30. In the first session of the Fortieth Congress, the remainder of the Massachusetts congressional delegation—Oakes Ames and William B. Washburn—were among those who had maintained a middle position between the radical and conservative wings of their party in the preceding Thirty-ninth Congress. Donald does not categorize Ames, but he classifies Washburn as an "independent radical." Another scholar labels Ames a "consistent centrist." Both Ames's and Washburn's districts were omitted from the analysis of the 1867 gubernatorial returns in order to sharpen the distinction between areas represented by radical and conservative Republicans. See Donald, *Politics of Reconstruction*, pp. 99—105; Benedict, *Compromise of Principle*, p. 22.

31. Boston *Pilot*, 16 March 1867; Boston *Daily Advertiser*, 8 November 1867; "Attention! Are you in favor of a law that deprives you of the right to sell the products of your farms? . . ." (Broadside 1867), Massachusetts Historical Society, Boston; Springfield *Republican*, 3 September 1870.

32. In 1867 the economic situation varied considerably from place to place. See

Frisch, "From Town to City," pp. 201–33; Holyoke *Transcript*, 1 June 1867. For evidence of Republican reverses resulting from the nationwide economic recession of 1866–67, see McCarthy, "Reconstruction Legislation and Voting Alignments," p. 252n.

33. Tyrrell, *Sobering Up*, pp. 87–124; Harmond, "Tradition and Change in the Gilded Age," pp. 257–59; Lane, *Policing the City*, quotation on p. 134; Abbott, "Maintaining Hegemony," pp. 8–9.

34. New York *Times*, 5 November 1867; Boston *Post*, 25 October 1867; Pittsfield *Sun*, 31 October 1867.

35. Brock, *American Crisis*, p. 277; Trefousse, "Acquittal of Andrew Johnson," p. 153; McCarthy, "Reconstruction Legislation and Voting Alignments," p. 318; Sumner, *Charles Sumner, His Complete Works*, 12:409.

36. Francis W. Bird to Charles Sumner, 9 June 1968, Sumner Papers; Charles Sumner to Francis W. Bird, 13 June 1868, Bird Papers; Charles W. Slack to Charles Sumner, 15 July 1868, Sumner Papers; O'Hare, "Public Career of Patrick Andrew Collins," p. 86.

37. Mirak, "John Quincy Adams, Jr.," p. 196; Edward L. Pierce to Charles Sumner, 24 July 1868, Sumner Papers; Duberman, *Charles Francis Adams*, pp. 334–35; Donald, *Charles Sumner and the Rights of Man*, pp. 345–46.

38. Edward L. Pierce to Francis W. Bird [n.d.], Fort Monroe (1862), and George S. Boutwell to Francis W. Bird, 10 January 1868, Bird Papers; Francis W. Bird to Charles Sumner, 17 January 1868, Sumner Papers; Donald, *Charles Sumner and the Rights of Man*, p. 344n. Bird's relationship with Bullock had never been very cordial. Bullock, as a member of the state legislature in 1861, opposed a resolution introduced by the radicals instructing the Massachusetts senatorial and congressional delegations to remove all obstacles to the enlistment of black troops. At the end of the war Bird urged Benjamin F. Butler to challenge Bullock for the governorship. See [By his children], *Francis William Bird*, p. 68n; Hoar, "Memoir of Alexander Hamilton Bullock," pp. xvi–xxviii; Butler, *Private and Official Correspondence of General Benjamin F. Butler*, 5:595–96.

39. Edward R. Tinker to Henry L. Dawes, 26 April 1868, box 19, Dawes Papers; Pittsfield *Eagle* quoted in the Pittsfield *Sun*, 1 November 1866; Horatio G. Knight to Henry L. Dawes, 26 March 1868, box 19, Dawes Papers.

40. [By his children], *Francis William Bird*, pp. 69–70; Charles Sumner to William Claflin, 9 August 1868, Claflin Papers; Whiting Griswald to Francis W. Bird, 6 August 1868, Bird Papers; Williard P. Phillips to Henry L. Pierce, 5 August 1868, Sumner Papers. If President Johnson had been removed from office in 1868, and if Sumner had been selected by Benjamin F. Wade (who as president pro tempore of the Senate would have become president if Johnson had been convicted following his impeachment) for a cabinet position, the Bird Club radicals would have welcomed either Loring or Dawes as a successor to Sumner in the Senate. Bird would not have been able to control a senatorial election in the state legislature that was elected in 1867. Fearing a strong challenge from Charles F. Adams, strategy dictated that Sumner, if he desired to accept a place in Wade's cabinet, would have to resign his Senate seat after the adjournment of the 1868 legislature. The choice of a successor to Sumner would then have devolved on Governor Bullock, who most likely would have appointed Dawes. See Francis W. Bird to Charles Sumner, 31 March 1868, and William S. Robinson to Charles Sumner, 13 April 1868, Sumner Papers.

41. *American Annual Cyclopaedia* (1868), p. 460; Boston *Post*, 11 September 1868, 9 July 1869; Springfield *Republican*, 6 January 1869.

42. Andrew Johnson to John Q. Adams, Jr., 26 September 1868 [copy], microfilm edition, reel 34, Johnson Papers; Mirak, "John Quincy Adams, Jr.," pp. 187–88; William L. Garrison to Samuel May, Jr., 25 October 1868, Garrison Papers.
43. Coleman, *Election of 1868*, p. 359; Boston *Post*, 2 and 3 September 1868; Boston *Herald*, 19 September 1868; Pittsfield *Sun*, 10 September 1868.
44. Boston *Pilot*, 25 July, 8 August, and 10 October 1868; Moses Bates to Andrew Johnson, 14 December 1867, microfilm edition, reel 30, Johnson Papers; Charles F. Adams, Jr., to Charles F. Adams, Sr., 21 February 1868, microfilm edition, reel 585, Adams Family Papers.
45. Springfield *Republican*, 8 July 1868.
46. Mantell, *Johnson, Grant, and the Politics of Reconstruction*, pp. 139–40.
47. Springfield *Republican*, 6 November 1867.
48. Boston *Daily Journal*, 6 November 1867.
49. Benedict, *Compromise of Principle*, pp. 322–24.
50. Boston *Daily Evening Transcript*, 4 November 1868. On the availability of split tickets at polling places, see the Boston *Post*, 4 November 1868.
51. Pittsfield *Sun*, 5 November 1868; Charles F. Adams, "Diary," 1 December 1868, microfilm edition, reel 82, Adams Family Papers; Mantell, *Johnson, Grant, and the Politics of Reconstruction*, table 1, p. 144.

Chapter 7. The Transition from Ideological to Pragmatic Politics, 1869–1871

1. Montgomery, *Beyond Equality*, p. 369; Abbott, "Maintaining Hegemony," p. 14.
2. Boston *Daily Journal*, 29 and 30 September 1869; Ira Steward to Friedrich A. Sorge, 4 December 1876, box 3, Steward Papers.
3. Boston *Post*, 28 September 1869, 2 November 1867; Boston *Pilot*, 20 January 1866; Harry Hopkins to George F. Hoar, 26 April 1871, Hoar Papers; Edward R. Tinker to Henry L. Dawes, 30 March 1866, box 19, Dawes Papers.
4. Boston *Post*, 5 October 1869.
5. Springfield *Republican*, 25 August 1869; Boston *Daily Journal*, 25 August 1869. On the "new departure" policy of the northern Democrats, see House, "Republicans and Democrats Search for New Identities," p. 474.
6. Hall, "Knights of St. Crispin," pp. 161–66; Boston *Post*, 25 October and 4 November 1869; Dawley, *Class and Community*, pp. 196–97; Ware, *Political Opinion in Massachusetts*, p. 382. In 1869, 5.2 percent of the electorate statewide voted the Labor Reform party ticket; but in the state's fifty-one predominantly "boot and shoe" towns, 15.5 percent of the eligible voters cast Labor Reform ballots.
7. Robinson, *"Warrington" Pen-Portraits*, p. 340; Boston *Post*, 3 November 1869; Charles F. Adams, "Diary," 3 November 1869, microfilm edition, reel 82, Adams Family Papers.
8. Edward Hamilton to Nathaniel P. Banks, 11 February 1870, box 81, Banks Papers; Harrington, *Fighting Politician*, p. 200.
9. Boston *Post*, 18 August 1870; Springfield *Republican*, 18 August, 3 September, 8 and 26 October 1870.
10. Boston *Daily Journal*, 10 and 13 September 1870; Wendell Phillips quoted in the Boston *Daily Advertiser*, 22 April 1872.
11. William L. Garrison to Oliver Johnson, 7 November 1870, and William L. Garri-

son to Wendell Phillips Garrison, 27 November 1870, Garrison Papers; Samuel May to Richard D. Webb, 24 August 1870, Anti-Slavery May Papers.

12. Montgomery, *Beyond Equality*, pp. 230–60; Abbott, "Maintaining Hegemony," p. 12; Wendell Phillips, *People Coming to Power!* p. 17.

13. Boston *Post*, 13 September 1870; Bartlett, *Wendell Phillips*, pp. 261–62, 265–66; Trefousse, *Ben Butler*, pp. 34–41; Wendell Phillips quoted in Harmond, "Tradition and Change in the Gilded Age," pp. 31–32; Robinson, *"Warrington" Pen-Portraits*, p. 445; Wendell Phillips quoted in ibid., p. 130.

14. Springfield *Republican*, 19 October 1870.

15. Springfield *Republican*, 20 October 1870; [By his children], *Francis William Bird*, p. 33; Stearns, *Cambridge Sketches*, pp. 177–78.

16. William Schouler to Henry L. Dawes, 24 October 1870, box 20, Dawes Papers; Robinson, *"Warrington" Pen-Portraits*, pp. 502–5; Springfield *Republican*, 24 August 1870.

17. William Claflin to George F. Hoar, 6 October 1870, Hoar Papers; Springfield *Republican*, 6 and 8 October 1870; Baum, "Woman Suffrage and the 'Chinese Question,'" pp. 60–77.

18. Springfield *Republican*, 13 October 1870; Boston *Daily Advertiser*, 13 October 1870.

19. Boston *Post*, 31 August 1870; Springfield *Republican*, 11 July, 2 September, 15 and 19 October 1870.

20. Adams, *Appeal to the Mechanics and Laboring-Men*, pp. 4, 16, 19–24.

21. "Warrington" in the Springfield *Republican*, 3 September 1870; Springfield *Republican*, 24 August 1870.

22. Charles F. Adams, "Diary," 9 November 1870, microfilm edition, reel 83, Adams Family Papers. The Republican majorities over the combined totals of their opponents in the gubernatorial contests from 1864 to 1870 were as follows:

Year:	1864	1865	1866	1867	1868	1869	1870
Majority:	76,022	48,506	65,209	27,946	68,771	9,702	8,861

23. The "pure" temperance vote is uncovered by counting the vote polled by former Know-Nothing Eliphalet Trask, the Prohibitionist party's candidate for lieutenant governor in 1870. Trask received 8,692 votes. Cf. Abbott, "Maintaining Hegemony," p. 9.

24. On attitudes toward drink in nineteenth century factory towns, see Dawley and Faler, "Working-Class Culture," pp. 466–80; Dodd, "Working Classes and the Temperance Movement," pp. 510–31; Faler, "Cultural Aspects of the Industrial Revolution," pp. 367–94; Tyrrell, *Sobering Up*, pp. 92–113, and "Temperance and Economic Change," pp. 45–67.

25. Ware, *Political Opinion in Massachusetts*, p. 386; New York *Times*, 9 September 1871; Springfield *Republican*, 6 May 1870, 24 July, 31 August, and 21 September 1871; Trefousse, *Ben Butler*, pp. 219, 313n; Samuel Shellabarger to George F. Hoar, 11 September 1871, and Benjamin F. Butler to George F. Hoar, 18 September 1871, Hoar Papers; Fall River *News*, 20 September 1871; Merriam, *Life and Times of Samuel Bowles*, 2:106. For a sample of Butler's ability to entertain an audience, see the Springfield *Republican*, 9 September 1871.

26. An account of Butler as a "machine" politician is contained in Mallam, "Benjamin Franklin Butler." For a reappraisal of Butler's career, see Crenshaw, "Benjamin F. Butler."

27. [Adams], "The Butler Canvass," pp. 147–70; Robinson, "General Butler's Campaign," pp. 742–50; Hoar, *Autobiography of Seventy Years*, 1:362ff; Pierce, *Memoir*

and Letters of Charles Sumner, 4:498; Nathaniel P. Banks to Mrs. Banks, 22 February 1871, box 3, Banks Papers; New York *Times*, 25 August 1871; Springfield *Republican*, 9 September 1871.

28. Peleg W. Chandler to Alexander H. Bullock, 15 September 1871, Bullock Papers; Nathaniel P. Banks to Mrs. Banks, 10 May, 25 July 1871, box 3, Banks Papers.

29. Boston *Post*, 31 July and 4 November 1871.

30. [Adams], "The Butler Canvass"; Butler, *Present Relations of Parties.*

31. Crenshaw, "Benjamin F. Butler," p. 136; Mallam, "Benjamin Franklin Butler," p. 184.

32. Because of the relatively small Democratic vote in Essex County in 1868, the actual number of Democrats who switched to Butler was approximately 1,670 or slightly less than 6 percent of the district's eligible voters. Statewide, about 6,050 former Democrats switched—slightly over 2 percent of the state's eligible voters. See Table 7.6.

33. Benjamin F. Butler to George F. Hoar, 18 September 1871, Hoar Papers; Henry L. Dawes to Edward L. Pierce, 21 June 1871, Pierce Papers; Edward R. Tinker to Henry L. Dawes, 28 June 1870, general correspondence to Dawes for January 1870, and Thomas Russell to Samuel Bowles, 18 February 1870, box 20, Dawes Papers; Boston *Post*, 25 January 1871.

34. Samuel Bowles to Henry L. Dawes, 20 June 1871, box 20, Dawes Papers; Edward L. Pierce to William Claflin [n.d.], Claflin Papers.

35. Donald, *Charles Sumner and the Rights of Man*, p. 522; Robinson, *"Warrington" Pen-Portraits*, p. 133; Abbott, *Cobbler in Congress*, pp. 239–40; Wendell Phillips quoted in the Boston *Daily Advertiser*, 5 October 1871.

36. Springfield *Republican*, 30 September 1871; Boston *Commonwealth*, 30 September 1871; Benjamin F. Butler to Charles Sumner, 2 October 1871, Sumner Papers; Henry Wilson to Benjamin F. Butler, 7 October 1871, box 86, series B, Butler Papers.

37. Henry C. Davis to Benjamin F. Butler, 2 October 1871, box 86, and Frank B. Martin to Benjamin F. Butler, 22 October 1871, box 86, series B, Butler Papers.

38. The temperance movement as a vehicle to create a greater sense of community is discussed in Chapman, "Mid-Nineteenth-Century Temperance Movement," pp. 43–50.

39. James M. Stone to Charles Sumner, 11 March 1871, Sumner Papers; Edgar J. Sherman to Benjamin F. Butler, 20 March 1871, Butler Papers.

Chapter 8. The Liberal Republican Movement and the Eclipse of Radicalism

1. Samuel Bowles to Henry L. Dawes, 21 May 1872, box 21, Dawes Papers; Goldman, *Rendezvous with Destiny*, pp. 9–23.

2. A satisfactory explanation of the Liberal Republican movement has proven elusive: see Gerber, "Liberal Republicans of 1872," pp. 40–73. Helpful works on the Liberal Republicans include Downey, "Rebirth of Reform"; Ross, *Liberal Republican Movement*; Sproat, *"Best Men,"* pp. 45–69. On the Republicans and the labor question, see Montgomery, *Beyond Equality.*

3. On the connection between reformism and "status anxiety," see Hoogenboom, *Outlawing the Spoils*, p. 21.

4. Stearns, *Cambridge Sketches*, pp. 165–66; [By his children], *Francis William Bird*, p. 77; Robinson, *"Warrington" Pen-Portraits*, p. 135.

5. Donald, *Charles Sumner and the Rights of Man*, p. 543; Samuel Bowles to Col. W. M. Grosvenor [copy of a letter], 9 March 1872, box 3, Atkinson Papers; Francis W. Bird to Charles Sumner, 11 April 1872, Sumner Papers.

6. Francis W. Bird to Charles Sumner, 15 April 1872, Sumner Papers; McPherson, *Abolitionist Legacy*, p. 25; Boston *Daily Advertiser*, 22 April 1872; Wendell Phillips to Charles Sumner, 11 April 1872, Sumner Papers.

7. Downey, "Horace Greeley and the Politicians," pp. 727–50; Duberman, *Charles Francis Adams*, pp. 352–85; Ross, *Liberal Republican Movement*, pp. 86–105; Edward R. Tinker to Henry L. Dawes, 17 May 1872, box 21, Dawes Papers.

8. Horace Greeley quoted in McPherson, *Abolitionist Legacy*, p. 27; Williamson, *Edward Atkinson*, pp. 89–91; Charles Francis Adams, "Diary," 7 January 1875, microfilm edition, reel 86, Adams Family Papers.

9. Robinson, *"Warrington" Pen-Portraits*, pp. 356–57; McPherson, *Abolitionist Legacy*, p. 29; Boston *Daily Evening Transcript*, 2 August 1872.

10. [By his children], *Francis William Bird*, p. 78.

11. Sumner, *Charles Sumner, His Complete Works*, 20:173–95; McPherson, *Abolitionist Legacy*, p. 31.

12. William Lloyd Garrison to William Wayland Clapp, 2 August and 21 December 1872, Clapp Papers; William Lloyd Garrison quoted in the Boston *Daily Journal*, 5 August 1872; William Lloyd Garrison to Wendell Phillips Garrison, 27 July 1872, Garrison Papers; Wendell Phillips quoted in the Boston *Daily Advertiser*, 16 August 1872.

13. Charles Sumner to Francis W. Bird, 25 April 1871, Sumner Papers; Nathaniel P. Banks to James S. Lewis, 31 July 1872, in the Pittsfield *Sun*, 7 August 1872; Francis W. Bird to Nathaniel P. Banks, 2 August 1872, Banks Papers.

14. Springfield *Republican*, 8 July 1870; Harrington, *Fighting Politician*, pp. 201–3.

15. Benjamin F. Butler to John B. Alley [draft of a letter], 12 August 1872, box 93, series B, Butler Papers; Charles Allen to Henry L. Dawes, 13 August 1872, Dawes Papers; Hart, *Commonwealth History of Massachusetts*, 4:600.

16. Merriam, *Life and Times of Samuel Bowles*, 2:179.

17. Springfield *Republican*, 10 and 12 September 1872; Boston *Daily Evening Transcript*, 12 September 1872; Boston *Post*, 12 September 1872; Charles Sumner to Francis W. Bird, 15 September 1872, Sumner Papers.

18. Boston *Globe*, 18 October 1872; Merriam, *Life and Times of Samuel Bowles*, 2:215; Springfield *Republican*, 29 August 1872.

19. Peden, "Charles O'Conor and the 1872 Presidential Election," pp. 80–90; Clark, *History of the Temperance Reform*, pp. 152–63; Boston *Daily Advertiser*, 5 November 1872.

20. William S. Jessup to George F. Hoar, 1 April 1872, Hoar Papers; McNeill, *Labor Movement*, p. 143; Montgomery, *Beyond Equality*, p. 373. Wilson, unlike Greeley, in 1870 had opposed the importation of Chinese laborers into North Adams to work in a shoe factory, an issue of great significance to the Knights of St. Crispin. See Rudolph, "Chinamen in Yankeedom," p. 19.

21. Welch, *George Frisbie Hoar*, p. 45; Blank, "Waning of Radicalism," pp. 87–122a; Abbott, "Maintaining Hegemony," pp. 20–21; Harrington, *Fighting Politician*, pp. 201–3; Donald, *Charles Sumner and the Rights of Man*, p. 554; Alexander H. Rice to Charles Sumner, 12 June 1872, Sumner Papers.

22. John Murray Forbes to Charles Sumner, 10 August 1872, in Forbes, *Letters and*

Recollections of John Murray Forbes, 2:178–83.

23. Samuel Gridley Howe to Andrew Dickson White, 8 August 1872, quoted in McPherson, *Abolitionist Legacy*, p. 31; Charles Sumner to Francis W. Bird, 13 September 1872, Sumner Papers; Stearns, *Cambridge Sketches*, p. 215.

24. Earlier interpretations of the 1872 election (written by historians who attached unwarranted importance to the shifts in voting choices of prominent men) claim that a relatively large amount of "independent" voting occurred at the polls in 1872 and that the anti-Grant sentiment marked the beginning of a fundamental realignment in Bay State politics. See Hart, *Commonwealth History of Massachusetts*, 4:597; Ware, *Political Opinion in Massachusetts*, pp. 374–75.

25. Robert C. Winthrop to John H. Clifford, 8 August 1872, microfilm edition, Winthrop Papers; George S. Hillard to William Schouler, 5 August 1872, Schouler Papers.

26. Baum, "'Irish Vote' and Party Politics," pp. 117–41.

27. James Peyton to Henry Walker, 24 October 1872, Banks Papers. Banks also enjoyed the support of some of Butler's followers. A victory for Banks would have given Butler additional control over dispersing patronage at the Charlestown Navy Yard because he would no longer have had to share appointments there with Gooch who, although a Republican, was on bad terms with Butler and the labor reformers. Josiah Snow to Benjamin F. Butler, 14 and 19 September 1872, and A. [W?] Richardson to Benjamin F. Butler, 10 September 1872, box 94, series B, Butler Papers. Regressing the vote for Grant upon the votes for Banks, Gooch, and all other congressional candidates yielded the estimate that 22 percent of Banks's vote was also in the Grant column. In 1872 Banks received 8,039 votes in the Fifth District.

28. Blank, "Waning of Radicalism," pp. 104–5; Pittsfield *Sun*, 2 October 1872.

29. Pittsfield *Sun*, 18 April, 7 August, 2 and 23 October 1872; Springfield *Republican*, 4 July 1872.

30. George F. Hoar, *Address of Hon. Geo. F. Hoar, August 13, 1872* [pamphlet], and A. A. Putnam to George F. Hoar, 15 August 1872, Hoar Papers.

31. Downs, *Economic Theory of Democracy*, pp. 36–50, 114–41.

32. Blank, "Waning of Radicalism," pp. 98–99; Boston *Daily Evening Transcript*, 28 October 1872; Donald, *Charles Sumner and the Rights of Man*, pp. 576–77; [By his children], *Francis William Bird*, p. 80; Marti, "Francis William Bird," pp. 85, 91.

Chapter 9. The Democratic Resurgence, 1873–1876

1. Charles F. Adams, "Diary," 4 November 1874, microfilm edition, reel 86, Adams Family Papers.

2. Springfield *Republican*, 5 November 1873. In 1873 Washburn won by only 12,823 votes, down by some 60,000 votes from the previous year.

3. Blank, "Waning of Radicalism," pp. 111–15.

4. Unidentified notes on the senatorial contest between Dawes and Boutwell in the "February 1873" folder, box 21, Dawes Papers; Springfield *Republican*, 21 February 1873.

5. Robinson, *"Warrington: Pen-Portraits*, pp. 360, 443; unidentified notes on the senatorial contest between Dawes and Boutwell in the "February 1873" folder, box 21, Dawes Papers; George S. Boutwell to William W. Clapp, 13 March 1873, and Thomas Russell to William W. Clapp, 22 October 1872, Clapp Papers; Boston *Daily Evening Transcript*, 12 March 1873.

6. George M. Stearns to Henry L. Dawes, 5 February 1873, Dawes Papers; Boston *Daily Evening Transcript*, 12 March 1873; New York *Times*, 18 March 1873.

7. Trefousse, *Ben Butler*, p. 224; Benjamin F. Butler quoted in Springfield *Republican*, 2 September 1873.

8. Blank, "Waning of Radicalism," pp. 125–27.

9. George F. Hoar quoted in Worcester *Evening Gazette*, 7 August 1873; John M. Forbes to George F. Hoar, 9 July 1873, Hoar Papers.

10. Ira Steward to George F. Hoar, 18 August [1873], Hoar Papers; Silvia, "Spindle City," pp. 77–78; Springfield *Republican*, 2 September 1873.

11. Boston *Post*, 28 July 1873.

12. O'Hare, "Public Career of Patrick Andrew Collins," pp. 111–13; Springfield *Republican*, 3 November 1873. In 1861 Gaston was elected mayor of Roxbury (annexed to Boston after the Civil War) in opposition to the "regular" Republican ticket. In 1868 the Democrats sent him to the legislature, and from 1871 to 1872 he served one term as mayor of Boston. *Biographical Encyclopaedia of Massachusetts*, 1:14–16.

13. New York *Tribune*, 17 September and 11 October 1873; Edward R. Tinker to Henry L. Dawes, 13 February 1872, box 21, Dawes Papers; William W. Rice to George F. Hoar, 7 January 1872, and William Thayer to George F. Hoar, 9 March 1874, Hoar Papers.

14. Springfield *Republican*, 5 November 1873.

15. Boston *Post*, 6 November 1873; Springfield *Republican*, 5 November 1873, 10 January 1874.

16. William W. Rice to George F. Hoar, 1 March 1874, Hoar Papers; Gardiner G. Hubbard to Henry L. Dawes, 24 February 1874, and Edward Atkinson to Henry L. Dawes [telegram], 17 February 1874, box 22, Dawes Papers; Otis Norcross, "Diary," 21 February 1874, Norcross Papers; John M. Forbes to Ulysses S. Grant, 27 September 1876, in Forbes, *Letters and Recollections of John Murray Forbes*, 2:186; Forbes, *Boston Collectorship*; Boston *Post*, 28 February 1874.

17. Samuel Bowles to Henry L. Dawes, 17 February 1874 and 15 October 1874, box 22, Dawes Papers; Pittsfield *Sun*, 18 March 1874; Albany [New York] *Argus*, 17 March 1874.

18. William A. Simmons to Edward R. Tinker, 1 March 1874, and Edward A. Atkinson to Henry L. Dawes, 18 March 1874, box 22, Dawes Papers; Boston *Daily Evening Transcript*, 17, 18, and 24 March 1874; Pittsfield *Sun*, 25 March and 22 April 1874; Edward Hamilton to Nathaniel P. Banks, 28 March 1874, box 92, Banks Papers; Blank, "Waning of Radicalism," p. 131.

19. Charles Eliot Norton to James R. Lowell, 13 March 1874, in Norton, *Letters of Charles Eliot Norton*, 2:36–38; Henry L. Dawes to Henry Wilson [copy of letter], 19 April 1874, and Henry Wilson to Henry L. Dawes, 22 April 1874, box 22, Dawes Papers. See also the letters received by Dawes in folders marked "March 21–31" and "April" for 1874, box 22, Dawes Papers.

20. Pittsfield *Sun*, 29 April 1874; Charles H. Doe to George F. Hoar, 4 January 1874, and S. S. Putnam to George F. Hoar, 5 March 1874, Hoar Papers.

21. Boston *Post*, 28 October 1874.

22. Worcester *Daily Spy*, 9 October 1874; Blank, "Waning of Radicalism," p. 149. On the abolition of school segregation in antebellum Massachusetts, see Litwack, *North of Slavery*, pp. 143–49.

23. William W. Rice to George F. Hoar, 4 March 1874, Hoar Papers; Welch, *George Frisbie Hoar*, p. 48–51.

24. Ware, *Political Opinion in Massachusetts*, pp. 193–95; Springfield *Republican*, 8 October 1874.

25. Merriam, *Life and Times of Samuel Bowles*, 2:271–72; Springfield *Republican*, 5 October 1874; Gardiner G. Hubbard to Henry L. Dawes, 28 July 1874, and D. E. Damon to Henry L. Dawes, 18 August 1874, box 22, Dawes Papers; William Lloyd Garrison to George W. Stacy, 31 August 1874, Garrison Papers.

26. Boston *Daily Advertiser*, 3 November 1874; E. C. Sherman to Henry L. Dawes, 12 October 1874, box 22, Dawes Papers; William S. Robinson to Francis W. Bird, 17 August 1875, Bird Papers.

27. On the variety of tickets at the Boston polling places in 1874, see Boston *Post*, 4 November 1874; Boston *Daily Advertiser*, 4 November 1874.

28. Because Talbot's Republican running mates for state offices defeated their Democratic counterparts, the "scratching" of Talbot's name from Republican ballots was the reason most frequently mentioned in newspaper accounts for Gaston's small margin of victory. A regression analysis of relationships between voting patterns in the 1874 congressional and gubernatorial races in 32 voting units (mostly wards) comprising Suffolk County and the city of Cambridge produced the following results: about 7 percent of the electorate split their tickets, about 4 percent voted in one contest but not in the other, and approximately 53 percent did not vote in either the gubernatorial or congressional election. Statewide, more split tickets were cast in 1874 than in 1884 when the extent of voter independence was exaggerated by the claims of Independent Republicans or Mugwumps. On the extent of split-ticket voting in 1884, see my "'Noisy but not Numerous,'" pp. 250–51.

29. Merriam, *Life and Times of Samuel Bowles*, 2:272; Boston *Post*, 6 November 1874; John K. Tarbox to Francis W. Bird, 27 August 1875, Bird Papers.

30. Boston *Daily Advertiser*, 10 November 1874; Merriam, *Life and Times of Samuel Bowles*, 2:272–73; Richard H. Dana, Jr., to F. D. Stedman, 4 November 1874, Dana Papers; Charles F. Adams, "Diary," 4 November 1874, microfilm edition, reel 86, Adams Family Papers; Blank, "Waning of Radicalism," p. 177; Boston *Post*, 4 November 1874.

31. Trefousse, *Ben Butler*, pp. 226–30; Springfield *Republican*, 6 and 13 November 1874.

32. Blank, "Waning of Radicalism," pp. 159, 161–62; Springfield *Republican*, 11 September, 9, 16, and 30 October, and 12 and 19 November 1874, quotation in 23 October 1874; C. C. Chaffee to Henry L. Dawes, 9 October 1874, box 22, Dawes Papers.

33. Boston *Daily Evening Transcript*, 10 September 1874; Springfield *Republican*, 29 October and 6 November 1874; Trefousse, *Ben Butler*, p. 320; Fall River *News*, 12 November 1874; Lowell *Weekly Journal*, 23 October 1874.

34. Henry L. Dawes to Henry D. Hyde, 28 November 1874, and William A. Simmons to Edward R. Tinker, 24 November 1874, box 22, Dawes Papers; Springfield *Republican*, 18 and 21 January 1875; Blank, "Waning of Radicalism," pp. 186–88.

35. Springfield *Republican*, 18 January 1874; Charles F. Adams, "Diary," 3 November 1874, and 20 January, 27 September, 25 October, and 3 December 1875, microfilm edition, reel 86, Adams Family Papers; Merriam, *Life and Times of Samuel Bowles*, 2:273–74.

36. Henry Cabot Lodge to Frank(?), 20 November 1874, Lodge Papers; Samuel Bowles to Henry L. Dawes, 29 January 1875, box 23, Dawes Papers; Merriam, *Life and Times of Samuel Bowles*, 2:273.

37. Holyoke *Transcript*, 3 April, 1 May, 19 June, and 25 December 1876; Massachusetts, Bureau of Statistics of Labor, *Ninth Annual Report*, pp. 3–4, 7–9; George F. McNeill to George F. Hoar, 17 May 1875, Hoar Papers.

38. Frisch, "From Town to City," p. 348; Brown, *Irish-American Nationalism*, pp. 46, 52–53.

39. Boston *Herald*, 3, 5, and 15 December 1875; Boston *Daily Evening Transcript*, 13 December 1875; Charles F. Adams, "Diary," 15 December 1875, microfilm edition, reel 86, Adams Family Papers.

40. Samuel Bowles to Henry Cabot Lodge, 21 December 1875, Lodge Papers; Winsor, *Memorial History of Boston*, 3:292; Lane, *Policing the City*, p. 196.

41. Springfield *Republican*, 30 September 1875; Alanson W. Beard to Henry L. Dawes, 14 June 1875, box 23, Dawes Papers; C. Curry to George F. Hoar, 20 October 1875, Hoar Papers.

42. John K. Tarbox to Francis W. Bird, 27 August 1875, 30 August 1876, Bird Papers.

43. William S. Robinson to Francis W. Bird, 17 August 1875, Bird Papers; Alanson W. Beard to Henry L. Dawes, 14 June 1875, box 23, Dawes Papers; Samuel Bowles to Gen. W. F. Bartlett, 8 October 1875, quoted in Merriam, *Life and Times of Samuel Bowles*, 2:347–48; Worcester *Daily Spy*, 28 October 1875.

44. William S. Robinson to Francis W. Bird, 12 February 1875, Bird Papers; Robinson, *"Warrington" Pen-Portraits*, pp. 382–90, quotations on pp. 387, 390.

45. Boston *Post*, 3 November 1875.

46. Alanson W. Beard to Henry L. Dawes, 3 and 11 November 1875, box 23, Dawes Papers.

47. Charles F. Adams, "Diary," 3 November 1875, microfilm edition, reel 86, Adams Family Papers; Springfield *Republican*, 3 November 1875.

48. Carl Schurz to Henry C. Lodge, 25 December 1875, and Samuel Bowles to Henry C. Lodge, 21 December 1875, Lodge Papers; John A. Norwell to Alexander H. Bullock, 24 April 1876, Bullock Papers; Henry L. Dawes, "Occasional Diary of H. L. Dawes, 1852–1876," Dawes Papers, Alanson W. Beard to Henry L. Dawes, 15 March 1876, box 23, Dawes Papers.

49. Roseboom, *History of Presidential Elections*, pp. 238–39; Carl Schurz to Charles F. Adams, 9 July 1876, microfilm edition, reel 595, Adams Family Papers; Henry Adams to Henry C. Lodge, 4 September 1876, and Henry C. Lodge, "Diary 1875–1885," 12 December 1876, Lodge Papers; George F. Hoar to Ruth A. Hoar, 17 and 19 June 1876, Hoar Papers.

50. Boston *Globe*, 29 July 1876; Boston *Pilot*, 29 July 1876; Charles F. Adams, "Diary," 6 and 8 September 1876, microfilm edition, reel 87, Adams Family Papers; O'Hare, "Public Career of Patrick Andrew Collins," pp. 119–20; Curran, *Life of Patrick A. Collins*, pp. 39ff.

51. Cincinnati (Ohio) *Commercial*, [?] October 1876 [newspaper clipping], microfilm edition, reel 606, Adams Family Papers; Collins, *Speech of the Honorable Patrick A. Collins*. For specific charges against Adams by Irish nationalists, see Thomas B. Hennessy, "Mr. Adams and the Fenians," [pamphlet dated "11 September 1876" and published in Boston], microfilm edition, reel 595, Adams Family Papers.

52. Baum, "'Irish Vote' in Massachusetts Politics," pp. 138–39; Charles F. Adams, "Diary," 4 October, 1 and 7 November 1876, microfilm edition, reel 87, Adams Family Papers; O'Hare, "Public Career of Patrick Andrew Collins," p. 124.

53. Presumably ballots were printed by Butler's supporters in this precise fashion. See Trefousse, *Ben Butler*, p. 233. Republican anti-Butlerites, who were incensed by Butler's nomination, staged a bolt led by Judge E. R. Hoar. For Butler's reaction, see his "open" letter to Hoar: Benjamin F. Butler to Judge Ebenezer Rockwood Hoar, 15 October 1876 [copy], Letterbook (box) 216, pp. 331–76, Butler Papers.

54. Benjamin F. Butler to Wendell Phillips, 22 October 1876 [copy], box 214, and Benjamin F. Butler to Reuben McFindley, 11 October 1876 [copy], box 216, Butler Papers.

55. Baum, "'Irish Vote' in Massachusetts Politics," p. 123.

56. Robinson, *"Warrington" Pen-Portraits*, p. 341; Massachusetts, Bureau of Statistics of Labor, *Census of Massachusetts: 1875*, 1:11–16, and *Thirteenth Annual Report*, pp. 97–168, 182–86.

Conclusion

1. Samuel Bowles quoted in Goodman, "Politics of Industrialism," p. 164.

2. James W. Hull to Henry L. Dawes, 14 February 1874, box 22, Dawes Papers.

3. Boston *Commonwealth*, 2 August 1873.

Bibliography

This bibliography is organized as follows:

I. Primary Materials

A. MANUSCRIPT COLLECTIONS

Boston, Massachusetts
  Boston Public Library
    Lydia and David Child Papers
    William Lloyd Garrison Papers
    Anti-Slavery May Papers
    William S. Robinson Collection
  Massachusetts Historical Society

Josiah G. Abbott Family Papers	Edward Kinsley Papers
The Adams Family Papers	Amos A. Lawrence Papers
Thomas Coffin Amory Papers	Henry Cabot Lodge Papers
John Albion Andrew Papers	John D. Long Papers
Edward A. Atkinson Papers	Theodore Lyman Papers
George Bancroft Papers	Grenville Howland Norcross Papers
George S. Boutwell Papers	Joel Parker Papers
Peleg W. Chandler Papers	William Schouler Papers
John Henry Clifford Papers	George Luther Stearns Papers
Richard Henry Dana, Jr. Papers	Amasa Walker Papers
William C. Endicott Papers	Emory Washburn Papers
Edward Everett Papers	Robert C. Winthrop Papers
George F. Hoar Papers	Horatio Woodman Papers

State House
  Secretary of the Commonwealth (Archives Division)
Cambridge, Massachusetts
  Houghton Library
    Francis W. Bird Papers
    William W. Clapp Papers
    Palfrey Family Papers
    Edward Lillie Pierce Papers
    Charles Sumner Papers
Chestnut Hill, Massachusetts
  Bapst Library of Boston College
    Patrick A. Collins Papers
Fremont, Ohio
  Rutherford B. Hayes Library
    William Claflin Papers
Madison, Wisconsin
  State Historical Society of Wisconsin
    Edward H. Rogers Papers
    Ira Steward Papers
Washington, D.C.
  Library of Congress
    Nathaniel P. Banks Papers
    Benjamin F. Butler Papers
    Henry L. Dawes Papers
    Andrew Johnson Papers
    Henry Wilson Papers
Worcester, Massachusetts
  American Antiquarian Society
    Alexander H. Bullock Papers
    Ginery Twichell Papers
  Dinand Memorial Library of the College of the Holy Cross
    Patrick R. Guiney Papers

B. NEWSPAPERS AND OTHER PERIODICALS:

Albany [New York] *Argus*, 1874
Boston *Commonwealth*, 1851–1854, 1861–1872
Boston *Courier*, 1854–1864
Boston *Daily Advertiser*, 1854–1872
Boston *Daily Atlas*, 1853–1854
Boston *Daily Bee*, 1857
Boston *Daily Evening Transcript*, 1854–1876
Boston *Daily Evening Voice*, 1865–1866
Boston *Daily Journal*, 1854–1876
Boston *Gazette*, 1873
Boston *Globe*, 1872–1876
Boston *Herald*, 1868, 1875–1876
Boston *Pilot*, 1854–1872
Fall River *News*, 1870–1871, 1874

Harper's Weekly, 1865
Holyoke *Transcript*, 1867, 1876
The Liberator (Boston), 1860–1863
Lowell *Weekly Journal*, 1874
New York *Herald*, 1867
New York *Times*, 1867
New York *Tribune*, 1855–1857, 1873
Pittsfield *Sun*, 1866–1876
The Right Way (Boston), 1865–1867
Springfield *Republican*, 1854–1876
Worcester *Daily Spy*, 1864–1875
Worcester *Evening Gazette*, 1868, 1873
Worcester *Palladium*, 1868

C. GOVERNMENT PUBLICATIONS

Boston, Massachusetts. Statistics Department. *The Municipal Register.* Boston:
1852–1929.
Massachusetts. Bureau of Statistics of Labor. *Annual Reports.* 1880–1885.
———. Bureau of Statistics of Labor. *The Census of Massachusetts: 1875.* Prepared
under the direction of Carroll D. Wright, Chief, Bureau of Statistics of Labor.
3 vols. Boston: Wright and Potter Printing Company, State Printers, 1887–1888.
———. Bureau of Statistics of Labor. *The Census of Massachusetts: 1880.* Compiled
by authority of the legislature, . . . , from the returns of the tenth census of the
United States. Boston: 1883.
———. Bureau of Statistics of Labor. *The Census of Massachusetts: 1885.* Prepared
under the direction of Carroll D. Wright, Chief, Bureau of Statistics of Labor.
3 vols. Boston: Wright and Potter Printing Company, State Printers, 1887–1888.
———. Bureau of Statistics of Labor. *Census of the Commonwealth of Massachusetts:*
1895. Prepared under the direction of Horace G. Wadlin, Chief, Bureau of Statistics of Labor. 7 vols. Boston: Wright & Potter Printing Company, State Printers,
1896–1900.
———. Bureau of Statistics of Labor. *Census of the Commonwealth of Massachusetts:*
1905. Prepared under the direction of the Chief of the Bureau of Statistics of Labor. 4 vols. Boston: Wright & Potter Printing Company, 1908–1910.
———. Bureau of Statistics of Labor. *A Compendium of the Census of Massachusetts:*
1875. Prepared by Carroll D. Wright, Chief, Bureau of Statistics of Labor. Boston:
A. J. Wright, State Printer, 1877.
Massachusetts. Executive Council. *The Report of Committee to Council on the Return*
of Yeas and Nays on Acceptance of the 20, 21, 22 Articles of Amendment to the
Constitution, May 16, 1857. Archives Division, State House, Boston.
Massachusetts. General Court. *Journal of the House of Representatives.* 1859–1876.
———. General Court. *Journal of the Senate.* 1860–1876.
———. General Court. *Manual for the Use of the General Court.* 1858–1915.
Massachusetts. House of Representatives. *Report of the Commissioners appointed to*
Inquire into the Expediency of Revising and Amending the Laws Relating to
Taxation and Exemption Therefrom. H.Doc.15, January 1875. Boston: Wright and
Potter, 1875.

Massachusetts. Secretary of the Commonwealth. *Abstract of the Census of the Commonwealth of Massachusetts, Taken with Reference to Facts Existing on the First Day of June, 1855.* Prepared under the direction of Francis DeWitt, Secretary of the Commonwealth. Boston: William White, Printer to the State, 1857.

————. Secretary of the Commonwealth. *Abstract of the Census of Massachusetts, 1860, from the Eighth U.S. Census, with Remarks on the Same.* Prepared under the direction of Oliver Warner, Secretary of the Commonwealth, by Geo. Wingate Chase. Boston: Wright & Potter, State Printers, 1863.

————. Secretary of the Commonwealth. *Abstract of the Census of Massachusetts, 1865: With Remarks on Same, and Supplementary Tables.* Prepared under the direction of Oliver Warner, Secretary of the Commonwealth. Boston: Wright & Potter, State Printers, 1867.

————. Secretary of the Commonwealth. *Acts and Resolves Passed by the General Court of Massachusetts, 1856–57.* Boston: William White, Printer to the State, 1857.

————. Secretary of the Commonwealth. *Acts and Resolves Passed by the General Court of Massachusetts in the Years 1858–59.* Boston: William White, Printer to the State, 1860.

————. Secretary of the Commonwealth. *Acts and Resolves Passed by the General Court of Massachusetts, 1862–1863.* Boston: Wright & Potter, 1863.

————. Secretary of the Commonwealth. *Historical Data Relating to Counties, Cities, and Towns in Massachusetts.* Prepared by Paul Guzzi, Secretary of the Commonwealth. 1975.

————. Secretary of the Commonwealth. *Report of the Committee on Votes of 24th Article of Amendment of Constitution, April 20, 1863.* Compiled by Francis W. Bird. Archives Division, State House, Boston.

————. Secretary of the Commonwealth. *Schedule of Votes Given on the 23rd Article of the Amendment of the Constitution in the Cities and Towns of the Commonwealth, on Monday the 9th Day of May, 1859.* Archives Division, State House, Boston.

————. Secretary of the Commonwealth. *Statistical Information Relating to Certain Branches of Industry in Massachusetts, for the year ending June 1, 1855.* Prepared from official returns, by Francis DeWitt, Secretary of the Commonwealth. Boston: W. White, Printer to the State, 1856.

————. Secretary of the Commonwealth. *Statistical Information Relating to Certain Branches of Industry in Massachusetts, for the Year Ending May 1, 1865.* Prepared from official returns by Oliver Warner, Secretary of the Commonwealth. Boston: Wright & Potter, State Printers, 1866.

U.S. Bureau of the Census. *Long Term Economic Growth, 1860–1965.* Washington, D.C.: Government Printing Office, 1966.

U.S. Census Office. *The Statistics of the Population of the United States: Ninth Census.* 3 vols. Washington, D.C.: 1872.

D. PUBLISHED COLLECTIONS OF LETTERS AND DOCUMENTS

Butler, Benjamin F. *Private and Official Correspondence of General Benjamin F. Butler During the Period of the Civil War.* Compiled by Jessie Ames Marshall. 5 vols. Norwood, Mass.: The Plimpton Press, 1917.

Forbes, John Murray. *Letters and Recollections of John Murray Forbes.* Edited by

Sarah Forbes Hughes. 2 vols. Boston and New York: Houghton Mifflin Co., 1899.

Higginson, Thomas Wentworth. *Letters and Journals of Thomas Wentworth Higginson, 1846–1906.* Edited by Mary Thatcher Higginson. Boston and New York: Houghton Mifflin Co., 1921.

Howe, Samuel Gridley. *Letters and Journals of Samuel Gridley Howe.* Edited by Laura H. Richards. 2 vols. Boston: Dana Estes and Co., 1909.

Lincoln, Abraham. *The Collected Works of Abraham Lincoln.* Edited by Roy P. Basler. 8 vols. New Brunswick, N.J.: Rutgers University Press, 1955.

Norton, Charles Eliot. *Letters of Charles Eliot Norton.* Edited by Sara Norton and M. A. de Wolfe Howe. 2 vols. Boston and New York: Houghton Mifflin Co., 1913.

Phillips, Wendell. *Speeches, Lectures, and Letters.* Boston: Lee and Shepard, 1891.

Schurz, Carl. *Speeches, Correspondence and Political Papers of Carl Schurz.* Edited by Frederic Bancroft. 6 vols. New York: G. P. Putnam's Sons, 1913. Reprint. New York: Negro Universities Press, 1969.

Sumner, Charles. *Charles Sumner, His Complete Works.* 20 vols. Boston: Lee and Shepard, 1883.

E. AUTOBIOGRAPHIES, MEMOIRS, AND DIARIES

Adams, Henry. *The Education of Henry Adams.* Boston: Houghton Mifflin Co., 1918.

Boutwell, George S. *Reminiscences of Sixty Years in Public Affairs.* 2 vols. New York: McClure, Phillips and Co., 1902.

Butler, Benj. F. *Butler's Book: Autobiography and Personal Reminiscences of Major-General Benj. F. Butler: A Review of his Legal, Political, and Military Career.* Boston: A. M. Thayer and Co., 1892.

Congdon, Charles T. *Reminiscences of a Journalist.* Boston: James R. Osgood and Co., 1880.

Griffin, Solomon Buckley. *People and Politics, Observed by a Massachusetts Editor.* Boston: Little, Brown, 1923.

Higginson, Thomas Wentworth. *Cheerful Yesterdays.* Boston and New York: Houghton Mifflin Co., 1898. Reprint. New York: Arno Press, 1968.

———. *Contemporaries.* Boston and New York: Houghton Mifflin Co., 1899.

Hoar, George Frisbie. *Autobiography of Seventy Years.* 2 vols. New York: Charles Scribner's Sons, 1903.

Sherman, Edgar J. *Recollections of a Long Life.* Boston: By the Author, 1909.

Stearns, Frank Preston. *Cambridge Sketches.* Philadelphia and London: J. B. Lippincott Co., 1905.

F. BOOKS, ARTICLES, AND PAMPHLETS BY CONTEMPORARIES

Adams, Brooks. "Oppressive Taxation of the Poor." *Atlantic Monthly* 42 (November 1878): 632–66.

Adams, Charles Francis, Jr. *Charles Francis Adams.* Boston: Houghton Mifflin Co., 1900.

[———.] "The Butler Canvass." *North American Review* 114 (January 1872): 147–70.

———. *Richard Henry Dana: A Biography.* 2 vols. Boston: Houghton Mifflin Co., 1890.

Adams, Henry. *The Education of Henry Adams.* Boston: Houghton Mifflin Co., 1918.

260 *Bibliography*

Adams, John Quincy. *An Appeal to the Mechanics and Laboring-Men of New England*. Boston: Rand, Avery, and Frye, 1870.

Andrew, John A. *The Errors of Prohibition: An Argument Delivered in the Representatives' Hall, Boston, April 3, 1867*. Boston: Ticknor & Fields, 1867.

[Andrew, John A.] "To the Voters of Massachusetts." In *Governor Andrew's Letter of Acceptance; Letter from George Bancroft, Esq.; Chas. Sumner as a Statesman*. Boston: Press of Geo. C. Rand & Avery, 1862.

[By his children.] *Francis William Bird, A Biographical Sketch*. Boston: By the Authors, 1897.

Bird, Francis W. *Facts vs. Illusions; Being a Reply to H. Haupt's Latest Misrepresentations Relating to the Troy and Greenfield Railroad*. Boston: Wright & Potter, 1862.

————. *Review of Gov. Banks' Veto of the Revised Code on Account of Its Authorizing the Enrolment of Colored Citizens in the Militia*. Boston: John R. Jewett and Co., 1860.

Bowen, James L. *Massachusetts in the War, 1861–1865*. Springfield, Mass.: Clark W. Bryan & Co., 1889.

Browne, Albert G., Jr. *Sketch of the Official Life of John A. Andrew*. New York: Hurd & Houghton, 1868.

Butler, B. F. *The Present Relations of Parties, Address at the Boston Music Hall, Nov. 23, 1870*. Boston: Marden & Rowell, Printers, 1870.

Chandler, Peleg W. *Memoir of Governor Andrew, with Personal Reminscences*. Boston: Roberts Bros., 1880.

Clark, George F. *History of the Temperance Reform in Massachusetts, 1813–1833*. Boston: Clarke & Carruth, 1888.

Clarke, James Freeman. "The Anti-Slavery Movement in Boston." In *The Memorial History of Boston, Including Suffolk County, Massachusetts, 1630–1880*, edited by Justin Winsor, 4: 369–400. 4 vols. Boston: Ticknor and Co., 1880–1881.

Collins, Patrick A. *Speech of the Honorable Patrick A. Collins at Marlboro, Mass., on Tuesday, September 14, 1876*. Boston: Post Publishing Co., 1876.

Cullen, James Bernard. *The Story of the Irish in Boston*. Boston: James B. Cullen & Co., 1889.

Curran, Michael P. *Life of Patrick A. Collins*. Norwood, Mass.: The Norwood Press, 1906.

Curtis, G. W. *A Memorial of Charles Sumner. . . .* Boston: Wright & Potter, 1874.

Forbes, John Murray. *The Boston Collectorship: Report of the Committee of Merchants*. Boston: Wright & Potter, 1874.

Frothingham, Octavius Brooks. *Boston Unitarianism, 1820–1850; Study of the Life and Work of Nathaniel Langdon Frothingham: A Sketch*. New York: G. P. Putnam, 1890. Reprint. Ann Arbor, Mich.: University Microfilms, 1961.

Greeley, Horace. "Charles Sumner as a Statesman." In *To the Voters of Massachusetts*. Boston: George C. Rand and Avery, 1862.

Guiney, Louise Imogen. *Colonel Guiney and the Ninth Massachusetts*. Worcester, Mass.: Harrigan Press, Inc., 1896.

Hale, Charles. *Our Houses Are Our Castles*. Boston: By the Author, 1855.

Hoar, George Frisbie. "Memoir of Alexander Hamilton Bullock." In *Addresses Delivered on Several Occasions by Alexander Hamilton Bullock*, pp. ix–xiv. Boston: Little, Brown, and Company, 1883.

Huse, Charles Phillips. *The Financial History of Boston from May 1, 1822 to January 31, 1909*. Cambridge: Harvard University Press, 1916.

Lawrence, William. *Life of Amos A. Lawrence, With Extracts From His Diary and Correspondence.* Boston and New York: Houghton Mifflin Co., 1888.

McNeill, George Edwin. *The Labor Movement: The Problem of To-Day.* New York: The M. W. Hazen Co., 1888.

Merriam, George S. *The Life and Times of Samuel Bowles.* 2 vols. New York: The Century Co., 1885. Reprint. 1970.

Murray, William Henry Harrison. *Prohibition v. License: A Review of ex-Gov. Andrew's Argument for License.* New York: J. J. Reed, Printer, 1867.

Nason, Elias, and Russell, Thomas. *The Life and Public Services of Henry Wilson.* Boston: B. B. Russell, 1876.

Northend, William D. *Speeches and Essays Upon Political Subjects, from 1860 to 1869.* Salem, Mass.: H. P. Ives, 1869.

Pearson, Henry G. *An American Railroad Builder, John Murray Forbes.* Boston and New York: Houghton Mifflin Co., 1911.

———. *The Life of John A. Andrew, Governor of Massachusetts, 1861–1865.* 2 vols. Boston: Houghton Mifflin, 1904.

Phillips, Wendell. *The People Coming to Power!* Boston: Lee & Shepard, 1871.

Pierce, Edward Lillie. *Memoir and Letters of Charles Sumner.* 4 vols. Boston: Roberts, 1877–1893.

Robinson, Mrs. William S., ed. *"Warrington" Pen-Portraits: A Collection of Personal and Political Reminiscences from 1848 to 1876, from the Writings of William S. Robinson.* Boston: Lee & Shepard, 1877.

Robinson, William S. "General Butler's Campaign in Massachusetts." *Atlantic Monthly* 28 (December 1871): 742–50.

Sewall, Samuel E. *The Legal Condition of Women in Massachusetts.* Boston: The New England Woman's Suffrage Association, 1869.

Stanton, Elizabeth (Cady); Anthony, Susan B.; and Gage, Matilda, eds. *History of Woman Suffrage.* 6 vols. New York: Fowler & Wells, 1881–1922.

Stearns, Frank Preston. *The Life and Public Services of George Luther Stearns.* Philadelphia and London: J. B. Lippincott Company, 1907.

Storey, Moorfield, and Emerson, Edward W. *Ebenezer Rockwood Hoar.* Boston: Houghton Mifflin Co., 1911.

Wadlin, Horace Greeley. *Citizens and Aliens.* Boston: Wright & Potter Printing Company, 1889.

———. "The Growth of Cities in Massachusetts." In *Publications of the American Statistical Association,* n.s. 13, 2 (March 1891): 159–73.

Weiss, John. *Life and Correspondence of Theodore Parker.* 2 vols. New York: D. Appleton Co., 1864.

Wilson, Henry. *History of the Rise and Fall of the Slave Power in America.* 2 vols. 3d ed. Boston: J. R. Osgood & Co., 1876–1878.

———. "The New Departure." *Atlantic Monthly* 27 (January 1871): 104–20.

Winsor, Justin, ed. *The Memorial History of Boston, Including Suffolk County, Massachusetts, 1630–1880.* 4 vols. Boston: J. R. Osgood and Co., 1880–1883.

G. OTHER PRINTED SOURCES

An Appeal to the Republicans of Massachusetts against Gag Resolutions and Forced Pledges, By a Republican. Boston: n.p., 1862.

The Congregational Quarterly. Boston: Congregational Library Association and

American Congregational Union. Vol. 3. January 1861.

Irish Central Executive Committee. *Address of the Central Executive Committee of Irish Citizens at Washington, D.C., to their Countrymen throughout the United States.* Washington, D.C.: McGill & Withebow, 1866.

Massachusetts Temperance Alliance. *Address of the State Temperance Alliance to the People of Mass., on a State Police for the City of Boston.* Boston: Wright & Potter, 1864.

Personal Liberty League of Massachusetts. *Constitution of the P.L.L. of Massachusetts Adopted by the Grand Council of the State of Massachusetts.* Boston: Printed for the Grand Council, 1867.

State Disunion Convention. *Proceedings of the State Disunion Convention, held at Worcester, Massachusetts, January 15, 1857.* Boston: Printed for the Committee, 1857.

II. Secondary Materials

A. REFERENCE WORKS

American Annual Cyclopaedia and Register of Important Events. New York: D. Appleton and Company, 1860–1872.

Barnes, William H. *The Fortieth Congress of the United States: Historical and Biographical.* 2 vols. New York: G. E. Perine, 1869.

Biographical Directory of the Governors of the United States, 1789–1978. 4 vols. Westport, Conn.: Meckler Books, 1977.

Biographical Encyclopaedia of Massachusetts of the Nineteenth Century. Vol. 1, New York: Metropolitan Publishing and Engraving Company, 1879; Vol. 2, Boston: Metropolitan Publishing and Engraving Company, 1883.

Candidate Name List and Constituency Totals, 1788–1979. Ann Arbor, Mich.: Inter-University Consortium for Political and Social Research (ICPSR 0002).

Dollar, Charles M., and Jensen, Richard J. *Historian's Guide to Statistics: Quantitative Analysis and Historical Research.* New York: Holt, Rinehart and Winston, Inc., 1971.

Eliot, Samuel Atkins. *Biographical History of Massachusetts.* 3 vols. Boston: Massachusetts Biographical Society, 1911.

Hart, Albert Bushnell, ed. *Commonwealth History of Massachusetts.* Vol. 4, *Nineteenth Century Massachusetts.* New York: The States History Company, 1930.

Hurd, D. Hamilton, comp. *History of Norfolk County, Massachusetts.* 2 vols. Philadelphia: J. W. Lewis and Co., 1884.

Lord, Robert H.; Sexton, John E.; and Harrington, Edward T. *History of the Archdiocese of Boston in the Various Stages of Its Development, 1604–1943.* 3 vols. New York: Sheed & Ward, 1944.

Massachusetts Register for the Year [1852–1874] & Business Directory. Boston: George Adams-Damrell & Moore Printers et al., 1853–1875.

Massachusetts State Record and Year Book of General Information, 1847–1851. Edited by Nahum Capen. Boston: J. French, 1847–1851.

Members of Congress Since 1789. Washington, D.C.: Congressional Quarterly, Inc., February 1977.

Nie, Norman H.; Hull, Hadlai C.; Jenkins, Jean G.; Steinbrenner, Karin; and Bent, Dale H. *SPSS: Statistical Package for the Social Sciences.* 2d ed. New York: McGraw-Hill Book Company, 1975.

Roseboom, Eugene H. *A History of Presidential Elections.* New York: Macmillan, 1957.
Sait, Edward McChesney. *American Parties and Elections.* 3d ed. New York: D. Appleton-Century Company, 1942.
Schlesinger, Arthur M., Jr., ed. *History of U.S. Political Parties.* Vol. 1, *1789–1860 From Factions to Parties*; Vol. 2, *1860–1910 The Gilded Age of Politics.* New York: Chelsea House Publishers, 1973.

B. UNPUBLISHED DOCTORAL DISSERTATIONS AND OTHER MANUSCRIPTS

Anderson, Godfrey Tryggve. "The Slavery Issue as a Factor in Massachusetts Politics, from the Compromise of 1850 to the Outbreak of the Civil War." Ph.D. dissertation, University of Chicago, 1944.
Baum, Dale. "The Massachusetts Voter: Party Loyalty in the Gilded Age, 1872–1896." Paper presented at the Symposium on Massachusetts History in the Gilded Age, John Fitzgerald Kennedy Library, Boston, 21 October 1982.
Bean, William Gleason. "Party Transformation in Massachusetts with Special Reference to the Antecedents of Republicanism, 1848–1860." Ph.D. dissertation, Harvard University, 1922.
Blank, Charles. "The Waning of Radicalism: Massachusetts Republicans and Reconstruction Issues in the Early 1870s." Ph.D. dissertation, Brandeis University, 1972.
Brown, Thomas H. "George Sewall Boutwell: Public Servant (1818–1905)." Ph.D. dissertation, New York University, 1979.
Crenshaw, William Vanderclock. "Benjamin F. Butler: Philosophy and Politics, 1866–1879." Ph.D. dissertation, University of Georgia, 1976.
Davis, Stuart John. "Liberty Before Union: Massachusetts and the Coming of the Civil War." Ph.D. dissertation, University of Massachusetts, 1975.
Denton, Charles Richard. "American Unitarians, 1830–1865: A Study of Religious Opinion on War, Slavery, and the Union." Ph.D. dissertation, Michigan State University, 1969.
Downey, Matthew T. "The Rebirth of Reform: A Study of Liberal Reform Movements, 1865–1872." Ph.D. dissertation, Princeton University, 1963.
Frisch, Michael H. "From Town to City: Springfield, Massachusetts, and the Meaning of Community, 1840–1880." Ph.D. dissertation, Princeton University, 1967.
Gambill, Edward Lee. "Northern Democrats and Reconstruction, 1865–1868." Ph.D. dissertation, University of Iowa, 1969.
Gravely, William Bernard. "Gilbert Haven, Racial Equalitarian: A Study of His Career in Racial Reform, 1850–1880." Ph.D. dissertation, Duke University, 1969.
Harmond, Richard Peter. "Tradition and Change in the Gilded Age: A Political History of Massachusetts, 1878–1893." Ph.D. dissertation, Columbia University, 1966.
Heslin, James J. "The New England Loyal Publication Society: An Aspect in the Molding of Public Opinion During the Civil War." Ph.D. dissertation, Boston University, 1972.
Kelso, John T. "The German-American Vote in the Election of 1860: The Case of Indiana with Supporting Data from Ohio." Ph.D. dissertation, Ball State University, 1967.
Kenneally, James J. "The Opposition to Woman Suffrage in Massachusetts, 1868–1920." Ph.D. dissertation, Boston College, 1963.
Kremm, Thomas Wesley. "The Rise of the Republican Party in Cleveland, 1848–1860." Ph.D. dissertation, Kent State University, 1974.

Lee, Richard Ellsworth. "The Rise of the Republican Party in Massachusetts." Ph.D. dissertation, University of Wisconsin, 1943.

Loubert, Daniel J. "The Orientation of Henry Wilson, 1812–1856." Ph.D. dissertation, Boston University, 1952.

McCabe, Robert Owen. "The Twilight of the Second Party System in Massachusetts: The Collapse of the Massachusetts Whig Party." Senior honors thesis, Harvard University, 1974.

McCarthy, John Lockhart. "Reconstruction Legislation and Voting Alignments in the House of Representatives, 1863–1869." Ph.D. dissertation, Yale University, 1970.

McCrary, Peyton. "After the Revolution: American Reconstruction in Comparative Perspective." Paper presented at the American Historical Association Convention, New York, 28 December 1979.

————. "The Civil War Party System, 1854–1876: Toward a New Behavioral Synthesis?" Paper presented at the Southern Historical Association Convention, Atlanta, Ga., 11 November 1976.

Mallam, William D. "Benjamin Franklin Butler, Machine Politician and Congressman." Ph.D. dissertation, University of Minnesota, 1941.

Mulkern, John Raymond. "The Know-Nothing Party in Massachusetts." Ph.D. dissertation, Boston University, 1963.

O'Hare, Sister M. Jeanne d'Arc, C.S.J. "The Public Career of Patrick Andrew Collins." Ph.D. dissertation, Boston College, 1959.

Parker, Albert Charles Edward. "Empire Stalemate: Voting Behavior in New York State, 1860–1892." Ph.D. dissertation, Washington University, 1975.

Petersen, Roger Dewey. "The Reaction to a Heterogeneous Society: A Behavioral and Quantitative Analysis of Northern Voting Behavior 1845–1870, Pennsylvania A Test Case." Ph.D. dissertation, University of Pittsburgh, 1970.

Purdy, Virginia Cardwell. "Portrait of a Know-Nothing Legislature: The Massachusetts General Court of 1855." Ph.D. dissertation, George Washington University, 1970.

Saunders, Judith Phyllis. "The People's Party in Massachusetts during the Civil War." Ph.D. dissertation, Boston University, 1970.

Senior, Robert Cholerton. "New England Congregationalists and the Anti-Slavery Movement, 1830–1860." Ph.D. dissertation, Yale University, 1954.

Shortridge, Ray Miles. "Voting Patterns in the American Midwest, 1840–1872." Ph.D. dissertation, University of Michigan, 1974.

Silvia, Philip Thomas, Jr. "The Spindle City: Labor, Politics, and Religion in Fall River, Massachusetts, 1870–1905." Ph.D. dissertation, Fordham University, 1973.

Siracusa, Carl Franklin. "A Mechanical People: The Worker's Image in Massachusetts Politics, 1815–1880." Ph.D. dissertation, Brandeis University, 1973.

Swenson, Philip David. "The Midwest and the Abandonment of Radical Reconstruction, 1864–1877." Ph.D. dissertation, University of Washington, 1971.

Sykes, Richard Eddy. "Massachusetts Unitarianism and Social Change: A Religious Social System in Transition, 1780–1870." Ph.D. dissertation, University of Minnesota, 1966.

Walsh, Francis R. "The Boston Pilot: A Newspaper for the Irish Immigrant, 1829–1908." Ph.D. dissertation, Boston University, 1968.

C. BOOKS

Abbott, Richard H. *Cobbler in Congress: The Life of Henry Wilson, 1812–1875*. Lexington: University of Kentucky Press, 1972.

Alexander, Thomas. *Sectional Stress and Party Strength: A Computer Analysis of Roll-Call Voting Patterns in the United States House of Representatives, 1836–1860.* Nashville, Tenn.: Vanderbilt University Press, 1967.

Anderson, Kristi. *The Creation of a Democratic Majority, 1928–1936.* Chicago and London: University of Chicago Press, 1979.

Barbrook, Alec T. *God Save the Commonwealth: An Electoral History of Massachusetts.* Amherst: University of Massachusetts Press, 1973.

Bartlett, Irving H. *Wendell Phillips, Brahmin Radical.* Boston: Beacon Press, 1961.

Beard, Augustus F. *A Crusade of Brotherhood, a History of the American Missionary Association.* Boston: The Pilgrim Press, 1909.

Benedict, Michael Les. *A Compromise of Principle: Congressional Republicans and Reconstruction, 1863–1869.* New York: W. W. Norton & Co., Inc., 1974.

Benson, Lee. *Toward the Scientific Study of History.* Philadelphia: J. B. Lippincott, 1972.

Benton, Josiah Henry. *Voting in the Field; A Forgotten Chapter of the Civil War.* Boston: By the Author, 1915.

Berthoff, Rowland Tappan. *British Immigrants in Industrial America, 1790–1950.* Cambridge: Harvard University Press, 1953.

Blalock, Hubert M., Jr. *Social Statistics.* 2d ed. New York: McGraw-Hill Book Company, 1972.

Blodgett, Geoffrey. *The Gentle Reformers: Massachusetts Democrats in the Cleveland Era.* Cambridge: Harvard University Press, 1966.

Blue, Frederick J. *The Free Soilers: Third Party Politics, 1848–1854.* Urbana: University of Illinois Press, 1973.

Bonadio, Felice A. *North of Reconstruction: Ohio Politics, 1865–1870.* New York: New York University Press, 1970.

Brauer, Kinley J. *Cotton Versus Conscience: Massachusetts Whig Politicians and Southwestern Expansion, 1843–1848.* Lexington: University of Kentucky Press, 1967.

Brock, William R. *An American Crisis: Congress and Reconstruction, 1865–1867.* New York: St. Martin's Press, 1963.

Brown, Richard D. *Massachusetts: A Bicentennial History.* New York: W. W. Norton & Co., 1978.

Brown, Thomas Nicholas. *Irish-American Nationalism, 1870–1890.* Philadelphia and New York: J. B. Lippincott Company, 1966.

Burnham, Walter Dean. *Critical Elections and the Mainsprings of American Politics.* New York: W. W. Norton, 1970.

Camejo, Peter. *Racism, Revolution, Reaction, 1861–1877: The Rise and Fall of Radical Reconstruction.* New York: Monad Press, 1976.

Carroll, Henry K. *The Religious Forces of the United States.* New York: Scribner, 1912.

Castel, Albert. *The Presidency of Andrew Johnson.* Lawrence: The Regents Press of Kansas, 1979.

Catt, Carrie Chapman, and Shuler, Nettie Rogers. *Woman Suffrage and Politics: The Inner Story of the Suffrage Movement.* 1st ed. New York: Scribner, 1923.

Chambers, William Nisbet, and Burnham, Walter Dean. *The American Party Systems: Stages of Political Development.* New York, London, and Toronto: Oxford University Press, 1967. Reprint. 1970.

Clubb, Jerome M., and Allen, Howard W., eds. *Electoral Change and Stability in American Political History.* New York: The Free Press, 1971.

Clubb, Jerome M.; Flanigan, William H.; and Zingale, Nancy H. *Partisan Realignment: Voters, Parties, and Government in American History.* Vol. 108. Sage Library of Social Research. Beverly Hills and London: Sage Publications, 1980.

Cole, Charles Chester, Jr. *The Social Ideas of the Northern Evangelists, 1826–1860.* New York: Columbia University Press, 1954.

Cole, Donald B. *Immigrant City: Lawrence, Massachusetts, 1845–1921.* Chapel Hill: University of North Carolina Press, 1963.

Coleman, Charles H. *The Election of 1868: The Democratic Effort to Regain Control.* New York: Columbia University Press, 1933.

Cullen, James B. *The Story of the Irish in Boston.* Boston: James B. Cullen and Co., 1889.

Curran, Michael P. *Life of Patrick A. Collins.* Norwood, Mass.: The Norwood Press, 1906.

D'Arcy, William. *The Fenian Movement in the United States: 1858–1886.* New York: Russell & Russell, 1947.

Darling, Arthur B. *Political Changes in Massachusetts 1824–1848: A Study of Liberal Movements in Politics.* New Haven, Conn.: Yale University Press, 1925.

David, Paul T. *Party Strength in the United States: 1872–1970.* Charlottesville: University Press of Virginia, 1972.

Dawley, Alan. *Class and Community: The Industrial Revolution in Lynn.* Cambridge: Harvard University Press, 1976.

Doherty, Robert M. *The Hicksite Separation: A Sociological Analysis of Religious Schism in Early Nineteenth Century America.* New Brunswick, N.J.: Rutgers University Press, 1967.

Donald, David Herbert. *The Politics of Reconstruction, 1863–1867.* Baton Rouge: Louisiana State University Press, 1965.

———. *Charles Sumner and the Coming of the Civil War.* New York: Alfred A. Knopf, 1960.

———. *Charles Sumner and the Rights of Man.* New York: Alfred A. Knopf, 1970.

Downs, Anthony. *An Economic Theory of Democracy.* New York: Harper & Row, Publishers, 1957.

Draper, Norman R., and Smith, Harry, Jr. *Applied Regression Analysis.* New York: John Wiley and Sons, Inc., 1966.

Duberman, Martin. *Charles Francis Adams, 1807–1886.* Stanford, Calif.: Stanford University Press, 1968.

Evitts, William J. *A Matter of Allegiances: Maryland from 1850 to 1861.* Baltimore: Johns Hopkins University Press, 1974.

Faler, Paul G. *Mechanics and Manufacturers in the Early Industrial Revolution: Lynn, Massachusetts, 1780–1860.* Albany: State University of New York Press, 1981.

Foner, Eric. *Free Soil, Free Labor, Free Men: The Ideology of the Republican Party Before the Civil War.* New York: Oxford University Press, 1970.

Formisano, Ronald P. *The Birth of Mass Political Parties: Michigan, 1827–1861.* Princeton, N.J.: Princeton University Press, 1971.

———. *The Transformation of Political Culture: Massachusetts Parties, 1790s–1840s.* New York: Oxford University Press, 1983.

Franklin, John Hope. *From Slavery to Freedom: A History of the Negro Americans.* rev. ed. New York: Alfred A. Knopf, 1974.

Freidel, Frank B. *Edward Everett at Gettysburg.* [Boston:] Massachusetts Historical Society, 1963.

Frisch, Michael H. *Town into City: Springfield, Massachusetts and the Meaning of Community, 1840–1880.* Cambridge: Harvard University Press, 1972.

Frothingham, P. R. *Edward Everett, Orator and Statesman*. Boston and New York: Houghton Mifflin & Co., 1925.

Gatell, Frank Otto. *John Gorham Palfrey and the New England Conscience*. Cambridge: Harvard University Press, 1963.

Goldman, Eric F. *Rendezvous with Destiny: A History of Modern American Reform*. New York: Alfred A. Knopf, 1952.

Gosnell, Harold F., and Merriam, Charles E. *Non-Voting: Causes and Methods of Control*. Chicago: University of Chicago Press, 1924.

Green, Constance McLaughlin. *Holyoke, Massachusetts: A Case History of the Industrial Revolution in America*. New Haven, Conn.: Yale University Press, 1939.

Gusfield, Joseph R. *Symbolic Crusade: Status Politics and the American Temperance Movement*. Urbana: University of Illinois Press, 1966.

Hammarberg, Melvyn. *The Indiana Voter: The Historical Dynamics of Party Allegiance During the 1870s*. Chicago and London: University of Chicago Press, 1977.

Handlin, Oscar. *Boston's Immigrants: A Study in Acculturation*. rev. and enl. Cambridge: Harvard University Press, 1941, 1959. Reprint. New York: Atheneum, 1972.

Harrington, Fred Harvey. *Fighting Politician: Major General N. P. Banks*. Westport, Conn.: Greenwood Press, 1948.

Harrison, Brian. *Drink and the Victorians: The Temperance Question in England, 1815–1872*. Pittsburgh: University of Pittsburgh Press, 1971.

Haynes, George H. *Charles Sumner*. Philadelphia: George W. Jacobs and Co., 1909.

Hixon, William B. *Moorfield Storey and the Abolitionist Tradition*. New York: Oxford University Press, 1972.

Holt, Michael F. *Forging a Majority: The Formation of the Republican Party in Pittsburgh, 1848–1860*. New Haven, Conn.: Yale University Press, 1969.

———. *The Political Crisis of the 1850s*. New York: John Wiley & Sons, 1978.

Hoogenboom, Ari. *Outlawing the Spoils: A History of the Civil Service Reform Movement*. Urbana: University of Illinois Press, 1961.

Howe, Daniel Walker. *The Unitarian Conscience: Harvard Moral Philosophy, 1805–1861*. Cambridge: Harvard University Press, 1970.

Hudson, Winthrop. *Religion in America*. 2d ed. New York: Scribner, 1973.

Jenkins, Brian. *Fenians and Anglo-American Relations During Reconstruction*. Ithaca, N.Y.: Cornell University Press, 1969.

Jensen, Richard J. *The Winning of the Midwest: Social and Political Conflict 1888–1896*. Chicago: University of Chicago Press, 1971.

Jones, Howard Mumford, and Jones, Bessie Zaban. *The Many Voices of Boston: An Historical Anthology 1630–1975*. Boston and Toronto: Little, Brown and Company, 1975.

Keller, Morton. *Affairs of State: Public Life in Late Nineteenth Century America*. Cambridge, Mass., and London: Harvard University, Belknap Press, 1977.

Kelley, Robert. *The Cultural Pattern in American Politics: The First Century*. New York: Alfred A. Knopf, 1979.

Kerlinger, Frederick Nichols. *Foundations of Behavioral Research*. 2d ed. New York: Holt, Rinehart and Winston, 1973.

Kerlinger, Fred N., and Pedhazur, Elazar J. *Multiple Regression in Behavioral Research*. New York: Holt, Rinehart and Winston, 1973.

Kirkland, Edward C. *Charles Francis Adams, Jr., 1835–1915: The Patrician at Bay*. Cambridge: Harvard University Press, 1966.

———. *Men, Cities, and Transportation, a Study in New England History 1820–1900*.

2 vols. Cambridge: Harvard University Press, 1948.

Kleppner, Paul. *The Cross of Culture: A Social Analysis of Midwestern Politics, 1850–1900.* New York: The Free Press, 1970.

———. *The Third Electoral System, 1853–1892: Parties, Voters, and Political Cultures.* Chapel Hill: University of North Carolina Press, 1979.

Knights, Peter R. *The Plain People of Boston, 1830–1860: A Study in City Growth.* New York: Oxford University Press, 1971.

Lane, Robert E. *Political Life: Why and How People Get Involved in Politics.* Glencoe, Ill.: The Free Press, 1959.

Lane, Roger. *Policing the City: Boston 1822–1885.* Cambridge: Harvard University Press, 1967.

Langbein, Laura Irwin, and Lichtman, Allan J. *Ecological Inference.* Sage University Paper series on Quantitative Applications in the Social Sciences, 07–001. Beverly Hills and London: Sage Publications, 1978.

Langtry, Albert Perkins. *Metropolitan Boston.* 5 vols. New York: Lewis Historical Publishing Co., 1929.

Leiby, James. *Carroll Wright and Labor Reform: The Origin of Labor Statistics.* Cambridge: Harvard University Press, 1960.

Levy, Leonard W. *The Law of the Commonwealth and Chief Justice Shaw.* Cambridge: Harvard University Press, 1957.

Lipset, Seymour Martin. *Political Man: The Social Basis of Politics.* Garden City, N.Y.: Anchor Books, 1963.

Litwack, Leon F. *North of Slavery: The Negro in the Free States, 1790–1860.* Chicago and London: University of Chicago Press, 1966.

McCaughey, Robert A. *Josiah Quincy, 1772–1864: The Last Federalist.* Cambridge: Harvard University Press, 1974.

McCormick, Richard P. *The Second American Party System: Party Formation in the Jacksonian Era.* Chapel Hill: University of North Carolina Press, 1966.

McCrary, Peyton. *Abraham Lincoln and Reconstruction: The Louisiana Experiment.* Princeton, N.J.: Princeton University Press, 1978.

McFarland, Gerald W. *Mugwumps, Morals, and Politics, 1884–1920.* Amherst: University of Massachusetts Press, 1975.

McKay, Ernest. *Henry Wilson: Practical Radical, a Portrait of a Politician.* Port Washington, N.Y.: Kennikat Press, 1971.

McKitrick, Eric L. *Andrew Johnson and Reconstruction.* Chicago: University of Chicago Press, 1960.

McLoughlin, William G. *New England Dissent, 1603–1833; The Baptists and the Separation of Church and State.* 2 vols. Cambridge: Harvard University Press, 1971.

McPherson, James M. *The Abolitionist Legacy from Reconstruction to the NAACP.* Princeton, N.J.: Princeton University Press, 1975.

———. *The Struggle For Equality: Abolitionists and the Negro in the Civil War and Reconstruction.* Princeton, N.J.: Princeton University Press, 1964.

McSeveney, Samuel T. *The Politics of Depression: Political Behavior in the Northeast, 1893–1896.* New York: Oxford University Press, 1972.

Mantell, Martin E. *Johnson, Grant, and the Politics of Reconstruction.* New York: Columbia University Press, 1973.

Mathews, Donald G. *Slavery and Methodism: A Chapter in American Morality, 1780–1845.* Princeton, N.J.: Princeton University Press, 1964.

Mayer, George. *The Republican Party, 1854–1964.* New York: Oxford University Press, 1964.

Mohr, James C. *The Radical Republicans and Reform in New York During Recon-struction.* Ithaca, N.Y.: Cornell University Press, 1973.

————, ed. *Radical Republicans in the North: State Politics During Reconstruction.* Baltimore: Johns Hopkins University Press, 1976.

Montgomery, David. *Beyond Equality: Labor and the Radical Republicans, 1862–1872.* New York: Vintage Books, 1967.

Morrison, Samuel E. *Three Centuries of Harvard.* Cambridge: Harvard University Press, 1936.

Neidhardt, W. S. *Fenianism in North America.* University Park: Pennsylvania State University Press, 1975.

O'Broin, Leon. *Fenian Fever: An Anglo-American Dilemma.* New York: New York University Press, 1971.

O'Connor, Thomas H. *The Disunited States: The Era of Civil War and Reconstruction.* 2d ed. New York: Harper & Row, 1978.

————. *Lords of the Loom: The Cotton Whigs and the Coming of the Civil War.* New York: Charles Scribner's Sons, 1968.

Perman, Michael. *Reunion Without Compromise: The South and Reconstruction, 1865–1868.* Cambridge: Cambridge University Press, 1973.

Pessen, Edward. *Riches, Class, and Power Before the Civil War.* Lexington, Mass.: D. C. Heath, 1973.

Polakoff, Keith Ian. *The Politics of Inertia: The Election of 1876 and the End of Recon-struction.* Baton Rouge: Louisiana State University Press, 1973.

Potter, David M. *The Impending Crisis, 1848–1861.* New York: Harper & Row, 1976.

Rice, Madeleine (Hooke). *American Catholic Opinion in the Slavery Controversy.* New York: Columbia University Press; London: P. S. King & Staples, 1944.

Ross, Earle Dudley. *The Liberal Republican Movement.* New York: H. Holt and Com-pany, 1919.

Schwartz, Harold. *Samuel Gridley Howe: Social Reformer, 1801–1876.* Cambridge: Harvard University Press, 1956.

Shapiro, Samuel. *Richard Henry Dana, Jr. 1815–1882.* East Lansing: Michigan State University Press, 1961.

Silbey, Joel H. *A Respectable Minority: The Democratic Party in the Civil War Era, 1860–1868.* New York: W. W. Norton & Co., Inc., 1977.

————. *The Transformation of American Politics, 1840–1860.* Englewood Cliffs, N. J.: Prentice-Hall, 1967.

Silbey, Joel H.; Bogue, Allan G.; Flanigan, William H., eds. *The History of American Electoral Behavior.* Princeton, N. J.: Princeton University Press Limited Paper-back Editions, 1978.

Siracusa, Carl. *Perceptions of the Industrial Order in Massachusetts, 1815–1880.* Mid-dleton, Conn.: Wesleyan University Press, 1979.

Smith, H. Shelton; Handy, Robert T.; and Loetscher, Lefferts A., eds. *American Christianity; An Historical Interpretation with Representative Documents.* Vol. 2, 1820–1960. New York: Scribner, 1963.

Smith, Timothy L. *Revivalism and Social Reform in Mid-Nineteenth-Century Amer-ica.* New York: Abingdon Press, 1957.

Sorauf, Frank J. *Political Parties in the American System.* Boston: Little, Brown and Company, 1963.

Sproat, John G. *"The Best Men": Liberal Reformers in the Gilded Age.* London and New York: Oxford University Press, 1968.

Sundquist, James L. *Dynamics of the Party System: Alignment and Realignment of*

Political Parties in the United States. Washington, D.C.: The Brookings Institute, 1973.

Swaney, Charles Baumer. *Episcopal Methodism and Slavery*. Boston: Richard G. Badger, Publisher, The Gorham Press, 1926.

Sweet, William Warren. *Methodism in American History*. rev. ed. New York and Nashville, Tenn.: Abingdon Press, 1953.

———. *The Methodist Episcopal Church and the Civil War*. Cincinnati: Methodist Book Concern Press, 1912.

Theil, Henri. *Principles of Econometrics*. New York: John Wiley & Sons, 1971.

Thernstrom, Stephan. *Poverty and Progress: Social Mobility in a Nineteenth Century City*. New York: Atheneum, 1973.

Thomas, Benjamin P. *Abraham Lincoln*. New York: Alfred A. Knopf, 1952.

Trefousse, Hans Louis. *Ben Butler: The South Called Him Beast!* New York: Twayne Publishers, 1957.

Tyack, David B. *George Ticknor and the Boston Brahmins*. Cambridge: Harvard University Press, 1967.

Tyrrell, Ian R. *Sobering Up: From Temperance to Prohibition in Antebellum America, 1800–1860*. Westport, Conn.: Greenwood Press, 1979.

Ware, Edith E. *Political Opinion in Massachusetts During Civil War and Reconstruction*. Vol. 74, no. 2. Columbia University Studies in History, Economics and Public Law. New York: Columbia University Press, 1916.

Weeden, William B. *War Government Federal and State in Massachusetts, New York, Pennsylvania, and Indiana, 1861–1865*. Boston: Houghton Mifflin & Co., 1906.

Welch, Richard E., Jr. *George Frisbie Hoar and the Half-Breed Republicans*. Cambridge: Harvard University Press, 1971.

Wheelwright, William Bond. *The Life and Times of Alvah Crooker*. Boston: By the Author, 1923.

Williamson, Harold Francis. *Edward Atkinson: The Biography of an American Liberal 1827–1905*. Boston: Old Corner Book Store, Inc., 1934.

Yearley, Clifton K. *The Money Machines: The Breakdown and Reform of Governmental and Party Finance in the North, 1860–1920*. Albany: State University of New York Press, 1970.

Zornow, William F. *Lincoln and the Party Divided*. Norman: University of Oklahoma Press, 1954.

D.   ARTICLES

Abbott, Richard H. "Massachusetts: Maintaining Hegemony," In *Radical Republicans in the North: State Politics During Reconstruction*, edited by James C. Mohr, pp. 1–25. Baltimore: Johns Hopkins University Press, 1976.

Arcanti, Steven J. "To Secure the Party: Henry L. Dawes and the Politics of Reconstruction." *Historical Journal of Western Massachusetts* 5 (Spring 1977): 33–45.

"Australian Ballot Law." *Proceedings of the Massachusetts Historical Society* 58 (Boston: Massachusetts Historical Society, 1925): 401–18.

Aylsworth, Leon E. "The Passing of Alien Suffrage." *American Political Science Review* 25 (February 1931): 114–16.

Baltzell, E. Digby. "The Social Insulation of the Traditional Elite." In *The Private Side of American History*, edited by Thomas R. Frazier, 2: 84–112. New York: Harcourt Brace and Jovanovich, Inc., 1979.

Baum, Dale. "The 'Irish Vote' and Party Politics in Massachusetts, 1860–1876." *Civil War History* 26 (June 1980): 117–41.

———. "Know-Nothingism and the Republican Majority in Massachusetts: The Political Realignment of the 1850s." *Journal of American History* 64 (March 1978): 959–86.

———. "'Noisy but not Numerous': The Revolt of the Massachusetts Mugwumps." *The Historian* 41 (February 1979): 241–56.

———. "Woman Suffrage and the 'Chinese Question': The Limits of Radical Republicanism in Massachusetts, 1865–1876." *New England Quarterly* 56 (March 1983): 60–77.

Bean, William G. "An Aspect of Know-Nothingism: The Immigrant and Slavery." *South Atlantic Quarterly* 23 (October 1924): 319–24.

———. "Puritan Versus Celt, 1850–1860." *New England Quarterly* 7 (March 1934): 70–89.

Benedict, Michael Les. "The Rout of Radicalism: Republicans and the Elections of 1867." *Civil War History* 18 (December 1972): 334–44.

Bennett, Lance W., and Haltom, William. "Issues, Voter Choice, and Critical Elections." *Social Science History* 4 (November 1980): 379–418.

Benson, Lee. "Research Problems in American Political Historiography." In *Common Frontiers of the Social Sciences*, edited by Mirra Komarovsky, pp. 113–81. Glencoe, Ill.: The Free Press, 1957.

Bergquist, James M. "People and Politics in Transition: The Illinois Germans, 1850–1860." In *Ethnic Voters and the Election of Lincoln*, edited by Frederick C. Luebke, pp. 196–226. Lincoln: University of Nebraska Press, 1971.

Blalock, Hubert M., Jr. "Correlated Independent Variables: The Problem of Multicollinearity." *Social Forces* 42 (December 1963): 233–37.

Brunet, T. Michael. "The Secret Ballot Issue in Massachusetts Politics from 1851 to 1853." *New England Quarterly* 25 (September 1952): 354–62.

Burnham, Walter Dean. "The Changing Shape of the American Political Universe." *American Political Science Review* 59 (March 1965): 7–28.

———. "Party Systems and the Political Process." In *The American Party Systems: Stages of Political Development*, edited by William Nisbet Chambers and Walter Dean Burnham, pp. 277–307. New York: Oxford University Press, 1967.

———. "Theory and Voting Research." *American Political Science Review* 68 (September 1974): 1002–23.

Campbell, Angus. "A Classification of Presidential Elections." In *Elections and the Political Order*, edited by Angus Campbell, Philip E. Converse, Warren E. Miller, and Donald E. Stokes, pp. 63–77. New York: John Wiley & Sons, 1966.

———. "Surge and Decline: A Study of Electoral Change." *Public Opinion Quarterly* 24 (Fall 1960): 397–418.

Chambers, William N., and Davis, Philip C. "Party, Competition, and Mass Participation: The Case of the Democratizing Party System, 1824–1852." In *The History of American Electoral Behavior*, edited by Joel H. Silbey, Allan G. Bogue, and William H. Flanigan, pp. 174–97. Princeton, N.J.: Princeton University Press, 1978.

Chapman, J. K. "Mid-Nineteenth-Century Temperance Movement in New Brunswick and Maine." *Canadian Historical Review* 35 (March 1954): 43–50.

Converse, Philip E. "Change in the American Electorate." In *The Human Meaning of Social Change*, edited by Angus Campbell and Philip E. Converse, pp. 297–99. New York: Russell Sage Foundation, 1972.

———. "Of Time and Partisan Stability." *Comparative Political Studies* 2 (July 1969): 139–71.

Cowart, Andrew T. "A Cautionary Note on Aggregate Indicators of Split Ticket Voting." *Political Methodology* 1 (Winter 1974): 109–30.

Crouch, Barry A. "Amos A. Lawrence and the Formation of the Constitutional Union Party in 1860." *Historical Journal of Massachusetts* 3 (June 1980): 46–58.

Curry, Richard O. "The Civil War and Reconstruction, 1861–1877: A Critical Overview of Recent Trends and Interpretations." *Civil War History* 20 (September 1974): 215–38.

Daniels, George H. "Immigrant Vote in the 1860 Election: The Case of Iowa." *Mid-America* 44 (July 1962): 142–62.

Davis, Horace B. "The Occupations of Massachusetts Legislators, 1790–1950." *New England Quarterly* 24 (March 1951): 89–100.

Dawley, Alan, and Faler, Paul. "Working-Class Culture and Politics in the Industrial Revolution: Sources of Loyalism and Rebellion." *Journal of Social History* 9 (June 1976): 466–80.

Dodd, Jill Siegel. "The Working Classes and the Temperance Movement in Ante-Bellum Boston." *Labor History* 19 (Fall 1978): 510–31.

Downey, Matthew T. "Horace Greeley and the Politicians: The Liberal Republican Convention in 1872." *Journal of American History* 53 (March 1967): 727–50.

Duberman, Martin B. "Behind the Scenes as the Massachusetts 'Coalition' of 1851 Divides the Spoils." *Essex Institute Historical Collections* 99 (1963): 152–60.

———. "Some Notes on the Beginnings of the Republican Party in Massachusetts." *New England Quarterly* 34 (September 1961): 364–70.

Elkins, David. "The Measurement of Party Competition." *American Political Science Review* 68 (June 1974): 682–700.

Faler, Paul. "Cultural Aspects of the Industrial Revolution: Lynn, Massachusetts, Shoemakers and Industrial Morality, 1826–1860." *Labor History* 15 (Summer 1974): 367–94.

Farrar, Donald E., and Glauber, Robert R. "Multicollinearity in Regression Analysis: The Problem Revisited." *Review of Economics and Statistics* 49 (February 1967): 92–107.

Ferejohn, John A., and Fioriana, Morris. "The Paradox of Not Voting: A Decision Theoretical Analysis." *American Political Science Review* 68 (June 1974): 525–36.

Flanigan, William H., and Zingale, Nancy H. "The Measurement of Electoral Change." *Political Methodology* 1 (Summer 1974): 49–82.

Foner, Eric. "The Causes of the Civil War: Recent Interpretations and New Directions." *Civil War History* 20 (September 1974): 197–214.

Formisano, Ronald P. "Analyzing American Voting, 1830–1860: Methods." *Historical Methods Newsletter* 2 (March 1969): 1–12.

———. "Deferential-Participant Politics: The Early Republic's Political Culture, 1789–1840." *American Political Science Review* 68 (June 1974): 473–87.

Gerber, Richard Allan. "Liberal Republicanism, Reconstruction, and Social Order: Samuel Bowles as a Test Case." *New England Quarterly* 45 (September 1972): 393–407.

———. "The Liberal Republicans of 1872 in Historiographical Perspective." *Journal of American History* 62 (June 1975): 40–73.

Goodman, Paul. "A Guide to American Church Membership Data Before the Civil War." *Historical Methods Newsletter* 10 (Fall 1977): 183–90.

———. "The Politics of Industrialism: Massachusetts, 1830–1870." In *Uprooted Americans: Essays to Honor Oscar Handlin*, edited by Richard L. Bushman, Neil Harris, David Rothman, Barbara Miller Solomon, and Stephan Thernstrom, pp. 161–207. Boston and Toronto: Little, Brown and Company, 1979.

Hall, John Philip. "The Knights of St. Crispin in Massachusetts, 1869–1878." *Journal of Economic History* 18 (June 1958): 161–75.

Haynes, George H. "The Causes of Know-Nothing Success in Massachusetts." *American Historical Review* 3 (October 1897 to July 1898): 67–82.

Hays, Samuel P. "Political Parties and the Community-Society Continuum." In *The American Party Systems: Stages of Political Development*, edited by William Nisbet Chambers and Walter Dean Burnham, pp. 152–82. New York: Oxford University Press, 1967.

Herriot, F. I. "The Germans of Iowa and the 'Two Year' Amendment of Massachusetts." *Deutsch-Amerikanische Geschichtsblätter* 13 (1913): 202–308.

Hofstetter, C. Richard. "Inter-Party Competition and Electoral Turnout: The Case of Indiana." *American Journal of Political Science* 17 (May 1973): 351–66.

Holt, Michael F. "The Democratic Party 1828–1860." In *History of U.S. Political Parties*, edited by Arthur M. Schlesinger, Jr., 1:497–571. New York: Chelsea House Publishers, 1973.

———. "The Politics of Impatience: The Origins of Know-Nothingism." *Journal of American History* 60 (September 1973): 309–31.

House, Albert V. "Republicans and Democrats Search for New Identities, 1870–1890." *Review of Politics* 31 (October 1969): 466–76.

Irwin, Galen A., and Meeter, Duane A. "Building Voter Transition Models from Aggregate Data." *Midwest Journal of Political Science* 13 (November 1969): 545–66.

Jensen, Richard. "The Religious and Occupational Roots of Party Identification: Illinois and Indiana in the 1870s." *Civil War History* 16 (December 1970): 325–43.

Jones, E. Terrence. "Ecological Inference and Electoral Analysis." *Journal of Interdisciplinary History* 2 (Winter 1972): 249–62.

———. "Using Ecological Regression." *Journal of Interdisciplinary History* 4 (Spring 1974): 593–96.

Kelley, Robert. "Ideology and Political Culture from Jefferson to Nixon." With comments by Geoffrey Blodgett, Ronald P. Formisano, and Willie Lee Rose. *American Historical Review* 82 (June 1977): 531–82.

Key, V. O., Jr. "Secular Realignment and the Party System." *Journal of Politics* 21 (May 1959): 198–210.

———. "A Theory of Critical Elections." *Journal of Politics* 17 (February 1955): 3–18.

Kirkland, Edward C. "Boston During the Civil War." *Proceedings of the Massachusetts Historical Society* 71 (October 1953–May 1957): 194–203.

Kleppner, Paul. "The Greenback and Prohibition Parties." In *History of U.S. Political Parties*, edited by Arthur M. Schlesinger, Jr., 2:1549–81. New York: Chelsea House, 1973.

Kousser, J. Morgan. "Ecological Regression and the Analysis of Past Politics." *Journal of Interdisciplinary History* 4 (Autumn 1973): 237–62.

———. "History – Theory = ?" *Reviews in American History* 7 (June 1979): 157–62.

———. "Key Changes." *Reviews in American History* 9 (March 1981): 23–28.

———. "The 'New Political History': A Methodological Critique." *Reviews in American History* 4 (March 1976): 1–14.

Kremm, Thomas W. "Cleveland and the First Lincoln Election: The Ethnic Response to Nativism." *Journal of Interdisciplinary History* 8 (Summer 1977): 69–86.

Lichtman, Allan J. "Correlation, Regression, and the Ecological Fallacy: A Critique." *Journal of Interdisciplinary History* 4 (Winter 1974): 417–33.

———. "Critical Election Theory and the Reality of American Presidential Politics, 1916–40." *American Historical Review* 81 (April 1976): 317–48.

———. "The End of Realignment Theory? Toward a New Research Program for

American Political History." *Historical Methods* 15 (Fall 1982): 170–88.

Lichtman, Allan J., and Langbein, Laura I. "Regression vs. Homogeneous Units: A Specification Analysis." *Social Science History* 2 (Winter 1978): 172–93.

Lipset, Seymour Martin. "The Emergence of the One-Party South: The Election of 1860." In *Political Man: The Social Basis of Politics*, by Seymour Martin Lipset, pp. 372–84. Garden City, N.Y.: Anchor Books, 1963.

Marti, Donald B. "Francis William Bird: A Radical's Progress through The Republican Party." *Historical Journal of Massachusetts* 11 (June 1983): 82–93.

McCormick, Richard L. "Ethno-Cultural Interpretations of Nineteenth-Century American Voting Behavior." *Political Science Quarterly* 89 (1974): 351–77.

McCrary, Peyton; Miller, Clark; and Baum, Dale. "Class and Party in the Secession Crisis: Voting Behavior in the Deep South, 1856–1861." *Journal of Interdisciplinary History* 8 (Winter 1978): 429–57.

McKay, Ernest A. "Henry Wilson and the Coalition of 1851." *New England Quarterly* 36 (1963): 338–57.

———. "Henry Wilson: Unprincipled Know-Nothing." *Mid-America* 46 (1964): 29–37.

Mirak, Robert. "John Quincy Adams, Jr., and the Reconstruction Crisis." *New England Quarterly* 35 (June 1962): 187–202.

Mulkern, John R. "Scandal Behind the Convent Walls: The Know-Nothing Nunnery Committee of 1855." *Historical Journal of Massachusetts* 11 (January 1983): 22–34.

———. "Western Massachusetts in the Know-Nothing Years: An Analysis of Voting Patterns." *Historical Journal of Western Massachusetts* 8 (January 1980): 14–25.

Osofsky, Gilbert. "Abolitionists, Irish Immigrants, and the Dilemmas of Romantic Nationalism." *American Historical Review* 80 (October 1975): 889–912.

Pease, Jane, and Pease, William. "Confrontation and Abolitionism in the 1850's." *Journal of American History* 55 (March 1972): 923–37.

Peden, Joseph R. "Charles O'Conor and the 1872 Presidential Election." *The Irish American Historical Society: The Recorder* 37 (1976): 80–90.

Pole, J. R. "Suffrage and Representation in Massachusetts: A Statistical Note." *William and Mary Quarterly* 14 (October 1957): 560–92.

Powell, Lawrence N. "The American Land Company and Agency: John A. Andrew and the Northernization of the South." *Civil War History* 21 (December 1975): 293–308.

———. "Rejected Republican Incumbents in the 1866 Congressional Nominating Conventions: A Study in Reconstruction Politics." *Civil War History* 19 (September 1973): 219–37.

Prindle, David F. "Voter Turnout, Critical Elections and the New Deal Realignment." *Social Science History* 3 (Winter 1979): 144–70.

Robboy, Stanley J., and Robboy, Anita W. "Lewis Hayden: From Fugitive Slave to Statesman." *New England Quarterly* 46 (December 1973): 591–613.

Rorabaugh, W. J. "Prohibition as Progress: New York State's License Elections, 1846." *Journal of Social History* 14 (Spring 1981): 425–43.

Rudolph, Frederick. "Chinamen in Yankeedom: Anti-Unionism in Massachusetts in 1870." *American Historical Review* 53 (October 1947): 1–29.

Rusk, Jerrold G. "The Effect of the Australian Ballot Reform on Split Ticket Voting: 1876–1908." *American Political Science Review* 64 (December 1970): 1220–38.

Sellers, Charles. "The Equilibrium Cycle in Two-Party Politics." *Public Opinion Quarterly* 29 (Spring 1965): 16–38.

Shade, William G. "'Revolutions May Go Backwards': The American Civil War and the Problem of Political Development." *Social Science Quarterly* 55 (December 1974): 753–67.

Shapiro, Samuel. "The Butler-Dana Campaign in Essex County in 1868." *New England Quarterly* 31 (September 1958): 340–60.

———. "The Conservative Dilemma: The Massachusetts Constitutional Convention of 1853." *New England Quarterly* 33 (June 1960): 207–24.

Shively, W. Phillips. "'Ecological' Inference: The Use of Aggregate Data to Study Individuals." *American Political Science Review* 63 (December 1969): 1183–96.

Shortridge, Ray M. "The Voter Realignment in the Midwest During the 1850s." *American Politics Quarterly* 4 (April 1976): 193–222.

Shover, John L. "The Emergence of a Two-Party System in Republican Philadelphia, 1924–1936." *Journal of American History* 60 (March 1974): 985–1002.

Silbey, Joel H. "The Civil War Synthesis in American Political History." *Civil War History* 10 (June 1964): 130–40.

Staiger, C. Bruce. "Abolitionism and the Presbyterian Schism of 1837–1838." *Mississippi Valley Historical Review* 26 (December 1929): 391–414.

Stark, Cruce. "The Development of a Historical Stance: The Civil War Correspondence of Henry and Charles Francis Adams, Jr." *Clio* 4 (June 1975): 383–97.

Storey, Ronald. "Class and Culture in Boston: The Athenaeum, 1807–1860." *American Quarterly* 27 (May 1975): 178–99.

Stout, Harry S., and Taylor, Robert. "Sociology, Religion, and Historians Revisited: Towards an Historical Sociology of Religion." *Historical Methods Newsletter* 8 (December 1974): 29–38.

Sweeney, Kevin. "Rum, Romanism, Representation, and Reform: Coalition Politics in Massachusetts, 1847–1853." *Civil War History* 22 (June 1976): 116–37.

Trefousse, Hans L. "The Acquittal of Andrew Johnson and the Decline of the Radicals." *Civil War History* 14 (June 1968): 148–61.

Tyrrell, Ian R. "Temperance and Economic Change in the Antebellum North." In *Alcohol, Reform and Society: The Liquor issue in Social Context*, edited by Jack S. Blocker, Jr., pp. 45–67. Westport, Conn.: Greenwood Press, 1979.

Vandermeer, Philip R. "Religion, Society, and Politics: A Classification of American Religious Groups." *Social Science History* 5 (February 1981): 3–24.

Williams, T. Harry. "Voters in Blue: The Citizen Soldiers of the Civil War." *Mississippi Valley Historical Review* 31 (September 1944): 187–204.

Wilson, Major L. "Of Time and the Union: Webster and His Critics in the Crisis of 1850." *Civil War History* 14 (December 1968): 293–306.

Wright, James E. "The Ethnocultural Model of Voting: A Behavioral and Historical Critique." *American Behavioral Scientist* 16 (May/June 1973): 653–74.

Index

"Half-breeds," 205, 216
Hallett, Benjamin F., 58
Hamilton, Edward, 60
Hampden County, 77
Hampshire County, 76–77
Hancock, John, 217
Harper's Ferry: John Brown's raid, 49
Harris, Benjamin W., 180
Hartford and Erie Bill, 152, 155
Harvard College, 28, 57, 90, 98
Haven, Gilbert, 95, 130
Haverhill, Mass., 195
Hawley, Mass., 66
Hayes, Rutherford B., 204–6, 208
Heinzen, Karl, 95
Higginson, Thomas Wentworth, 55, 74
Hillard, George S., 173
Hoar, Ebenezer Rockwood, 159, 189,
    198–99, 253 (n. 53)
Hoar, George Frisbie, 24, 159, 161, 164,
    181–82, 187, 191, 216–17; on Butler,
    185–86; on Hayes's nomination, 205
Holy Cross, College of the, 57
Holyoke, Mass., 200
"Honest Man's" ticket, 37–39, 48, 232
    (n. 29)
Hooper, Samuel, 117, 132
Hoosac Tunnel, 65–66, 68
Howe, Samuel Gridley, 55–56, 166, 172
Hull, Mass., 74, 236 (n. 4)
"Hunkers," 65, 117, 202

Illinois, 173
Immigrants, 28, 75, 78, 80, 93, 95, 108–
    11, 126, 128, 132, 165, 175–76; natural-
    ization of, 13–15, 31; voting restrictions
    upon, 43–48. *See also* Foreign-born
    population
Independent Republicans. *See*
    Mugwumps
Indiana, 140, 173
Indians, 11
Industrial workers, 83, 85, 87, 90, 92–93,
    114, 117, 126, 134–35, 146, 151–54, 156,
    159, 165, 171, 175–76, 186, 200–201, 213;
    voting behavior of, 114–16, 134–35, 155,
    157, 159–60, 176, 178. *See also* Occupa-
    tional identifications of voters
Iowa, 69
Ireland, 109–11, 127, 132
Irish-Americans, 15, 29, 45, 49, 53, 75,

78, 93, 94, 108–12, 125–26, 128, 132,
    139, 153, 156, 159, 176, 201, 205–7, 215;
    voting behavior of, 95, 100, 110, 112–13,
    159–60, 176–77, 205–9, 213. *See also*
    Birthplace of population

Johnson, Andrew, 62, 100, 102, 111–12,
    117–18, 122–24, 131, 138, 141, 184, 191,
    245 (n. 40); attempts to forge anti-
    radical coalition, 103–4, 106–8, 114,
    119–21, 215; radical disappointment
    with acquittal of, 135
Joint Committee on Reconstruction, U.S.
    Congress, 184
Jones, Edward J., 127–28

Kansas, 3, 37
Kansas-Nebraska Act, 27, 93
Knights of St. Crispin (KOSC), 146–47,
    152–53, 249 (n. 20)
Know-Nothing party, 15, 20, 69, 90, 95,
    126, 128, 150, 164, 212, 214; and realign-
    ment of 1850s, 24, 26–43, 52–54; voter
    support for, 27–28, 32–33, 232 (n. 22),
    factionalism in, 30–32, 34, 37, 43; and
    suffrage restriction, 31, 43–48; demise
    of, 35–37, 41; despised by Bird Club,
    47–49, 213; and Constitutional Union-
    ists, 50–53; behavior of constituency in
    1860s, 94, 108
Koerner, Gustave, 48
Ku Klux Klan, 156, 163, 172

Labor reform movement, 28, 57, 114–18,
    151, 153–54, 165, 171, 186, 202, 212, 215,
    250 (n. 27). *See also* Workingman's
    party
Labor Reform party, 146–47, 150–52,
    154–55, 161–62, 178–79, 246 (n. 6)
Lane, Joseph, 50
Lawrence, Amos A., 51–52, 62, 67, 117
Lawrence, Mass., 110
Lenox, Mass., 73
"Liberal Republican and Democratic"
    ticket, 170, 173, 179, 181
Liberal Republicans, 185, 215; motiva-
    tions of, 164–66; and 1872 Cincinnati
    convention, 166–67; and Grant's re-
    election, 167–74, 176, 178–79, 181–82;
    behavior of, after 1872, 186, 193, 200,
    209, 216